A TRANSNATIONAL STUDY OF LAW AND JUSTICE ON TV

This collection examines law and justice on television in different countries around the world. It provides a benchmark for further study of the nature and extent of television coverage of justice in fictional, reality and documentary forms. It does this by drawing on empirical work from a range of scholars in different jurisdictions. Each chapter looks at the raw data of how much 'justice' material viewers were able to access in the multi-channel world of 2014 looking at three phases: apprehension (police), adjudication (lawyers), and disposition (prison/ punishment).

All of the authors indicate how television has developed in their countries. Some have extensive public service channels mixed with private media channels. Financing ranges from advertising to programme sponsorship to licensing arrangements. A few countries have mixtures of these. Each author also examines how 'TV justice' has developed in their own particular jurisdiction. Readers will find interesting variations and thought-provoking similarities. There are a lot of television shows focused on legal themes that are imported around the world. The authors analyse these as well.

This book is a must-read for anyone interested in law, popular culture, TV, or justice, and provides an important addition to the literature due to its grounding in empirical data.

A Transnational Study of Law and Justice on TV

Edited by
Peter Robson and Jennifer L Schulz

·HART·

OXFORD · LONDON · NEW YORK · NEW DELHI · SYDNEY

HART PUBLISHING

Bloomsbury Publishing Plc

Kemp House, Chawley Park, Cumnor Hill, Oxford, OX2 9PH, UK

HART PUBLISHING, the Hart/Stag logo, BLOOMSBURY and the Diana logo
are trademarks of Bloomsbury Publishing Plc

First published 2016
Paperback edition, 2019

A catalogue record for this book is available from the British Library.

Library of Congress Cataloging-in-Publication Data
A catalogue record for this book is available from the Library of Congress.

ISBN: HBK: 978-1-50990-568-3
PB: 978-1-50992-798-2
ePDF: 978-1-50990-570-6
ePub: 978-1-50990-569-0

Typeset by Compuscript Ltd, Shannon

TABLE OF CONTENTS

CONTRIBUTORS' BIOGRAPHIES

Michael Böhnke works as an editor for the law firm of Dr Ulbrich & Kaminski Rechtsanwälte, Bochum and as editor's assistant for *The German Journal of Law and Society*. He has studied Cinema Studies and Sociology at the Ruhr-Universität Bochum and is currently working on a 'History of the American Film 1930–65'. Publications: 'Myth and the Law in the Films of John Ford' (2001) 28 *Journal of Law and Society*, Special Issue: Law and Film and 'Young Tom Edison—Edison, the Man: Biopic of the Dynamic Entrepreneur' (2003) 12(3) *Public Understanding of Science* (together with Stefan Machura).

Christine A Corcos is the Richard C Cadwallader Associate Professor of Law, Louisiana State University Law Center and Associate Professor of Women's and Gender Studies, Louisiana State University A&M, Baton Rouge, Louisiana. She has published numerous law review articles in the area of media law, human rights, European legal history, and law and popular culture. Among her recent publications are: 'Seeing It Coming Since 1945: State Bans and Regulations of "Crafty Sciences" Speech and Activity' (2015) 37 Thomas *Jefferson Law Review* 39; *The Law of the European Union: A New Constitutional Order*, 2nd edn with Alain A Levasseur et al (Durham, NC, Carolina Academic Press, 2013); and *Law and Popular* Culture, 2nd edn with David Ray Papke et al (LEXIS/Matthew Bender Publishing, 2012). She is a member of the editorial board of the *International Journal for the Semiotics of Law*, a member of the Law and Humanities Institute board of governors, and she edits the Media Law Prof Blog, the Law and Magic Blog, and the Law and Humanities Blog.

Kathleen Custers, PhD, studied Communication at the University of Leuven in Belgium. She has worked as a researcher at the University of Antwerp, Belgium and as a post-doc at the University of Leuven. She was a Visiting Professor at the Brian Lamb School of Communication at Purdue University, Indiana, USA. She is a Research Fellow at the University of Leuven and works as a research consultant for GfK. She is interested in media violence, emotion effects of media use, and methodology.

Anja Louis completed her undergraduate and postgraduate degrees in Hispanic Studies at Birkbeck College (University of London). She is Senior Lecturer/Associate Professor in Spanish and Intercultural Studies at Sheffield Hallam University, UK, where she is a member of the Cultural Communication and Computing Research Institute. She has published widely in the field of 'law and culture', with particular emphasis on gender studies and popular culture. Her monograph *Women and the*

Law: Carmen de Burgos, an Early Feminist analyses the representation of law in
the work of Spanish feminist Carmen de Burgos. Most recently, she has co-edited
a collection of essays that brings together leading international specialists of
Burgos's work. (Louis and Sharp (eds), *Femininity and Feminism: Carmen de Burgos
Defines the Modern Woman*. Routledge, in press). Dr Louis' current research project examines the representation of female lawyers and law enforcement officers
in Spanish film and television. It surveys relatively early representations of women
lawyers in the 1960s, followed by archetypal lawyers of the transition to democracy
in the 1980s, and more recent representations of women lawyers and law enforcement officers in the 2000s.

Stefan Machura is Professor of Criminology and Criminal Justice at the School
of Social Sciences, Bangor University, Wales. Previously, he was at the Law Faculty
of the Ruhr-Universität Bochum/Germany. He has been teaching classes in Crime
and the Media, and Law in Film since 1995. Since 2014, Stefan Machura has been
a board member of the Research Committee on Sociology of Law, International
Sociological Association. From 2000 to 2008, Stefan Machura served as speaker of
the Sociology of Law Section, German Sociological Association. Some of his books
include: *Eugen Ehrlich's Sociology of Law* (ed) with Knut Papendorf and Anne Hel-
lum (2014); *Understanding Law in Society* (ed) with Knut Papendorf and Kristian
Andenæs (2011); *Krieg im Film* (*War in Film*) (ed) with Rüdiger Voigt (2005);
Ehrenamtliche Richter in Südrussland (*Lay Judges in South Russia*) with Dmitrij
Donskow and Olga Litvinova (2003); *Recht im Film* (*Law in Film*) (ed) with Stefan
Ulbrich (2002); and *Law and Film* (ed) with Peter Robson (2001).

Lukas Musumeci is a Lecturer at the Faculty of Law, University of Hamburg,
Germany and at the Faculty of Law, University of Basel, Switzerland, where he is
also a PhD candidate. At the time of writing, he was a Researcher at the Zentrum
für rechtswissenschaftliche Fachdidaktik (Centre for Legal Education) at the
University of Hamburg, Germany. Before that, from 2008 until 2013, he was a
Research Assistant in Basel. Lukas Musumeci teaches courses in constitutional,
administrative and public international law. In 2011, he won the Credit Suisse
Teaching Award for Best Teaching (together with Dr. Mareike Schmidt). His publications cover the fields of public international law, constitutional law and legal
education.

Nickos Myrtou is Specialised Teaching Personnel in the Department of Communication & Media Studies at the National and Kapodistrian University of Athens
(NKUA) where he teaches Television and Radio Production as well as Documentary Production. As a member of the Audiovisual Media Laboratory of the Department he is in charge of student productions and research on new technologies and
practices. He holds a BA and an MA degree from the Department of Communication & Media Studies. He is a guest lecturer on the yearly project 'Dialogue
of Civilizations: Greece: Then and Now—The Greek Media' of the Northeastern
University. He is also a videographer and editor and has worked on a number of

short films and documentaries. He edited the book, *Television Production, Video Montage, Technology-Art and Technique* and he writes articles for the magazines *Photographer* and *PhotoBusiness* about montage techniques and post-production.

Panagiota Nakou is a graduate of the London School of Economics. She holds a Master of Science from the Media and Communications Department of the London School of Economics and a BA from the Faculty of Communication & Media Studies at the National and Kapodistrian University of Athens (NKUA). She has taken part in media research and media monitoring using content and critical discourse analysis; her MSc dissertation focused on the media representation of Greece's far-Right political party, Golden Dawn, and its spokesman, Ilias Kasidiaris. She has participated in the Hellenic Political Science Association conference (HPSA, December 2014) and the Political Science Association conference (PSA, March 2015).

Fabian Odermatt is a Research Assistant and PhD candidate at the Institute of Criminal Law and Criminology at the University of Berne, Switzerland. His research focuses mainly on the field of law and popular culture.

Glen Odgaard is a Danish lawyer and film historian who has worked with law & film since 2009. This is his first contribution to a book. Glen Odgaard has arranged and held lectures on various topics at conferences in Europe including: political philosophy; international politics; mediation; the history of the American Supreme Court; and law & film. Since 1992 he has been a board member of various national and international organisations, including Mensa. In August 2006 he became the first Dane to be elected chairman of Mensa International's election committee. In addition to Glen's work to introduce and promote law & film in Denmark, he had experience of working in the Danish Parliament and the Danish Ministry of Defence before starting his own law firm in 2015.

Stamatis Poulakidakos, PhD, is Senior Research Associate and Teaching Assistant at the Department of Communication & Media Studies of the National and Kapodistrian University of Athens (NKUA). He holds a BA and a PhD degree from the Department of Communication & Media Studies, and an MA degree in New Media, Information and Society from the London School of Economics (LSE). He works at the Laboratory for Social Research in Mass Media, Department of Communication & Media Studies, specialising in media monitoring and quantitative content analysis. At the same time he is a tutor on the BA in Media Production programme of the Athens Metropolitan College, in collaboration with Queen Margaret University of Edinburgh. He has taken part in many research projects and has participated in various Greek and international conferences. He authored the book *Propaganda and Public Discourse: The Presentation of the MoU by the Greek Media* (Athens, DaVinci Books, 2014). In addition, he has published several papers on political communication, propaganda, social media and the public sphere, political advertisements, protests and other media-related issues.

Itay Ravid is a doctoral candidate (JSD) and a John M. Olin Fellow in Law and Economics at Stanford Law School. His research interests include administrative law, criminal law, judicial decision making, the design of legal institutions, and the relationship between law and mass media. Itay holds an LL.B. in Law and Communication and Journalism (Hebrew University of Jerusalem), an LL.M in Public and International Law (Joint degree—Northwestern University and Tel-Aviv University), and a JSM in Law (Stanford Law School, SPILS fellow). His master's thesis, which studied narratives of obedience to legal norms in popular TV shows, was awarded the Colin B. Picker Prize by the American Society of Comparative Law. In his JSD dissertation Itay is quantitatively assessing the effects of the media on sentencing decisions in US trial courts, focusing, among other things, on racial inequalities in sentencing outcomes. Itay's scholarship has been published in journals such as the *Stanford Journal of International Law*, the *Cardozo Arts and Entertainment Law Journal* and the *Berkeley Journal of Entertainment and Sports Law*.

Before coming to Stanford Itay was an attorney at the Israeli Solicitor General's office. He represented the Israeli government in constitutional and administrative matters and litigated before the Supreme Court in its capacity as the High Court of Justice. Itay also served as a senior legal clerk to Justice Dorit Beinisch, the President of the Israeli Supreme Court.

Peter Robson is Professor of Social Welfare at the University of Strathclyde, Glasgow. He works on housing law, in which he has written a number of books, the most recent being *Housing Law in Scotland* (2011) and *Residential Tenancies* (2012). He has annotated statutes—Housing (Scotland) Act 1988, 2001, 2006, 2010—and is currently completing the Housing (Scotland) Act 2014 and the Private Housing (Tenancies) (Scotland) Act 2016. He also works on law and popular culture. He is the co-author of *Film and the Law* (2010) and co-editor of *Law and Justice on the Small Screen* (2012). He is the author of essays in 2015 and 2016 popular culture collections and journals on 'Popular Fiction and Lawyers', 'Theatre and the Law in the 21st Century', 'Vigilantes in Film' and 'Women Lawyers on TV'. Meanwhile, he has co-written a book on the architecture of courts in Scotland entitled *The Spaces of Scottish Justice*. He is a solicitor and judge in the Scottish Tribunals Service working on disability benefits. He was chair of the leading homelessness charity, Shelter, from 1999 to 2005 and from 2005 has been chair of the West Lothian Social Landlord organisation, WESLO, with some 2,500 houses.

Valentin Rolando has his Master's degree in International Media from University Paris 8. He is currently passing a second Master's degree in Brand Strategy and Innovation at CELSA, Paris Sorbonne. Valentin is interested in digital communication, visual studies, and questions the way images are broadcasted and received on French television and its digital extensions. His Master degree's thesis centred on the construction of reality through the prism of television programming.

Jennifer L Schulz, SJD, is Associate Professor at the Faculty of Law, University of Manitoba, Canada and a Fellow of the Winkler Institute for Dispute Resolution at Osgoode Hall Law School, Toronto. From 2010 to 2012 she was Associate Dean

(Research & Graduate Studies) and the Executive Director of the Manitoba Legal Research Institute. She is currently writing a book entitled *Mediators in the Reel World*, which she researched in spring 2013 while a Faculty Visitor at the Faculty of Law, University of Cambridge and a Research Fellow at Birkbeck College School of Law, University of London. In autumn 2014 Dr Schulz was a Visiting Scholar in Residence at the Centre for the Legal Profession at the Faculty of Law, University of Toronto and from 2003 to 2004 she was the first Canadian invited Research Fellow at the Program on Negotiation at Harvard Law School. Dr Schulz has taught at four Canadian law schools and has won teaching awards at two of them. She is a federal and international research grant recipient and the author of many refereed articles and chapters on mediation and popular culture topics.

Cassandra Sharp, PhD, is Senior Lecturer in the School of Law, Faculty of Law, Humanities and the Arts, University of Wollongong, Australia, and a member of the Legal Intersections Research Centre. Cassandra's research draws on cultural studies, literary theory, criminology, and legal theory to interrogate public interaction with legal consciousness. She is co-editor, with Marett Leiboff, of *Cultural Legal Studies: Law's Popular Cultures and the Metamorphosis of Law* (Routledge, 2015). Her primary research interest lies in the expression and transmission of law within the public imaginary through mediated popular fictions, and she has developed an interdisciplinary empirical methodology to explore the ways in which the concept of justice is challenged and/or maintained through contemporary stories of law.

Ferdinando Spina is an Assistant Professor at the University of Salento, Italy, where he teaches courses on Crime and the Media, and Sociology of Law. He has conducted research on Italian judges and lawyers, fear of crime and the media, and environmental conflicts. He is author of several publications, including the books *Sociologia dei Nimby. I conflitti di localizzazione tra movimenti e istituzioni* (*The Sociology of NIMBY. Locational Conflicts between Social Movements and Institutions*) and *Il doppio codice. Diritto e tecnologie della comunicazione* (*The Double Code. Law and Media Technology*).

Hilde Van den Bulck, PhD, studied Communication at the University of Leuven in Belgium and at Leicester University in the UK. She has been a Lecturer at Leicester University and a Visiting Fellow at the Annenberg School for Communication at the University of Pennsylvania. She is a full Professor at the University of Antwerp, Belgium. She specialises in European and Belgian media policy, but also has a keen interest in celebrities and celebrity activism.

Jan Van den Bulck, PhD, DSc, studied Communication at the University of Leuven in Belgium, Political Science at Hull University (UK), and Epidemiology at the University of Rotterdam, Netherlands. He is a Professor of Media Psychology at the Department of Communication Studies at the University of Michigan. He is interested in the effects of media use on worldviews, perceptions, and behaviour. In recent years a large part of his research has focused on the effects of media use on healthy sleep.

Barbara Villez is Professor of Legal Language and Culture and Teaching Science at University Paris 8. She directs the research centre Justices, Images, Languages, Cultures (www.jilc.fr) which focuses on the representations of law and justice through images ranging from television series to contemporary art performances. 'Performing the Law', a project she co-directed, was financed by the Labex Arts H2H at University Paris 8 and culminated with an international conference hosted at France's Cour de cassation in December 2015. Professor Villez is also Associate Researcher at the Institut des Hautes Etudes sur la Justice in Paris and the Laboratoire de communication et politique-Irisso (CNRS), where she created and directs a network of television series scholars. Among her many publications are three books: *Séries télé:visions de la justice* (PUF, 2005); *Television and the Legal System* (Routledge, 2009); and *Law & Order, New York Police Judiciaire: La justice en prime time* (PUF, 2014).

Zofia Zawadzka is a barrister. She provides services in individual counselling on civil law and intellectual property law at a law office in Białystok, Poland. She worked as a Lecturer in Law at the Intellectual Property Law Unit, Faculty of Law, University of Białystok from 2011 to 2014, where she taught courses in intellectual property law and media law. Her doctoral thesis, completed in 2011, examined legal regulation of the rights and conflicts between freedom of the press, privacy, and image protection of public figures. Zofia's research interests include various areas of intellectual property law. She is the author of the monograph *Press Freedom and Right to Privacy of Public Figures: A Problem of Solving the Conflict of Rules* (2013); co-author of two student books on the subject of 'Intellectual Property Rights and Media Law'; and numerous law review articles concerning aspects of intellectual property and human rights.

1

A Transnational Study of Law and Justice on TV

PETER ROBSON AND JENNIFER L SCHULZ

Introduction

Images tend to be more compelling than words. Another reason for the peculiar power of visual images is that they often get treated as 'windows' opening onto reality, rather than as the visual constructions that they are.[1]

Imagination and fiction make up more than three quarters of our real life.[2]

The images of popular culture are recognised as powerful. Viewership and consumption of these images, whether in film, television, video games or other image-based media, continue to grow rapidly. Since the mid-1980s there has been a rapid growth of published material by scholars on the relationship between law and popular culture. Much work has examined the ways in which looking beyond the legal text can provide both interest to students of law as well as insights into the influences at work on the content and application of the law. This has its roots in cultural legal studies and in the notion that law and lawyering is about more than mere rote learning of rules and following them blindly. From the middle of the twentieth century legal education has stressed that the beliefs and perceptions of those applying the law, whether in the courts or on the streets, has an important influence on how law operates.

The early work in English on law and popular culture started from the recognition that the world was so suffused with media images that this was where people actually obtained their knowledge and attitudes in relation to the legal system.[3] It was suggested that the extent of programming and coverage was so vast that it must have an influence on how people view and understand the law.[4] At first, scholars of

---

[1] Sherwin (2014) xxxiii.
[2] Weil (1947).
[3] Macaulay (1987); Friedman (1989).
[4] Stark (1987); Sherwin (2000).

popular legal culture did not make any distinction between film and television as sources of study.[5] This early work drew no particular distinction between law and justice as it appeared on film and on television, and could be described as employing a literary approach. The trend for the first 20 years was principally to examine and assess film.[6] At the time of this writing, spring 2016, there have been no fewer than 20 books published which are focused on law, film and justice.[7] There have also been a number of special editions of journals which have taken law and film as their theme.[8] An overview of the scholarship reveals that the vast majority of these essays and books took as their focus either an individual film or a group of films.

Television, by contrast, has been covered in only two essay collections and two books.[9] The approach to TV has been, rather like its counterpart on film, principally concerned with cultural/literary analysis. Individual programmes and series have been scrutinised in terms of their significance to such issues as the representation of women,[10] the impact of reality television on perceptions of justice[11] and specific issues such as rape.[12] In addition, there have been overviews of how TV lawyers and problem-solvers have evolved over time.[13] The literary approach continues to develop into such areas as superheroes and graphic novels,[14] although the world of PS4 and Xbox and the exploits of those such as Phoenix Wright: Ace Attorney,[15] have yet to be explored.

Simply put, there has not been a concerted and organised movement of legal scholarship although some writers have interpreted the work on film, for instance, as 'the law and film movement'.[16] Most of the work has looked at film and television from a cultural studies perspective, with a focus on meaning. Most scholars have a legal background but some come from the social sciences and the humanities.[17] There have also been some explorations from the perspective of film studies. These have emphasised the different techniques which film uses to construct effective narratives.[18]

The legal personnel examined are almost always lawyers and occasionally judges. Negotiators, mediators or arbitrators are rarely mentioned.[19] In terms of police officers, scholars suggest that popular culture emphasised that 'crime does

---

[5] Macaulay (1987); Friedman (1989).

[6] Greenfield, Osborn and Robson (2001).

[7] See references in: Robson and Silbey (2012); Robson, Osborn and Greenfield (2014); and Wagner and Sherwin (2014).

[8] University of San Franciscio Law Review (1996); *Vermont Law Journal* (2003); *Baltimore Law Journal* (2007).

[9] Jarvis and Joseph (1998); Robson and Silbey (2012); Rapping (2003); and Villez (2009).

[10] Schulz (2009).

[11] Robson and Silbey (2012).

[12] Bergman (2012).

[13] Robson (2007a); Robson (2007b).

[14] Dailly and Davidson (2012); Ramiro Avilés, Rivaya and Barranco Avilés (2014).

[15] www.amazon.co.uk/Phoenix-Wright-Ace-Attorney-Nintendo/dp/B000EOTWSI.

[16] Machura (2016b).

[17] Clover (1992); McNeely (1995).

[18] Moran, Christie, Sandon and Loizidou (2004); Sarat, Douglas and Umphrey (2005); Black (1999).

[19] Schulz (2008); Menkel-Meadow (2004) 583.

not pay'[20] and thus the public received an 'image of crime and justice that typically supports a policy of crime control mechanisms ahead of due process protections'.[21] Policing is often 'depicted as glamorous, with a great deal of independence and access to tremendous resources, with an extremely high rate of success'.[22] The assumption that there is a link between older series and modern day offerings is one which is often taken for granted. A common cultural heritage stretching from *Perry Mason* through *LA Law* down through *the practice* to *The Good Wife* and *Suits* underpins discussions about changes in the nature and identity of the TV lawyer.[23] Similar sorts of overviews exist in the scholarship on police and detective series on television.[24] The issue of what is the 'lifespan' of a television series is one which needs to be addressed, as the assumption that there is link between shows may not be borne out with new, younger audiences.

The empirical work that exists has examined the impact of film and television on their audiences. One of the earliest texts drew attention to the importance of cinema and the messages of films about law. Vicenzo Tomeo, in his 1973 exploration of the influence of Italian film on the theme of justice, *Il giudice sullo schermo* (*The Judge on the Screen*),[25] noted how films influenced peoples' views of the legal system based on empirical studies undertaken in the late 1960s and early 1970s. Tomeo was well ahead of other scholars with his interest in the impact of popular culture on people's beliefs and attitudes. This kind of detailed empirical work has been taken up in other studies in the United States, most notably by Podlas on reality television.[26] The views of younger generations of lawyers were also covered in a number of studies,[27] and an international study looked at the sources of law students' ideas about justice and how these varied between cultures.[28] Overall, however, there has been a dearth of empirical work.

Against this limited empirical backdrop comes our current transnational work. Work on film and television to date has largely focused on the United States.[29] We aim to extend the coverage to other areas of the world. Thus our study, undertaken in 14 different countries, maps out exactly what kind of law-centred television programming there was in November 2014. The chapters look at the raw data of how much 'law and justice' material television viewers were able to access in the multi-channel world of 2014. The Index describes all of the law-themed television shows on the air—something not available anywhere else. Contributors examined all three phases of the legal process—apprehension (police focus); adjudication

---

[20] Carlson (1985).
[21] Surette (1992).
[22] McNeely (1995).
[23] Asimow and Mader (2004).
[24] Turnbull (2014).
[25] Tomeo (1973).
[26] Podlas (2008); Podlas (2009).
[27] Salzmann and Dunwoody (2005); Sharp (2005).
[28] Asimow, Greenfield and Guillermo et al (2005).
[29] Francophone writing such as *La Justice sure l'ecran* and the extensive Spanish language material focus primarily on US material too.

(lawyer focus) and disposition (prison/punishment focus) in all forms of legally themed programming (dramas, reality shows, documentaries, etc). Across all 14 countries the heaviest television focus rests upon the first phase of the legal process, namely apprehension or police work.

Another finding that is consistent across many jurisdictions is the over-representation of American legally themed television programming. In Greece 83% of the police shows on television were American. In Canada 71.7% of all the legal shows airing on television were American and in Spain, 65% were American. In Australia, Denmark and Poland 62% of the law and justice themed shows were imported from the United States, in Germany 60% of the shows were American, and almost 50% of the shows in Switzerland were American. Israel, Italy and Britain had far fewer American imports.

Uniquely, in this collection the results are related to the TV production and content control systems existing in each country. One of the problems common to all the work on law on television is that the readership is assumed to have knowledge and understanding of the nature of television systems. What has been lacking is any indication of what limitations there are on which kinds of programmes are likely to be made in the first place. Also missing is a sense of what kind of justice television has been available over the years and how the programmes and issues have changed over time. Finally, the financing of the television services in different countries is an issue which has not featured in the books and articles which have looked at law and justice on the small screen. Here, our authors examine the history, development, statutory backdrop and financing behind the television broadcast in their countries.

We are curious as to how legally themed television programmes provide a window into why the justice system operates as it does. We, like others,[30] seek to understand and teach the law in context, rather than as some abstract set of rules unconnected with politics, economics or social forces, and thus our collection highlights socio-cultural context. Contributing authors describe changes in representations of women, people of colour and other under-represented groups on television. Readers will discover a commonality between jurisdictions with more than one language: the minority language speakers watch less dominant TV, preferring programming in their minority language. So, for example, French-speaking Canadians and Flemish-speaking Belgians are much more loyal to their local minority language TV, whereas English-speaking Canadians and French-speaking Belgians embrace dominant foreign TV shows. Finally, we subscribe to the view that lawyers need to be fully rounded individuals rather than narrow technicians. The early curricula of common law degree programmes contained coverage of jurisprudence with the intention that this examination of the nature and function of law would enrich its practitioners.[31] Now, in the twenty-first century, an

---

[30] Osborn (2001).
[31] Robson (1979).

understanding of the cultural imagery of law—especially of televised popular culture—is crucial to becoming fully rounded, reflective legal practitioners.

The original impetus to modern law and popular culture studies was the underlying assumption that what was shown on television is of significance in shaping the public's ideas about and reactions to the justice system. Steven Stark noted that by the time an American child reaches the age of 18 she or he will have seen 18,000 murders on TV.[32] However, as Stark points out, gauging the specific influence of watching those murders is far from straightforward. We do not know how significantly TV is shaping the public's views on crime. What we can offer with this collection, however, which is absent from all previous scholarship, is a detailed explication of how extensive the TV material on law and justice is in many jurisdictions in the world. What we seek to do with this transnational study is to provide a basis for empirically assessing whether or not the assumptions about the significance of television law bear scrutiny.

It is worth saying that our personal interest in the relationship between law and popular culture arises from a very simple practical question: how is it that social structures which are manifestly unjust and exploitative can be sustained effectively over long periods of time with minimal challenge? Our interest in the role of popular culture is as crudely functionalist as this. It is not concerned with the aesthetics of the cultures for their own sake. We are concerned that scholarship in the field runs the risk of becoming an end in itself, with its language and objects of study becoming so esoteric as to defy understanding to all but a tiny coterie of scholars.

Instead, we hope that our collection of empirical research will provoke and promote new questions and understandings. Readers of our collection will find, across the whole range of the different countries examined, that lawyer-focused television is very much a minority offering. Despite the fact that there have been very many TV shows featuring a host of lawyers in dramas and in reality TV shows, these shows do not actually feature extensively in the empirical studies collected in this book. On the other hand, police and detective series dominate in *all* jurisdictions and a great deal of the programming stems from the United States.

In a world of multiple channels, 'catch-up' TV, or binge watching, the physical task of providing data on what is available to watch becomes problematic. Indeed, accessing television is in a process of evolution. Accessibility platforms and viewing habits have changed. The rise of viewing through streaming, Netflix and boxed sets, along with the proliferation of niche channels, means that traditional ideas about the extent and nature of law and justice on television must be considered quite carefully. What we have done in this collection is limit ourselves to those channels which are free to air. At present, pay-per-view TV still occupies a limited part of the market in most of the countries we cover and for that reason it has been excluded from the data.

---

[32] Stark (1987) 231.

In mapping out what is actually available to watch in detail, and the context in which it is available, means we can start to address the kinds of issues Bergman identified as crucial. He talked about whether or not popular legal culture reflected, reinforced or revised beliefs about law, lawyers and the legal system.[33] What seems clear from this empirical study is that popular culture scholars need to go further and include the police and law enforcement if they want to know about perceptions of the legal system. The thing that emerges clearly from our study is the overwhelming dominance of the first aspect of the legal process, namely, apprehension or police process, both in drama and in reality forms.

Asimow, Brown and Papke talk of 'the ways in which cultural products can shape expectations about legal systems and contribute to critical debates about lawmakers, justice and the exercise of state power', and 'ways in which popular representations of law mediate legal practices and conceptions of justice'.[34] We respond that the extant emphasis on portrayals of lawyers has diverted scholars from work on the police, and this needs to be addressed if we are to fully debate conceptions of justice, fairness, the exercise of state power, the content of legal rules, and the processes by which law is made and is seen to be made in the world today.

[33] Bergman (2012) 153.
[34] Asimow, Brown and Papke (2014) 1.

2

Australia

CASSANDRA SHARP

In 2016 Australia celebrates the sixtieth anniversary of television broadcasting. The Australian television landscape is dominated by three free-to-air commercial networks and three national public broadcasters. The development and expansion of television in Australia however had somewhat slow beginnings, having been significantly delayed by the Second World War. Although experimental transmissions using the Radiovision system[1] had been conducted in the 1920s and 1930s, the introduction of full-scale television broadcasting did not occur until 1956—timed well to enable coverage of the Melbourne Olympics.[2] At that time a mere 5% of Melbourne households and 1% of Sydney homes owned a TV set.[3] In comparison, a 2014 survey showed that 72% of Australians 'binge watch' television—watching three or more episodes of one series in one sitting—and that nearly 50% download or rent television shows online.[4] Of course, the technologies of production have changed, and while televisions still seem to dominate the Australian living room with ever-increasing large screens, the diverse modes of watching now also enable viewing from even the smallest of hand-held screens. Doubtless, this is a far cry from the post-war setting in which the true development of Australian television began.

The Development of Australian Television

With television broadcasting having already emerged in the US and UK, Australia looked to each country's industry model for inspiration. In June 1948, the federal government proposed to follow the British model by establishing a

---

[1] Bielby (1981) 173; Luck (2006) 15.

[2] November 1956.

[3] Televisionau.com, *The History of Australian Television—1950–59*, 'Timeline', see: televisionau. com/timeline/1950-1959.

[4] Deloitte Media Consumer Survey 2014: www2.deloitte.com/au/en/pages/technology-media-and-telecommunications/articles/media-consumer-survey-2014.html.

government-controlled TV station in each capital city, which would derive its revenue from compulsory licensing fees, rather than the US commercial model, which was based on privately owned networks earning profits from advertising. For this reason the government created the Australian Broadcasting Act 1948[5] which specifically prohibited the granting of commercial TV licences. It was not until 1953 (following a change in government)[6] that a Royal Commission report recommended that television services should be introduced gradually, to allow for the granting of commercial licences. The resultant Broadcasting and Television Act 1956[7] provided 'the legislative framework for a dual system of TV ownership',[8] with a national, government-funded TV network run by the Australian Broadcasting Commission (ABC) operating alongside privately owned commercial stations. The practical implication of this legislative change was that it paved the way for a comparatively mild system of government regulation of commercial TV.[9]

In 1955, the government established the Australian Broadcasting Control Board (ABCB)—an agency responsible for the regulation of broadcasting standards and practices and the allocation of TV licences. On 16 September 1956 mainstream television was launched in Australia with network TCN-9 Sydney. This new Australian communications medium was famously introduced by Bruce Gyngell with the words 'Good evening, and welcome to television'.[10] In the late 1950s and early 1960s the television was a warmly received technological advance in Australian culture, and it fast became a growth industry with both entertainment and advertising potential.

By 1960, 70% of homes in Sydney and Melbourne had a television set.[11] Following the establishment of television in most major metropolitan centres and capital cities, television continued to expand to regional and remote areas, significantly reaching even those in the most northern and western parts of Australia. Some highlights of Australian television development during this time included: (i) in 1966, being able to receive daily news reports via satellite; (ii) in 1969, along with the rest of the world, being able to watch the live broadcast coverage of the Apollo 11 moon landing; and (iii) in 1970, the official opening of a microwave link between the east and west coast, enabling transmission of material across the country. This fostered a sense of national unity following the devastating effects of Cyclone Tracy, most evident by high viewership of a national 28-hour telethon broadcast on 31 December 1974 to raise money for Cyclone Tracy relief.

---

[5] Cth No 64, 1948.
[6] Curthoys (1991) 154.
[7] Cth No 33, 1956.
[8] Curthoys (1991) 155.
[9] ibid, 156.
[10] Erin McWhirter, 'Australia celebrates 50 years of television' *News Limited* (5 September 2006).
[11] ibid.

From the 1970s Until Now …

In 1972 the Australian government announced that all stations would convert to colour on 1 March 1975. Despite significant cost, and in what is said to be one of the fastest changeovers to colour in the world, by 1980 almost 80% of homes owned a colour television set.[12] The changing social and political landscape that was characteristic of the 1970s and 1980s was reflected in TV broadcasts on Australian television during that period. It had a particular impact on Australia's developing multicultural population. The launch in 1980 of Australia's second national public broadcaster—the Special Broadcasting Service (SBS)—prioritised subtitled and foreign language content, and 'emphasised what was seen as the lack of responsiveness among Australia's media institutions to an increasingly culturally diverse society'.[13]

Of course, by the 1980s, technological advancements also began moving quickly, and in 1986 AUSSAT satellites were launched in order to relay radio and TV networks to very remote areas of rural Australia, allowing country viewers the same options as city viewers.[14] The 1990s began with the nation in a recession, impacting the budgets of TV networks which affected the profitability of local production,[15] yet this decade still managed to usher in the era of 24-hour transmission—starting with the ABC in 1993 and Pay TV or subscription television in 1995.

The twentieth century ended with the growing popularity of reality TV and game shows in Australia and the emergence of community television stations, including in 2007 the National Indigenous Television Network (NITV). Significantly, the turn of the millennium also introduced the possibilities of digital television and the options of widescreen, standard definition and high-definition production. In the years between 2001 and 2009 all networks began transmitting in HD digital with several providing 'more viewing choice than ever before' by operating a second standard definition digital channel.[16]

In the last five years, Australian television has seen the complete shutdown of all analogue services, the introduction of 3D transmissions, and the availability of services which provide TV on demand. Doubtless, Australians have embraced television with significant passion, and the last 60 years have facilitated the production of many favourite Australian TV shows. The next section of the chapter reflects on the nature of crime and justice TV shows produced locally over this period.

---

[12] ibid. The slogan used to sell colour television to the Australian public was 'March first into colour'.
[13] Cunningham and Turner (2010) 156.
[14] Televisionau.com, *The History of Australian Television—1980–89*, 'Timeline', see: televisionau.com/timeline/1980-1989.
[15] ibid.
[16] ibid.

Law and Justice in Australian Television History

In the early years of Australian television, following the first issue of TV licences, there was no enforcement of local content quotas by the government or the ABCB, and so US and British imports seemed to be the dominant products shown on air. This was particularly the case within the dramatic genre, with nearly all dramas scheduled on the commercial networks being produced in the United States (*Perry Mason* was a favourite), and British programmes dominating the ABC. Because at this time it was not convenient or cost-effective for networks to produce local content, only the most basic shows in the variety or quiz formats were produced in Australia, and these were usually developed by the ABC. 'By the early 1960s at least 80% of all Australian TV content was sourced from the USA and not surprisingly American programs (sic) consistently topped the ratings'.[17] As a result, concerns began to be raised about the lack of local content on Australian commercial television, and this eventually led to a federally commissioned report in 1963, which identified 97% of television drama content as imported from the United States.[18] This was especially egregious because the Broadcasting and Television Act 1956 had required licensees to 'as far as possible, use the services of Australians in the production and presentation of radio and television programs'.[19]

Eventually, in 1970 the ABCB introduced regulations that imposed a local content quota (45% of evening programmes had to be produced within Australia)[20] in order to prevent the television industry being overly 'Americanised.' This paved the way for an Australian identity to be established, with shows such as *Bandstand*, *IMT*, *Homicide* and *The Mavis Bramston Show* forming a big part of Australian pop culture.[21] In 1976–77 the ABCB was superseded by the Australian Broadcasting Tribunal (ABT) and since that time, although quotas for Australian content have increased to 55%,[22] many 'still believe that the bar for Australian content has been set too low'.[23] Nevertheless, over the last 60 years Australian television has produced numerous notable television series and miniseries, many of which were framed around dramatic issues of law and justice. These programmes have historically canvassed the three aspects of the law and justice process identified for this transnational collection: criminal detection; adjudication; and punishment.

---

[17] skwirk.com, 'American and British Cultural Influence': see Skwirk.com.au.

[18] Curthoys (1991) 157.

[19] ibid.

[20] ibid, 157.

[21] Televisionau.com, *The History of Australian Television—1970–79*, 'Timeline', see: televisionau.com/timeline/1970-1979.

[22] Mandated by the Broadcasting Services (Australian Content Standard) 2005 created under the Broadcasting Services Act 1992 (Cth) and regulated by the Australian Communication and Media Authority.

[23] Australian National Film and Sound Archive, Digital Learning 'TV and Family Life', see: dl.nfsa.gov.au/module/645/; see also Cunningham and Turner (2010) 175.

However, it is clear that both twentieth and twenty-first century Australian audiences have exhibited a clear fascination and penchant for crime stories (true and fictitious) and police dramas.

Police Dramas and Crime Stories

One of the earliest and most famous Australian police drama series was *Homicide*, produced between 1964 and 1977 by Crawford Productions for the Seven Network. Widely known for changing the landscape of Australian TV, and for constituting a 'major stimulus to local TV production',[24] *Homicide* was an immediate and profitable success story primarily because 'viewers enjoyed seeing stories played out in their own familiar suburban backdrops and without an American or English accent'.[25] The series was set in a real location—Melbourne's Russell Street police headquarters—and although it followed a fictional homicide squad, many episodes were based directly on real cases. The success of the series (which holds the record as one of the two longest running Australian drama series)[26] demonstrated that even in these early days of Australian television there was a market for locally produced dramas. Crawford Productions followed *Homicide* with a police drama titled *Division 4* (1969–75) for the Nine Network, and another drama for Ten called *Matlock Police* (1971–76). *Division 4* was a melodrama set in Yarra Central, a fictitious inner Melbourne suburb with a broad demographic, and in a similar fashion to *Homicide* presented the inner workings of a police station dramatised with realism and authenticity.[27] *Matlock Police*, however, differentiated itself from its predecessors by focusing on the drama-filled personal lives of the police officers working in the fictional small country town of Matlock.

This trend towards the more 'soap opera' element, with an emphasis on personal relationships within the police force, enabled Crawfords to have further production success with *Cop Shop* (1977–83). Exploring the nature of social and romantic relationships at a time of significant social transformation, *Cop Shop* took viewers twice a week into the lives and homes of both uniformed police officers and the plainclothes detectives of the fictional Riverside Police.[28] In these series, the police were for the most part portrayed extremely positively and writers were often assisted by members of the Victorian Police Force.

This positive portrayal (and relationship with) Australian police officers began to change however in the 1980s. For example, in 1983, the ABC produced the

---

[24] Curthoys (1991) 157.

[25] Televisionau.com, *Feature Articles—Cop Shows*, see: televisionau.com/feature-articles/cop-shows. The series even managed to sell overseas.

[26] *Blue Heelers* was allowed to produce its final episode at 510—the same number of episodes as *Homicide*.

[27] *Classic Australian Television—Division 4*, see: www.classicaustraliantv.com/div4.htm.

[28] Less successful attempts at police dramas during this time included *Bellamy* (1981), *Special Squad* (1984) and *Waterloo Station* (1983).

controversial *Scales of Justice*—a series of three self-contained, character-linked dramas that painted a less positive picture of Australian law enforcement than its predecessors. The series attracted criticism (from the police and commentators alike) for its portrayal of entrenched, systemic corruption at all levels of law enforcement, and for its observational, 'docudrama' style. The concern was that its realism would confuse audiences who were not capable of distinguishing fiction from fact. Despite the criticism, the 'authentic' style of *Scales of Justice*, that blurred boundaries between real-life events and fictional accounts, contributed in the late 1980s and early 1990s to Australian audiences increasing their appetite for stories based on 'real-life' events and true crime. In 1989, the recreation of the Fitzgerald Inquiry[29]—*Police State*—was largely based on transcripts of the Inquiry itself.[30] This was quickly followed by *Phoenix* (1992–93), which recounted the investigation of the bombing of a Victorian state police headquarters, loosely based on the real-life circumstances of the Russell Street bombing in 1986. These two series used documentary style cinematography and were favourably received by critics.[31]

In the mid-1990s, the ABC continued the emphasis on 'real-life' storytelling with *Blue Murder* (1995), a miniseries that portrayed the relationship between controversial NSW detective Roger 'the Dodger' Rogerson and notorious criminal Arthur 'Neddy' Smith. The series presented 'a world where co-dependence and cooperation between cops and criminals is a normal part of police culture'.[32] Narrated by the major characters, *Blue Murder* featured a naturalistic style and the observational camera techniques that had flavoured earlier ABC productions. It tapped into the public's apparent enthusiasm for true-crime stories—the key tagline used to advertise the series was: 'one of the most shocking characters in the history of law enforcement—a true story'. Interestingly, this miniseries was completed while its real-life counterparts were very much a part of the Australian criminal landscape—Neddy Smith was facing murder charges at the time and an injunction was granted to postpone the broadcasting of the series until after the trial in an attempt to mitigate possible prejudice and subjectivity in the outcome.

In addition to the ABC, the late-1990s saw a boom in Australian-made crime detective series on commercial television. Some of these shows included the Nine Network productions *Stingers* (1998–2004) and *Water Rats* (1996–2001); and the long running Seven Network police drama *Blue Heelers* (1993–2006). *Stingers* was a gritty, brisk series that followed agents in a police undercover unit who create false identities to get close to their targets; while *Water Rats* differentiated itself by

---

[29] This was a 'Commission of Inquiry into Possible Illegal Activities and Associated Police Misconduct', from 1987 to 1989, into the Queensland police force that resulted in the deposition of a premier and the incarceration of three former ministers and a police commissioner.

[30] Kate Matthews reports: 'In one curious sequence that further complicates the distinction between real and represented events, Sergeant Colin Dillon plays himself, delivering his own testimony once more for the screen': Kate Matthews, 'Reality and TV Crime' *Australian Screen*, online resource of the Australian National Film and Sound Archive. See: aso.gov.au/titles/collections/reality-and-tv-crime/.

[31] ibid.

[32] ibid.

uniquely focusing on the Sydney Water Police as they investigated crimes around visually stunning Sydney Harbour locations. Seven's *Blue Heelers*, however, was by far the audience favourite for many years, and equalled the record set by *Homicide* for longest running series. It followed in the early tradition of *Matlock Police* by depicting events in a rural Victorian setting of fictional Mount Thomas, and its success sparked a flurry of production in the new millennium surrounding police driven crime series, including: *Young Lions* (2002) on Nine; *White Collar Blue* (2002–03) and *Rush* (2008–11) on Ten; and *City Homicide* (2007–11) on Seven.

Australia's second national broadcaster, SBS, also found some success in the production of crime dramas with two variations of the traditional police format. The first, *East West 101*, premiered in 2007 and again deployed techniques of gritty naturalism using dream and flashback sequences. The series provided a fresh take on criminal activities occurring in Sydney's multicultural west by tackling the complex and nuanced issue of race relations surrounding the police force. With the second SBS production series *Carla Cametti PD* (2009), the network took a different approach to the genre by basing the story on an Italian-Australian female police detective who was descended from the Mafia and found herself investigating her own gangster family. It was however short lived.

In the late-2000s, the popularity of 'real-life' crime depictions fuelled a change in emphasis—from crime detection to crime perpetration. The Nine Network's *Underbelly* franchise (beginning in 2008) was based on tales that were drawn directly from the Australian criminal underworld. The first series dramatising Melbourne's 'gangland wars' was stylised heavily on the US drama series *The Sopranos*,[33] and was favourably received by audiences and critics alike. *Underbelly* was a massive ratings success for Channel Nine, being hailed as 'Australia's best ever crime drama'.[34] However, ironically reminiscent of the legal circumstances surrounding *Blue Murder*, an injunction was also filed against the screening of *Underbelly* in Victoria. Key underworld figures involved in these gangland wars were about to begin criminal trials and the concern was that the fictionalised re-enactments of several events and characters would be unfair to those accused.[35] As a result, *Underbelly* began screening on 13 February 2008 on the Nine Network in all parts of Australia *except* Victoria. It was not until 2011 that the series could finally be screened in Victoria as *Underbelly: Uncut*.[36]

The *Underbelly* series continued to enjoy ratings success with the production of five more seasons in recent years—each one covering a different time period

---

[33] Turnbull (2014) 4.

[34] Daniel Ziffer, 'Underbelly Wins Ratings War' *The Age* (Melbourne, 14 February 2008); Marcus Casey, 'Butterflies in the Underbelly for gang show on Channel Nine' *The Daily Telegraph* (31 January 2008).

[35] Interestingly, the screening of *Underbelly* (and its potential to produce bias) was used by one of the underworld criminals, Tony Mokbel, as a justification to fight his extradition from Greece. It was also suggested that another major criminal featured in the series, Carl Williams, could have his appeal jeopardised on the basis of unfair prejudice: www.australiantelevision.net/underbelly/legal.html.

[36] For a quick, concise summary of the legal issues surrounding this series, see: www.australiantelevision.net/underbelly/legal.html.

in Australia's sordid criminal history.[37] Importantly, the popularity of the *Under-belly* series continues to demonstrate an almost insatiable public appetite for true-crime storytelling that fuelled the production of local crime drama series over the last 60 years.

Stories About Adjudication and Punishment: Focus on Female Lawyers

Interestingly, the most prominent and successful series developed locally within both the adjudication and punishment categories have revolved around key female figures. In the early-1980s, *Prisoner* (1979–86) was a powerful and unique drama series based around the lives of the inmates and staff of the maximum security Wentworth Detention Centre. As the only Australian television series to really deal with incarceration, the opening scenes were charged with emotion and gritty realism as two terrified new inmates entered the prison. The premise was that as women from diverse backgrounds are confronted by life in a prison cell, the rules and boundaries that keep the isolated community together are pushed to extremes. As a result the struggle for power, for friendship and for rehabilitation became dominant storylines. *Prisoner* was one of Australia's most popular series, and has become a cult classic.

During the time *Prisoner* was on the air, other female legal characters were being conceived. Known primarily for its successful and popularly received police dramas, Crawford Productions again struck gold in the early-1980s, with its dramatic soap opera for the Ten Network, *Carson's Law* (1983–84). Set in the 1920s, its protagonist was an independent 'progressive' lawyer and mother of three, who had to constantly fight prejudice within a male dominated legal world after her husband suddenly died. It was critically acclaimed for its attention to period detail and high technical standard; however the biggest criticism of the series was 'the scant regard paid to real life legal practice'.[38] However, *Carson's Law* depicted the every-day struggles that female lawyers face (and still do) in fighting prejudice and ste-reotypes. Since this time several other popular Australian female characters have found their place within the fictional law firm or courtroom, as most evident in the late-1990s production of ABC's *SeaChange* (1998–2000).

In *SeaChange*, Laura Gibson is a successful city corporate lawyer with an all-consuming career when her world implodes. After a series of personal crises, Laura packs up her life, and with her two children in tow, takes up a position as a local magistrate in the small and sleepy coastal town of Pearl Bay where she hears many eccentric cases. 'Gaining record-breaking audiences for a non-commercial

---

[37] *Underbelly: A Tale Of Two Cities* takes us back to 1976; *Underbelly: The Golden Mile* is set in Sydney's Kings Cross from 1988 to 1999; *Underbelly: Razor*—the 1920s; *Underbelly: Badness* takes place in Sydney from 2001 to 2012; *Underbelly: Squizzy* spans the years 1915 to 1927.

[38] Aussie Soap Archives: members.ozemail.com.au/~fangora/index.html.

drama, it became the most popular Australian series on air',[39] and part of its appeal was the focus on the characters' struggles with what is actually required to have a meaningful life. Interestingly, Laura's courtroom provided the perfect venue for a small town to balance the relationship between the rule of law and the rules of community and friendship.[40] *SeaChange* was a whimsical series with quirky characters that attracted popular attention because of its anti-materialistic, small town message. In a beguiling way, it not only popularised the idea of city dwellers moving to a more relaxed coastal lifestyle,[41] but it also again demonstrated the difficulties female lawyers/judges face in a traditionally male dominated arena.

ABC's *Crownies* (2011) on the other hand, followed five young solicitors fresh out of law school (three of whom were women), as they began work at the Crown Prosecutor's Office and made decisions about the prosecution of alleged wrongdoers. As is seemingly a tradition in ABC legally themed dramatic productions, the series is based on the real-life NSW Office of the Director of Public Prosecutions (DPP)—a frantic workplace where discussion of murders, political corruption and sexual abuse of minors is not only commonplace, but mandatory.[42] The series thus highlights the moral dilemmas facing public prosecutors in a world that craves retributive justice,[43] and the storylines show these young men and women attempting to negotiate the pressures of balancing (at times) conflicting personal values and legal principles. With strong female characters becoming more prevalent on television in contemporary times, the ABC has introduced us to several interesting and complex female characters in *Crownies*, not least of which has been Senior Crown Prosecutor Janet King (Marta Dusseldorp), described as 'one of the most feared and admired advocates at the bar. Steely and immovable, with an armour-piercing gaze and a tongue that can eviscerate a poor argument, she is a consummate professional'.[44]

The spin-off production of *Janet King* (2014, ABC) in an eight-hour legal/political thriller explored the dilemmas of this fiercely independent woman who returns to work after maternity leave[45] and is flung into a shocking prosecution that involves intrigue, twists and revelations that become quite impactful on her life. The portrayal of Janet King in both these series demonstrates that Australian audiences are extremely receptive to storylines involving complicated yet professional and highly competent female lawyers.

It is interesting to note that another ABC production *Rake* (2010–) uses the unprofessionalism of a male criminal defence barrister to serve as stark contrast.

---

[39] Kate Matthews, *SeaChange—One of the Gang, Curators Notes*: aso.gov.au/titles/tv/seachange-one-of-the-gang/notes/. 'With audiences that sometimes topped two million, *SeaChange* knocked current affairs show 60 Minutes (1979–current) from its previously comfortable perch atop the ratings in the Sunday night 7.30 pm family viewing timeslot'.

[40] ibid.

[41] Murphy (2002).

[42] Graeme Blundell, 'DPP lawyer drama a Crownie achievement for ABC' *First Watch, The Australian* (9 July 2011).

[43] Sharp (2014).

[44] The official *Crownies* website on *Janet* (2011): see abc.net.au.

[45] The character of Janet King is in a same-sex relationship and has a child through IVF.

The main character, Cleaver Greene, is a brilliant barrister whose life is spiralling out of control. At once charismatic and self-destructive, he is a gambler in debt, he participates in many questionable activities, and he defends the indefensible: from bigamists to cannibals, drug lords to murderers, and somehow still seems to keep his career afloat. Yet, the series gained popularity for the way his character was portrayed (and acted by Richard Roxborough)—charming, garish, colourful and exasperating all at once. Rather than the usual legal drama which is procedural and formulaic, *Rake* thrives and survives on the sometimes shocking overlap between Greene's personal and professional lives. The show has had further success in other jurisdictions, for example airing on Netflix in the US, UK and Canada.[46]

Law and Justice on Australian Television in November 2014

The extent and nature of 'justice', both formal and informal, observed during the collection period on Australian TV, was consistent with the approach across this collection—that being classified both in terms of the phase of the justice process portrayed as well as by the kind of programme. As was demonstrated in the previous section, the three distinct categories within the 'justice' genre (police and crime detection; lawyer and court or adjudication; and punishment) are not represented equally in terms of programming. It is clear from the history of Australian television production that Australian audiences have a distinct penchant for true-crime stories and police detection material. That was especially true in 2014—whether within imported or locally produced material.

The empirical data summarised below covers the designated sample time of November 2014. The time period was determined as the primary viewing hours between 6.30 pm and 11.30 pm, and the coverage was across all free-to-air television stations. Shows selected for inclusion were measured against the three generic categories (police and detective; lawyer and court; prison and post-prison) and also cross-referenced across the style of show (drama, comedy, reality, or documentary). As will be demonstrated by the data referenced in the table below, the overwhelming network preference during this time period was to prioritise police and crime detection shows, with minimal screen time allocated to shows depicting either lawyer and court-focused material, or prison and post-prison productions. This is the case for both Australian and imported series, and it must be noted that across the selected month and time frame, the ratio of imported series to home-grown Australian productions was 10:1. Interestingly, 62% of the law and justice themed shows airing during the month of November were imported from the US; while 28% originated in the UK. While this might not seem to correlate

---

[46] Interestingly, the Fox Network in the US has produced an American version starring Greg Kinnear in the title role.

with the ABCB quotas identified earlier of 55% local production, it should be remembered that the shows identified for this research only canvass series with a law and justice theme. It is to be expected that the remaining 45% of Australian produced TV shows would fall within other categories and genres.[47]

Table 1: Shows relating to law and justice on Australian TV

Police and detective material	Dramas	Comedies	Reality-based entertainment
WEEK 1 (3–9 Nov)	**Australian productions (1)** *Doctor Blake Mysteries* **US productions (17)** *Blue Bloods* *Fargo* *Grimm* *Criminal Minds* *Law and Order: SVU* *CSI* *CSI: Miami* *Breaking Bad* *NCIS* *NCIS: LA* *NCIS: New Orleans* *Gotham* *Castle* *The Blacklist* *Homeland* *Marvel's Agents of Shield* *Cold Case* **British productions (11)** *Inspector Lynley* *New Tricks* *Scott and Bailey* *Agatha Christie's Poirot* *Midsomer Murders* *Rosemary and Thyme* *A Touch of Frost* *The Fall* *Dalziel and Pascoe* *Happy Valley* *Silent Witness*	**US productions (1)** *Brooklyn Nine-Nine*	**Australian productions (4)** *Gold Coast Cops* *Territory Cops* *Highway Patrol* *Crash Investigation Unit* **US productions (2)** *COPS* *COPS: Adults Only*

(continued)

---

[47] Australians also have a desperate fascination for the reality genre and home improvement shows.

Table 1: *(Continued)*

Police and detective material	Dramas	Comedies	Reality-based entertainment
WEEK 2 (10–16 Nov)	Same as week 1 plus: **US productions (4)** *Medium* *Arrow* *Hawaii Five-O* *Covert Affairs* **British productions (1)** *Jonathan Creek*	Same as week 1	Same as week 1
WEEK 3 (17–23 Nov)	Same as week 1	Same as week 1	Same as week 1
WEEK 4 (24–30 Nov)	Same as week 1 plus: **British productions (1)** *Death in Paradise*	0	Same as week 1
Total 4 wks	35	1	6

Lawyer and court-focused material	Dramas	Comedies	Reality-based entertainment
WEEK 1 (3–9 Nov)	**US productions (2)** *The Good Wife* *Reckless* **British productions (1)** *Judge John Deed*	0	
WEEK 2 (10–16 Nov)	Same as week 1 minus: *Reckless*		
WEEK 3 (17–23 Nov)	Same as week 1 *minus:* *Reckless*		
WEEK 4 (24–30 Nov)	Only *Judge John Deed* aired during this week		
Total 4 wks	3	0	

(continued)

Table 1: *(Continued)*

Prison and post-prison material	Dramas	Comedies	Reality-based entertainment
WEEK 1 (3–9 Nov)	**US productions (1)** *Crisis*	0	**US productions (1)** *America's Hardest Prisons*
WEEK 2 (10–16 Nov)	There were 0 dramas during weeks 2–4 in this category		0
WEEK 3 (17–23 Nov)			**US productions** *America's Hardest Prisons*
WEEK 4 (24–30 Nov)			**US productions** *America's Hardest Prisons*
Total 4 wks	1	**0**	1

The Australian Fascination with Crime Detection

As evidenced in Table 1 above, during the sample month, very few Australian productions appeared. In terms of the three categories designated for this international comparison, there were zero local productions within the adjudication (lawyers, court-focused) and punishment (prison and post-prison) categories. Clearly, the most dominant source of material in relation to law and justice (formal and informal) was found to be within the category of crime detection (police and detective material). Only 12% of the police and detective material that screened during the month of November 2014 was locally produced. Significantly, out of this home-grown material, four out of the five were located within the reality-based entertainment classification (with the remaining show *Dr Blake Mysteries* (2013–) in the drama category). The four series of *Gold Coast Cops* (2014–), *Territory Cops* (2012–), *Highway Patrol* (2009–) and *Crash Investigation Unit* (2008–11) form the core group of reality-based shows that led Australian produced prime-time viewing on Monday and Tuesday nights during the sample month.

Gold Coast Cops produced by the Ten Network, follows the day to day activities of police officers from the newly created Rapid Action & Patrols Group (RAP) on the Gold Coast in Queensland. Given unprecedented access to what is described as an 'elite' taskforce responsible for 'policing everything from biker gangs and street violence to drug heists and organised crime', the series gives viewers 'a compelling insight into the RAP and the men and women fighting crime on the Gold Coast'.[48]

---

[48] Network Ten Chief Programming Officer, Beverley McGarvey, Network Ten Promotional online material for *Gold Coast Cops*: tenplay.com.au/channel-ten/gold-coast-cops/about.

Interestingly, despite its popularity *Gold Coast Cops* has attracted significant attention in social media for the disunity it has provoked within the police force. Many police officers external to the RAP unit have taken umbrage at the use of the term 'elite' as a descriptor for this taskforce, and have argued that RAP alone is not responsible for the success of the Queensland Police Force.[49]

Territory Cops, also airing on the Ten Network in the time slot after *Gold Coast Cops*, mirrors a similar pattern to its prime-time bedfellow. Following police officers in the Northern Territory of Australia (described in one episode as 'one of the last Frontiers'), the unique criminal problems of that area are highlighted: problems with alcohol and drugs in more remote communities; the large distances between towns in the outback; and the native wildlife. It is worth noting the 'Australianness' of both these series. Australian slang ('fair dinkum') and the Australian tradition of assigning nicknames ('Wombat', 'Macca') are especially emphasised, as is the stereotypically 'Aussie' laid-back casual attitude that is evident in the police officers' interactions with suspects.

The fascination Australian audiences have with the 'real-life' work of police officers continues with both *Crash Investigation Unit* and *Highway Patrol*. Each of these series, produced by the Seven Network, focuses on road crimes and serious traffic incidents. Depicting the investigations into serious traffic offences and incidents that occur on our major roads, including high-speed police chases, attending major road accidents, and confronting out-of-control drunk drivers, these series follow a documentary style presentation designed to demonstrate 'real-time' police activity.

Finally, as mentioned above, the only home-produced production in the drama classification of crime detection was the *Dr Blake Mysteries* produced by the ABC. In this series, set in the former gold rush town of Ballarat in 1959, Dr Lucien Blake returns to town to take over his dead father's medical practice and the connected role as on-call police surgeon. Dr Blake inevitably gets caught up in the investigation of various criminal mysteries that need solving within a community that is rebuilding itself, and the series provides an interesting take on Australia's social history and development during the 1950s.

Concluding Remarks

It is interesting to note that despite the wealth of Australian TV series production over the last 60 years, the month of November 2014 does not adequately reflect

---

[49] Amy Remeikis, 'Gold Coast Cops mocked by colleagues' *Brisbane Times* (30 September 2014): www.brisbanetimes.com.au/queensland/gold-coast-cops-mocked-by-colleagues-20140929-10nr7q. html. This is despite the unit increasing the level of successful public 'tip-offs' since it began airing: Cartwright, D, 'Gold Coast Cops attracts public tip-offs' *News Corp Australia Network* (16 March 2015) www.news.com.au/national/queensland/gold-coast-cops-attracts-public-tip-offs/ story-fnk7yze2-1227264927373.

that. As one would expect, traditionally the majority of locally produced comedy and drama on commercial networks is shown during the ratings period[50] and November (as the final ratings opportunity for the year) is often seen as a key time for commercial networks to wind up their flagship series. However, 2014 seems to have witnessed a particular slump in the screening of local productions—and it did not go unnoticed. One journalist commented:

> Aussie TV networks are in a slump with hardly any shows getting above the crucial one million viewers in recent weeks. Nothing looks likely to stop the rot even though there is more than a month left to go until the end of the ratings year. It can't come quick enough.[51]

In a year that produced several good law and justice themed Aussie dramas (eg, *Dr Blake Mysteries, Rake, Janet King*), the month of November was a major let-down. Certainly, the 2014 ratings revealed that the most watched programmes during the year were sport and locally produced reality/competition shows (*My Kitchen Rules, The X-Factor, The Block, MasterChef* and *The Bachelor*).[52] So despite the fact that the shows that reached the largest audiences in 2014 were locally produced, the only home-grown 'law and justice' themed series to earn a place on the top 50 most watched shows was a Seven Network telemovie entitled *The Killing Field* (2014). This production featured a female detective sergeant who brings her team to a small town to solve a missing person/murder case. Rebecca Gibney (one of Australia's most beloved actors) played the starring role of Detective Winter, and the series was so well received that Gibney returned in Australia's most recent production to reprise her role for her own spin-off: *Winter* (2015). The success of this series would suggest that the Australian enthusiasm for crime detection series, and strong female leads, has not abated as time has passed.

While the month of November 2014 may not have demonstrated a thriving local demand for law and justice themed series, the history of Australian television production to date would indicate that Aussie audiences have a distinct penchant for crime detection series (whether imported or not) and particularly enjoy home-grown dramas that are based on real-life events/crimes. Perhaps it might be argued, that as our history and heritage is so closely tied up with a convict narrative, we cannot help but exhibit an enduring and unwitting fascination of that which is in our blood—but of course only time will tell if our penchant for crime will one day wane.

---

[50] Ratings data is collected every week excluding a two-week break during Easter and 10 weeks over summer (December, January and the start of February).

[51] Vickery, C, 'TV networks asking "where have all the viewers gone" as shows fail to break the one million viewer barrier' *News Corp Australia Network* (3 November 2014): www.news.com.au/entertainment/tv/tv-networks-asking-where-have-all-the-viewers-gone-as-shows-fail-to-break-the-one-million-viewer-barrier/story-fn8yvfst-1227110018622.

[52] Read more about 2014 ratings: www.smh.com.au/entertainment/tv-and-radio/seven-wins-2014-tv-ratings-battle-but-nine-on-target-with-advertisers-20141130-11w2ms.html#ixzz3V6dA51Ex.

3

Belgium (Flanders)

HILDE VAN DEN BULCK, KATHLEEN CUSTERS
AND JAN VAN DEN BULCK

Introduction

Flanders is the northern, Dutch-speaking part of Belgium, with over half of the 11 million Belgian population. It shares its language only with its northern neighbour, the Netherlands, and a limited number of former Dutch colonies such as Aruba and Suriname. Its small region and language has always affected Flemish television, which has a history of limitations inherent to small media markets but also of ambition and strong local roots.

As in most Western European countries, television in Belgium started as part of public service broadcasting. Following the political structure of the Belgian State, the public service broadcaster was founded in 1930 as one institute with two semi-autonomous departments: the Flemish NIR and the French-speaking INR. The introduction of the 1960 Broadcasting Bill split Belgian public service broadcasting into two separate institutions, one Flemish and one Walloon, each developing their own policies with regard to the producing and programming of fiction.[1] Following the federalisation of the competence of media policy in the 1980s, both regions increasingly developed their own distinct broadcasting policies. In both cases, the public service broadcasting monopoly was ended legally in 1987 after which Flanders saw the introduction of a commercial channel, VTM, owned by a holding of Flemish publishing companies, while in French-speaking Belgium the Luxembourg RTL took charge of commercial television.[2] This is reflective of an enduring policy trend in Flanders, characterised by an emphasis on Flemish ownership and content and on a *pax media* between public service and commercial media players. Nevertheless, both followed European trends[3] and grew into multichannel markets in the 1990s, providing a growing number of commercial home and international channels. More recently, the television markets witnessed

---

[1] Van den Bulck (2001).
[2] Saeys (2007).
[3] Siune and Hultén (1998).

a convergence of old and new media following digitisation, introducing new services that move beyond traditional, linear television through time shift options and VOD and new players such as OTT services (eg, Netflix). This chapter focuses on Flemish television but, where data are available, contextualises this by making reference to French-speaking Belgian and wider European television markets.

The availability, characteristics and reception of TV law shows in Flanders over time has been influenced by the characteristics of its media market. Flanders is a small region with a globally little used language. This influence must be understood within the tension between home-made versus imported programmes, between cultural proximity and cultural imperialism, between homogenisation and hybridisation, all processes that typically can be seen to be at work in a small television market such as that in Flanders.[4]

To this end, this chapter provides a theoretical framework that discusses the position of small television markets in what has always been a boundary crossing industry and how this can affect the availability, characteristics and reception of TV law shows. Against this backdrop, we provide a historical overview of Flemish TV law shows, indicating two distinct historical periods: the public service broadcasting monopoly (1953–89) and the period of competition and commercialisation (1989–2005). The final section will look at the contemporary digital era and provides a number of case studies and the result of a quantitative content analysis of Flemish channels in November 2014. Throughout, we focus on the production of TV law shows, the characteristics and the reception hereof, looking at home-made as well as imported programmes.

Production, Import, Imperialism and Cultural Proximity

Governments, as well as public and commercial broadcasters, always have valued highly the production of domestic audiovisual content for a mix of economic and cultural reasons. Traditionally, public broadcasters tried to fulfil their threefold responsibility to inform, educate and entertain through qualitative and, preferably, home-made programmes. Special attention was given to the enhancement of the educational and cultural capital of the audience, hence the high professional standards, and to the articulation and promotion of national identity.[5] The latter definitely applied to entertainment fiction, seen as a crucial platform to (re) create, maintain and stimulate national identity and cultural specifics. The arrival of commercial television did not put an end to this, as many local commercial channels too attached great importance to providing recognisable home programming to compete with foreign channels. Today, home production continues

---

[4] Lowe and Nissen (2011).
[5] Scannell and Cardiff (1991); Tracey (1998); and Van den Bulck (2001).

to be key to television stations and governments around the world, as a means of economic wellbeing of the production sector, as a showpiece of cultural specifics and as popular with audiences.[6] Even at the EU level, the opening up of television markets was always combined with a stress on home-made programmes, to foster the creative industries and the cultural diversity in Europe.

This preference for home-made programmes on the policy and production side is mirrored by a preference of audiences for home productions. This is explained through the concept of cultural proximity. Straubhaar describes this as 'the tendency to prefer media products from one's own culture or the most similar possible culture',[7] and empirical research recognises that audiences search for cultural proximity in audiovisual services.[8] Audiences indeed seemed to give preference to domestically produced programmes, or at least to programmes incorporating familiar personal and group affiliations, lifestyle, language and social norms, and values relating to gender, religion, ethnicity and family.[9] Audiences also preferred local adaptations of US television shows.[10]

Moreover, the proximity of the geographic location shown in media content may contribute to the degree of impact a TV show has on its audience. Viewers will be more likely to notice similarities between themselves and characters of domestically produced TV shows than between themselves and characters of internationally produced TV programmes. These similarities may enhance identification, i.e, the process through which people become engrossed and 'experience reception and interpretation of the text from the inside, as if the events were happening to them'.[11] Flemish characters might thus elicit greater identification in a Flemish audience than do American characters. In turn, American crime drama shows diminished appeal elsewhere as viewers find it difficult to identify with styles, values, beliefs, institutions and behavioural patterns of the material in question.[12]

This has financial implications. Television production, and especially the production of fiction, is an expensive affair, due to its specific cost structure with high development and original costs and low to no reproductive costs. This results in a need for economies of scale (and scope) to be profitable, also by selling programmes in different (and consecutive) markets. Creating such economies of scale, however, is not evident for small broadcasters from small cultures and countries, as the home market is limited, and co-production and sales are limited due to a high cultural discount. The latter refers to the fact that Flemish programmes will not have great appeal outside Flanders.

Even in the days of public service monopolies, budgets and opportunities pushed public broadcasters, particularly smaller ones, to acquire part of their

[6] Syvertsen et al. (2014).
[7] Straubhaar (2003) 85.
[8] Straubhaar (1991).
[9] Straubhaar (2003).
[10] De Bens and de Smaele (2001); and Straubhaar (1991).
[11] Cohen (2001) 245.
[12] Hoskins and Mirus (1988) 503.

programming from elsewhere.[13] As the number of channels grew, following the end of public service monopolies, and the number of broadcasting hours extended, more and more programming needed to be acquired to fill all the slots.[14] Many studies in communication sciences have dealt with the issue of selling and acquiring audiovisual content, focusing on the uneven nature of programme flows characterised by a dominance of US programming, especially fiction, on the world market.[15] Reasons for the international success of US programmes include that they are relatively cheap to acquire as these programmes can break even in their large home market; tend to be in English, a worldwide lingua franca; and the characteristics of the American TV market which gives US shows an advantage due to synergies with the Hollywood film industry.

From a political economy perspective, the uneven flows are determined by the process of cultural imperialism, insisting that inequality in information, communication and content flows reproduce economic power structures.[16] Many studies have empirically illustrated the one-way traffic in content flows from the United States to other parts around the globe.[17] One underlying problem with these flows is the potential harm they cause to (particularly smaller) national cultures and identities, and to cultural diversity with the presumed impact ranging from cultural homogenisation to cultural appropriation.[18] Despite extensive criticism, modification and contextualisation of the notion of cultural imperialism[19] and despite the realisation that cultural imperialism is no longer a matter of cultural dominance of one but several centres in the world, the idea of cultural imperialism, and its many diverging manifestations, has remained highly relevant. It continues to be backed by data pointing not only at the dominance of US, but also UK audiovisual exports, in particular vis-a-vis the south/developing countries, but also vis-a-vis smaller European countries that fail to escape the economic and cultural dominance of US and UK players in the audiovisual market.[20]

Fiction on Flemish Television between 2006 and 2013

The proportion of fiction is highest in the programming found on commercial television channels. In Flanders, 15.7% of the leading public services channel, Eén, is devoted to fiction programmes of which 12.2% consists of series. Ketnet, the public children's television channel, devotes 41.4% of its airtime to fiction

---

[13] Van den Bulck (2001).
[14] Spada (2002).
[15] See Dupangne and Waterman (1998).
[16] Schiller (1976); and Boyd-Barrett (1977) 116–36.
[17] See, eg, Varis (1985); and Boyd-Barrett (1977) 116–36.
[18] Hannerz (1992).
[19] Tomlinson (1999); and Thussu (2007).
[20] Van Poecke and Van den Bulck (1994); and Banarjee (2003) 57–79.

whereas Canvas, the public cultural channel, devotes much less airtime to fiction (12.2%). In total, the Flemish public broadcasting channels devote 69.3% of their total schedule time to fiction.

Concerning the commercial channels in Flanders, the principal commercial channel, VTM, devotes 36.2% of programming time to fiction, of which 26.2% consists of series. The channels 2BE and Vier score higher with proportions of fiction of 48.6% and 43.8% respectively. Similar patterns are visible in the French community.

Regarding the origin of fictional programming, the proportion of national works in Flanders increased from 6.6% in 2007 to 8.8% in 2013, whereas the proportion of non-European works decreased from 26.2% to 23.6% in the same period. The proportion of national works in Wallonia was considerably lower with 0.7% in 2007 and 1.9% in 2013, whereas the proportion of European works was significantly higher in 2007 (38%) and 2013 (38.6%). The proportion of non-European fiction programmes broadcast by Flemish television channels did not change between 2007 (67.2%) and 2013 (67.5%). In Wallonia, there was a slight decrease from 61.3% in 2007 to 59.5% in 2013.

The Flemish situation is in line with the global European pattern between 2006 and 2013. Overall, across 17 European countries,[21] European-produced fiction shows an increasing trend going from 36.3% in 2006 to 39% in 2013. This is largely due to a rise of nationally broadcast fiction programmes across all countries in the same period, going from 13.1% in 2006 to 17% in 2013. Before 2011, the countries with the largest proportion of national fiction programmes were France (28.1%), Spain (22.6%), the United Kingdon (17.5%), Italy (16.8%) and Germany (13.4%). In 2013, national works were prevalent in Poland (47.6%) and Portugal (42.6%). Overall, the United States is the main origin of non-European fiction. In 2013, Denmark had the largest proportion of non-European fiction (81.0%) followed by Sweden (77.5%) and the United Kingdom (71.3%). Countries with the least proportion of non-European fiction are Luxembourg (39.3%), France (39.4%) and Portugal (48.4%).[22]

Large differences exist regarding the use of dubbing between European countries. Northwestern Europe (United Kingdom, Ireland, the Netherlands, the Nordic countries and the Dutch-speaking part of Belgium) prefer subtitling to dubbing. Only movies and children's TV shows are dubbed; movies and TV shows for older audiences are subtitled. In France, Spain, Italy and the Germanophone countries (Germany, Austria and the German-speaking part of Switzerland) the dubbing market is the largest; nearly all movies and TV shows are released dubbed in the language of origin.

A report of the Flemish Center for Information about Media (CIM) indicated that home-made fiction programmes ranked highly in Flanders. The top 10 fiction

---

[21] Austria, Belgium, Switzerland, Germany, Denmark, Finland, France, the United Kingdom, Ireland, Italy, Netherlands, Norway, Sweden, Spain, Luxembourg, Poland and Portugal.
[22] Lange (2014).

series broadcast on the principal public and commercial channels in Flanders in 2013 were all home-made. Examples are *Eigen Kweek, Salamander, De Ridder, Twee tot de Zesde Macht, Danni Lowinski, Zone Stad, Aspe, Zuidflank*, and *Thuis*. The availability, characteristics and reception of Flemish TV law shows must be understood against this background of tension between home-made versus imported programmes, between cultural proximity and cultural imperialism, and between homogenisation and hybridisation.

Historical Overview of TV Law Shows in Flanders

The Public Service Monopoly Years (1953–89)

As a classic example of European public service broadcasting,[23] Flemish television aimed to provide a mix of information, education and entertainment within the boundaries of high professional standards and aimed at contributing to national identity and a cultural-educational logic. Priorities in the early years thus were clear: information, high culture and grand entertainment, including TV plays (one-off fictional drama) and high quality fiction, were to provide the basic ingredient, while other programmes were to serve as stopgaps.[24] Analysis of actual programming in 1953 and 1957[25] reveals that entertainment took up 35.7% and 39.1% respectively of all broadcast time. Within entertainment, there was 5% and 21% respectively reserved for TV plays (one-offs, based mostly on theatre plays). Among the early TV plays, only one 'detective style' story could be identified: *Een Inspekteur voor U (An Inspector Calls)*, based on a 1945 British play by John B Priestley revolving around a suicide and a police detective. Series were rare with only two original home-made productions in the 1950s that had popular Flemish folk content; most series were American in origin. According to Anthierens, the key characteristics of these US series were 'cheap empathy and superficial heroism'.[26] Cop shows such as *I am the Law* (1955) and *Highway Patrol* (1958) and a western series, *Tales of the Texas Rangers* (1957) dominated and were liked because they were well made and relied on 50 years of Hollywood experience.[27] Later, British fiction was broadcast as it was believed to provide better quality stories and stronger acting.[28]

It was not until the 1960s, when public service television came of age both financially and in terms of programming, that entertainment in general and

---

[23] Van den Bulck (2001).
[24] Van den Bulck (2009).
[25] Van den Bulck (2000) 219.
[26] Anthierens (1965) 159.
[27] Bal (1985).
[28] Van Casteren (1978).

fiction in particular really took off. The latter was helped by the introduction in 1963 of videotape, allowing taping and editing programmes.[29] In the 1960s and 1970s, entertainment took up between 34.6% (1961) and 20.6% (1973) of all broadcast time.[30] Within entertainment, the percentage of fiction varied, with single plays going down from 21.8% of all entertainment in 1961 to 7.1% in 1973, while series (excluding miniseries that were overall very rare) showed a reverse trend going from 13.8% in 1961 to 39.6% by 1973.[31] Indeed, a key evolution in the growing relevance of fiction was the move from single play to serialisation. A good example was *Hof van Assisen 1886–* (*Court of Assizes 1886–*), a range of historical reconstruction single plays dealing with historical Flemish court cases of which the first, *De zaak Versmissen* (The Versmissen Case), was broadcast in 1965. In 1971, this was serialised into fictional court cases in the series *Beschuldigde Sta Op* (Defendant, Please Rise).[32]

However, most Flemish fiction was far removed from the law show genre. Instead, the need for identification with Flemish culture was translated into a strong focus on adaptations of Flemish theatrical and literary classics and Flemish culture. In the 1960s, this resulted in many popular series focusing on nostalgic interpretations of village and farming life and 'ordinary folks', while in the 1970s, as public service television became more elitist, high-quality drama revolving around well-to-do families were produced as well (eg, *Vorstinnen van Brugge* (*Princesses of Bruges*)). Flemish law shows were very rare, limited to an original home-made children's series *Axel Nort* (1966) about a private investigator, and a co-production with Dutch public service broadcasting pillar organisation KRO called *Centraal Station* (*Central Station*, 1974) about railway detectives. The latter is an interesting example of hybridisation, as it incorporated genre characteristics of US and British police detective shows. As a result, it had a contemporary and even cosmopolitan feel, funky music and spectacular chases, and therefore was very different from most of the fiction produced at the time.[33] This trend continued in the 1980s with a majority of home-made drama continuing the focus on history, 'ordinary folk' and farmers, and a few notable police shows.

The 1980s sitcom *De Kolderbrigade* (*The Slapstick Brigade*, 1980) was set in a police station in Ghent; and *Beschuldigde sta op* from 1981 onwards was replaced by *Met voorbedachte rade* (*Premeditated*), now based entirely on original Flemish fictional police scenarios. *Centraal Station* was followed by *Langs de kade* (*Along the Waterfront*), which focused on harbour policing and, following US trends, on the protagonists' personal lives as much as police action.

---

[29] Dhoest (2004) 49.

[30] Van den Bulck (2000) 271–72.

[31] Van den Bulck (2001).

[32] Van Casteren, A. (1978). *25 dozijn rode rozen. Een kwarteeuw Vlaamse televisie.* [25 Dozen red roses. A quarter century of Flemish television] Gent: Het Volk; Grossey, R. (1995) *Groot lexicon van de tv series uit de fabuleuze Jaren 50-60.* [Lexicon of TV series from the fabulous 50-60s]Antwerp: Standaard Uitgeverij; and Grossey, R. (1997) Groot lexicon van de tv series uit de spetterende jaren 70. [Lexicon of TV series from the rousing 70s] Antwerp: Standaard Uitgeverij.

[33] Dhoest (2004) 57.

Imported fiction to a large extent compensated for the absence of home-made law shows. The additional broadcast hours required more programming, and selection criteria became less strict and more openly focused on entertainment over the cultural education logic. Imported law shows were dominated by the United States; police and detective shows were omnipresent and extremely popular. These included: *87th Precinct, Mannix, Jake,* and *Columbo,* amongst others. The 1960s introduced the subgenre of special agents, such as in *The Man from UNCLE* (1966), *Mission Impossible* (1967), *Get Christie Love* (with a female lead, 1975), and provided law shows with a certain moral story as in *The High Chaparral* or *The Untouchables* (1965).[34] In the 1970s, there were a number of imported law shows introducing the sub-genre of outlaws and private individuals fighting for justice such as *The Persuaders* (1971) and *Alias Smith and Jones* (1972). Of course there were European cop shows too such as British series *Sherlock Holmes* (1965) and *The Sweeney* (1987); French series *L'Heure de Linge U* (1978) and *Commissaire Moulin* (1978).[35] The 1980s also saw the international success of German 'Krimi' series such as *Derrick* and *Der Alte,* extended to Flemish television.

Competition and Commercialisation (1989–2006)

The end of the Flemish public service broadcasting monopoly in 1987, the result of technological, economic, political and cultural factors as well as a general level of criticism with regard to the bureaucratised and culturally hermetic public service institution that had lost touch with its audience,[36] and the introduction of the first Flemish commercial television station VTM, resulted in a considerable shift in programming, also with regard to law shows. Wanting to be 'Flemish and Popular', VTM introduced a wide range of Flemish fiction but, different from the old public service television's stress on quality drama, VTM opted mostly for popular fiction and for long-running series that could tie audiences to the station.[37] Between 1990 and 2002 it introduced no less than 15 new, home-made sitcoms, mostly about 'ordinary people'. Following the enormous success of soap operas abroad, it introduced its own daily soap *Familie* (*Family,* 1991–), which was fashioned along the lines of British ordinary people soaps such as *Eastenders,* and the twice weekly *Wittekerke* (1993–2008), focusing on a particular, but fictional, community near the seaside.

VTM also invested in law shows, thus giving the genre not just a boost but a make-over, albeit with varying success.[38] The various productions suffered from the difficult balance between reasonable production costs, credible action and audience appreciation. The majority of shows focused on the police detective

---

[34] Buxton (1990).
[35] Grossey (1995); and Grossey (1997).
[36] Van den Bulck (2007); and Blumler (1992).
[37] Dhoest (2004) 65.
[38] ibid, 69.

sub-genre, first with a low-cost production *Commissaris Roos* (*Detective Roos*, 1990), fashioned along the lines of the German Krimi genre, followed by *Bex & Blanche* (1993) about a detective (Bex) who was a distinctly Flemish and credible anti-hero. Audiences loved the show but this could not sufficiently compensate for its high production costs. The cheaply made 1997 *Gilliams & De Bie* failed to lure audiences. To the extent that VTM did provide prestigious quality drama in this period, it was never based in the law show genre.

Public service broadcasting at first was slow to respond to this commercial competition. However, from the mid-1990s onwards, following a thorough reorganisation of the public service institution, public television started to invest more heavily in contemporary, quality popular drama, including law shows. *Heterdaad* (*Red Handed*, 1996) was a typical cop show, set in the Brussels criminal investigations department, and was strongly influenced by US and UK police and detective shows. *Heterdaad* proved very popular with audiences due to its credible scenarios and quality acting. It was the start of a real revival of law shows, including the lawyer series *Recht op Recht* (*Right To Justice*, 1998) and courtroom drama *Court of Assizes* (1998), a 'turbo' version of *Beschuldigde sta op*, as well as police shows such as the short-lived detective series *Sedes & Belli* (2002).[39] Of special interest is the public service broadcaster's scenarios *Flikken* (*Cops*) that ran from 1999 until 2009 and was set in a Ghent police station. Its success extended Flemish borders as (in line with the cultural proximity notion explained above) the series was first bought and broadcast by Dutch public service broadcasters, and later was sold as a format to Dutch public service broadcasters that translated it into *Flikken Maastricht* (2007–) and *Flikken Rotterdam* (2016). In 2004, the public service general interest channel launched its original detective series *Witse*, comparable in set-up to the UK production *Frost* with a grumpy chief constable (Witse) and his team.[40] The series was a huge success, with regular viewing figures of over 1.6 million, and lasted until 2012. The series was sold to Dutch public broadcaster AVROTROS. Also in 2004, the main commercial channel VTM introduced *Aspe*, based on the books of Flemish author Pieter Aspe, similarly focusing on a chief constable (Van In) and his team. The series ran successfully for 10 years.

The extension of the Flemish television market in the 1990s and early 2000s with additional Flemish channels did not translate into a proliferation of Flemish law shows as the smaller size of the audiences of many of these channels (and thus the smaller amount of commercial revenues) did not warrant the investment in (expensive) original fiction. One notable exception was *Vermist* (*Missing*), first broadcast in 2006 as a production of VT4 (in collaboration with production company Eyeworks) that revolved around the Missing Persons Division of the Belgian federal police.

The arrival of the new channels, particularly those originating in the mid-1990s (Kanaal Twee (now 2BE) and VT4 (now VIER)), created a considerable increase

---

[39] ibid, 74.
[40] Dhoest (2007).

in the availability of US crime fiction on Flemish television stations. Aimed at younger audiences and working with limited budgets, they depended heavily on imported programmes, including law shows, sometimes broadcasting them daily in a vertical scheduling technique and buying multiple repeat options. Furthermore, VT4 was the first in Flanders to introduce the programming technique of 'stacking', ie, programming several episodes of one programme or programmes of the same genre right after each other. This created a weekly crime night with series such as *CSI* and *NCIS* and their spin-offs, and *Homeland*, etc.[41] Through the years some US law shows, ranging from *Twin Peaks* in the early 1990s to, more recently, *Homeland* proved considerably successful with audiences. However, and confirming the above-discussed notion of cultural proximity, most of the US series, including those obtaining top ratings in the United States, never reached more than 700,000 viewers in Flanders. In comparison, *Witse* consistently reached over 1.6 million viewers and in its season finale, almost 2 million viewers. General interest channels such as public service channel één and commercial VTM, accommodating older audiences watching television in the afternoon, broadcast reruns of old law shows such as *Columbo* or shows such as *Murder, She Wrote*.

While these examples seem to support the idea of US dominance in foreign fiction TV, there are also clear indications of other programme flows. While the success of the German Krimis died down in the twenty-first century, they were replaced by a dominance in the 1990s and 2000s of UK shows including *Miss Marple* and *Poirot* (based on characters of UK writer Agatha Christie), *Inspector Morse* (based on a character in the work of Colin Dexter) and its sequel *Lewis* and, more recently, its prequel *Endeavour*, *Midsomer Murders*, *Frost* and many others. Many of these were first broadcast on Canvas, the public service channel for audiences looking for added value, and thus were branded as quality fiction. In terms of audience ratings, they often did better than US series. Despite being scheduled on the lesser-watched Canvas, they often reached around 900,000 viewers. In more recent years, this channel has broadcast Nordic crime series such as *Wallander, The Killing* and *The Bridge*, following the Nordic Noir vogue in the wake of the huge success of the *Millennium* trilogy (books and films).[42]

TV Law Shows in Flanders Today

The results of our content analysis of what was on offer on Flemish channels in November 2014 offers an interesting view of the contemporary Flemish television landscape. We analysed all the channels commonly available through most cable

---

[41] Van den Bulck, Tambuyzer and Simons (2014).
[42] AM Waade and PM Jensen (2013) 'Nordic Noir production values: *The Killing* and *The Bridge. Akademisk kvarter* 7': www.akademiskkvarter.hum.aau.dk/pdf/vol7/13a_AWaadePMJensen_Nordic-Noir.pdf, 188–201.

companies. This included één and Canvas (the public broadcasting channels) and the commercial channels: VTM, 2be, vier, vijf, and Acht.

In total 383 hours and 10 minutes of relevant material were broadcast during the period we studied. Only four programmes had prison-based storylines. These were four two-hour made-for-television movies, one per week. They were broadcast after 10.00 pm. There was no Flemish material. There were five hours and 10 minutes of lawyer and court-based shows in the reference period. This included four episodes of a Flemish show during prime time (7.30 pm to 10.00 pm), for a total of three hours and 40 minutes. There were two episodes of an American show for a total of one hour and 50 minutes, after 10.00 pm.

The majority of the material was police and detective related, 368 hours and 40 minutes in total. A small proportion of the material was comedy (4.02%) and slightly more was reality TV (8.27%), but the majority was drama (87.7%). Of this, 9.7 % was Flemish. This picture changed somewhat during prime time, when the proportion of Flemish material increased to 20.2%.

Conclusions and Discussion

The results of our content analysis are unsurprising and reproduce largely what earlier studies of international programme flow across Europe and in Belgium have shown. The proliferation of TV channels since the advent of cable TV means that more channels now have more hours to fill. TV shows produced in North America are invariably cheap. They have recouped their production costs in a large home market and are prolific during off-peak viewing hours in Flanders.

The findings of our content analysis have to be seen in their proper context. A number of observations can be made. First, content broadcast is not the same as content received. This is particularly relevant when comparing Flemish shows with American and other international shows. It may appear that Flemish shows are under-represented. As mentioned above, the picture changes somewhat when the viewing rates are added to it. Flemish police shows such as *Witse* or *Vermist* attract large audiences and have a prime-time audience share that no American or other show ever reaches. Even combined, the *CSI* or *NCIS* franchises, for instance, only reach a small part of the viewing audience, on the smaller channels. Unfortunately, viewing rates are rarely available for individual shows, but if they were it would be interesting to compare the raw data of content analysis with weighted data that take the viewing rates into account. The percentage of Flemish shows as a proportion of the viewing audience would likely be a lot higher in that case.

Second, what is available on television undergoes strong seasonal changes. Even the most popular shows only produce 12 or 24 new episodes each year. While a random month in a random year is likely to reproduce the large trends (such as the emphasis on police and detective drama we found in the current study), smaller trends may be more variable. Depending on the time and the year, the picture our content analysis drew could have been very different. For instance, the commercial channel VTM aired *Danni Lowinski*, a Flemish remake of a German show with the same name. This comedy show about a female lawyer ran for two seasons in 2012 and 2013, for a total of 26 episodes, each reaching about a 39% market share during prime time. A large proportion of the viewing audience was therefore exposed to a comedy show about a lawyer for part of the year during two years. This finding points at a second weakness of content analysis. It is extremely vulnerable to seasonal variation. While genres that are omnipresent, such as police shows, will probably always yield similar high percentages, regardless of the sample and the sample size, the same cannot be said for the other genres in this study. A single successful, but short-lived series may suggest that more prison comedy or courtroom reality drama is present than there usually is. Conversely, our current study suggests that courtroom reality TV is absent in Flanders, even though at least one series ran for five seasons, for a total of 26 episodes, on één (public channel) and Vier (a commercial channel) since 2011. A similar phenomenon is well known among media planners. Channels with a small audience are said to suffer from the law of 'Double Jeopardy': they have a smaller audience, which is also less loyal.[43] At the level of individual genres (such as lawyer comedies), the Double Jeopardy concept suggests that rare genres are less likely to show up in a sample of TV shows. Content analyses should take this into account.

Finally, the abundance of police and detective drama begs the question of its popularity. On one level this is clearly the most popular of the genres discussed in the contributions to this book. It is probably even the most popular genre all round, even when compared with other types of TV content. It is important, however, to note another concept from econometric audience research. Until fairly recently, viewer choice was relatively limited. Even though buying and renting films and TV series has been possible for a while, as is the recording of programmes for viewing later, studies of viewer behaviour suggest that people tend to 'watch by the hour'.[44] When people feel the need to watch TV they often prefer watching a 'least objectionable programme' over not viewing at all and thus may end up watching something they do not particularly like because nothing they like more appears to be on offer.[45] However, more recent developments may challenge this view. Today people are not limited to broadcast and cable channels. There are many different types of pay-per-view and other 'on demand' systems. In addition, there are many more platforms on which to consume TV programmes, such as laptops, tablets, or even mobile phones. In the coming years, audience research will have to try to determine whether viewing patterns that are as old as television survive the onslaught of new technologies and new content delivery systems.

---

[43] Van den Bulck (1995).
[44] ibid; and Van den Bulck (2006).
[45] ibid.

Will police, law and law-breaking television remain the mainstay of our audio-visual diet? Or will more choice show that much of the time the police drama, the prison reality show, or the lawyer comedy was just the 'least objectionable programme': a choice viewers made in the early decades of television because it was cheap, it was exciting, and because 'nothing else was on'.

4

Britain

PETER ROBSON

TV and its Development in Britain

Overview

The world's first regular high-definition television service was launched in Britain in November 1936 by the British Broadcasting Company (BBC).[1] The emergence of TV in Britain followed the successful experiment with radio and the decisions taken back then about funding and how to control this new medium. The strong commitment to public service broadcasting continues and although its demise has been forecast on a number of occasions, its services continue to enjoy very wide public support.[2]

The British Broadcasting Company Ltd was set up in November 1922 and became a corporation in 1927 funded by a licence fee[3] and with a public service ethos.[4] Its mandate, as expressed by its first Director General, John Reith, emphasised both entertainment and information.[5] These goals were later expressed in the 'soundbite' that the function of broadcasting was to 'educate, inform and entertain' and this remains embedded in the BBC's current charter.[6] In the post-war era, when television became a functioning reality, the concept of a public television service was accepted with a licence fee to fund it and a ban on advertising

---

[1] For details of the other more spasmodic services around in other countries at this time see Smith (1998) 18; for the beginnings of American television see Smith (1998) 23–37; and on its development Smith (1998) 147–61.

[2] British Audience Research Bureau (hereafter BARB) shows it as attracting around a third of the total TV audience today in the multi-channel digital age: www.barb.co.uk/whats-new/weekly-viewing-summary.

[3] Sykes Committee (1923) para 76(14).

[4] Crawford Committee (1926) para 20(a).

[5] Reith (1924) Pt 1, ch 1 'The Function of Broadcasting' 15–19.

[6] BROADCASTING, *Copy of Royal Charter for the continuance of the British Broadcasting Corporation* (2006) para 5(1). The BBC's main activities should be the promotion of its Public Purposes through the provision of output which consists of *information, education and entertainment* (my emphasis).

and programme sponsorship.[7] The view taken then was that advertising would 'endanger the traditions of public service, high standards and impartiality which have been built up over the past 25 years'.[8]

With a move to the political Right in 1951, however, legislation was introduced to establish a commercially funded system of television broadcasting to be overseen by a new regulatory body, the Independent Television Authority. On 22 September 1955 the first commercial channel, ITV, started broadcasting.[9] It was funded by 'spot advertising'. The advertising was inserted within and between its programmes as opposed to what was perceived by the Committee to be the more manipulative model of sponsorship. It was given, however, a serious public service remit which has led to it being described as a 'commercial public service broadcaster'.[10]

The programmes broadcast by the new commercial channel had both good taste and quality requirements as well as a requirement not to serve the interests of any particular political party. There was also a requirement that there be locally produced British material and that local interests be served. The notions of political balance and impartiality were also included.[11] It was acceptable for arguments of a political character to be expressed as long as these were included in 'programmes of properly balanced discussions or debates'.[12]

The Pilkington Committee, which was tasked to review the new system in July 1960, was critical of the narrowness of the programming of ITV and in order to encourage quality and diversity in programming chose to recommend an expansion of the public service channel.[13] The result was the Television Act 1963 and the launch of a second public service channel, BBC2, in 1964. The broad topic of the future of broadcasting was considered by the Annan Committee in the 1970s whose task was to consider the whole issue of the 'constitutional, organisational and financial arrangements and what conditions should apply to the conduct' of both existing and new services.[14]

The upshot of these concerns was a new way of encouraging independent productions with a diversity of programming within Channel 4. This fourth channel had a public service responsibility[15] and was funded by the commercial TV channels which had access to the airtime of Channel 4 to place their advertising. The fifth channel, Channel 5, was a rather simpler proposition. It went on air in 1997 and was conceived as and remains a purely commercial channel.

---

[7] *Broadcasting Committee Report* (1951).

[8] ibid, para 376.

[9] It was originally referred to as ITV—Independent Television—but since 2003 it has been technically referred to as Channel 3 to avoid confusion—BARB however and the public tend to still use the term ITV.

[10] Johnson and Turnock (2005a) 3.

[11] Television Act 1954, s 3.

[12] ibid, s 3 (1)(g)(ii).

[13] Pilkington Committee (1961–62) paras 901–02.

[14] Annan Committee (1976–77).

[15] Communications Act 2003, s 265 (3).

In the twenty-first century the availability of Freesat and Freeview has brought a wide variety of unregulated channels to over 26 million households. Of the 26 million homes receiving television in 2014, 11.4 million were receiving TV through satellite, 4.1 million through cable and 19.3 million through aerials.[16] BBC, ITV Channel 4 and Channel 5 can be accessed free of charge either through having a digital satellite receiver or aerial and these account for some 70% of audience share with the subscription services BSkyB having some 8% of the market and UK Channel Management around 4%.[17] There is no obligation on these commercial channels to provide a broad or well-thought-out range of programmes or have any news or documentary content as required in the BBC's Charter or the Television Act 1954 and its successors. Commercial channels can provide, as some like Dave, GOLD and Yesterday do, nothing but repeats of old material previously seen on other channels. Most are free but some involve subscription. The big difference here, as reported to the Hunt Committee in 1982, was that these channels were not subject to the same kind of detailed regulation as the existing channels.[18]

British Television Policy in the Twenty-First Century

The Formal Legal Regulation Framework of Television Providers in the Twenty-First Century

As noted, the BBC was set up with a public service goal or mandate. It was given a Royal Charter in 1926 and this has been renewed by successive governments. The current Charter from 2006 states that 'the BBC exists to serve the public interest'[19] and that its 'main object is the promotion of its Public Purposes'.[20] These public purposes are extremely broad and timeless:

a. Sustaining citizenship and civil society.
b. Promoting education and learning.
c. Stimulating creativity and cultural excellence.
d. Representing the UK, its nations, regions and communities.
e. Bringing the UK to the world and the world to the UK.
f. In promoting its other purposes, helping to deliver to the public the benefit of emerging communications technologies and services.[21]

---

[16] BARB, *Trends in Television Viewing*, Table 4.
[17] ibid, Table 5.
[18] Hunt Committee (1981–82).
[19] BROADCASTING, *Copy of Royal Charter for the continuance of the British Broadcasting Corporation* (2006) para 3(1).
[20] ibid, para 3(2).
[21] ibid, para 4.

By contrast, commercial television was originally regulated by the Television Act 1954 which laid down slightly less ambitious guidelines. The original regulatory body, the Independent Television Authority, had to be satisfied that

> nothing is included in the programmes which offends against good taste or decency or is likely to encourage or incite crime or to lead to disorder or to be offensive to public feeling or which contains any offensive representation of or reference to living person.

News coverage must be balanced, accurate and impartial.[22]

Under the current legislation, the Communications Act 2003, in deciding whether programmes meet the relevant criteria OFCOM (the Office of Communications) the current regulator is also charged with looking at ensuring the same kind of mix of 'information, education and entertainment' as were found in the Reith principles for the BBC.[23]

Financing TV in Britain

There are quite distinct differences between the funding of the public service channels—BBC and Channel 4—and the commercial channels. The BBC obtains its funds directly from all owners of television sets being required to buy a licence to watch their televisions legally.[24] The principle of the licence fee as a way of funding television was discussed by the Peacock Committee in the 1980s. The Committee noted that the flat-rate licence fee was regressive and unfair to those who might choose to watch only commercial channels. Its advantages were the security of funding that was provided for the BBC and the independence and freedom from political interference which it provided for this universal public service. One by-product was programmes of high quality being produced. The Report recommended that the licence fee be retained, with a move to a system of subscription in the future.[25] Subsequent examinations of the system in the 1990s[26] and in the twenty-first century[27] looked at various alternatives. These ranged from the licence fee status quo, funding from taxation, advertising, subscription and mixed sources.[28] The licence fee remains in place at the time of writing and is the subject of intense discussion in the run up to the 2016 BBC Charter renewal and appointment as Secretary of State for Culture, Media Sport of John Whittingdale on 11 May 2015. He previously chaired the Culture, Media and Sport Select Committee which indicated in February 2015 that, while in Whittingdale's words, 'in

---

[22] Television Act 1954, s 3(1).
[23] Communications Act 2003, s 264(6).
[24] ibid, s 363—those over 80 are exempt in terms of Regulations made under s 363(6).
[25] Peacock Committee (1986).
[26] Department of National Heritage, *The Future of the BBC* (1992).
[27] Culture, Media and Sport Committee (2015).
[28] *The Future of the BBC*, paras 6.6–6.25.

the short term, there appears to be no realistic alternative to the licence fee', the Committee concluded there was no 'long-term future for the licence fee in its current form'.[29]

Content Regulation

For the BBC the Charter states that the BBC 'shall be independent in all matters concerning the content of its output'.[30] At a working level, guidelines in relation to content standards have to be approved by the BBC Trust[31] as derived from the Communications Act 2003. These cover protection of persons under the age of 18, omission of material likely to encourage or incite any crime or disorder, exercise of responsibility with respect to the content of religious programmes, application of generally accepted standards so as to provide protection for members of the public from the inclusion of offensive and harmful material, and refraining from the use of techniques which exploit the possibility of conveying a message to viewers or listeners, or otherwise influencing their minds, without their being aware, or fully aware, of what has occurred.[32]

Changes in the Sector

Television in 1946 was available to 0.2% of the population in Britain[33] and by the end of the century this had risen to 96%—with 57% of homes having two or more TV sets.[34] As noted above, the range of providers has changed in the past 60 years from the single public service channel, the BBC, to a huge number of small providers along with the six major ones in terms of audience share—BBC (32.35%), ITV (23.05%), Channel 4 (10.77%), BSkyB (8.39%), Channel 5 (5.99%) and UK Channel Management (4.51%).[35] The audience shares of each of the smaller channels are all under 2%.

The British TV world divides into two distinct zones. On the one hand we have the public service commitment sector comprising about 70% of the audience with a commitment to balance in both programmes and limitations on content, whilst the unregulated sector has the ability to schedule what it wishes in the way it wishes.

---

[29] At: www.parliament.uk/business/committees/committees-a-z/commons-select/culture-media-and-sport-committee/.

[30] BBC Charter, para 6.

[31] BBC Agreement, para 43; the Trust is the governing body under the current 2006 Charter.

[32] Communications Act 2003, s 319.

[33] Briggs (1979) 242.

[34] European Audiovisual Observatory (1999) 37.

[35] This is itself owned by the BBC and includes Alibi HD (a detective channel).

The Development of Law, Crime and Justice on British Television

Along with family sagas and medical dramas, legally focused dramas have been ever present on British television. All aspects of the law and justice process have featured in the dramas from the police and detective apprehension stage, through the adjudication trial stage featuring lawyers, and finally to the disposition stage of the prison drama as well as the aftercare probation service. This has been the case in both home-grown and non-British material. Whilst Turnbull perceptively points out that this history has never been strictly linear and 'the trajectory of the television crime drama is one of loops, spirals and returns',[36] there are, nonetheless, certain developments and patterns that can be usefully noted.

Police Dramas

The nature of the first dramas was described as 'rosy and reassuring'[37] and took a non-threatening perspective on the politics of policing. This era, characterised after one of the first and longest-running series, *Dixon of Dock Green* (1955–76) portrayed police as straightforward and upstanding and criminals as largely decent people whom circumstances had pushed into antisocial activities. Written by Left-leaning Labour stalwart Ted Willis, this modestly social realist perspective[38] was also found in his screenplays for the cinema such as *No Trees in the Street* (1951) and *Flame in the Streets* (1961). The contrast with the American import shown on commercial channel, ITV, *Dragnet* (1955–68) was marked. Here we had a fast-paced documentary-style police series. The police were again, of course, unimpeachable but the production standards were high and use of outside broadcast locations was more extensive. Home-produced series, with single crimes committed, investigated and solved in 30 or 60 minutes from commission to apprehension, however, dominated airtime in the 1960s UK. These included *No Hiding Place* (1959–66) and *Echo Four Two* (1961) among the commercial channel offerings and from the BBC, *Maigret* (1960–63), *Z Cars* (1962–65; 1967–78) and *Softly Softly* (1966–76). An even more hardnosed style of policing along with the personal conflicts in the lives of the police were showcased in *The Sweeney* (1975–76; 1978).

Women also featured in this programming most notably with *Juliet Bravo* (1980–85), *The Gentle Touch* (1980–84) and *CATS Eyes* (1985–87). *Juliet Bravo* introduced a woman police inspector as the principal protagonist. The focus was

---

[36] Turnbull (2014) 42.

[37] Cooke (2003) 33.

[38] Although Turnbull suggests that it 'portrayed a "conservative attitude to crime" viewing crime as the result of individual failing rather than as a product of social conditions' (2014) 40, this is not my reading of the show except as regards the upstanding nature of the police and their general probity.

on the day to day grind of community policing rather than major criminals and their world. It was centred on a woman in charge of an all-male force. A rather different kind of approach with a woman leading the team is found in the murder-focused *Prime Suspect* (1991–93; 1995–96; 2003; 2006).

In fiction, the work of British police detectives has, from the days of Sherlock Holmes in the 1880s, been complemented by amateurs like Hercule Poirot, Miss Marple, Lord Peter Wimsey and Albert Campion and we find this too on television.[39]

Police shows continue to be a prominent part of the television schedules into the twenty-first century. These include ensemble pieces that have a focus on the non-glamorous elements of day to day policing. These come in both contemporary form (*The Bill*, 1984–2010) as well as with a nostalgic twist (*Heartbeat*, 1992–2010). The most common structure is to use a slightly mismatched pair of detectives focusing on murder—Endeavour Morse and Robbie Lewis (*Inspector Morse* 1987–93 plus five specials between 1995 and 2000); DI Robert Lewis and DS James Hathaway (*Lewis* 2006–); George Wexford and Mike Burton (*The Ruth Rendell Mysteries* (1987–2000); Andy Dalziel and Peter Pascoe (*Dalziel and Pascoe* (1996–2007); *Murder City* (2004–06 DI Susan Alembic and DS Luke Stone). Lone men and lone women working with difficulty in a team also feature in *Wycliffe* (1994–98), *A Touch of Frost* (1992–2010), *Prime Suspect* (1995–2000) and *Vera* (2009–).

In these shows the settings enable us to reflect on possible changes in the modes of policing and the changing nature of crime and society. We find this in the wartime work of Chief Inspector Christopher Foyle (*Foyle's War* 2004–15), the rationed post-war world of 1950s Cambridge in *Grantchester* (2014–), the not quite swinging sixties of the North East centred Inspector George Gently (*Inspector George Gently*, 2007–), the North York Moors (*Heartbeat*) and the Oxford of raw recruit, Detective Constable Endeavour Morse (*Endeavour* 2012–).

The opportunities to provide contemporary perspectives on social change have not been lost on writers and producers with the strong female presence in *Scott and Bailey* (2011–). The same kinds of challenges provided by family and police work—and the twenty-first century world in general—are confronted by Janine Lewis (*Blue Murder*, 2003–09) and Catherine Cawood (*Happy Valley* 2014–).

In addition, in the 1970s the import of selected American series started a trend of gritty material with *The Streets of San Francisco* (1973–80) and *Kojak* (1973–78); in the 1980s, *Hill Street Blues* (1981–87); and in the 1990s, *NYPD Blue* (1993–2005). In the current century we have the *CSI* franchises (2000–). American law enforcement, then, has also been ever present in British homes. Whilst these may have had a great impact on the collective memory, they were not shows at the expense of locally produced material, and many of the American series produced during these decades have never been seen in Britain. Hence, looking simply at

---

[39] Agatha Christie's *Poirot* (1989–93, 1995, 2000, 2002–04, 2006, 2008–12); *Miss Marple* (1984–87, 1989, 1991–92, 2000–06); *Lord Peter Wimsey* (1972–75); *Campion* (1989–90).

series starting with the letter A, British audiences never saw *The Andy Griffith Show* (1960–68), *Angel Street* (1992) or *Angela's Eyes* (2006) and the list of American series never seen by British audiences is staggering. More recently, though, we have had Scandinavian crime dramas making an appearance in both their original form—*The Killing* (2007–12) from Denmark, *The Bridge* (2011–), and *Wallander* (2005–13) from Sweden, as well as in reworkings in the English language version of *Wallander* (2008–14). *Inspector Montalbano* (1999–) from Italy and *Spiral* (2005–) from France have also been shown, albeit in the case of the latter in a very late night slot.

Lawyer-Focused Programmes

The first lawyer focused offering did not come until 1958's *Boyd QC* (1958–64). Although courtroom based, this show often involved Boyd solving crimes in the style of his American contemporary, Perry Mason. In Richard Boyd's case this was achieved without Mason's detective and secretarial team.

The first female legal protagonist in any prime-time television programme was found in the series *Justice* (1971–74). This show focused on the trials and personal tribulations of a middle-aged female barrister in the male-dominated legal world. The courtroom drama with the focus on what happens in a courtroom has been a constant feature of British produced programmes for the past 50 years.[40] Within the three distinct British legal systems—England/Wales, Scotland,[41] and Northern Ireland—the distinction between lawyers who practise only in the courts under the instructions of other office-based lawyers is encountered. The court-based barristers and advocates in wigs and gowns in impressive court settings have been the focus of most of the dramas made for British television. Their colleagues based in offices who deal with wills, land transactions and divorces do in fact appear in the lower courts but their work has been less visible in the media. Long-running series focused on barristers include *Rumpole of the Bailey* (1975–92), *Kavanagh QC* (1995–2001), *Judge John Deed* (2001–07), *New Street Law* (2006–07) and *Silk* (2011–14). There are other offerings which did not last more than a single series, despite the employment of stars with a following of fans from other TV or film work. Some of the series, like *North Square* (2000) and *Outlaws* (2002), have gone beyond the tried and trusted David and Goliath courtroom battle in the style of Perry Mason and provided a more nuanced view of lawyers, their clients and their adversaries and are available on DVD.[42] This roster of British lawyers has been complemented over the years by a modest contribution from the United

---

[40] Robson (2007).

[41] Three series focus on Scotland—*Sutherland's Law* (1972–74); *The Justice Game* (1984); and *The Advocates* (1993–95).

[42] See also a comic eccentric view of British justice in *Kingdom* (2007–09).

States, starting in 1959 with *Perry Mason* (1957–64; 1973–74) and *The Defenders* (1961–65). Britain has only been given access to a small number of the vast range of over 250 American TV lawyer dramas produced.[43] These have included prime-time showings of *Petrocelli* (1974–76) and *LA Law* (1986–94), but most other US programmes have been allocated late night or afternoon slots. Hence it was possible to see *The Trials of Rosie O'Neill* (1990–92), *Judging Amy* (1999–2005), *the practice* (1997–2004), *The Client* (1995–96) and *Ally McBeal* (1997–2002). Even the first series of *Matlock* (1986–95) was shown, albeit 20 years after it started. More recently, *Damages* (2007–12), *The Good Wife* (2009–), *Franklin and Bash* (2011–14) and *Suits* (2011–) have been available on late-night slots.

Prison Dramas

It was the Probation Service which was the first other justice-orientated organisation to be featured on the BBC, in *Let Justice be Done* (1950) and on commercial television in *Probation Officer* (1959–62). It was not until 1974 that the specific theme of prison life appears again on British television in both drama form— *Within These Walls* (1974–76; 1978)—and in comedy—*Porridge* (1974–77). The life of a post-release prisoner is covered, again principally for laughs, in *Going Straight* (1978). For those with an interest in prison and the issues raised by this phase of the justice process, there has been reliance on imported material from Australia and the United States in the shape of *Prisoner in Cell Block H* (1979–86), *Bad Girls* (1999–2006), *Wentworth* (2013–) (shown as *Wentworth Prison* in the UK, 2014–) and *Orange is the New Black* (2013–). Prison shows have never been a major feature of British television and the empirical study both at the time selected and over a much longer time frame bears this out.

Documentaries

Documentaries have been a feature of British TV and there have been series dedicated specifically to the legal system and its failings like *Rough Justice* (1982–2007). In recent years these have been complemented by the emergence of programmes focusing on the lurid details of notorious child serial killers like Fred and Rose West.[44] Beyond these there is also a smattering of actual documentaries on a range of ad hoc issues covering unsolved murders, serial killers and rather more domestically, consumer protection.

---

[43] Erickson (2009).
[44] criminalminds.wikia.com/wiki/Fred_and_Rosemary_West.

Reality Shows

Changes in technology have allowed the use of small cameras in a whole range of locations to record aspects of human life. The area of law, crime and justice has seen a whole range of programmes produced which focus on the day to day operations of police and other law enforcement personnel. These groups have welcomed an opportunity for the public to get a glimpse of their work and a new kind of reality show has been born. These are documentary in style but they resemble more a promotional video for the service featured. Whilst they track the reality of policing and other areas of law enforcement, they do not provide any context or appraisal of the work being undertaken. What we see is the action on the streets with no attempt to provide a rationale of why the officers are deployed how they are. These documentaries, then, are interesting glimpses of what the police or other semi-autonomous branches of the state apparatus are happy for the public to see. They do not provide any kind of documentary analysis of the choices and politics of policing and law enforcement. From Britain these include: *Brit Cops, Motorway Patrol* (2001–), *Police Interceptors* (2008–) and *UK Border Force* (2008–09); and from the elsewhere: *Border Security: Canada's Front Line* (2012–), *World's Wildest Police Videos* (1998–2002; 2012) and *Dog and Beth* (2013–15).[45] When done well such series can attract praise, as in a series shown outside the period of our study called *The Detectives* (2015). *The Detectives* is a three-part series shown on prime time on BBC2. It followed the same pattern as these other 'reality' programmes and garnered praise for its coverage of historic sex crimes which came to light in the UK in 2014. Its powerful depiction of the daily work of the police was described as 'shaming the typical police procedural'.[46]

Law, Crime and Justice on British TV in 2014

This study looks at the month of November 2014. Examination of the television schedules before and since then indicates that this month is pretty representative of the programming throughout the rest of the year and not a 'rogue' month.[47]

The extent and nature of 'justice', both formal and informal, on TV is classified both in terms of the location of the material in the process of justice as well as by the kind of programme. These categories are not represented equally in terms of programming, as we shall see. In the section on the development of law, crime and justice on TV in Britain we saw how there were many more police shows than lawyer shows and even less prison and post-prison material. This is not simply

---

[45] See Programme Index in this volume.
[46] *The Guardian* (19 May 2015) Television, G 2, 21.
[47] cf Belgium, ch 3 in this volume.

an historical issue but one which persists in the twenty-first century programme decisions. It ties in with surveys on what kind of television the public have indicated they prefer.[48]

Table 1: Shows relating to law and justice on UK TV

1. Police and detective material					
	Dramas	Comedies	Reality	Reality entertainment	Documentaries
WEEK 1 (3–9 Nov)	178 hours	.5 hours	50 hours		6 hours
WEEK 2 (10–16 Nov)	189 hours	1.5 hours	97 hours		24 hours
WEEK 3 (17–23 Nov)	192 hours	2 hours	112 hours		30 hours
WEEK 4 (24–30 Nov)	216 hours	1.5 hours	130 hours		36 hours
Monthly total	775 hours	5.5 hours	389 hours		96 hours

2. Lawyer and court-focused material					
	Dramas	Comedies	Reality	Reality entertainment	Documentaries
WEEK 1 (3–9 Nov)				39 hours	
WEEK 2 (10–16 Nov)				44 hours	
WEEK 3 (17–23 Nov)				41 hours	
WEEK 4 (24–30 Nov)	3 hours			37 hours	
Monthly total	3 hours			161 hours	

(continued)

---

[48] BARB Survey (2015).

Table 1: *(Continued)*

3. Prison and post-prison material					
	Dramas	**Comedies**	**Reality**	**Reality entertainment**	**Documentaries**
WEEK 1 (3–9 Nov)	1 hour				2 hours
WEEK 2 (10–16 Nov)	1 hour				1 hour
WEEK 3 (17–23 Nov)	1 hour				1 hour
WEEK 4 (24–30 Nov)					1 hour
Monthly total	**3 hours**				**5 hours**

a. Police and Detective Material

Drama stood alone and was distinguished from comedy on the basis that the notions of Macaulay[49], Friedman[50] and Sherwin[51] about citizens learning about the legal system were much less likely to occur with the former than the latter. In any event, the comedy contribution was minimal amounting to only 5.5 hours over the whole month as compared with some 775 hours of drama. More recent police shows combine procedural elements as well as 'detecting', although the emphasis varies, unlike the amateur sleuths assisting the police like *Poirot* and *Miss Marple*.

Within the police and law enforcement material which is based directly on real life rather than fictional, a distinction has been made between those programmes where a narrative structure and analysis is employed which have been categorised as 'documentaries' and those which do not. Those, like *Police Interceptors* and *Cops* where, typically, hand-held cameras simply follow the work of an agency with limited comment and context and often no presenter, are classified as 'reality'. They are, in essence, promotional material for the organisation featured. The line is not always quite as clear with such material as *24 Hours in Police Custody* (2014–) which, whilst it affects a fly-on-the-wall style, is more than the recorded highlights of a day's policing.

b. Lawyer and court focused material

As for lawyer and court-focused material, there is precious little available on British television in the month we examined. The full coverage only produced

---

[49] Macaulay (1987).
[50] Friedman (1989).
[51] Sherwin (2000).

three showings of the relatively recent minor American comedy drama, *Franklin and Bash*. This has been an area of life which has produced many long-running and iconic series over the years. Although lawyer dramatic portrayals figure prominently in the law and television literature they do not have a major presence on screen when compared with other aspects of the law, crime and justice system.

As far as other lawyer material is concerned, one can see the wide extent and narrow range of reality entertainment shows featuring courtroom themes. Reality entertainment featured on a regular daily basis except on Sundays. These amounted to some 161 hours over the month out of a total coverage of 1,135 hours, or 12%. Although over the years similar shows have been essayed in Britain,[52] this kind of format has yet to find an audience for a British version. At the time of writing in 2015, there is a British series, *Judge Rinder* (2014–) operating on mainstream afternoon commercial television, but it was not on air during the time of the November survey. Oddly, despite the availability of very different kinds of reality entertainment shows along the lines of *Judge Judy* (1996–),[53] the surprise perhaps is that only Judge Judy Sheindlin appears before the British public. Although, as mentioned, she has been joined more recently by Judge Robert Rinder, during our survey the full 161 hours of reality entertainment were comprised of American *Judge Judy*.[54]

c. Prison and post-prison material

The coverage of prison and post-prison material is very limited. Again, the whole month of November 2014 yielded three hours of the Australian drama *Wentworth Prison*. This is in line with the limited coverage of such shows generally on British television noted above. There were also some five hours of documentary coverage of prison issues—*Broadmoor* from ITV1, a series focusing on the British prison for the criminally insane, along with one hour from Channel 5, *Inside Holloway*, looking at the London women's prison, Holloway.

Summary of the Material

The most dominant source of material in relation to law and justice (formal and informal) was found to be drama about the police. Of the 775 hours under the broad heading 'police and detection' some 80% is devoted to police detection and 20% to police procedurals, although as noted already this line is becoming somewhat blurred in twenty-first century offerings. As we shall see, however, the vast majority of these offerings were 'second hand' from earlier eras. The sources of the programming featured 50% of home-produced material. The actual figures

---

[52] Robson (2007).
[53] Marder (2012) 233 cites eight other contemporary 'television judges'—Judge Pirro, Judge Hatchett, Judge Lynn Toler, Judge Marilyn Milian, Judge Mazz, Judge Joe Brown, Judge Alex and Judge Mathis.
[54] Marder (2012); Terzic (2012).

for home-produced material on British channels is 85%. It is only the existence and availability of the specialist crime Channel 5 USA which increases the external input, principally from the United States, during the month surveyed.

The crude assessment of the hours of material must also be seen in the context of' fresh' material in peak viewing slots as opposed to daytime and late-night scheduling. Again, the number of prime-time shows shown on channels other than ITV3, 5 USA, CBS Reality and True Entertainment, was limited. On BBC1 prime time we had old episodes of the 'cold cases' police show *New Tricks* (2003–15). Of the new material we only had a missing person mystery, *The Missing* and the fantasy ancient/modern detection of *Sherlock*. ITV showed one new police series set in the early 1950s featuring a young vicar helping a policeman friend to solve crime in rural Cambridgeshire in *Grantchester*.

The original hope was that one would be able to contrast the way in which issues like gender, race and class had been covered in the past with the present. The position is, however, rather unusual in that these representations are with us every day in the offerings from the crime channels. What has happened has been that the trends noted in the overview of the development of crime programmes on British television can actually be observed rather than described. The principal change has been not to the storylines and issues covered, but to who is covering them in police procedurals and detective material. Women have assumed a much higher profile although the raw statistics disguise this with the continued modern screen presence of reruns of *Columbo* (1971–78; 1989–2003), *Kojak*, *Wycliffe*, *Frost* and their like, alongside contemporary female police officers like Scott and Bailey, Jane Tennison and Vera. What is also interesting is that of the older pioneering women series, the only one which occurs in this survey is the 1980s American import *Cagney and Lacey*. No sight of *Juliet Bravo*, *The Gentle Touch* or *CATS Eyes* in this month or since.

Focus of Law, Crime and Justice Material

The statistic that seems the most revealing is the split between the three broad categories. In the month surveyed there was only a handful of dramas with lawyers and the court system at their centre—three hours in the whole month—and the nearest we have to lawyers on TV is the 161 hours of *Judge Judy*. There was even less coverage of the prison system and the process of dealing with those breaching the rules—eight hours. On the other hand, the daily coverage of police and law enforcement material over all channels was on average 45 hours amounting to 1,265 hours in the month and 95% of output on law, crime and justice. Within this category of police and apprehension, the dominance of dramas was notable at 60% with reality programmes at 30% and documentaries at just under 10%.

New material is swamped by the backlog from over the past 40 years of old police dramas and detective stories. That is complemented by a stream of 'reality' views of law enforcement at work at some unspecified time and place protecting the citizenry from a range of problems which are implicitly of great concern but whose scale and significance are never analysed. Alongside these are a limited number of documentaries on the more lurid and sensational aspects of life. If, indeed, Macaulay, Friedman, McNeely and Sherwin's suggestions that the screen is where the public learn about law and justice, then the picture is disturbing and likely to stoke fears of crime at a time when statistics suggest that many areas of crime are in decline.[55]

Changes in the Personnel and Issues

The elements which did look as though they might throw up interesting material were around gender, race and ethnicity. The preponderance, however, of older material from earlier decades mean that an enquiry on these themes is problematic. The paucity of new material means an in-depth reading of the new programmes offers little. Rather, what the material allows us to see is the way in which these issues were covered in the past. The results are in line with the overview of the development of law, crime and justice television outlined above. Women changed from being virtually invisible as protagonists in the justice system in the days of *Z Cars* and Regan and Carter's *Sweeney* to fronting their own series. Interestingly, the only female headed series encountered in the November survey was the American *Cagney and Lacey* police procedural. Thus, whilst we have noted that modern police shows now contain a number of female leads their relative absence in the past is highlighted in the selected material on the rerun channels.

By the same token, the absence of lawyer series in our survey adds little to the existing observations from those scholars who have examined the field that this is an area where men have dominated. With the exception of Margaret Lockwood's pioneering Harriet Peterson in *Justice* in the early 1970s, British viewers waited 40 years for a female lead to appear as a principal protagonist in *Silk*. The same kind of gap is found in the United States between *Kate McShane's* 1975 woman lawyer and Patty Hewes and Alicia Florick in the 2000s in *Damages* and *The Good Wife*, respectively.[56]

There are also a number of issues that are absent. Race and ethnicity were matters which scarcely featured in the white world of *Dixon of Dock Green*, *The Sweeney* or *Heartbeat*. Whilst they make an appearance in *The Bill*, they are not encountered in the retro world of *Grantchester*. There is, though, a possibility in certain circumstances of racial issues being hinted at with references to 'colour bars' and implied fears of miscegenation appearing in 1960s set *Inspector George*

---

[55] www.theguardian.com/uk-news/2015/apr/23/crime-rate-ons-lowest-level-england-wales-police.
[56] *The Trials of Rosie O'Neill* and *Judging Amy*—a soapy self-help series with limited focus on legal practice and the wacky world of *Ally McBeal*.

Gently. These are, however, subtle hints as are any change in the causal explanations of crime and disorder to be gleaned from this viewing. Just as George Dixon implied that 'there but for the grace of God' was all that separated criminals from the respectable in 1950s Britain, that mantra remains steadfastly in place 60 years on—along with the mad and bad who populate the worlds of *Agatha Christie* and *Midsomer*.

5

Canada

JENNIFER L SCHULZ

Introduction

In Canada, the law on television is actually overwhelmingly American and is dominated not by lawyer shows, but by police shows. This chapter traces the history and development of Canadian legal television and then describes past and current Canadian legal television offerings. It then outlines the methodology adopted and describes and analyses what law and justice television was available in Canada in November 2014.

History and Development of Canadian Television

The first television available in Canada was television from our neighbouring country, the United States of America. Canada's first public television, the Canadian Broadcasting Corporation (CBC), came four years *after* American networks began regular broadcasting in Canada.[1] This means that there has never been a time when Canadians did not watch American TV.

The CBC was and is public and government funded. It first opened public television stations in Toronto and Montreal in 1952, and later expanded to Vancouver, Winnipeg, Ottawa and Halifax. The CBC obtained its operating funds through Parliamentary Operating Appropriations[2] and advertising. Smaller markets gained television access through private sector companies that acted as CBC

---

[1] Tate (2000) 6, emphasis added.

[2] Parliamentary Operating Appropriations are acts authorising government expenditure. Under Canada's political system, Parliament has supreme authority over taxation and government spending. This means that the executive (which includes the Prime Minister and the Cabinet) and the public service cannot raise taxes or spend monies without first obtaining Parliament's explicit approval or authority through a Bill known as an appropriation act. Spending legislation takes the form of appropriation acts, which enable the government and its agencies to spend money. From 1990 to 2014 there has been a significant decline in total grant and operating dollars from Parliament to the CBC.

network affiliates. These affiliates were expected to provide both local programming and national CBC programming to their designated regions.[3] In 1958 the Broadcasting Act authorised commercial television in Canada, and the Canadian Television Network (CTV) was created in 1961. The CTV was the beginning of private, advertising-funded Canadian television. When the development of Canadian programming did not occur as quickly as the Board of Broadcast Governors hoped, it introduced Canadian content regulations. English-speaking Canadians have always watched more American television for entertainment than Canadian television[4] and thus the Canadian government had a fear of American cultural domination. In Québec, Canada's French-speaking province, French Canadian TV is most commonly watched and there are many more Canadian made and Canadian viewed French language programmes than English programmes.[5]

The fear of American cultural domination is why Canadian television has always, and continues, to exist in a context of protective legislation.[6] In 1968 the Canadian Parliament passed a new Broadcasting Act and replaced the Board of Broadcast Governors with the Canadian Radio and Television Commission, which later became the Canadian Radio-Television and Telecommunications Commission, or the CRTC. The CRTC's goal is to ensure that the telecommunications and broadcasting systems serve the Canadian public by encouraging 'the creation of programming that reflects Canada's diversity and enables Canadians to participate in their country's democratic and cultural life'.[7]

Pursuant to private sector lobbying for increased network choices, Global Communications received a broadcasting licence for Ontario in 1972. By the 1980s, private television broadcasters provided 60% Canadian content in the day (6.00 am to midnight) and 50% Canadian content in prime time (6.00 pm to midnight). Unfortunately, however, Canadian content points could be achieved by hiring Canadian technical and creative personnel; it was not necessary to produce a programme that 'felt' or appeared to be Canadian, or had specific Canadian content. Additionally, there was very little Canadian drama available to view during prime time due to simultaneous substitution, or simulcasting.

Simulcasting allows Canadian broadcasters to broadcast an American programme in Canada at the same time it is being broadcast in the United States if it is on a Canadian signal. Canadian networks buy the broadcasting rights for American shows and air them at the same time, except with Canadian advertisements; this practice continues to this day. The result is that private stations are able

---

[3] Brinton (2001) 32.

[4] The Canadian television preferred by Canadians is news reporting and sports coverage—otherwise English-speaking Canadians greatly prefer American television for their drama/entertainment viewing. See Schulz (2012) 426.

[5] Yves Boisvert, host of two Québec legal television shows said, '48 or 49 of the most-watched shows are produced [in Québec]. In the rest of Canada, 50 of the 50 most-watched shows are produced in the United States'. See S Goldberg: www.thestar.com/life/technology/2013/04/26/canadians_watch_30_hours_of_tv_but_for_many_web_dominates_free_time.html.

[6] Schulz (2012) 427.

[7] *Communications Monitoring Report* (2013) 5.

to make the greatest profit via 'the familiar mode of offering popular American programming through peak viewing hours and making minimal investment in Canadian programmes'.[8]

In response, the CRTC attempted to incentivise the production of Canadian drama series in 1984. It offered a 150% credit towards Canadian content requirements (ie, a one-hour programme would count as a one-and-a-half-hour programme) if broadcasting companies would air a dramatic programme between 7.00 pm and 10.00 pm that met Canadian content criteria. 'This was a significant incentive, for Canadian private broadcasters could in effect reduce the total required hours of Canadian programming in their evening schedules', leaving more room for American shows in prime time.[9]

In the late 1980s, independent regional broadcasting companies entered the market, such as CanWest in Winnipeg and Allarcom in Edmonton. CanWest eventually purchased the Global Network in 1990 and was renamed CanWest Global Communications Corporation. A new Broadcasting Act was passed in 1991; this new legislation maintained its commitment to the promotion of Canadian cultural objectives, particularly 'national identity and cultural sovereignty'.[10] It also stated that the 'Canadian broadcasting system should serve to safeguard, enrich and strengthen the cultural, political, social and economic fabric of Canada'.[11]

In the 1990s, national companies began to acquire many of the small independent stations and in 1995 the CRTC gave independent companies Atlantis and Alliance 'speciality channel' broadcasting licences. Throughout the 1990s the CRTC also released an annual report on Canada's broadcasting and telecommunications sectors called the 'Communications Monitoring Report', or CMR. The CMR attempted to assess the impact of market and technological developments on the cultural, social and economic policy objectives of the Broadcasting Act and the Telecommunications Act. The CMR also reviewed the effectiveness of the CRTC's regulatory frameworks and its success in achieving its objectives. In 1999, the CRTC eliminated minimum Canadian programming spending requirements for private broadcasters, but increased requirements for Canadian priority programming in prime time.[12] The definition of priority programming was widened beyond drama, music and variety to include documentaries and Canadian entertainment magazine programmes. Since variety, documentary and educational programmes are cheaper to produce than dramas, private broadcasters focused on the lowest possible cost approach to Canadian content, which led to a reduction in Canadian drama production overall.

More recent developments in the history of Canadian television include the fact that the Canadian Association of Broadcasters set out guidelines for voluntary

---

[8] Brinton (2001) 38.
[9] ibid, 43.
[10] Broadcasting Act, SC 1991, c 11, s 3(1)(b).
[11] ibid.
[12] Brinton (2001) 91–93.

cultural diversity. The guidelines state that 'private broadcasters shall make an effort: to reflect, … The … multicultural and multiracial nature of … Canadians, and the special place of aboriginal peoples within Canadian society'.[13] The review of Canadian television that follows indicates that broadcasters are not taking this voluntary guideline seriously because Canadian legal television programming does not reflect Canada's multicultural and multiracial nature.

Canadian Legal Television

A review of the history of English language Canadian TV demonstrates that there are few law shows. This chapter focuses on English Canadian TV as nine out of 10 of our provinces and all three of our territories are overwhelmingly English speaking.[14] Law shows, or legally themed television that focuses on law and/or lawyers, while prolific in the United States, are almost non-existent in Canada. The most accurate description of Canadian legal television is that it is sparse. Canada has produced limited amounts of programmes about its own legal systems, preferring instead to import extensively from the United States.

The most famous of all Canadian legal dramas, and in fact, perhaps the most famous prime-time Canadian drama, is *Street Legal. Street Legal* ran from 1987 to 1994 on CBC. It was the longest-running one-hour scripted drama series in the history of Canadian television, holding the record for 20 years, before being surpassed by *Heartland*'s 125th episode on 18 October 2014.[15] *Street Legal* focused on the professional and private lives of the partners in a small Toronto law firm. The primary stars were Sonja Smits as Carrington Barr, Eric Peterson as Leon Robinovitch and C David Johnson as Chuck Tchobanian. Produced at the same time as *LA Law* in the US, *Street Legal* was distinctively Canadian in its use of Canadian court customs and procedures. In its last six seasons, it regularly drew about a million viewers, the benchmark of a Canadian hit. *Street Legal* also aired in Spain as *Los Abogados*, in Russia as *Лабиринт правосудия* and in West Germany as *Die Waffen des Gesetzes*; wide international reach for a Canadian television programme.

There have been a few other Canadian law shows but none of them are currently on the air. *This Is Wonderland* was a Canadian legal drama with comedic elements which aired on CBC from 2004 to 2006. It highlighted the multicultural nature of Toronto and demonstrated the shortcomings of the judicial system, regularly

---

[13] Murray (2002) 14.

[14] Québec has developed more legal shows than English-speaking Canada because it has a different legal system. Québec's legal system is a civil system (based on France's legal system) while the rest of Canada has a common law system (based on England's) that is similar to the United States' legal system. As such, American shows make more 'legal sense' to English Canadian viewers than French Canadian viewers.

[15] *Heartland* is a Canadian family drama produced by the CBC; it is not a legally-themed television show.

depicting it as a blunt instrument ill-equipped to respond to the needs of a diverse and changing society.

The Associates was an hour-long prime-time dramatic series that ran for two seasons on CTV, in 2001 and 2002. CTV commissioned the show at a cost of about $1 million per episode.[16] It featured five new associates in a large Toronto Bay Street law firm.[17] This show also did not hide its Canadian-ness. Interestingly, *The Associates* was full of instances where lawyers chose to use alternative dispute resolution (ADR) processes such as negotiation, mediation and arbitration instead of litigation.[18] Almost half of the first season's episodes had mediation-themed storylines and mediation was made to look as interesting and as exciting as courtroom work—something extremely rarely seen on television. *The Associates* depicted an unprecedented amount of ADR as compared with American and Canadian legal dramas of the time.

Family Matters with Justice Harvey Brownstone was a Canadian show that billed itself as the only TV show hosted by a real sitting Ontario provincial court family law judge.[19] This was English Canada's *only* reality court TV show. It aired on CHCH TV, an independent Ontario channel and on CHEK TV, an independent British Columbia channel, from 2011 to 2013. *Family Matters* focused on the relationship between modern family issues, divorce and the justice system, and had an online legal Q&A which provided free legal information from lawyers and other legal professionals.

Billable Hours was a Canadian comedy series that aired on the pay-per-view Showcase channel from 2006 to 2008. It too was set in a Toronto law firm and focused on three young lawyers struggling to balance their expectations of life with the difficult realities of building a career in law. The show was accompanied by a 10-part webisode series entitled *Billable Minutes*. *Billable Hours* also aired in Australia on ABC2.

In 2002, there was a one-hour docudrama called *History's Courtroom* on History Television. It explored landmark Canadian legal decisions in an effort to educate the public. In 2003 there was *The Docket*, a half-hour legal affairs show produced in Halifax which aired nationally on CBC Newsworld. The show had a documentary plus panel format that aimed to document the effects of legislation on ordinary Canadians. Similarly, there was a French language half-hour legal issues show called *Justice*[20] that ran from 2004 to 2005 in Québec, with a view to bringing legal topics to the French-speaking public's attention. In 1999, there was a programme called *Understanding the Law*, a series of short animated National

---

[16] S Adilman, 'Backroom drama: cast, crew invested months of effort to refine *The Associates* for a second season, but will the show's audience take notice?' *Toronto Star* (6 January 2002): search.proquest.com/docview/438394925?accountid=14569.

[17] Bay Street in Toronto, Ontario is Canada's equivalent to Wall Street in New York City, New York.

[18] For more information on *The Associates*, see Schulz (2012); and Schulz (2011).

[19] www.familymatterstv.com/about.

[20] archives.radio-canada.ca/emissions/1428.

Film Board films about landmark legal decisions, such as *The Worm*, about the classic tort case *Donohue v Stevenson*.[21]

There were also some Canadian police shows set in Toronto that are no longer on the air such as *Played*,[22] *Cracked*[23] and *The Bridge*.[24] Related programmes, although not police shows in the usual sense, were *Fraud Squad TV* and *Cra$h and Burn*, about insurance fraud. There was a French-language police procedural called *Omerta* produced by the CBC from 1996 to 1999; another French police procedural called *19-2* which first aired on Télévision de Radio-Canada in 2011; and in April 2014 a show about Crown Prosecutors called *Tout la Verité* debuted in Québec.

Methodology

In this book we are concerned with legally themed television that is currently broadcast. In order to obtain Canadian data I conducted an empirical study of the television available to English Canadian viewers in Manitoba, Canada in November 2014. Regular, free television, not pay-per-view channels were examined.[25] All law and justice programming, broadly defined, including fictional dramas and comedies, reality and documentary shows, and even children's programming were included. Law and justice programming and/or legally themed shows means TV programmes with law as their primary topic and does not include shows that dealt with law only in passing. Shows with law as the primary topic included shows focusing on police procedure and criminal investigation (apprehension), the lawyer and judge phase of the legal process (adjudication) and incarceration (disposition).[26]

Although November 2014 is the month of analysis in every chapter in this book, November 2013 was also examined to see if there were any significant changes. The data was collected from television listings filtering out certain channels and categories of programming, such as sports, music, Fashion TV, Treehouse and Teletoon (children's channels), HGTV (home and garden programming), Food Network, and pornography. Shows were included that, according to the episode summary

---

[21] www.nfb.ca/film/understanding_the_law_the_worm.

[22] www.ctv.ca/Played.aspx.

[23] www.cbc.ca/cracked/.

[24] en.wikipedia.org/wiki/The_Bridge_(Canadian_TV_series).

[25] As at the time of writing, no Canadian television content appears on the Canadian version of Netflix. American, and to a lesser extent, British shows continue to make up the bulk of the offerings on Canadian Netflix.

[26] The author thanks the Legal Research Institute of Manitoba for funding that enabled her to hire two excellent research assistants: Rachel Beaupré, JD (2014), Rosenblatt Immigration Law, Toronto; and Paul Kathler, JD (2016), D'Arcy and Deacon LLP, Winnipeg, who both did outstanding jobs of data collection for this chapter.

or general show description, were likely to involve an element of apprehension, adjudication or disposition. The raw data of how much 'justice TV' viewers were able to access in Manitoba, Canada in November 2013 was recorded.

A year later, each day in November 2014, the actual month of analysis for this book, the same process was followed. The data points collected were:

— Show title
— Country of origin
— Language
— Day of the week aired
— Date aired
— Time aired
— Network and channel
— Description/classification

Data were entered on a daily basis using an online TV guide[27] in conjunction with the on-screen television guide. In addition, when supplementary information about programmes was required, the Internet Movie Database (imdb.com) was searched. The description or classification of each show was one of the following:

— Police drama
— Crime drama
— Legal drama
— Reality/reality court
— Documentary
— Comedy
— Children's show
— Live court hearings

Findings

In November 2014 in Manitoba, Canada, there were 5,003 law-related TV shows and 17 law-themed films broadcast over 103 television channels, for a total of 5,020 law-related programmes. When averaged over four weeks this means there were 1,255 law-related programmes per week on television in Manitoba. This does not include the law-related content that would have been found on news programmes and magazine programmes. This is an incredible amount of law-themed television and indicates a vast area of popular culture in need of further study.

---

[27] affiliate.zap2it.com/tvlistings/ZCGrid.do?fromTimeInMillis=1414818000000&aid=shawca.

The findings from Manitoba in November 2014 are generalised to English-speaking Canada for that period.[28]

Of the shows, 99.5% (4,996 out of 5,020) were in English, 13 shows, or 0.3%, were in French, and 11 shows, or 0.2%, were bilingual. There were slight differences between the levels of French language material collected in 2013 as compared with 2014.[29] Although there was a lot of legal television available to be watched in Canada in November 2014, only 26.6%—just slightly more than a quarter—of the shows were Canadian. Nearly 72% (71.7%) of all the legal shows available on television were American. The countries of origin of the 5020 law television shows and movies available in November 2014 were as follows:

Table 1: Country of Origin of Law Shows shown on TV in Canada

United States	3,597	71.7%
Canada	1,337	26.6%
United States/Canada	34	0.7%
New Zealand	26	0.5%
Australia	16	0.3%
United Kingdom	9	0.2%
United States/France/Germany	1	0.02%
Total	**5,020**	**100.00%**

Analysis

Analysis of the data immediately reveals two very important facts. First, there is a vast amount of American programming in Canada. This is not surprising; I have noted it before[30] as have others;[31] the dominance of American programmes on Canadian television is well documented. Over 70% (71.7%) of legally themed television available to watch in Canada is American.

---

[28] Susan Brinton has written that 'region is an important component of our collective Canadian identity and culture' in Brinton (2001) iv, and of course that is true. There are regional, provincial and territorial differences in the TV broadcast across the country, but cataloguing those differences is beyond the scope of this chapter.

[29] The low quantity of French programming may be the result of the cable package used in the 2014 survey, Shaw Communications, which is headquartered in Calgary, Alberta, a non-bilingual Canadian province, whereas in 2013 MTS was used. MTS is headquartered in Manitoba, a bilingual province, which may therefore have broadcast more French programming in 2013 than Shaw Communications did in 2014.

[30] Schulz (2012) 425–40.

[31] For one example see S Goldberg, 'I Want My Law TV' *The National*, an online publication of The Canadian Bar Association: cba.org/cba/national/janfeb03/PrintHtml.aspx?DocId=6369.

The second significant finding is that over 80% (81%) of the law-themed television is about police officers, not lawyers. In November 2014 the most prevalent American legally themed TV shows on Canadian television were focused on policing rather than lawyering:

— *Forensic Files*
— *Criminal Minds*
— *NCIS* (multiple iterations)
— *Law & Order* (multiple iterations)
— *CSI* (multiple iterations)
— *Cops* and *Cops Reloaded*
— *Hot Bench*
— *Campus PD*

Of the 5,020 law shows and films found on TV in November 2014, 3,501 were related to police procedure and forensics carried out in police labs. A further 503 of 5,020 shows were about border policing. The several variants of *Law & Order* totalled 103 shows. Given that roughly half of each *Law & Order* episode is about policing and the other half is court room drama, *Law & Order* was counted as 52 policing shows. Combined, this means that there were 4,056 of 5,020 shows focused on policing, or 81% of law-themed television available in Canada in November 2014 focused on police. Most Law & Popular Culture scholars have focused on depictions of lawyers. The fact that over 80% of law television in Canada is about police officers indicates that scholars might consider shifting their foci. Indeed, it is not particularly accurate to talk about 'TV Law in Canada'. It is actually American policing that we see on television.

As mentioned, in Canada there were on average 1,255 law-related shows per week on television. According to the Bureau of Broadcasting Measurement, Canadians spend an average of 30 hours per week watching television.[32] This means it is likely Canadians are watching between several and many law-related shows every week. If we accept that much of what people think they know about law is derived from television's depictions,[33] we may conclude that the 'law' most Canadians think they know about is actually American policing, or perhaps American criminal law. Of course, even then, it is American *television* policing and criminal law, not 'real' Canadian policing or criminal law. Thus, it is completely accurate to say that the vast majority of law-related TV that English-speaking Canadians are watching is American, and it is focused on policing.

If Canadians were watching Canadian television in November 2014, the law-themed shows they were most likely watching were *Border Security: Canada's Front Line*, *Murdoch Mysteries* and *Flashpoint*, as these three Canadian programmes

---

[32] M Oliveira, 'Canadians watch 30 hours of TV but for many web dominates free time' *Toronto Star* (26 April 2013): www.thestar.com/life/technology/2013/04/26/canadians_watch_30_hours_of_tv_but_for_many_web_dominates_free_time.html.
[33] Asimow and Mader (2004) 7; and Penney (2004) 211, fn 43.

aired the most in 2014. Interestingly, all three of these shows are also police shows. *Border Security* is a documentary/reality show that follows the work of the men and women who protect Canada's borders (and was also broadcast in the UK during November 2014). *Murdoch Mysteries* is a period piece crime drama set in 1890s Toronto. William Murdoch uses radical forensic techniques (for the time), including fingerprinting and trace evidence, to solve murders. (*Murdoch Mysteries* could be watched in some regions of the United States on niche networks in November 2014). *Flashpoint* is a one-hour prime-time drama about the Strategic Response Unit or SRU, a handpicked team of elite police officers. These officers are different from other SWAT teams because their arsenal also includes a gift for words, manifested in excellent negotiation skills. Therefore, no matter whether English-speaking Canadians are watching American or Canadian law-themed television, the vast majority of it is focused on policing.

In addition to *Border Security: Canada's Front Line*, *Murdoch Mysteries* and *Flashpoint*, there were 18 other Canadian law-themed shows broadcast in November 2014, for a total of 21 shows. Five, like *Border Security*, were documentary programmes (*Crime Stories*,[34] *Dark Waters of Crime, Motives & Murders, Murder She Solved* and *To Serve and Protect*). Thus, there were a total of six documentaries out of 21 law-themed shows. Ten shows were prime-time police or detective dramas (*Cold Squad, Da Vinci's Inquest*,[35] *Da Vinci's City Hall, Intelligence, Missing, Motive, Republic of Doyle, Rookie Blue, The Border, The Listener*). Together with *Murdoch Mysteries* and *Flashpoint*, that makes 12 crime dramas focused on policing out of the total of 21 shows. Rounding out the programmes were live, televised hearings at the Supreme Court of Canada on CPAC and two comedic programmes, *Due South* and *Overruled!*

Due South was a mid-1990s comedy, now in reruns, which by Canadian standards, was a relatively famous show. It pitted a cynical American police detective against an upright Royal Canadian Mounted Police constable (played by Paul Gross) in the city of Chicago. The show was created by Paul Haggis who subsequently went on to become an Oscar-winning screenwriter for *Million Dollar Baby* and *Crash*, which he also directed. Finally, in November 2014 one could also watch *Overruled!* on the Family Channel. This show is a teen comedy about the trials of Cooper, a smooth-talking teen who puts his charm and principles to good use as a lawyer in his high school's after-school court. Thus, only two shows out of 21—live Supreme Court of Canada hearings and a teen show—were about lawyers rather than police officers. The law on screen in Canada in November 2014 was overwhelmingly focused on criminal law and policing. Lawyers and courts, the usual foci of Law & Popular Culture studies, hardly showed up at all.[36]

---

[34] Anja Louis, in her chapter in this book, reports that *Crime Stories* is broadcast in Spain under the title *Informe Criminal.*

[35] Christine Corcos, in her chapter in this book, reports that *Da Vinci's Inquest* was the only non-American law show on TV in the US in November 2014.

[36] This is true with respect to films aired on television in Canada in November 2014 as well. The Canadian film, *An Officer and a Murderer*, is the true story of a respected Canadian military officer who committed numerous brutal crimes and was eventually brought down by a tenacious small town police

In my own work in Law & Popular Culture I have been focused on questions of gender, on use of alternative dispute resolution processes, and on bringing profile to Canada in a field dominated by Americans. My analysis of Canada's November 2014 data has therefore presented me with a dilemma. If I want to focus on the picture in Canada, and the picture in Canada is policing, what of my research interest in alternative dispute resolution? Most TV policing is done by men, so what about my interest in the role of women?

When analysing the data with a view towards gender, one sees that in the 21 Canadian shows there were more depictions of women and people of colour than there have been in the past on Canadian television. However, the legally themed television available to be viewed in Canada in November 2014 certainly did not demonstrate gender equality. While the diversity of characters depicted has increased, there are still very few women in leadership roles or women protagonists in television shows. This is perhaps not surprising given TV's overemphasis on police work, an area heavily dominated by men. Of the 21 Canadian television shows, only five featured women protagonists (*Intelligence, Missing, Motive, Murder She Solved: True Crime,* and *Rookie Blue*),[37] which suggests that future work on gender in the context of Canadian television might focus on those five programmes. Overall there were also very few characters of colour, almost no LGBTQ characters, and class differences and physical disabilities were also rarely portrayed.

What about my interest in alternative dispute resolution (ADR)? Is there any ADR to be found on Canadian television? This research reveals very little ADR depicted on legally themed television programmes. French Canada has a reality TV show with a dispute resolution focus called *L'Arbitre*. This show stars lawyer Anne-France Goldwater. It is filmed in Québec and produced by Québec Network V Télé.[38] The title of the show translates to *The Arbitrator*, so it is a rare, overtly ADR programme. Regrettably however, *L'Arbitre* is not available in Manitoba.

Some episodes of American law-themed television, such as *The Good Wife*, depict ADR processes such as negotiation, mediation and arbitration. However, most legally themed television is focused on policing or secondarily, on the courtroom, and ADR does not figure prominently, if at all. This is strange because 'over 90% of all legal cases in Canada and the United States settle before going to trial, yet neither country's current television broadcasting depicts this reality of settlement and mediation'.[39]

For two seasons in the early 2000s there was a Canadian prime-time drama, *The Associates*, which included many alternative dispute resolution storylines,[40] but

---

detective. The second Canadian film that aired in November 2014 was *Blind Trust*, wherein a woman is convicted of killing her boyfriend in the heat of passion. She flees after the trial in order to learn who framed her, conducting investigatory work on her own.

[37] The Canadian film, *Blind Trust*, also featured a woman protagonist.
[38] vtele.ca/emissions/l-arbitre/episodes/.
[39] Schulz (2014) 53.
[40] For more information on *The Associates*, see Schulz (2012); and Schulz (2011).

this show is no longer broadcast. There was also an American prime-time drama called *Fairly Legal* that ran for two seasons in Canada and the US. The show was the first prime-time English language show actually about an ADR process, and it featured a woman mediator protagonist. However, *Fairly Legal* was off the air in both countries in 2014.[41]

For a researcher interested in ADR, the dearth of television programming in the area is disheartening and strange. The reality of legal practice is the opposite of what we see on TV. In real life much of law revolves around ADR processes such as negotiation, and takes place without police officers and without trials. For example, in 2006 there were 2,539 statements of claim filed in Manitoba, Canada. There were 257 trials set and 223 judicially assisted dispute resolution (JADR) meetings set.[42] Only 83 trials were actually heard however, while 181 JADR meetings occurred.[43] This means that trials occur less than half the number of times that cases are settled with judicial assistance. In addition, of course, there are hundreds of cases that settle without the assistance of a judge. For example, in 2009 in Manitoba only 2–3% of the statements of claim filed actually proceeded to trial.[44] The remaining 97–98% of statements of claim filed were settled, discontinued or abandoned.[45] More cases settle, usually via an ADR process, than are resolved via a trial in Canada. Law is more than police chases and verdicts but television in Canada in November 2014 did not reflect that reality, nor does it today.

Conclusion

Canadians now have a greater ability than ever before to choose exactly what they want to watch. In November 2014 in Manitoba, Canada, there were 1,255 law-related programmes per week broadcast on television and the vast majority—71.7%—were American. Thus, our television watching choices, both historically and today, are mainly American.

Canadians who enter Canadian law schools and courtrooms with expectations based upon American legally themed television will be greatly surprised by all the differences between American and Canadian courtroom procedure, and even more likely, they will be bored. Real law is never as scintillating as television law.

---

[41] In November 2013, however, *Fairly Legal* was dubbed in French and shown on Manitoba television as *Le Negotiator*.

[42] JADR meetings are akin to case conferences or settlement conferences with judges. The judge assists the parties and counsel to attempt to reach a settlement.

[43] GA Derwin, 'Judicially Assisted Dispute Resolution: Ten Years of Success' *Possibilities: CBA National Alternative Dispute Resolution Section Newsletter* (April 2008), The Canadian Bar Association: www.cba.org/cba/newsletters/adr-2008/news.aspx#article3.

[44] www.cfcj-fcjc.org/inventory-of-reforms/manitoba-judicially-assisted-dispute-resolution-jadr.

[45] With respect to the statements of claim set down for trial in 2009 in Manitoba, only 23% to 32% of the cases actually proceeded to trial.

Moreover, if Canadians take information about law from what they watch on television, they will mainly 'learn' about American criminal law and policing. If Canadians choose to watch Canadian programming about law, they will still predominantly only encounter police officers, not lawyers. The reality is that 81% of the law-themed television in Canada is about police officers, not lawyers. Finally, whether Canadians watch American or Canadian TV law, they are overwhelmingly presented with white male police officers and little to no alternative methods of dispute resolution.

Canadian television will never become as global as American television. However, as a more marginal country, Canada is well placed to increase its focus on the marginalised. Canadian television might be the place to begin to create a larger cultural legal space for alternative dispute resolution,[46] women, people of colour and other marginalised legal processes and actors. I am interested in engaging with these topics. What is less clear to me is whether my interest, or the interest of other Law & Popular Culture scholars, will be piqued by examining Canadian legally themed television. The picture in Canada is predominantly focused on police officers. Will Law & Popular Culture scholars be willing to research and write about them?

---

[46] Schulz (2011).

6

Denmark

GLEN ODGAARD

Introduction and Method

This study covers law and justice related programmes on Danish television over one month starting on Saturday 1 November 2014. The gossip and TV magazines *Her og Nu* and *Billedbladet* were scrutinised for law-related programmes. In addition to the TV magazines, IMDB, websites of TV channels and production companies, Wikipedia and other sources were used. For each programme title, channel, date and time of screening, length in minutes (excluding commercials), country of origin and genre (police and detective material, lawyer and court-related material, prison and post-prison material) were noted.

Films about the army or about weapons in general were not included. Westerns series like *Bonanza* were not included but a western film like *The Outlaw Joey Whales* was included because it has a clear legal theme. TV series that were not about law but contain lawyers (the main character or one of the leading characters is a lawyer) were included. If a minor character is a lawyer then it was not included. Hence, *How I Met Your Mother* was included because one of the five main characters, Marshall Eriksen, is a law student from Columbia University and later a lawyer, and *Joey* was included because the title character, Joey's neighbour and main love interest, is the lawyer Alexis (Alex) Garrett. *Desperate Housewives*, however, was not included though one of the main characters is married to a lawyer.

The Danish TV Channels

The Channels and Their History

DR

DR (Danmarks Radio) is Denmark's national broadcasting corporation and is still Denmark's largest electronic media enterprise and started in 1925 as a radio station. Experimental television broadcasts started in 1949, with regular programming from 1951 and daily programmes from 1954. Colour television test broadcasts were started in March 1967 and in 1978 it was switched entirely to colour. DR's monopoly on national television lasted until 1988, when TV2 started broadcasting (see under TV2 below).

DR added a second television channel DR2 in August 1996. On 7 June 2007, DR added an all-day news channel DR Update. At the Danish changeover to over-the-air digital signals, DR added the following three new channels to their line-up on 1 November 2009: DR HD—a channel with high definition transmissions; DRK—dedicated to culture and history, sometimes also alternative films. The 'K' stands for 'kultur', the Danish word for culture; DR Ramasjang—a children's channel.

On 28 January 2013 DR HD was shut down and replaced by DR3. The DR3 programmes are directed towards the youth and young adult audience. On 4 March 2013 DR Update was closed down and replaced by yet another children's channel DR Ultra meaning that DR Ramasjang targets children aged 6–10 and DR Ultra targets children aged 7–12.[1]

TV2

On 1 October 1988 Denmark's second TV station TV2 began broadcasting, thereby ending the television monopoly previously exercised by Danmarks Radio (DR). It is still publicly owned and is based in Denmark's third largest city Odense. Today TV2 has its main channel and five subsidiary stations. They are: TV2 Zulu, targeted at the youth; TV2 Charlie, oriented towards older audiences; TV2 News, a 24-hour news channel (launched on 1 December 2006); TV2 Fri, a leisure and hobby channel (launched on 5 May 2013) and TV2 Sport, a dedicated sports channel (launched on 9 January 2015); as well as the internet-based pay-per-view channel TV2 Sputnik which started broadcasting in December 2004. Before TV2 Sport there was also TV2 Film, a non-stop movie channel (launched on 1 November 2005). However, in August 2014 TV2 announced that TV 2 Film was to be closed down and replaced by their new sports channel in January 2015.[2]

Viasat / Modern Times Group

Viasat is broadcast from London and is owned by the Swedish media conglomerate Modern Times Group (MTG) targeting the Nordic and Baltic countries. Their main channel in Denmark, TV3, was launched in 1987 (a year before TV2).[3] In April 1996 they launched their sister channel TV3+ and in March 2009 TV3 Puls. The channels generally shows a lot of British and American TV shows. Apart from these channels they also have specialised channels such as TV3 Sport1 (launched in July 2013) and TV3 Sport2; film channels, Viasat Film, Viasat Film Nordic, Viasat Film Action, Viasat Film Family, Viasat Film Classic, Viasat Explorer and Viasat History.[4]

---

[1] Today DR has the following six channels: DR1, DR2, DR3, DRK, DR Ramasjang and DR Ultra.
[2] The relevant channels for this study are: TV2, TV2 Zulu, TV2 Charlie and TV2 Film.
[3] The reason why it was called TV3 and not TV2 in Denmark was that at the time it was launched Sweden already had two publicly owned TV channels.
[4] The relevant channels for this study are: TV3, TV3+ and TV3 Puls.

SBS

Their TV channels are broadcast in Denmark by satellite from London and comprise Kanal 4 (founded April 2006) profiling themselves as Denmark's only 'women's channel' with programmes such as *Denmark's Next Top Model* and *Gossip Girl*; Kanal 5 (founded April 2001) focusing on sport, film and American drama shows; and 6'eren (launched in January 2009) advertising as the only channel for men with offerings of football and *American Chopper*.

Popularity

According to TNS Gallup the older established main channels DR1 and TV2 are by far the most popular. Looking at the period from 2000 to 2009 then the viewing share for TV2 is between 30% and 36%; for DR1 it is between 24% and 30%; for TV3 it is between 5% and 9%; and for DR2 between 3% and 5%. All others usually have between 0% and 3%.

Law-Related TV on the Various Channels

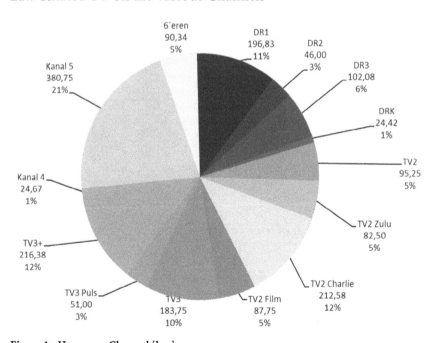

Figure 1: Hours per Channel [hrs]

As seen above the private TV channel Kanal 5 with 380 hours and 45 minutes contains by far the greatest amount of law-related programmes followed by TV3+ (216 hours and 25 minutes), TV2 Charlie (212 hours and 35 minutes) and DR1 (196 hours, 50 minutes). Kanal 5's leading position is mainly explained by its large number of American police series such as *Criminal Minds, CSI, Mike & Molly, Special Victim's Unit.* DRK is at the bottom with only 24 hours in a month due to their main focus on cultural and historical documentaries.

Time of the Week and Time During the Day

Definitions: Programmes shown between midnight and 5.00 am is a new date but is considered to be a part of the day before because that is the way it is mentioned in the weekly TV magazines I used as a source. Hence a programme running from 0.05 to 0.55 am is registered under Saturday 1 November though the actual date is Sunday 2 November.

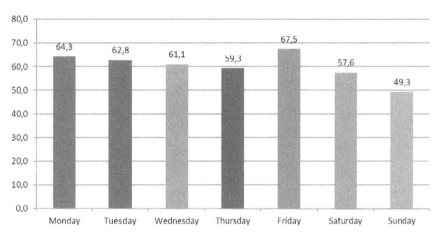

Figure 2: Average hours per weekday

We see above that law-related programmes are shown regularly throughout the week for between 49 hours 20 minutes (Sunday) and 67 hours 30 minutes (Friday) per day. This is explained by the fact that many of the TV series are on a constant rerun every day of the week.

What Time of the Day are Law-Related Programmes Shown?

It was decided to focus on the starting point of a programme regardless of when the programme ends.

— 'Night' is defined as a programme starting between midnight and 4.59 am.
— 'Morning' is defined as a programme starting between 5.00 am and 11.59 am.
— 'Afternoon' is defined as a programme starting between 12.00 noon and 5.59 pm.
— 'Evening' is defined as a programme starting between 6.00 pm and 11.59 pm.
— 'Prime time' is defined as a programme starting between 8.00 pm and 8.59 pm and is hence just a subdivision of 'evening'.

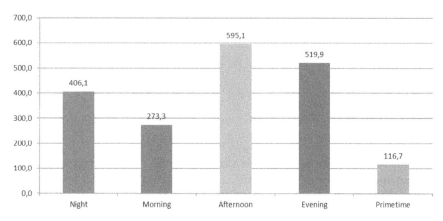

Figure 3: Time of the day [hrs]

Here we see that afternoons have the highest amount of law and related TV (595 hours and 5 minutes), followed by evenings (519 hours and 50 minutes) and that mornings have the lowest amount of law-related TV (273 hours and 20 minutes).

Countries of Origin

It was possible to find the country of origin of all programmes except a few *Border Security* programmes. Among the *Border Security* programmes it was in most cases specified whether it was *Border Security USA, Canada or Australia* but in a few cases it was unfortunately not, hence these are of unknown origin though they are from one of these three countries.

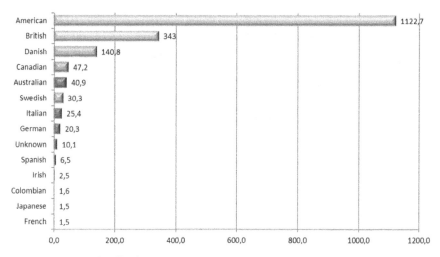

Figure 4: Nationality [hrs]

Looking at the above figure we see that law-related TV in Denmark is clearly dominated by American programmes: 1.122 hours and 40 minutes or 62.5% are American. We also see a clear number two, Britain, with 343 hours followed by the home country Denmark in third place with 140 hours. Canada (47 hours) and Australia (40 hours and 55 minutes) take fourth and fifth place.

Common American programmes include: *CSI, CSI Miami, CSI: New York, NCIS, Bones, Special Victims Unit, How I Met Your Mother, Without a Trace, Criminal Minds* and *Hawaii Five-0. Bones*, for example, had a total of 101 episodes on either TV3 or TV3+: a new episode on Wednesday 9.00 pm with reruns the following Saturday at 7.00 pm. In addition, older episodes was shown every weekday at 1.00 pm with a rerun the next day at noon plus further reruns at the weekend. There were 49 episodes of *Criminal Minds* showing every evening at 9.00 pm on Kanal 5 with a rerun later the same evening. *CSI* was on a constant rerun on Kanal 5 with two episodes every afternoon in addition to another rerun Saturday afternoon and evening.

Common British programmes included 78 episodes of *The Bill* on TV2 Charlie, 60 episodes of *Heartbeat* (two episodes every afternoon of the week on TV2 Charlie) and 17 episodes of *Midsomer Murders* on DR1.

The most common Danish programmes were the documentaries *Razzia*, *Station 2*, *Politijagt* and *Krimi5*.

Razzia follows real task forces of a variety of Danish government agencies on the job including the Danish Tax Authority, Food Agency or Environmental Agency as they try to find people seeking to break the law. There were 34 half-hour episodes shown on TV2 every weekday afternoon and in the evening at 9.25 pm.

Station 2 follows the work of real Danish policemen as they solve a variety of crimes. The first episode on TV2 was in 1993 and has since been shown in a variety of formats. In November 2014 a total of 12 episodes were shown on TV2, prime-time Thursday evening plus reruns another day later in the evening or at night. One of the formats is *Station 2 Efterlyst* (*Station 2: Wanted*): a live TV programme where the host informs the viewer about crimes the Danish police are currently trying to solve. The hosts function as middlemen between the audience and the police indicating that the police are ready by the phone to take calls from the public. Viewers are also told regularly about developments in the respective cases.

Politijagt (literally, *Police Hunt*) is a Kanal 5 programme about the Danish traffic police. A camera is put on a police car and the viewer can follow how the police chase cars that are driving too fast. A total of 17 episodes are shown throughout the month—prime time every Wednesday and Friday evening from 8.00 pm to 9.00 pm with reruns either in the afternoon or later in the evening.

Krimi5 is Kanal 5's equivalent to TV2's *Station 2*. Twenty-one episodes of one hour were shown but always in the middle of the night.

All the above-mentioned programmes are very police and/or government friendly. They give a feeling of safety (crime does not pay) and a sense that the police, TV and the good citizens of Denmark are all working together to solve crimes.

Common Canadian programmes include *Border Security Canada* (21 episodes on TV2 at night), *Rookie Blue* (20 episodes on DR3 at night), *Continuum* (nine episodes on TV3+ at night); and common Australian programmes include 15 episodes of *The Doctor Blake Mysteries* (always a little after midnight on DR1).

Swedish programmes cover a little more than 30 hours: five 1.5 hour episodes of *Annika Bengtzon* every Sunday at 10.10 pm; four 1.5 hour episodes of *Wallander* every Tuesday at 10.30 pm; and four 1.5 hour episodes of *Maria Wern* in the afternoon, all on DR1. Sweden and Denmark are neighbours and the national TV channels of Sweden and Denmark often cooperate. It is hence of no surprise that all the Swedish programmes are shown on DR. It is interesting, however, that the other Scandinavian neighbour, Norway, did not have a single law-related programme on Danish TV in November 2014. The German presence is due to 20 episodes of *Kommissar Rex*, one episode on TV2 Charlie every afternoon in the five weekdays on a constant rerun. The Italian presence is due to the reruns of the Bud Spencer and Terrence Hill films on TV2 Film at different times of the day.

With Denmark having a population of just 5.4 million and a language almost only spoken in Denmark, it is of no surprise that many programmes are of foreign origin. The market is simply too small.

Looking at languages we see that the English language is clearly dominant: 1,566 hours (87.3%) contain programmes from a country where English is the native language. Comparing that with the other five official languages of the UN (French, Spanish, Russian, Arabic and Chinese) we see that there is a little in French (two hours 30 minutes) and Spanish (eight hours 10 minutes) but nothing in Russian, Arabic or Chinese. No programmes came from Eastern Europe and only one programme came from Asia (the Japanese documentary *Silent Shame* from 2010 about war crimes, shown in the middle of the night); one came from South America (the Colombian co-production *Maria Full of Grace*); and there were no programmes from Africa.

Genre

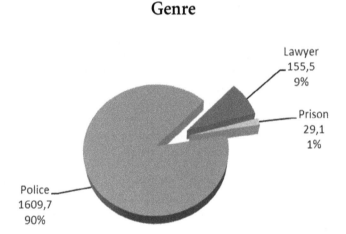

Figure 5: Duration per genre [hrs]

We see above that police and detective-themed material far exceeds the other two genres: lawyer and court-related material, and prison and post-prison material. Of the 1,794 hours and 20 minutes of law-related material, 1.609 hours and 45 minutes deal with police and detectives in different forms.

Due to the volume it was necessary to make a further division into drama, comedy and documentary. For dramas and comedies, it was noted whether it was a film or a TV series.

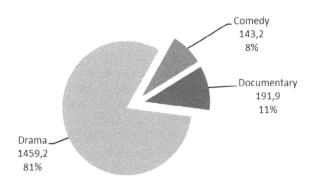

Figure 6: Duration per subgenre [hrs]

Of the three subgenres, drama, comedy and documentary we see that drama with over 1.459 hours (81%) far exceeds comedies and documentaries.

It is also interesting to notice that unlike in the United States actual court cases are completely absent from Danish TV.

Police and Detective Material

Dramas

Police and detective dramas came to a total of 1.372 hours and 10 minutes. Of these, 905 hours and 50 minutes (66%) were of American origin. Due to the volume it was decided to divide them into the further subcategories of film or TV series.

Films About Police and Detectives

Dramatic film portrayals of police and detectives were shown for 205 hours and 50 minutes. Among these US material was shown for 166 hours and five minutes (81%).

TV Drama Series About Police and Detectives

Drama TV series of police and detectives were shown for 1.166 hours and 20 minutes. Among these, US material was shown for 739 hours and 45 minutes (63%) and British 290 hours and 20 minutes (25%). Native Danish programmes accounted for just 22 hours and 40 minutes.

Of the five most common of all law-related programmes on Danish TV, four of the five are in the category American police drama series including the most common of all, *CSI*. If you combine *CSI*, *CSI New York* and *CSI Miami* then these add up to 129 hours and 10 minutes. *CSI* is followed by *NCIS* (99 hours and five minutes), *Bones* (98 hours and five minutes) and *Special Victims Unit* (57 hours).

The second most common of all law-related programmes on Danish TV and the most common of British origin is *The Bill*, also a police drama series. A total of 103 hours and 50 minutes (120 episodes) was shown on TV2 Charlie, usually two episodes every afternoon with reruns at night. Another police drama series of British origin worth mentioning is the 53 hours and 20 minutes (60 episodes) of *Heartbeat* also shown on TV2 Charlie but in the late afternoons.

Danish police drama series include *Dicte* and *Rejseholdet*.

Rejseholdet (*Unit One*) was a 32-episode Emmy award-winning TV series made by DR running for four seasons in the period from 2000 to 2004. In November 2014 it was shown for 13 hours and 50 minutes on DRK. Until 2002 *Rejseholdet* was a real unit within the Danish police with the purpose of solving complex and national cases. Many episodes are supposedly based on true crime stories from Rejseholdet.

Dicte is a 2013 series based on novels by Elsebeth Egholm and follow the criminal reporter Dicte Svendsen (played by Iben Hjejle) as she tries to solve crimes. TV2 showed it at prime time every Wednesday with additional reruns on Sunday afternoons.

Comedies

For the period analysed, comedies on police and detectives were rarer. Of the total of 55 hours and 30 minutes, US material covered 33 hours and 40 minutes. Examples include *Mike & Molly* (two episodes almost every morning on Kanal 5).

Documentaries

A total of 182 hours and five minutes concerned documentaries on police and detectives. Of these the majority were not American but Danish. In this category, 110 hours and 55 minutes (61%) were of Danish origin, followed by British (23 hours and 40 minutes, 13%), American (20 hours and 45 minutes, 11%) and Australian (six hours and 30 minutes, 4%). The Danish programmes include *Razzia*, *Station 2*, *Politijagt* and *Krimi5* (see above under 'Countries of Origin').

Lawyer and Court-Focused Material

Lawyer and court focused material covered a total of 155 hours and 30 minutes. Of these almost all (146 hours and 35 minutes, 94 %) were American. Only three hours and 45 minutes were Danish (*Gift ved Første Blik* (*Married at First Sight*)) but shown at prime time every Tuesday evening on DR1.

Dramas

Dramas on lawyers ran for some 61 hours and 10 minutes. Of these 18 hours were from the American TV series *The Whole Truth* (Kanal 5, all at night). The majority, however, was accounted for by the many different American films shown on many different Danish TV channels and at various different times of day too.

Comedies

All comedies about lawyers are American and there was a total of 87 hours and 25 minutes. In contrast to other categories there are actually more lawyer comedies than lawyer dramas on Danish TV. This is mostly due to the constant reruns of the popular TV series *How I Met Your Mother* (TV3+), *Dharma and Greg* (every morning on TV2 Zulu) and *Joey* (every afternoon on TV2 Zulu). Every weekday TV3+ shows at least four episodes of *How I Met Your Mother*: from 5.00 pm to 6.00 pm with reruns from the previous day followed by the next two episodes from 6.00 pm to 7.00 pm with additional reruns at the weekends, amounting to 120 episodes for just one month.

Documentaries

The category covered a total of six hours and 55 minutes. Among them was a two-part documentary about the Nuremberg Trials following the Second World War and the above-mentioned Danish programme *Gift ved Første Blik*.

Prison and Post-Prison Material

Prison and post-prison material is rarely dealt with on Danish TV. Just 29 hours and five minutes were in this category for a whole month. Of this 15 hours and 55 minutes (55%) were American, nine hours and 40 minutes (33%) were British, and three hours and 30 minutes (12%) were Danish. The American presence mainly stems from film classics such as *Silence of the Lambs, Hannibal, The Shawshank Redemption* and Jim Jarmusch's *Down by Law*.

Summary and Analysis

All in all, 1,794 hours and 20 minutes of law-related programmes were found on Danish TV channels in November 2014.

— Kanal 5 was by a clear margin the channel with the most law- and justice-related TV: 380 hours and 45 minutes were shown on that channel—164 hours and 20 minutes more than the second place: TV3+. DRK was the channel with the least law- and justice-related TV.

— Law-related programmes are shown regularly throughout the week. There is not much difference between the least common day (Sunday) and the most common day (Friday). This is explained by the fact that the most common programmes are on a constant rerun every day of the week.
— Afternoon is the most common time of day to show law-related TV: 595 hours and five minutes were shown on in the afternoon, more than twice as much as the least common time of the day, morning.
— The US is by far the most common country of origin: 62.5% of all law-related TV was of American origin followed by Britain and Denmark. Of all the material, 87.3% is from a country where English is a native language. The US leads in all categories except documentaries where most were of native Danish origin. In contrast to more than 30 hours of TV of Swedish origin and more than 20 hours of TV of German origin there was surprisingly no programmes from our other neighbour Norway.
— Drama and specifically American police drama series is by far the most popular genre: 1.459 hours (81%) can be categorised as drama; 1.372 hours and 10 minutes are in the category of police drama; and 739 hours and 45 minutes are in the specific category of American police drama series. Actual court cases are absent from Danish TV.

Combining all these factors then the most typical programme is an American police drama on Friday afternoon on Kanal 5. *CSI* fits all these criteria and also happened to be the single most common of all law-related programmes on Danish TV in November 2014.[5]

---

[5] Sources: *Billedbladet* 44, 30 October 2014—77th year; *Her & Nu* week 45, 5 November 2014; *Her & Nu* week 46, 12 November 2014; *Her & Nu* week 47, 19 November 2014; *Her & Nu* week 48, 26 November 2014.

7

France

BARBARA VILLEZ (WITH VALENTIN ROLANDO)

On any given weekday in France, a television viewer can watch a multitude of crime fictions, documentaries on the police or a televised 'magazine' report on a famous case or an issue of social justice. The French television viewer has a choice of 24 'free' television channels belonging to the TNT (*télévision numérique terrestre*, or terrestrial digital television).[1] Seven of these are public channels, the other 17 are privately owned, but free of charge, outside the licence fee. Everyone pays a licence fee of €136, included on the yearly council tax form.

French Television History, Financing and Organisation

French television started to broadcast programmes in the late-1930s. A few years later, General Charles de Gaulle with the help of the Ministry of Information set up a state-regulated audiovisual service, RTF (Radiodiffusion Télévision Française). Created by law in 1949, RTF provided for the spending, investment and management of television and radio. It was also in charge of regulating television content and overseeing journalistic behaviour. The decision to develop a public television service clearly indicated the will to monitor the flow of information. Three additional objectives for French television were that programmes had to inform, educate and entertain the audience. Broadcasts like *5 Colonnes à la Une* offered the first TV reports and dealt with social issues at home, and foreign policy through the coverage of international conflicts (eg, the Algerian War).

Television has never been high in the French cultural hierarchy and it was not a standard household feature until well into the 1960s. In 1960 only 13% of families had a television set at home. By 1970 this figure had increased to 70% even though

---

[1] There are 25 TNT (*télévision numérique terrestre*) stations in France today. The TNT was introduced in 2005 and extended to the whole territory in 2011. The public stations belong to the France Télévision holding (France 2, France 3, France 4, France 5 and France ô which provides news from France's overseas departments and territories, sometimes broadcasting news on francophone Africa as well).

the audiovisual offer remained limited. French television was a single channel service (Télévision Française 1) broadcasting regularly for 40 hours a week until April
1964 when a second channel, Antenne 2, was created, initially broadcasting only
a few hours a day. In December 1972, a third channel was launched, covering the
whole country but with regional content.

In 1964, a few months after the launch of the second channel (Antenne 2), RTF
was transformed into ORTF (Office de radiotélévision française), which provided
greater autonomy in relation to the government. In 1974 the ORTF was replaced
by seven independent subsidiaries: the three television channels as independent
organisms (Télévision Française 1, Antenne 2, France 3 Régions), Télédiffusion de
France (responsible for technical material), Société Française de Production, Radio
France, and INA (Institut national de l'audiovisuel, responsible for archives). An
independent commission was created to redistribute the licence fee among these
seven public companies.[2]

French television remained a totally public institution until 1981. During his
campaign for the presidency, François Mitterand, promised to give more freedom
to the audiovisual sector. Canal+, the first pay television station (with encrypted
periods during the evening and parts of the day) was created in 1983 and started
broadcasting in the following year. In 1984 the first French language satellite
channel TV5 was created. Today public television is financed by the licence fee
(60%) and advertising (40%). Advertising was introduced into the system in
1968. During Nicolas Sarkozy's presidency, advertising was limited on the public (state owned) channels, permitted during the day, except between 8.00 pm
and 6.00 am. However, certain companies can sponsor programmes during this
time slot. Private companies and advertising finance private stations. Some private channels also rely on subscriptions (eg, Canal+, Orange Séries, etc). In 1983
the *Cosip* (*Compte de soutien à l'industrie des programmes*) was created to collect
a tax on all channels making them contribute to cinematic and other audiovisual
productions.

Although programmes linked to subjects of law and justice can be seen on all
channels, some smaller channels tend to specialise in these themes as part of their
offerings. Here there is a more regular coverage of crime, especially police work.
For example, Planète+ carries documentaries on organised crime, 'magazines'
dealing with famous cases and related subjects such as prison escapes or banking fraud. Much of their scheduling, however, consists of reruns during the week.
TMC (Télé Monte-Carlo, financed through capital from France and Monaco) is a
non-specialised channel, yet most evenings (during prime time and afterwards),
police shows are broadcast (the *CSI*, and *Law & Order* shows, *90' Enquêtes*, a 'magazine' on police activity). Polar,[3] is a channel, which regularly broadcasts crime

---

[2] 'Chronologie de la politique de l'audiovisuel': www.vie-publique.fr/politiques-publiques/
politique-audiovisuel/chronologie/.
[3] 'Polar' is a French slang term for crime fiction.

series and films. Many programmes dealing with law and justice are imported, but as we note below, strict quotas are imposed on all the channels as to imported content.

The French Legal Context

French justice is inquisitorial, not adversarial. Like most systems outwith the Anglo-American tradition, the judiciary is a separate profession within the civil service. More serious crimes are dealt with by superior courts consisting of a judges, two legal assessors and a jury of six citizens seated on either side of the three judges. Trials are judge led, rather than lawyer led, which means that the direction of speech is always to and from the presiding judge. One particular judge often encountered in TV programmes mentioned in this study is another feature of the continental system, the investigating magistrate (*le juge d'instruction*). He or she is a *juge du siege* responsible for investigations in criminal cases for more serious crimes, and sometimes in less serious matters. Their investigatory role results in rather shorter and different trials from the Anglo-American system.

History of Law Material on French Television

The first regular French programme on the theme of justice was *En votre âme et conscience*, first aired on 28 February 1956 (RTF). It ran until 13 December 1969 (by then on the first channel of ORTF). Based on famous cases, each broadcast reconstructed parts of the trials and the public was invited at the end of the show to act as jurors and re-judge the accused. Each episode told a different story and there were no recurring characters; the judges and lawyers played by different actors in an exaggerated style.

Despite this long history of fictional reconstructions, French television programmes on justice, over the past 60 years, have principally taken the form of documentaries, also about famous cases already dealt with in the media (*l'affaire Grégory*), judicial scandals (*l'affaire Outreau*), important cases in French history (*l'affaire Dreyfus* or the Eichmann trial) or current crime issues (recidivism after prison) or foreign justice (prisons in the United States). The content of these reports has centred on the investigations prior to trial or a historical narrative of the cases. Interviews with the lawyers, police officers, journalists who covered the cases and news archives were used, but there are no actual films of trials because a 1954 law forbids cameras of any sort to be used in, or even brought to, courtrooms.

During the last 60 years, there have been twice as many documentaries, docu-dramas or magazines about famous cases as legal dramas.[4] Three kinds of magazine can be found on French television: TV reports (*Terrain d'investigation, 90' Enquête, Révélation*); programmes with educational purposes (*Des droits pour grandir*); and filmed reconstructions of human-interest stories, from the police investigation to the trial (*Faites entrer l'accusé, Chroniques criminelles, Passions criminelles, Les Enquêtes impossibles, Crimes*). TV reports mainly represent the daily routine of various police departments. Technical devices, such as hidden cameras, are frequently used allowing a journalist to participate in sometimes dangerous operations.

The early years of television were marked by an effort to bring culture to the public as well as to create cultural content especially for television.[5] Thus, in 1955 Albert Camus was invited on an important literary programme entitled *À livre ouvert* (RTF) to read passages of his book *The Stranger* from the dock of a mock courtroom.[6] In 1956 a first 'series' of historical mystery was aired in which various hypotheses were dramatised and a jury of historians determined the most plausible solution at the end (*Enigmes*, sometimes called *À chacun sa vérité*, RTF). Occasional plays, like a French adaptation of Rose's *Twelve Angry Men* or Racine's *Les Plaideurs*, have been televised from the early years of regular broadcasting. Robert Hossein directed a number of procedural plays in which the audience was invited to pronounce a verdict at the end. At least one of these, *L'affaire Seznec: c'est vous qui allez le juger*, a famous miscarriage of justice, was aired on France 3 in April 2010 and 94% of the television audience of 3 million that evening voted to acquit Seznec.[7] Parodies have been used as a way to criticise the institution of justice and experimental trial performances have been broadcast, like comedian Patrick Sébastien's 'real false trial' (France 2, 19 May 2006, 20:50) in which a popular singer was charged with murder. Again here, the television audience pronounced a verdict. This staged fictional trial, entitled *Intime Conviction*[8] was originally a project for several shows in which a famous personality would be accused of a crime and real lawyers would play their professional roles. Sébastien presided over the court assisted by two (actor) *assesseurs*, bringing the public a more exact picture, at least, of la Cour d'Assises dealing with serious offences.

Numerous feature films from the United States dealing with the police, lawyers and the courts or prisons have been available on television a year or two after playing in the cinema. In fact, on TF1, France 2 and Arte (the Franco-German

---

[4] 'La Justice saisie par la télévision' (2003) 69–72.

[5] Delavaud (2012).

[6] Brochand and Mousseau (1987) 58.

[7] *20 Minutes* (21 April 2010: www.20minutes.fr/culture/399341-20100421).

[8] Jurors are told to give a verdict according to their 'intime conviction' or what they deeply believe. Here again an important difference in legal culture appears between the continental tradition and the common law where juries are not to convict if they have a **reasonable** doubt.

channel), Sunday night prime time is often dedicated to such films. *Kramer v Kramer* (Robert Benton, 1979), *The Verdict* (Sidney Lumet, 1982), *Find Me Guilty* (Sidney Lumet, 2006), *The Witness* (Peter Weir, 1985) and many more have been broadcast with multiple reruns over the years. Nevertheless, the main source of material dealing with justice has been television series, such as *Ivanhoe, Zorro, Starsky and Hutch, Kojak, Hill Street Blues (Capitaine Furillo), Miami Vice, The Untouchables, Perry Mason, LA Law (La Loi de Los Angeles), Ally McBeal, the practice (Bobby Donnell et associés)* and, very late at night, even Sidney Lumet's *100 Centre Street (Tribunal central)*. All the series of the *Law & Order* franchise have appeared on several channels at various times of the day and evening. The more recent series like *Close to Home, Drop Dead Diva* or *Suits* have also been aired on TNT channels.

The French have very few courtroom series of their own,[9] but they have produced numerous police and detective series. Many of these, and certainly all the earlier shows, follow a 90-minute format, corresponding to a cinematic time slot. Today the 52-minute format is also used. Some investigators are loose adaptations: *Thierry la fronde* (RTF 1963–64; ORTF 1964–66) based on the adventures of Robin Hood; or *Arsène Lupin* (ORTF, 1971–74) from Maurice Leblanc's 'gentleman thief' known to take on other criminals and save damsels in distress; Léo Malet's *Nestor Burma* (Antenne 2, 1991, later France 2 and until 2003, reruns on M6). *Louis la brocante* (France 3, 1998–2014), an antique dealer turning detective in each episode proved French viewers' affection for sleuths. There is an impressive corpus of police fictions: *PJ (Police judiciaire*, France 2, 1997–2009); *Commissaire Moulin* (TF1, 1996–2008); *La Crim'* (France 2, 1999–2006); *Diane, femme flic* (TF1, 2003–10); *Julie Lescaut* (TF1, 1992–2014); *Navarro* (TF1, 1989–2007; D8 2012–14); *Les Bleus, premiers pas dans la police* (M5, 2006–10).[10] Frequent reruns on various channels run alongside new shows, such as *Deux flics sur les docks* (France 2, 2011–); *Candice Renoir* (France 2, 2013–); and *Chérif* (France 2, 2013–).

Une femme d'honneur (TF1, 1996–2008) attempted a different approach to police drama as it takes place in the *gendarmerie*[11] and *Alice Nevers, le juge est une femme* (TF1, 1993–) is about an investigating magistrate (*juge d'instruction*). Given that Alice Nevers' particular type of work would correspond more to police work in the common law system, this series is classified as a police series.

---

[9] Two important exceptions to this were *Tribunal* (TF1, 1988–90) in which Judge Garonne presided over a different case each episode and *Avocats et Associés* (France 2, 1990–2010) about a small law firm in Paris. (For details see Villez (2009) 48– 52, 59).

[10] It must be remembered that for many French series, a season may only contain six or eight episodes. There can be a considerable lapse in time between seasons and therefore if broadcast dates span 12 years, this will not mean that the series is composed of 12 seasons.

[11] France has two concurrent police forces, one with civil status and the gendarmerie with military status. Both are composed of several departments which sometimes appear to have the same responsibilities.

The series of made-for-television-movies *Femmes de loi* (TF1, 2000–09) centres on the particular collaboration between two women: an assistant prosecutor and a police lieutenant in the criminal brigade (*Brigade anti-criminalité*). Since one of the main characters is a prosecutor (*magistrat debout*) the series offers courtroom scenes. These scenes, however, do not provide a reliable picture of French trials. The production team seems more concerned with what they assume television viewers expected after watching American courtroom dramas. Hence, jury members sit in a box separate from the bench of judges and the witness is questioned and cross-examined in another box. This may be an attempt at producing an experience of the real or an 'effect of the real'[12] but it is not a French reality.

Many members of the French legal professions have expressed their exasperation over the habits that telecitizens[13] here have acquired with their frequent exposure to American courtroom series. Demanding a warrant from the police, invoking a Fifth Amendment right to silence or calling French judges '*Votre honneur*', because of bad dubbing, led in 2005 to Dominique Perben the Minister of Justice appealing to television writers and producers to rectify the situation by creating good French alternatives for these imported series. Canal+ heard his plea, but they were already working on *Engrenages*, a series project with sales in foreign markets in mind. Despite its slow start, the show sold in Great Britain and new scriptwriters, more knowledgeable of French criminal justice, assured a successful run as of season three. *Engrenages*[14] has received a more positive reception from some members of the legal profession and from the police for its realism and respect shown to these professions.[15] They also feel that the series gives a truer picture of the collaboration among different services and the reality of the politics of the judicial hierarchy.

The vast majority centre on the apprehension of criminals. There have been few courtroom dramas and virtually no prison series produced in France.[16] On the other hand, the French have dealt with all three stages of criminal justice management in documentaries. Documentaries are rarely serialised and although reruns are frequently sold to other channels, they tend to be aired late at night. The ratings for imported fictions (police series, courtroom dramas and films dealing with prison), however, attest to the popularity of these themes with French audiences. Given the rules governing quotas on foreign material during prime time, the interest in questions of justice and the French television industry's preference

---

[12] Barthes (1968); and Barthes (1982) 81–90.

[13] Villez (2009).

[14] *Engrenages* is seen in the UK and the US under the title of *Spiral* and received an Emmy Award as best foreign series, for its fifth season, in 2015.

[15] See interview of Judge Sylvie Perdriolle, Paris, June 2013 in Villez (2014).

[16] It is forbidden to film prisoners or shoot films in prison, thus there have been more feature fictions on this subject produced in France than documentaries. Recently, permission to film within the walls of prisons has been obtained and a few prisoners have been part of documentaries.

to produce documentaries and buy foreign fictions, revealed that imported material accounted for well over half of all the justice material shown on French television.[17]

The Empirical Study of Justice Material on Television in France in November 2014

We covered only those programmes clearly related to the subject of justice (police focus, courtroom focus or prison focus). This included fictional dramas and documentaries as well as 'television magazines' combining interviews, archives and discussion among guests on the set. In, for example, *Faites entrer l'accusé*, past cases are analysed; this is neither a reality programme, nor a documentary. The work carried out on French television covered the programmes carried by 66 channels: 23 TNT,[18] the rest on satellite or ADSL-TV (from internet service providers). Actually of these 66 channels, only 49 offered programmes concerned in our study. This is because the others are niche channels specialising in sports, opera or animal documentaries.

A total of over 4,000 programmes in November 2014 constituted the body of broadcasts in which justice was central, either with a focus on police work, on the courts and the legal professions, or on the outcomes of court decisions. The programmes were analysed according to genre, to country of origin, content (apprehension, adjudication, outcomes) and scheduling (prime-time or daytime slots). The genre analysis revealed that justice material constituted 12.1% of the content on all the channels of the 49 channels examined.

Distribution of Programmes Per Day According to Genre

Table 1, and the accompanying graph (Figure 1) give the number of all the programmes found during the first week of November 2014, per day and according to genre. Thus, for the first Saturday (the first days of the television week in *Télérama*) there was a total of 170 broadcasts dealing with justice, separated into four

---

[17] See Table 2.

[18] Some of Canal+ programmes are broadcast unencrypted, mostly talk shows or news programmes such as *Le Grand Journal*, *Le Petit Journal*, *La Nouvelle Édition* or satirical and comedy programmes like *Le Zapping* or *Les Guignols de l'Info*. These subscription-free programmes are considered a part of the TNT service.

categories: drama series, movies, documentaries and 'magazines'. For the first week the total of all such shows was 997 programmes.

Table 1: Distribution of programmes per day according to genre

	TV Series	Movies	Documentaries	TV Reportage/ Magazines	Total
Saturday	122	19	14	15	170
Sunday	92	25	4	4	125
Monday	108	9	9	11	137
Tuesday	101	16	11	8	136
Wednesday	107	12	6	11	136
Thursday	116	12	11	8	147
Friday	122	10	2	12	146

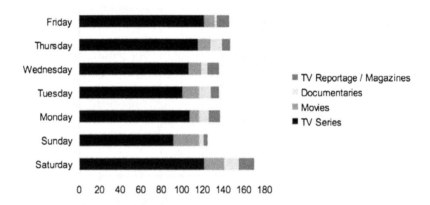

Figure 1: Programmes per day according to genre

Distribution of Programmes Per Day According to Nationality

The following table (Table 2) and graph (Figure 2) give the number of programmes per day according to their country of origin. It is clear from this table that during week one, a total of 692.5 programmes were of foreign origin and 304.5 were produced by France. Some programmes were co-produced by two European countries; in that case, the percentage was divided equally between the two producing countries. Thus, the quotas imposed on French channels concerning imported material are more or less followed as 50% of the content was foreign.

Table 2: Distribution of programmes per day according to nationality (week 1)

	USA	France	Germany	Great Britain	Other
Saturday	68	63,5	21,5	10	7
Sunday	59	32	13	13	8
Monday	71	41	15	7	3
Tuesday	66	45	17	2	6
Wednesday	71	39	15	7	4
Thursday	75	40	17	8	7
Friday	73	44	18	8	3

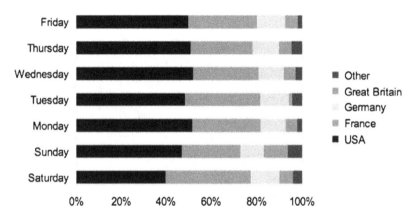

Figure 2: Programmes per day according to country of origin

Distribution of Programmes Per Genre According to Nationality

The table (Table 3) and graph below (Figure 3) give the number of shows per genre according to country of origin. The majority of drama series are American whereas France remains the major source of production of documentaries and the only source for "magazines". The most striking finding concerns Great Britain. Here, although the programmes they export may be fewer than those of the United States or Germany, they are almost all fictional dramas, particularly in series form. France, thus, seems to have maintained its reliance on documentary and 'magazines' to deal with issues of justice. Through the interview of key characters and filmed reconstructions, programmes such as *Crimes*, broadcast on NRJ12 or *Faites entrer l'accusé* (France 2) tend to develop a particular approach to justice, avoiding sensationalism, concentrating on story.[19]

Table 3: Programme genres according to country of origin

	TV Series	Movies	Documentaries	TV Reportage/ Magazines
USA	418	49	16	0
France	154	41	40.5	69
Germany	116	0	0,5	0
Great Britain	53	2	0	0
Other	27	11	0	0

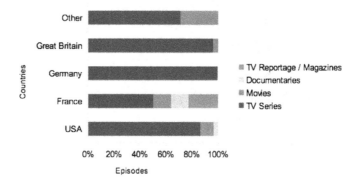

Figure 3: Distribution of programmes per genre according to nationality

Data collected during the first week of November was checked against various days chosen at random from the following weeks of the month. Each check confirmed the initial findings: the number of programmes according to genre and according to nationality remained the same. Indeed the variation of material in terms of genre and quantity varied little (+/-5%) from week to week and this is probably still the case months later. For instance, a comparison between Thursday 6 November and Thursday 20 November (see Figure 4) highlights this fact.

The organisation of the French programme schedules was stable all through the month, despite some small variations on major channels (TF1, France 2, France 3, Arte, M6 and Canal+) depending on live specials or sporting events. Documentaries did not constitute a significant source of material on justice

---

[19] This is the story given by the journalists conducting the interviews for the show when contacting potential interviewees, as reported by Clément Domas interning with the production company of *Crimes* NRJ12, February 2015.

during the period studied and those that were broadcast during the whole month were essentially French productions. Series, on the other hand, were the most frequent source of representations of justice on the 49 channels during the month of November (see Figure 4).

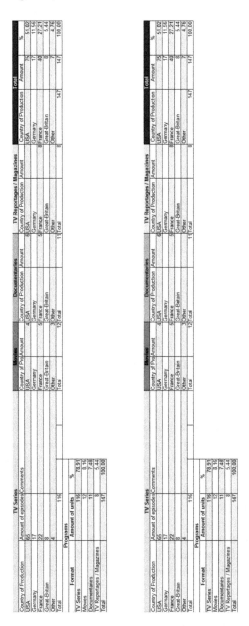

Figure 4: Comparison between Thursday 6th November and Thursday 20th November

Scheduling policies were reactive. If TF1 devoted most of its weekday prime time to crime drama series, other channels, such as France 3 or M6 scheduled crime drama series on Saturday night. Moreover, the type of content (apprehension, adjudication, outcomes) of the series also differ from one channel to another.[20] France 2, a public subsidiary channel of the *France Télévision* holding, broadcast a new episode of *Commissaire Magellan* on Saturday, whereas the private channel M6 devoted its entire Saturday evening (from 8.50 pm to 1.10 am) to the American crime series *NCIS: Los Angeles.* The NCIS programmes command the highest ratings on M6 and this is largely the reason for such a scheduling decision.[21] This also means, however, that the first episode broadcast in the evening is new, but the later ones are generally reruns.

The balance between the high proportion of American drama series and those of France and Europe can be explained by the imposed quotas of French and European productions on French television. It must be remembered that 60% of the programmes broadcast on French television must be European productions and 40% of that must be produced in France. These quotas were introduced by the French government in the early 1970s in order to promote local culture. The kind of material imported from the United States and broadcast on French television, however, is different from the programmes produced in France and the rest of the European Union. More than 90% of the American material on law and justice comprises fictional drama. Private channels in France like TMC, Paris Première and Série Club devote the main part of their schedules to series like *Charlie's Angels, Numb3rs, CSI: New York* and the *Law & Order* universe (see: Table 4: content per genre).

Content (Title) Per Genre

Table 5 gives the titles of the shows dealing with law and justice during the first week of November 2014. As already noted, the theme most encountered is police work. The most frequent genre is drama series, some old, some new, produced in France and elsewhere. Law and court material appears in seven drama series and all of them are American. Movies (feature films and made-for-tv-movies) constitute the second most significant group of shows aired during that week. Here again, the majority dealt with police work. Of the five movies that week with a courtroom focus, two were French. The theme of prison was covered in seven films of which three were produced in France. There were few comedies, all of them films, and mostly with a police focus again. It is very important that all these comedies were French productions which tends to confirm the sceptical view of

---

[20] See, eg, a channel like Polar which specialises in this type of content as opposed to the main channels which air more varied programmes.
[21] Interview with Christine Bouillet, head of programming at M6 (Villez (2014)).

Table 4: Police and Detective material

Dramas (Series)	Dramas (movies)	Comedies	Reality	Documentaries	TV Reports/ Magazines
Castle, Numb3rs, Monk, Murder, She Wrote, CSI: New York, Magnum, The Bridge, Continuum, Blue Bloods, The Pretender, Those Who Kill, Criminal Minds, Hannibal, Ray Donovan, Body of Proof, Mentalist, Lilyhammer, Brooklyn Nine-Nine, Sex Crime, Justified, Profilage, Navarro, Commissaire Moulin, Julie Lescaut, Engrenages, Soeur Thérèse, Paris, Enquêtes Criminelles, PJ, Maigret, Crimes en série, Quai n°l, Les crimes d'Agatha Christie, Charlie's Angels, Les Cordiers, juge et flic, Commissaire Cordier, Commissaire Magellan, La Commune, Alice Nevers, le juge est une femme, A Case for Two, SOKO Leipzig, Mick Brisgau, 112 Unité d'Urgence (112 Emergency, *informal title*), Alarm for Cobra 11—The Highway Police, Waking the Dead, Hercule Poirot, Midsomer Murders, Luther, Rush, Mongeville, The Murdoch Mysteries, The Gates, Lines of Duty	Loss of faith, Hidden Away, Je fais le mort, Pawn, Hercule Poirot, Hunted, L.A Confidential, Le Parfum de la Dame en Noir, L'Arme Parfaite, Party Girl, Codi 60, Taking lives, Confessions d'un commissaire de police au procureur de la République, L'hypnotiseur, Night Sins, Wild Things 2, Lieutenant, Paul Gruninger le Juste, L'heure du crime, Légitime défense, Pile ou face, Kick-Ass 2, The Raid, La disparue du Pyla, Fausses disparitions, Ransom, L627, Alex Cross, A Crime, L'ange du crime, Flic Story, I confess, Deceiver, Chinatown, Gunn, Carnal Innocence, Lethal Weapon 4, Mystic River, Coup d'Eclat	Associés contre le crime, Les keufs, Bouche cousue, RIP Department, Jamais 2 sans 3		Le petit guide de l'empoisonneur, Une femme à la Gendarmerie Royale du Canada, Les Dossiers Karl Zéro, Les faits Karl Zéro, Montmartre du plaisir et du crime, Le Casse (1,2,3), Ice Crime, La nouvelle vague du polar scandinave, Crimes en Haute Société, Ripoux Story, Blood Relatives: petits meurtres en famille	Faites entrer l'accusé, Terrain d'investigation, Révélations, Passions Criminelles: le magazines des faits- divers, Enquête exclusive, Les enquêtes de l'impossible, Crimes, Enquête d'action, La Brigade, 90' Enquêtes

(continued)

Table 4: *(Continued)*

Law and Court material						
Dramas (Series)	Dramas (movies)	Comedies	Reality	Documentaries	TV Reports/ Magazines
Ally McBeal, Suits, Drop Dead Diva, Law and Order: Special Victims Unit, Law and Order: Criminal Intent, Law and Order, Scandal	Trial: The Price of Passion (Double Verdict), Cruel Justice, The Counselor, Coupable?, Vérité Oblige	9 mois ferme		Avocat des étrangers, Viol, elles se manifestent, Simone Veil: une loi au nom des femmes, Narco-finance: les impunis	Des droits pour grandir, L'écho des lois

Prison & post-Prison material						
Dramas (Series)	Dramas (movies)	Comedies	Reality	Documentaries	TV Reports/ Magazines
Rectify, Misfits	Prisoners, Bird on a Wire, Présumé coupable, Death Race, You don't Know Jack, Illégal, Médecin Chef à la Santé		Pit Bull and Parolees	Perpétuité pour les enfants d'Amérique, Mon père est un criminel	

the French towards their judicial institution, which is seen as a simple institution of the government rather than independent of the State.

Documentaries were largely French and some from other parts of Europe. Police work was the theme found most often although there were four broadcasts on the courts and two on prisons. There was only one reality programme during this period: an episode of a six season American production, *Pit Bull and Parolees* (*Pitbull et prisonniers*). The show tells the story of men on parole, hired by Mrs Torres who runs a kennel for abused and abandoned pitbulls. The parolees take care of the animals thus permitting the mutual rescue of these men and the unpopular dogs. This reality show was aired on station No 23 and the same 42-minute episode was rebroadcast several times. In the category of 'magazines' aired during week one of the study, all were French and all concerned past crime investigations.

Prime Time and Daytime Distribution

'Prime time' runs from 8.00 pm to 11.00 pm and 'daytime' covers all remaining programming. Twenty-four hour broadcasting began in the late 1980s on the private channels. This did not happen all at once, but was the result of progressive experimentation[22] by the different private stations, followed later by the public ones. Before this, broadcasting stopped in France at 11.30 pm. It is significant that most justice content, during the prime-time slot, is on Wednesdays and Fridays, despite a CSA rule that television content must not adversely affect film releases in cinemas which take place on Wednesdays.

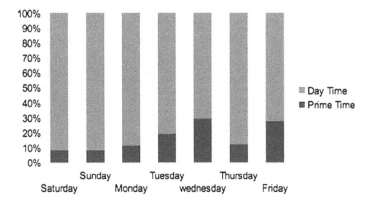

Figure 5: Programme distribution according to broadcast periods

---

[22] Sauvage and Veyrat-Masson (2012) pp.222–223.

Table 5: Programme distribution according to broadcast periods

	Prime-Time(%)	Day-Time(%)
Saturday	8,28	91,72
Sunday	8,29	91,71
Monday	11,14	88,86
Tuesday	19,37	80,63
Wednesday	29,38	70,62
Thursday	12,42	87,58
Friday	27,63	72,37

Prime Time

As seen in Table 6 and Figure 6 below, programmes on justice during prime time are concentrated at the end of the working week. This corresponds to broadcasting traditions going back a good 20 years. The most frequent genre encountered is the drama series. Documentaries and magazines, however, are less often aired during prime time than daytime or late at night.

Table 6: Programme distribution per genre according to broadcast periods (prime time)

	TV Series	Movies	Documentaries	TV Reports/Magazines	Total
Saturday	17	2	1	0	20
Sunday	13	4	0	0	17
Monday	15	1	2	0	18
Tuesday	13	3	2	2	20
Wednesday	22	5	2	2	31
Thursday	26	2	0	1	29
Friday	23	4	5	0	32

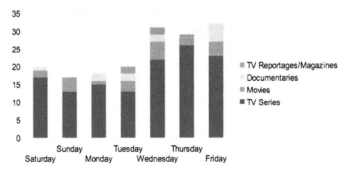

Figure 6:

Daytime

Saturday is curiously the day during which all genres feature in shows with a focus on law and justice. There are several reasons for this, but the most obvious is that the broadcasts are essentially reruns. Channels pay a licence fee, decreasing over time, for any drama series purchased. Smaller stations have quite small budgets and even though they pay to re-broadcast an episode of a series, this costs them less than airing recent shows (all genres combined) or producing any. The drama series shown during the day on weekends were for example, *Hercule Poirot, Magnum, Columbo*.

Table 7: Programme distribution per genre according to broadcast periods (daytime)

	TV Series	Movies	Documentaries	TV Reportages/Magazines	Total
Saturday	105	14	14	14	147
Sunday	79	17	4	4	104
Monday	93	7	9	9	118
Tuesday	88	11	6	9	114
Wednesday	85	6	9	4	104
Thursday	90	9	8	10	117
Friday	99	4	7	2	112

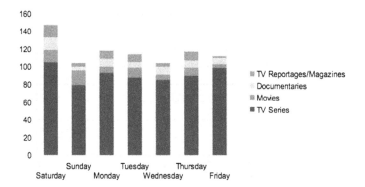

Figure 7: Programme distribution per genre according to broadcast periods (day-time)

Sex, Sexuality, Social Issues, Ethnicity, Gender, Race, Class

On the whole, social issues have been dealt with in the coverage of law and justice on television over the years, both in French and foreign dramas, so French audiences are well exposed to them. Ethnicity and class are themes particularly present in the French crime series, *Engrenages*.[23]

Many suspects in French crime series are Arab or black even if it turns out in the story that they are not the actual perpetrators. Les *tontons* or police informants are also mostly of Muslim origin even if their habits would not make them devout members of this religious group. White-collar crimes are rarely dealt with in French crime series. Such stories, however, involving French provincial bankers or traders or important businessmen, can be found with greater frequency in films which end up on the small screen a year or so after being featured in cinemas. Canal+ gets them first and then, after another year or so, the major TNT channels are able to broadcast them. Since French cinema has always been less fearful of controversial subjects, gender, sexuality and most social issues including racism and hate crimes are dealt with in film. Such questions are handled in documentaries as well. For example, on 1 November on Planète+[24] at 7.00 pm a documentary on crimes related to racism and discrimination in the army was broadcast[25] (with reruns late in the night on 5, 8 and 14 November). The film shows a surprising number of cases in which young recruits, coming from the country's housing projects[26] and often of Muslim origin, were victims of racist attacks by fellow soldiers or neo-Nazi groups.

Subjects such as illegal immigration, prostitution or drug trafficking are quite often treated in French documentaries, TV reports and in small budget films either made for television or broadcast shortly after appearing in theatres. Recent issues such as paedophilia are most often left to American series and films.[27] This subject has been at the centre of television *magazines* such as *Faites entrer l'accusé* (France 2) following cases with a high media profile in France and Belgium in the early 2000s.[28] *Magazines* often choose not to deal with sensitive material. Subjects,

---

[23] Canal+ (2005–). On BBC4, under the title of *Spiral*.

[24] Part of the Canal+ group, Planète+ is currently a pay television channel which broadcasts mostly documentaries, but fictions and magazines, such as re-showings of *Faites entrer l'accusé*, are also part of the programming.

[25] *Racisme et discriminations: l'armée au rapport.* This documentary by Marianne Kerfriden was originally broadcast on Canal+ in 2012.

[26] Social housing estates or in some cases slum belts.

[27] French films have used such themes as a watermark, for example in *Simon Werner a disparu*, 12 November on Arte at 8.50 pm where an adolescent's disappearance is feared to have something to do with drugs or kidnapping by a paedophile; but this is not the case in the end.

[28] Marc Dutroux (2004, Belgium), Anger (2005 and 2007—several defendants), Outreau (2005, several defendants), Michel and Monique Fourniret (2008).

such as the recent confrontations between supporters and opponents of same-sex marriage, are avoided by programmes like *Crimes*, which deliberately chose not to stage the reconstruction of criminal cases related to LGBT issues. In addition, issues of religion are not represented and remain taboo subjects in French society. The contrary is true, however, with respect to class and social issues.

A recent theme represented on French television was the issue of young girl gangs who engage in violent crime. Gangs have been in the news, related to hate crimes, some of them displaying their aggression on Youtube. *Engrenages* in season five made a group of girls from a housing project carry out a series of criminal actions, being alternatively both victims and perpetrators of extreme violence.

Concluding Remarks

In the light of both broadcast habits over the past 60 years and production quotas, the programmes found during the month of November showed a majority of police fictional dramas and imported material more or less within the limits imposed. France was the main producer of the documentaries broadcast during this period. The country pays a lot of respect to journalists and thus considers documentaries and its *magazines* as serious sources of information about the law and justice, but they do not watch these as much as they do films or drama series. Prime-time slots are mostly filled with fictional dramas while documentaries appear later at night for viewers more committed to these subjects, or bad sleepers. Documentaries or talk shows dealing with trials with a high media profile, or judicial scandals attract some attention and may be broadcast during prime time. They fill in the background rapid news coverage misses out. Some of these cases will end up as made-for-tv movies portrayed from a historical perspective, names, dates, places preserved—any reference to real people is voluntary.

Most representations of the judicial process on French television deal with apprehension: police and detective work. Adjudication is mostly found in drama series and films imported from other countries, mainly the United States with its long experience of fictionalising law and justice. The important observation here is that when looking at the coverage of justice on national television, it is necessary to consider, not only representations or content, the number of hours of programming and the schedules, but also production policies. The decision to broadcast imported programmes, the question of whether it is cheaper to produce or buy, does not only rest on financial considerations. National tastes and attitudes also play a major role. The French have always liked problem solving, so police and detective series have been regularly successful.

An important aspect of the French tendency to produce police fictional dramas rather than courtroom dramas derives from the fact that scriptwriters have very little, if any, legal knowledge. In the United States an impressive number of scriptwriters have been lawyers, public defenders, prosecutors, or simply law students who tried their hand at writing for television or film. Again *Engrenages* is a rare series where although not having first-hand experience, the principal writer, Anne Landois, had worked on legal material before coming to Canal+ and once working on this series surrounded herself with a team of *magistrats*, lawyers and members of the specialised *police judiciare*—judicial police—department to write with as much realism as possible.

Finally, France's inquisitorial tradition takes a vertical approach to the law and justice. The judge represents the authority of the state and the state is the seat of power. The French see justice as an instrument of the state. Edgar Quinet, the nineteenth-century French historian wrote that France was antilegalist.[29] This does not mean 'anti- law or justice', but interest does not lie there. *Engrenages* expresses this idea often in both its textual and iconic discourse. American courtroom dramas may criticise the system, but they often finish on a note of confidence; 'the system works' even if the people who run it are weak and foolish. Justice is seen as a means to organise relations between people, to deal with conflict. In France, this is the realm of the state. Solutions to conflicts come from laws aimed at foreseeing types of conflicts with solutions from the top down. Rules do not come from court decisions. In France justice is not a system of separate services, but a collegial affair. The procedure before trial, as seen above, is much more circular and usually much longer. Judges do not take decisions in their own name and are therefore not seen as clearly independent. This has not encouraged French writers to consider judicial dilemma in films or series, which is a pity since French judges have much to say on the matter.

In France, most things are state business. It is thus logical that the state fathered television and has continued to raise it since its birth, seeing it through various national and international developments. This has not always allowed French television to thrive in a competitive, commercial, or recently, global context. Television and justice in France have more in common than one would expect.

---

[29] Quinet (1857).

8

Germany

STEFAN MACHURA AND MICHAEL BÖHNKE

Introduction

German television operates within a specific political as well as media-economic and aesthetic framework. Following the Second World War, West German radio and TV were modelled on the BBC with its fee-based economy, emphasis on the educational function, political independence and respectability. Nevertheless, TV politics were intertwined in power struggles in the Federal Republic of Germany. The first public channel, ARD, was in the hands of the provinces which had their respective broadcasters contributing to the schedules. There was the Westdeutscher Rundfunk (WDR), Bayerischer Rundfunk (BR), Hessischer Rundfunk (HR) among others. In the 1960s, the nationwide second channel ZDF entered the scene along with regionalised third channels, like WDR3, BR3 and HR3. With little competition, prime-time crime programmes dominated the small screen in the 1960s and 1970s. Backed by steady revenues and the cultural mission, ARD and ZDF started to co-finance films made for the silver screen to support the industry and to be able to make high-profile content. Acclaimed international TV series, like the Swedish *Wallander* resulted from co-production.

During its 40-year lifetime, East German television had to work as the mouthpiece for the Socialist Unity Party following Soviet guidance. Productions were censored and some film makers played hide and seek with the authorities, allowing the audience to read between the lines. In Marxist-Leninist states, crime was considered a remnant of bourgeois society soon to disappear once people were educated and committed to socialism.

In West Germany, with the advent of cable technology, private channels were gradually introduced from 1984. They aimed at filling gaps left by the public broadcasters: showing more US-produced series and movies. Limited only by cable capacity, the initially regionalised third channels of the ARD family competed beyond provincial boarders. We also find Arte, a Franco-German public culture channel. After the fall of the Berlin Wall, the West German model was transferred to the former East German provinces. For a brief period, private broadcasters invested in their own productions to match the quality of ARD and

ZDF. More recently, however, many of them reverted to just endlessly repeating US series. In the private sector, channels centred on two competing media trusts: the RTL Group owned by media giant Bertelsmann and ProSiebenSat.1 Media-AG. In 2014, the private channels had a share of 55.1% of the viewers.[1] Despite the availability of pay TV, free-to-view terrestrial/cable television still forms the main source for news and entertainment.

German provinces kept a careful eye on their regional TV stations, public or private, while the German cities tried to attract media companies. Here there had always been competition with theatres. A dispersed media structure benefited from a wealth of acting, directing and scriptwriting talent. German TV productions like *Ein Fall für zwei* (*A Case for Two*) or *Tatort* (*Crime Scene*), discussed below, were exported to numerous countries, making German crime fiction, especially police-centred ones, accessible to a world audience.

Over the decades there has been a substantial shift from educational topics to entertainment. Earlier law-related formats like ZDF's *Ehen vor Gericht* (*Marriages in Court*), or *Verkehrsgericht* (*Traffic Court*) showed aspects of law with minimal amount of drama. Later private channel TV 'judge' shows by contrast are noted for displays of aggressive behaviour and bizarre cases. The German legal system combines a highly bureaucratic pattern in which the judge investigates the case with adversarial aspects. Court procedures follow a paternalistic, inquisitorial style making do with the Constitution's 'social state of law'.[2] Not much of this is seen on screen.

At the 8.15pm prime-time slot on a Sunday, the German audience is used to watching the latest episode of *Tatort*. It is the flagship of the German public ARD channel family. Affiliated regional broadcasters contribute sequels, including occasional Swiss and Austrian productions, reaching a total of about 900.[3] Three facts stand out especially: that not only on many Sunday evenings a new entry is shown, but older episodes are on constant rerun. Viewer rates are high throughout and often top the list of the most popular programmes of the week.[4] It is a time-honoured tradition in crime fiction to pit a working class police officer against a wealthy, upper-class suspect and *Tatort* often adopts this rule, particularly as it allows for a certain amount of social criticism.

The public channel ZDF also gained a reputation for crime series, especially at prime time on Friday nights. In the past, there were famous and popular police officers in series like *Der Kommissar* (*The Inspector*) (1969–76), *Der Alte* (*The Senior*) (1977–) and *Derrick* (1974–98). Inspector Derrick especially showed a world audience the activities of an upright police officer. Here, the police did not cross the boundary between office and private life. Storylines also often emphasised the dangers lurking behind unconventional lifestyles.

---

[1] Verband Privater Rundfunk- und Telemedien (2015).

[2] Arts 20(1) and 28(1), first sentence of the German Federal Constitution.

[3] M Maurach, 'Was ist los im "Tatort"?' *Frankfurter Allgemeine Zeitung* (25 June 2013) 31.

[4] One *Tatort* in the period analysed was seen by one in four TV viewers, 9.86 million: J Overkott, 'Wie "Tatort"–Fahnder abtreten' *Westdeutsche Allgemeine Zeitung* (18 November 2014).

ZDF's series *Ein Fall für zwei* (*A Case for Two*) (1981–2013, 300+ episodes) paired a Frankfurt lawyer (changing over time) with private eye Josef Matula. German lawyers normally do not work in this way. In criminal cases, investigations are left to the police. The ZDF thus made the home audience familiar with a foreign—US—pattern.[5]

Polizeiruf 110 (*Police Call 110*) was the East German answer to the *Tatort* series. Its meta-narrative followed the lines laid out by the Socialist Unity Party, basically showing how the collective aided by its impeccable 'Volkspolizei' stood up to depraved elements still influenced by bourgeois patterns of behaviour. The old '110' opened a window into a now distant frugal way of life, in which 'people's property' had to be defended. After Unification, the '110' team continued their work for the ARD. Some of these more recent episodes are unique, as they dramatise how East German society and especially the former 'People's Police' came to terms with the new situation.

German private channels RTL and Sat.1 have made a name for reality entertainment series. These series combine fictitious cases following two models. In one group there is some involvement of 'real' professional personnel who are acting in a realistic way. German TV judge shows are the prime example. Alternatively, they are stylised as if real cases were addressed, most notably by the use of non-legal actors ('compressed reality').[6]

Large production companies like Constantin and Filmpool cater to the seemingly insatiable appetite of private channels for reality entertainment. Episodes are very efficiently and cheaply mass produced for a fraction of what an episode of *Tatort* costs.

German court TV is different from the initial US formats. Although Judge Judy's small claims court became a role model for Sat.1's *Richterin Barbara Salesch*, the model which proved most popular was the 'criminal court' concept. These TV courts combined an adversarial type of procedure with the TV judge in a more passive role than actual German judges. Real lawyers played lively prosecutors and defenders and there were quite aggressive displays by defendants and witnesses (usually lay actors). The TV judge has a say in the choice of case scripts and later 'rules' as if they were still in a state court.

TV judge shows are not taken too seriously by the public and even more so by the professionals who find themselves quite often incorrectly represented. Nevertheless, the shows had their core of dedicated followers. Viewers are led to believe that courts are places where insults are rife, the innocent are ridiculed initially, and tearful last minute confessions are standard fare.[7] If fellow citizens are this dangerous, the help of lawyers as well as the steady hand of the judge are needed. TV judges are stars, and serve as trustees of the people, setting things right.[8] Therefore,

---

[5] Machura and Ulbrich (2001a) 129. The show was watched by up to 7 million viewers: F Bossy, 'Keine Rente für Matula' *Frankfurter Allgemeine Zeitung* (15 September 2006) 44.

[6] Brauck (2009) 88.

[7] Thym (2003); Machura (2012) 261–66.

[8] Porsdam (1999) 102–04; Machura (2016b) 180–81.

the message to the audience is ambivalent: the world is a dangerous place but justice can be achieved in the end. The audience cannot get the assuring bit without having to endure the threatening aspects.

For the present chapter, we are testing a series of hypotheses:

1. Law-related TV content is dominated by police and detective material, more specifically even: fictional portrayals of police.
2. American TV series are most frequently broadcast when it comes to police and detective fiction.
3. Material on lawyers and courts tends to be characterised mainly by the TV judge shows.
4. Documentaries and fictional drama on serious topics are mainly shown by public TV channels.
5. Overall, the message to viewers is that police, lawyers and courts can be trusted.

Method

This study covers television over four weeks, starting on 3 November 2014. The leading TV guide *Gong* was scrutinised for law-related programmes. Additionally, we used the TV guide *Bunte Wochenzeitschrift*, a supplement of newspapers in the Ruhr valley and Southern Westphalia, as well as websites of TV channels, production companies, the Internet Movie Database and other sources. For each film or episode, we noted title, date and time of screening, length in hours (advertisements not deducted for practical reasons), country of origin and if the programmes were a series or not. For police and detective material, lawyer and court material as well as prison and post-prison material, we used the subcategories 'dramas', 'comedies', 'reality programmes', 'reality-based entertainment' and finally, 'documentaries'. The outcome was skewed towards one type of product, requiring further subdivision. In a group setting, we watched some shows for details of content and style.[9]

Police and Detective Material

Police and detective-themed shows made up a full 1,190 hours in the four weeks of the study. Of these, US material amounted to 51.6% with 614 hours of airtime.

---

[9] The authors would like to thank Dr Olga Litvinova and Julia Mieden for their participation in viewing sessions.

Dramas

The dramatic portrayal of police and detective work came to a total of 908 hours. Of these, with 546 hours, US material amounted to 60.1%. Because of the sheer volume, the TV shows are further divided into subcategories: films, German, US and finally (other) European TV series.

Films on Police and Detectives

Films on police and detectives were mainly shown in the late-night slot. Among the 41 hours of film in this subgenre, US productions added up to 23.5 hours, forming a 57.4% share. They included for example *Mississippi Burning* and *Robocop*.

Non-US films included the Swiss production *Die Akte Grüninger* on the public culture channel Arte about a Swiss police officer helping Jews to escape from the Nazis. French films (often co-produced with neighbouring countries) add another seven hours. Two German TV films lasted 3.5 hours. Among them the acclaimed Stasi story *Das Leben der Anderen* (*The Life of Others*). Films from Romania, Denmark and the Netherlands add a further 310 minutes. All the films not originating from the US were found on public channels.

TV Drama Series on Police and Detectives

Police and detective-themed TV series (excluding comedies and reality formats) alone added up to 867 hours in total, 60.2% of these were of US origin.

German Drama Series on Police and Detectives

German drama series on police and detective work were shown for 307 hours. Only occasionally these series, such as *Mordkommission Istanbul*, were set in other countries. Among the dramas focusing on police and detectives, a few series are of paramount importance.

In Gefahr—ein verhängnisvoller Moment (*In Danger—a Fatal Moment*) on Sat.1 is the most broadcast series in this category from a private channel. Shown regularly at 6.00 pm and again late in the night, here sometimes with two sequels in a row. In the four weeks, the series occupied some 38 hours of the schedules. This, however, is an exception as generally the public stations of the ARD family and the ZDF clearly dominate this series category.

When it comes to the amount of material broadcast and co-productions with Germany's southern neighbours, ZDF's *SOKO* (*Special Police Unit*) series family, stands out with 70 hours. They ranged from *SOKO 5113* with 27 episodes often in the late morning or late afternoon but never at prime time, totalling 21 hours, to *SOKO Köln* with just over four hours. The Austrian offspring *SOKO Kitzbühel* was represented with 33 episodes amounting to a little over 26 hours of airtime, symmetrically placed at 4.10 pm with repeats at 4.10 am. It was complemented by *SOKO Wien* with just over three hours.

In the four weeks monitored, no less than 42 *Tatort* episodes were shown by ARD and its affiliates (63 hours). On Thursday, 27 November, during prime time from 8.15 pm to 9.45 pm, WDR 3 repeated *Am Ende des Tages* (*At the End of the Day*) from 2010. It shows some fairly typical characteristics of the *Tatort* series. A retiring police officer witnesses the brutal murder of his lover, and becomes himself the main suspect. A night club owner is the next victim, then the police-man's daughter. It turns out to be the revenge of a murderer released from prison. The police officer had arrested him years ago and shot the gangster's pregnant wife. The main protagonists, as in every *Tatort*, are the Kommissare of the murder squad: here Friedrich Dellwo and the Charlotte Sänger. This time, they take longer to identify the real culprit. Dellwo arrives too late at the scene of the third crime. Typically for the Dellwo/Sänger duo both get themselves in danger. In the dramatic finale, on a bridge, the killer, the ex-officer and his two younger colleagues meet with weapons drawn. When Dellwo incapacitates his former superior, preventing the staged duel, the killer—already knowing he is dying from cancer—commits suicide. 'Death proneness' according to Daniel Hermsdorf is a recurring feature of modern crime series. It can be characterised as the prevalence of morbid themes, bleak *mise en scène*, broken characters and drastic violence.[10] *The End of the Day* thus resembles the feel of modern Swedish TV crime, like *Wallander* (shown 13 times in November). Apart from this, as in many a *Tatort*, chief police officers are presented as feeble and superfluous personalities, in contrast to the admirable qualities of the *Tatort* inspectors. Because of the revenge setting, law features most prominently in this entry in the form of the archaic 'an eye for an eye'. As is stand-ard for law and crime-related stories, the heroes follow their own codes of ethics rather than the law.

GDR-episodes of *Polizeiruf 110* appeared nine times on parts of the ARD chain in slots around midnight. Fifteen post-unification episodes, mostly reruns, were also screened during evening and night time, one at the 8.15 pm prime time. Alto-gether, the ARD chain screened 34.5 hours of *Polizeiruf*.

US Drama Series on Police and Detectives

Finding a large number of US series, mainly on the private channels, was not unexpected. American productions added up to 522 hours over the four weeks of the study. For example, Sat.1 clearly considered *Navy CIS* one of its strongest offerings as it showed 71 episodes, at various times, even at the 8.15 pm prime-time slot. Single episodes and packages of episodes added up to over 74 hours. As a result, *Navy CIS* was the most frequently aired police and detective-related TV series, beating even *SOKO* and *Tatort*. Other US series follow suit. Fifty-four hours of airtime on Kabel 1 over the morning and early afternoon were filled with 54 almost exclusively single episodes of *Cold Case* (with repeats). S-RTL added another 51 hours with 30 blocks of *Monk*, mostly two at a time, quite often at the

---

[10] Hermsdorf (2010) 257–94.

8.15 pm prime-time slot, but generally well dispersed. They were the three most often broadcast US series in this category.

Other European Drama Series on Police and Detectives

A further five series originated from European countries. Some of these were co-productions and accounted for 28 episodes and 38 hours. They were usually screened around midnight. The majority were Scandinavian—19 hours. They included 16 hours of *Wallander* on the ARD member channels. The second most screened series was the British Inspector Barnaby (*Midsomer Murders*) each Thursday night at 00.45 on ZDF. The Austrian series *Schnell ermittelt* (*Fast Forward*) also figured with eight episodes, six hours in total, on the 'third programmes' HR3 and RBB. This has a female main character and continues the tradition of satirical Austrian police detective series started by Koffan ermittelt.

Comedies on Police and Detectives

Comedies featuring police and detectives were rarer in the period of analysis. Of their 25 hours, 10.5 hours (41.8%) were accounted for by repeated screenings of the US comedies *Beverly Hills Cop* and *The Other Guys* on Kabel 1, as well as *Top Dog* on Tele 5. Most of the remaining comedies were of German origin.

Reality Programmes on Police and Detectives

Four series made in Germany completely dominated the 'reality' category among police and detective material. They ran for 131 hours altogether over the four weeks. Camera crews followed real police and their cases. In terms of frequency, Sat.1's *Auf Streife* (*On Patrol*) was most notable: it was scheduled 49 times, for between 40 minutes and four hours. Episodes ran all through the morning to midday. In these four weeks, airtime added up to a total of 54 hours. At various times from midday to late afternoon, another private channel, Kabel 1, offered the series *Achtung Kontrolle!* (*Attention Control!*) with one, two, or even four episodes in a row, amounting to 52 hours. Episodes of *Schneller als die Polizei erlaubt* (*Faster than the Police Allows*) were played a total of four hours on the private Vox channel.

Within the reality programmes, *Toto & Harry—Die Zwei vom Polizeirevier*, literally: *The Two from the Precinct*, marks a low point. Nevertheless, on Sunday 23 November from 8.15 pm to 10.25 pm the episode was pitched against the prestigious ARD *Tatort*. The move to prime time on a Sunday highlights their persistent popularity in some quarters, but possibly indicates also that Kabel 1 had given in to ARD's almighty flagship series.

The most outstanding of their 16 cases is the first one. Two juveniles are suspected of having robbed a street musician. However, the victim has disappeared making Toto & Harry's work difficult. In a scene, mild-mannered Toto accompanied by a colleague reports to their boss Kommissar, Kerstin, an attractive blonde many years his junior, to hear advice about the legal aspects of the case. At issue is the all-important legal basis of arrest. If they get it wrong, the case will go nowhere. These scenes, shot in the police headquarters, allow the viewer to get a glimpse into the actual workplace of the law enforcers. During the interrogation, the main suspect has the upper hand over the two seasoned coppers and even sends them to copy a list of his previous convictions. However, the last laugh is with Toto & Harry, as soon after, a new victim comes forward accusing the juveniles of having attempted a robbery right after their release from police custody.

The series illustrates that the police intervene in the small crises of life, rescuing an injured hedgehog, addressing three instances of noisy neighbours, returning a disoriented elderly person to their hospital bed. 'The police are your friend and helper' is a saying in Germany—and Toto & Harry are mastering this discipline. Therefore, we can understand why the Bochum police force enjoys public support. On the other hand, the jocular mode of the presentation combined with the frequent use of the local vernacular is a little reminiscent of Abbott & Costello.

Reality-Based Entertainment on Police and Detectives

Three German TV series[11] came to a total of 49 hours. RTL employs private eyes to play themselves after midnight into the early morning. *Die Trovatos— Detektive decken auf* (*The Trovatos—Detectives Reveal*) occupied 37 hours, usually with two episodes screened back to back. Predominantly shown between 3.00 am and 6.00 am, aimed certainly at a student audience, RTL sent out the social workers and policemen of *Die Schulermittler* (*The School Detectives*). Luckily, the cases are solved quickly, so they only worked for 2.5 hours over the four-week period. More prominently placed with a regular spot at about 6.00 pm and reruns after midnight, the police officers of *K11 Kommissare im Einsatz* (*K11 Commissioners in Action*) appear six times on the TV programme, clocking up 9.5 hours on the Vox channel.

Documentaries on Police and Detectives

Within the police and detective material, documentaries accounted for 77 hours of screen time. They were dominated by the US series *Medical Detectives*, broadcast by the private Vox channel in 28 bundles in the middle of the night and early morning, amounting to 58 hours of airtime—74.8% of the documentaries.

---

[11] Another two German series broadcast by RTL, *Verdachtsfälle* with 65 screenings, 106 hours, and *Betrugsfälle*, 22 episodes, 18 hours, were excluded from the analysis as it remained unclear in how many of the episodes police, detectives, lawyers or other legal personnel actually appear. Simple dishonesty, adultery and suspicion seem to dominate in these two series.

The German documentary series coming closest was *Lebenslänglich—Mord, Kommissar Wilfings Kriminalfälle* (*Life in Prison: Murder, Inspector Wilfings's Criminal Cases*) on BR3, with four episodes, a mere 3.75 hours.

The German equivalent of the British *Crime Watch*, the monthly *Aktenzeichen XY*, ran at prime time on ZDF with a repeat in the middle of the night—three hours combined. In this series, containing re-enactments of crimes, original CCTV footage and pieces of evidence, interviews with law enforcement staff working on a case, as well as mug shots of suspects, the public is asked to come forward with information. The similar themed *Kriminalreport Hessen* on H3 was somewhat forlorn and short (25 minutes) before midnight on one day.

The remaining 12 documentaries (with two repeats) making up a further 12 hours, are scattered over the four weeks and rarely ran at prime time. Some of the titles allude to crime at certain places, be it the *Terror of the Berlin Woods* (RBB), drug crime in Moscow (N24), to *The Power in Cyberspace* (RTL). Notably, three documentaries dealt with historic topics: the crimes of Klaus Barbie (BR 3), *Der Fluch des Edgar Hoover* (*The Curse of Edgar Hoover*) (Arte) and the operations of the Stasi in schools (WDR).

Lawyer and Court-Focused Material

Broadcasts specifically on lawyers and courts added up to a total of 215 hours. Interestingly, only 5.5 hours were from US productions, 2.6%. The distribution among categories is skewed towards reality TV shows and reality entertainment. Of all German channels, Sat.1, followed by Vox, dominated lawyer- and court-focused material.

Dramas on Lawyers and Courts

Ten broadcasts of dramas, including at least two repeats, amounted to 13 hours of airtime, of which two hours were from the only US film: *The Life of David Gale*. Two German drama series stand out: *Der Staatsanwalt hat das Wort* (*The Public Prosecutor has the Word*) and *Ein Fall für zwei* (*A Case for Two*). The public Hessen 3 channel contributed four screenings from the TV series, *The Public Prosecutor has the Word*, in slots before midnight. The series was produced under the East German communist regime and still finds its way into the TV schedules.

ZDF's *A Case for Two*, was broadcast in the study period, lasting 60 minutes per episode. In an episode aired on the Saturday night slot at 9.40 pm (29 November), the proprietress of a stately vineyard is killed in an accident just after she had hired private eye Matula for a princely sum to investigate her husband's philandering. Suspicion falls on her husband who under their prenuptial agreement would be barred from any inheritance if he commits infidelity. In an illogical twist, this man chooses Matula's lawyer partner Markus Lessing for his defence. Dr Lessing years ago had also fallen in love with the lady, before she married the philanderer. The main legal issue is 'Parteiverrat' (breach of fiduciary duty to client): the lawyer will lose his licence if he acts against the interests of his client.[12] The series' attraction is the teamwork of an unlikely couple, the more working class private eye and the well-bred lawyer. American scholars have argued that a luxurious lifestyle detracts from the audience's trust in lawyers.[13] Here, Lessing is seen playing golf, driving a Mercedes, frequenting gourmet restaurants and living in an upmarket apartment surrounded by modern art. Significantly, it is his knowledge of fine wines which finally solves the case. Therefore, the audience might well see his wealth in a positive light.

In the end Matula, with whom the audience is likely to have empathy, prevents the victim's son Martin killing the guilty husband. With a quick move, Matula disarms Martin and calms him down declaring that the culprit will get his comeuppance. Not only does the hero express his trust in the legal system but he also suggests that the audience can safely share his view.

The same national public broadcaster ZDF announced the drama *Das Zeugenhaus* (*House of Witnesses*) as the TV event of the year.[14] The plot was based on a book dealing with a little known detail around the Nuremberg Trials of major war criminals.[15] In 1945, a grieving Hungarian countess was required to act as hostess for witnesses testifying before the Nuremberg tribunal for either prosecution or defence. The story is a parable on the uneasy coexistence of those who served the Nazi regime in various roles and those who had been persecuted by them. Both groups clash in the stately mansion. Partly based on fact, the film mixed historical and fictitious elements. Director Matti Geschonneck is quoted as having used the traumatic experiences his father endured after he survived the concentration camps as part of the film's narrative.[16] In gripping scenes, the victims and witnesses agonise about being alive while their comrades perished. There are no scenes at all with lawyers inside the court other than snippets from historical newsreels and radio broadcasts. Nevertheless, the shadow of the trial always looms over the protagonists up to the point that some are left guessing whether they will only appear as witnesses or might end up in the dock themselves. The founder of the Gestapo, Rudolf Diels, slickly utters: 'There is no innocence any more, no guilt either, only grey in grey'. Visually, *Das Zeugenhaus* again features the dim lighting and bleak colours of *Wallander*-type films. Although there are elements of suspense, the overwhelming theme is the effect of the totalitarian Nazi state on the individuals involved.

[12] Art 356, German Criminal Code.
[13] Pfau, Mullen, Diedrich and Garrow (1995) 326.
[14] Monday, 24 November, 8.15 pm to 10.00 pm, also available on DVD. It was followed by a 45-minute documentary about the real *Zeugenhaus*.
[15] Kohl (2005).
[16] Powelz (2014).

Comedies on Lawyers and Courts

Comedies on lawyers and courts were almost absent from the schedule in these four November weeks in 2014. They only added up to 3.5 hours, all accounted for by the US production *Franklin & Bash*, all shown on the private Kabel 1 channel at 11.20 pm and 2.10 am.

Reality-Based Entertainment on Lawyers and Courts

Reality-based entertainment on lawyers and courts made up a total of 196 hours.[17] The German TV judge shows have to be counted in here. Their heyday seems to be over, with mainly two shows *Richterin* (Judge) *Barbara Salesch* and *Richter* (Judge) *Alexander Hold* remaining on the schedule. Salesch and Hold sat in judgement on the Sat.1 channel, 21 and 22 times respectively (between them 43 hours, of 60-minute episodes). *Das Strafgericht* (*The Criminal Court*), produced by the private arch rival RTL, came to a meagre two episodes with just 110 minutes. All the TV judge shows were reruns.

In this subcategory of 'reality-based entertainment' there are not only judge shows. Vox's *Verklag mich doch!* (*Sue Me!*) had a record number of 92 screenings on weekdays at midday and early in the morning adding up to a total of 88 hours. Each episode is introduced and commented on by one of three studio lawyers from a legal and ethical point of view. To give it the feel of authenticity, lay people are employed to enact the fictional cases.

With daily episodes once again around fictitious cases, two Sat.1 lawyer series running at 3.00 pm and 4.00 pm with repeats late in the night were noted: first *Im Namen der Gerechtigkeit—Wir kämpfen für Sie* (*In the Name of Justice—We Will Fight For You!*) was shown on 42 occasions. The lawyers in this series are known to the audience from the *Richter Alexander Hold* show. Here, they work outside the courtroom.[18] In addition, *Anwälte im Einsatz* (*Lawyers in Action*) was screened 31 times. A well-populated website introduces the protagonists as real-life lawyers with their own firms and even offers legal advice on issues such as marrying in a foreign country, cybermobbing, and conflicts with landlords or at the workplace.[19]

Documentaries on Lawyers and Courts

Only four documentaries on lawyers and courts were offered to the viewers, amounting to a little less than three hours in all. One of them complemented the 'TV drama of the year' discussed above.

---

[17] There were no reality programmes, for example, following real lawyers or judges in their work.
[18] Constantin Entertainment (nd).
[19] Sat.1 (nd).

Prison and Post-Prison Material

German television rarely deals with prisons and what comes after. We counted 13 hours altogether, of which 10 hours were from US material, a full 77.8%. Comedies, reality programmes and reality-based entertainment were not spotted. In the four weeks investigated, there were only five dramas on prison and post-prison experience, altogether running for a meagre 8.5 hours. Bar one, they were US productions. Three appeared on public channels. Documentaries on these issues were equally sparse, six shows adding up to a running time of 4.5 hours. Of these, three were of German origin and on public channels. All prison and post-prison material was presented during the evenings and nights.

Summary and Analysis

All in all, for 85,065 minutes, or 1,417.75 hours, the equivalent of 59 days, law-related broadcasts were noted in German TV schedules in the four weeks of November 2014. In all likelihood, there will have been even more coverage as we did not investigate TV news and TV magazines. There is also law-related content in other genres. The density of scheduling would allow anyone, even those returning from shift work at the most unusual times, to get their dose of law, crime, police and detective work, of lawyering and courts. TV stations routinely repeat shows in the early morning and night time slots, midday and in the afternoon.

Our first hypothesis assumed that law-related TV content is dominated by police and detective material, more specifically even: fictional portrayals of police. The first part is confirmed by the sheer weight of more than 916 hours in this category, the second by a look at the actual content of these series and films. The variety of the cop film/series subgenre is very broad.

The second hypothesis is also supported, as American TV series are most frequently broadcast when it comes to police and detective fiction. Their market share is 60%. The remaining section is produced mostly in Germany and some co-produced by German public TV channels. In addition, even to the uneducated viewer, Austrian, Swiss and even Scandinavian police series are not exactly alien and set in a similar and recognisable legal and social system.

Our third hypothesis was that material on lawyers and courts tends to be characterised mainly by the TV judge shows. When it comes to quantity, they were, however, clearly beaten by a proliferation of new 'reality-based entertainment', most notably Vox's *Verklag mich doch!* (*Sue Me!*). In these series, lawyers have replaced TV judges as the centre of attention.

Our fourth hypothesis suggested that documentaries and fictional drama on serious topics are mainly shown by public TV channels. Our sweep of the TV schedules has confirmed this assumption. Public broadcasters still honour their educational mission by producing and placing on the schedule topics which remind Germans of social injustice, political oppression and other issues, not only in the country itself. Neither do they shrink from the horrendous crimes committed in the name of German people in the last century.

Finally, we assumed the overall message to viewers to be that police, lawyers and courts can be trusted. This hypothesis is supported. Analysing TV judge shows suggests that the judge figures as a trustee of the public and demonstrates a form of authority which is acceptable to broad audiences. Dramas need to have antagonists. Rogue and incompetent police officers, biased judges (very rare) and irresponsible lawyers serve as obstacles which have to be overcome by the 'justice figure'.[20] These come in the form of the hero police officer, or lawyer. This basic structure is found time and again and plots almost always end with the 'right' side winning. Popular TV programmes thus are a legitimating force when it comes to people's belief in the legal professions, institutions and the law itself.

Some further observations can be added. Maybe because of the prevalence of recently produced TV content, women no longer appear as unequal or inferior to male colleagues. The success of post-war feminism finds its expression on the small screen. Notably, the genres of TV judge shows and TV police series now take female authority figures for granted.

Lawyer- and court-related material in general was clearly second to police and detective formats. This distribution also corresponds to the prominence of criminal law among lay people. Scholars have studied classic courtroom dramas like *To Kill a Mockingbird* or *Young Mr Lincoln*[21] for many years and in great detail. However, in the four weeks analysed, none of these films was listed in the TV guides. This would suggest that efforts to analyse TV series[22] and especially the new reality entertainment varieties, need to intensify.

Life behind bars and its effect on those who are released form only a very small portion of TV content. While certainly part of the public imagination, those topics do not form an object of hot debate in today's Federal Republic. Prison and probation affairs are largely left to professional experts, charitable organisations and the churches.[23]

When they do not produce their own 'reality-type' formats, private channels mainly resort to broadcasting US series. As for TV drama, it is the public sector which invests in fresh local produce. Some of the content is clearly influenced by Hollywood examples. We have described the unusual cooperation of lawyers with private detectives for ZDF's *Ein Fall für zwei*. There are not only US influences, however. Fertilisation also occurs from neighbouring European countries. Most notably, the *Wallander* series has been copied a lot when it comes to bleak and gloomy scenes, brooding characters and a heavy dose of nihilism. The more

---

[20] Rafter (2006) 136.
[21] Böhnke (2001).
[22] eg, contributions in Asimow (2009); Robson and Silbey (2012).
[23] As penal policy generally, Savelsberg (1999).

upbeat overall message of law-related films—yes, there are problems, but they can be overcome by the right people with the aid of the law[24]—however, prevails.

In the end, the popularity of law-related television may be rooted in the audacity of using law to advance one's good cause. In symbolically satisfying this need, the programmes make sure they have an audience and as a side effect, contribute to a legitimation of the existing social order, its legal institutions, the professions working with them and the law itself.

---

[24] Greenfield, Osborne and Robson (2001) 27.

9

Greece

NICKOS MYRTOU, STAMATIS POULAKIDAKOS
AND PANAGIOTA NAKOU

The First Years of TV in Greece 1944–67

Modern Greece is a result of consecutive wars that formed the borders but post-poned social changes. In the aftermath of the Second World War a bitterly fought civil war took place, which ended with the prevalence of the right-wing nation-alists. Greece entered the Western Bloc under the auspices of the United States and adopted the capitalistic economic model. The post-civil war governments marginalised the part of the population that was on the losing communist side[1] and focused on suppressing pro-communist notions rather than rebuilding the country.[2] In that problematic socio-economic context, we find the reasons for the delayed development of television in Greece and the rationale under which TV has been created and developed.

Greece has a history of state controlled media.[3] Radio had been under state control since 1938, when the government established the Radio Broadcasting Ser-vice.[4] Greek broadcasting is embedded in a culture of state presence; television in particular, has followed similar footsteps of political patronage and opportunism.[5]

In 1951 law 1663 mentioned for the first time officially the word 'television'. The law described the creation and operation of radio and television stations with the purpose of education and amusement for the army. In a military country there was no place for private or public television.[6] Two years later, law 2312/1953 described the organisation and operation of the National Institution for Radio Broadcasting (henceforth NIRB) in Greece, as totally controlled by the government. Since 1952, under article 14 of the Constitution, freedom of the press did not apply to cinema, radio, theatre and public appearances in general.[7] In addition, law 3778/1957 set

---

[1] Detailed information on the subject can be found in Komninou (2002); and Tsoukalas (2005).
[2] Valoukos (2008).
[3] Papathanassopoulos (1999) 382; Sims (2003).
[4] Sims (2003) 5; Tsaliki (1997).
[5] Tsaliki (1997) 35.
[6] Valoukos (2008).
[7] Dagtoglou (1989).

forth the right of the government to be informed beforehand of the content of all programmes with the right to pre-emptive censorship.[8]

During the 1950s television was just a futuristic dream for most Greeks.[9] Despite the existence of a legal framework for the operation of television broadcasts and the sporadic appearance of television sets in major appliance stores the first—unsuccessful—broadcasting experiments took place in 1958. All political parties had doubts about the new medium; the newspaper publishers did not want to risk their power and the entertainment industry disliked the idea of more competition.[10]

In 1960 the first successful experimental broadcast took place. The Public Electricity Company set up a small television studio and broadcast the first Greek television content with the use of a Philips 500W transmitter that had a reach of about 45 kilometres. Konstantinos Karamanlis, the then Prime Minister, was present at the beginning of the broadcast and gave the first televised speech marking the beginning of experimental broadcasting in Greece.[11]

In the following years the broadcast domain in Greece would be tied in with political parties and interests. The newly appointed chairman of the Board of Directors of the Athens Economic Research Center, Andreas Papandreou was knowledgeable about the importance of television control and put pressure on his politician father, Georgios Papandreou, to appoint a party-friendly person as director of the NIRB.[12]

After an unsuccessful attempt at installing a transmitter, due to pressure from press tycoons,[13] Lord Thomson was invited to Greece by Giorgos Mavros, President of the Greek National Bank, in February 1965 to discuss the possibility of a private sector funded broadcast network. That led to the first experimental broadcasts which took place in May 1965. For the first time after the initial legislation back in 1951, Greek television was on its way, though not having overcome political resistance.[14] The Palace was not fond of the way the NIRB handled the situation;[15] the press was still wary of the technology and it was very much believed that the new medium was under the complete control of the Prime Minister, Georgios Papandreou, and it would support him against the Palace.

The Papandreou Government was overthrown in July 1965.[16] The NIRB found an opportunity to fight back while the new government was being set up. On the morning of 21 September 1965 the first broadcast took place. The response of the press ranged from indifference to outrage and the new government was quick to

---

[8] Valoukos (2008).
[9] Valoukos (2008).
[10] Komninou (2002).
[11] More on this in both Valoukos (2008); and Karter (2004).
[12] Valoukos (2008); Dampasis (2002).
[13] More on the events in Peponis (2002).
[14] Valoukos (2008).
[15] An uncle of the king was representing Dutch interests for the installation of a broadcasting network, according to Valoukos (2008).
[16] Peponis (2002).

order the end of broadcasts. Strangely, though, while the press was against television, the radio industry believed that its survival was possible only alongside the advancements in broadcasting. So the decision to forbid the progressing of experimental broadcasting was met with an immediate strike.[17] The new government had no choice but to give in and withdraw the ban on broadcasting provided experimental television did not include newscasts. It was obvious that in order for the experiment to be successful it was necessary to broadcast a regular schedule.[18] With a tight budget, the 1966 Football World Cup rights were bought and broadcast in the afternoon, not live of course but the next day. The success was impressive, since in the next days about 15,000 TV sets were sold.[19]

Apart from the NIRB, private investors in Thessaloniki took it upon themselves to create the first private television station in Greece.[20] In Thessaloniki there were about 2,500 TV sets and a total of 8,000 TV sets in all northern Greece, thus a model of advertising-supported channels was feasible. They used the International Show of 1965 as a starting point and they went on broadcasting, including some imported television series like *Lassie* and *Peyton Place*. Channel 3 kept on broadcasting until 1970 when the junta shut it down.[21]

It is evident that despite the previous laws, the inauguration of Greek television set forth the problems that are still in existence. First, there was a precedent of illegality both on the public and private front; second, there was a mixed economic model of government and advertising funds.[22]

Soon after an experimental period, the broadcasting turned to a daily one from 11:30 to 13:30.[23] Fourteen years after the first law was put in effect, on 23 February 1966, this first broadcast (of the National Institute of Broadcasting) took place under the name Channel 5. The two-hour broadcast consisted of an international newscast, the show *For You, My Lady*, two documentaries, an orchestral performance and a short film. The Greek press remained highly unimpressed and hostile to the beginning of Greek television.[24]

In the same year, the Greek armed forces launched their own station, named Television of the Army (ToA), making Greece the only country with a fully operational military television service.[25] The armed forces had been working on this project since the 1950s, having manufactured the first completely Greek transmitter in 1959. The army had the legal right to operate a television station (law 1663/1951), being at the same time extremely suspicious of Georgios Papandreou and his disagreements with the Palace. When Papandreou lost power, the

---

[17] Karter (2004).
[18] Dampasis (2002).
[19] Valoukos (2008).
[20] Anastasiadis (1994)
[21] Valoukos (2008).
[22] More in Papathanassopoulos (1993); and Panagiotopoulou (2004).
[23] Karter (1979).
[24] Valoukos (2008); P Kounenaki, 'Greek Television: The 30-year course from the first broadcast to contemporary polyphony' *Kathimerini* (10 March 1996).
[25] Heretakis (1997).

armed forces had no resistance and with the benefit of lots of equipment from the United States they were able to broadcast experimentally in September 1965. A few months later, the armed forces used Channel 10 and began broadcasting on 27 February 1966.[26]

While Greece already had two main 'competing' stations on air, it lacked a regulatory framework.[27] No laws were put forward to protect pluralism, there was no economic model of operation and no newscasts were allowed. Channel 5 aired its first newscast called *Echo of Events* in April 1966. While it started as a weekly show, it soon aired on a daily basis. From 1966 to 1967 both stations (Channel 5 and ToA) had a number of regular broadcasts. Alongside the Greek programmes one could find shows like *Lassie, The Saint, Fury, The Dick Powell Show* and *The Baron.* American and British law and action shows were selected very early for broadcast in Greece. This kind of content was further enhanced by the Junta.[28]

Television under the Junta (1967–73)

The Junta took power on 21 April 1967. At first the new regime worked on controlling the press and radio broadcasts, since it knew the power of television as a propaganda tool.[29] The new-born television was under the dictators' direct control,[30] with a plan to change the extrovert Greek society to an introverted entertainment-based one.[31]

The two channels had different uses for the Junta.[32] NIRB was technically upgraded in order to broadcast the European Athletics Championship of 1968 that took place in Athens. ToA focused on public entertainment and political propaganda. The televised schedule consisted of shows that promoted nationalism, especially the Junta's idea of Greek Christianity alongside anti-communist and anti-Turkish propaganda.[33] A number of TV series provided the main vehicle for the familiarisation of the public with the 'army uniform'. *The House with the Phoenix* featured a colonel as a positive role model and the series *Unknown War*, promoted a friendly and heroic image of the Greek soldier.

The heavy use of television as a mechanism for ideology emphasised the necessity for economic planning. In 1968 the Junta passed a law that made it mandatory

---

[26] Valoukos (2008).

[27] ibid.

[28] Karter (2004); and Valoukos (2008).

[29] Kastoras (1978) 87, 93; Koukoutsaki (2003) 724.

[30] Papatheodorou and Machin (2003) 36; Tsaliki (1997).

[31] Komninou (2002).

[32] Valoukos (2008).

[33] Anti-Turkish propaganda has been used by previous governments as well, but during the Junta a number of parades, shows and series were used to promote the idea of the barbaric Turkey alongside with the notion that Greece has never been an imperialistic nation but has to defend itself against the Turks.

for the public to pay a licence fee for the operation of NIRB via their electricity bills, while ToA was funded through secret funds of the Ministry of Defence. When the need for more money emerged, under advice from American experts, the use of advertising revenue in the form of sponsorship was implemented.[34] The private sector met the production cost of televised shows and received 80% of the advertising revenue while the station would use the remaining 20% for other purposes. The first adverts made their appearance in September 1967 during the airing of *Mission Impossible*. The economic model of ToA enabled the station to gather the best Greek producers and to obtain the rights to many foreign series like *The Fugitive* and *The Untouchables*.

Besides content changes in 1968, another major change was the successful installation and upgrade of the broadcast network with 17 new transmission points covering the whole of Greece. The new broadcast network improved the signal quality, leading to a significant increase in TV sets. In 1968 the total number of sets was about 100,000 and the following year reached 200,000.[35] By the end of 1969, the experimental phase of Greek television was officially over, since there was a modern network and well-trained technicians.

The end of the experimental period came with regulations set out by the Junta regime. Law 722/1970 (with an amendment 1307/1972) renamed the Television of the Army, the Information Service of the Armed Forces (ISAF). They were given the right to install and operate television stations in order to inform and entertain the armed forces personnel and the public, under the supervision of the Ministry of Defence. The fiction programmes were shaped to fit the needs and goals of the military regime. The new entity was not restricted to radio and television broadcasts, but was entitled to produce movies and publish newspapers. The same year with Law 745 the National Institute of Broadcasting changed to the National Institute of Radio and Television (NIRT), gained the right to advertising revenues and was set under the control of three ministries: Presidency, Finance and Transportation.[36]

Programmes had to be entertaining and 'neutral'. The values promoted were those of the dictatorship's credo: 'Nation, Religion, Family'.[37] Censorship was constantly exerted throughout the process of production, from screenwriting to the final edit.[38] Entertainment genres, such as fiction, fitted perfectly the dictatorship's ideological project. Apart from their entertaining character, adventure and crime fiction had a complementary function: they served to highlight the role and importance of the National Police Force as well as that of policemen's devotion to the law.[39]

---

[34] Valoukos (2008), Kounenaki, P, 'Greek Television: The 30-year course from the first broadcast to contemporary polyphony' *Kathimerini* (Athens, March 10, 1996).
[35] ibid.
[36] Dagtoglou (1989).
[37] Koukoutsaki (2010).
[38] Koukoutsaki (2003) 724.
[39] ibid, 724, 732.

In May 1970 the first Greek law comedy, *Mister Defender*, was aired and lasted for two years with 256 episodes. This was the first comedy series in Greek television.[40] Until the fall of the Junta, the televised entertainment programmes were mainly musical shows, quiz games and sports, especially football.[41] In addition, both channels broadcast a number of theatre plays predominantly with nationalist content.

It is worth noting that during the Junta regime the ISAF had the legal right to advertising revenues through sponsorship deals, thus making the ISAF able to make shows with better production values.[42]

The State TV Era 1974–89

The new government led by Konstantinos Karamanlis, decided on 'national unity'.[43] The new Prime Minister removed the law that made the Communist Party illegal, but at the same time did not strike down the army or the Junta affiliates. In that same spirit the changes in television were not radical, since no one was fired or moved. In addition, the best of the art and intellectual world were appointed to managerial positions with actor Dimitris Horn being the new director. The new managers had to work with outdated equipment, about 2,000 unqualified personnel, a huge debt and programmes over-saturated with the junta ideology.[44] The need for legal reform was apparent in order for television to become independent.

The 1975 Constitution set radio and television under direct government control, in order secure objectivity. Law 230/1975 created Hellenic Radio and Television (ERT) in order to inform and entertain the Greek public. The same law set the obligatory—for every household—licence fee payable through electricity bills. It is important to note that even though the integration of the ISAF was clearly set out, the conservative parts of Greek society and the new government were in complete disagreement; the former considered the Act as treason.[45]

The rise of new political forces (PASOK—social-democrats as the major opposition party) in the 1977 elections led to a tightening of government control over public television. In 1979 Greek television chose SECAM as the standard of colour broadcasting[46] and, until the 1981 elections, public television was regarded by the press as part of the government propaganda arsenal.[47]

---

[40] Valoukos (2008).
[41] More in Koukoutsaki (2010).
[42] More in Valoukos (2008); and Komninou (2002).
[43] Komninou (2002).
[44] Valoukos (2008).
[45] Valoukos (2008), Kounenaki (1996).
[46] The selection of the French technology SECAM instead of the superior German PAL was a personal choice of Karamanlis as a gesture of goodwill towards France, since France was supporting Karamanlis' vision of Greece entering the European Community. Later on when private channels appeared they would select PAL offering better picture quality than public broadcasts.
[47] Valoukos (2008).

PASOK won the 1981 elections. Back in 1978 the new Prime Minister, Andreas Papandreou, had given a speech in Parliament against government control of public television, raising high hopes for a change to the legal framework. Indeed, the new director of public television had direct orders to conclude the integration of the ISAF and reform the schedules, which he did by setting out a new content triptych: socialism, village life, and women. The reform unfortunately did not bring about objectivity and diverse viewpoints in the newscasts. Despite the many new faces, newscasts were still under the control of the governing party. Instead of removing notions of party control over public TV, a solution of allowing all political parties airtime was selected.[48]

In a law on health (Law 1288/1982), a section was added which ended the ISAF renaming it ERT-2 while ERT was now ERT-1. ERT-2 had significantly fewer programmes than its counterpart, a gap that was reduced by the broadcasting of both Greek and foreign films. A number of problems, including corruption and party favouritism, were supposed to be dealt with by the creation of a unified organisation for public television. This was expected to happen in 1984, but never took place.[49]

In 1985 the deregulation of broadcasting was mentioned as a solution to the lack of diverse viewpoints. PASOK tried to loosen the control of public television and appointed non-party members to its leadership. A short-lived period of pluralism ended in the aftermath of serious student riots and the way they were televised.[50]

While the EU had given a directive on the deregulation of broadcasting and the end of public monopolies, PASOK resisted this change using rhetoric about 'loss of aesthetic quality' and 'dangers from abroad'. The municipal authorities wanted municipal radio and television and were assisted by the press which was now attacking the public monopoly. Building on previous strategies, the mayor of Athens created the first radio station even though the government had not yet set a legal framework. A few months later, the private and municipal radio stations in Greece numbered more than a thousand. PASOK had no choice but to accept the new situation and with Law 1730/1987 reformed ERT into one publicly owned body,[51] allowing existing private and municipal radio stations to remain on air. This law was still not enough to reform the broadcasting situation in Greece. A year later—again illegally—the municipality of Thessaloniki set up its own television station, TV-100, and started broadcasting. At the same time, the press conglomerates were putting pressure on the government to get the right to broadcast, declaring that only the press could guarantee pluralism and objectivity.[52]

---

[48] For more Panagiotopoulou (2010); and Vovou (2010) esp chs 4 and 13.
[49] Valoukos (2008).
[50] Valoukos (2008).
[51] ibid.
[52] Papathanassopoulos (1997).

In June 1989, during the run-up to the elections, a private TV station—ANT1—starts experimental broadcasting.[53] PASOK lost the elections and press owners pushed forward their plans for achieving the right to broadcast locally and experimentally without a change in the legal framework. Privately owned TV stations were again a reality in Greece, like public television had been in previous decades.[54]

The new government tried to reform ERT without removing surplus staff. A new team for newscasts was created and the director of information was promised the possibility of working without party ties in order to reinstate ERT as the objective information station. In the autumn of 1989, existing radio stations were legalised. Temporary licences were given to MEGA and ANT1 to broadcast. The National Council of Broadcasting was also established as the independent organisation to regulate broadcasting.[55]

To summarise, in the years after the dictatorship, the national stations continued being government controlled, first by the conservative party of New Democracy, which was in power from 1975 to 1981, and then by the socialist PASOK, which ruled the country until 1989.[56] The television boards were appointed by the government. Each time the government changed, the television boards would change too.[57]

The Deregulation Era

Public television's inability to change and reform led to its complete devaluation, allowing the private stations to conquer the field.[58] The duopoly of MEGA and ANT1 had to face the competition from the SKAI and STAR channels, the first Greek television stations with no evident political affiliation promoting an 'infotainment' style. The decline of the newspapers provided more advertising revenue for television owners and a number of channels changed ownership with no significant impact on content and ratings. In 1994 the first subscription channel appeared, owned by NetMed, providing a competitive model with no advertising, and broadcasting movies and sport events. The lack of adverts and the sport events—basketball championship and selected football games—helped the company gain about 300,000 subscribers.[59]

While MEGA and ANT1 were gaining power over public broadcasting, the rest of the broadcast scene was in a state of chaos. A number of stations started

---

[53] ANT1 is the result of businessman Minos Kiriakou to pre-emptively set a precedent and win over the more powerful press owners who are pushing for private television.

[54] Panagiotopoulou (2010).

[55] More in Papathanassopoulos (1997), Komninou (2002) and Panagiotopoulou (2010).

[56] Koukoutsaki (2003) 722; Papatheodorou and Machin (2003) 39.

[57] Koukoutsaki (2003) 722; Papatheodorou and Machin (2003); Tsaliki (1997).

[58] Heretakis (1997).

[59] Valoukos (2008).

broadcasting and asked the National Council for Broadcasting for licences. In the ongoing confusion no control over who was broadcasting at what frequency was achieved.[60] The large number of local and unregulated channels which broadcast illegally, led to the United States naming Greece as number one in film piracy in 1997 and threatened them with an embargo if intellectual property rights were not properly protected. Under this pressure the Greek government started charting all the frequencies and closed down several local channels.[61] A new law (2863/2000) tried to empower the National Council for Broadcasting but was not fully implemented. In an attempt to control corruption and conflicts of interest, Law 3021/2002 sought to put limitations on the percentage of ownership in media companies.

In Greece, up until the end of the 1980s, the evolution of Greek television was notable for the political, social and cultural symbolism of television. Consequently, the emergence of the entertainment model of the 1990s was the result of a combination of factors that were external to television production. These factors need to be linked to the political turbulence in Greece at the end of the 1980s, with the country being incorporated into the framework of general European television deregulation.[62]

The abolition of the state monopoly in broadcasting led to the rampant commercialisation of radio and television with hundreds of new channels and stations mushrooming at the national, regional and local levels. Broadcasting turned into a dynamic, rapidly growing industry, expanding from analogue, to cable, satellite and digital television services.[63] Fast-paced industrialisation and spectacular market growth,[64] however, failed to cut the umbilical cord that traditionally tied media organisations to the state. Thus, although the government's grip of radio and television was considerably loosened, the media–state relationship, though adapted to the new conditions, remained an intimate one.[65]

From the Olympics to Crisis

The period after the Olympic Games of Athens (2004–09) was a very optimistic one. The success of the games, a city full of new infrastructure and an international economic climate that provided cheap loans, gave Greek society a sense of security and contentment. Law 3592/2007 stated that legally operating stations

---

[60] Papathanassopoulos (1993).
[61] Valoukos (2008); more on peripheral TV stations in Panagiotopoulou (2004).
[62] Koukoutsaki (2003) 730; Kountouri (2010); Leandros (1996); Papathanassopoulos (1990a), Papathanassopoulos (1990b) 117–18; Papathanassopoulos (1993); Papathanassopoulos (1997); Papathanassopoulos (2005).
[63] Papatheodorou and Machin (2003) 32.
[64] Heretakis (1997); Heretakis (2010).
[65] Papatheodorou and Machin (2003) 35.

were those that were already in operation and in compliance with previous Laws 2644/1998, 3051/2002 and 3444/2006. The same law covered the transition to digital television (DVB-T) and how the new technology would be regulated. The law gave an advantage to public television with more frequencies and the flexibility to act as service providers for others.[66] Two years later, in June 2009, the private channels ALPHA, ALTER, ANT1, MAKEDONIA TV, MEGA, SKAI and STAR created DIGEA, a company to act as digital provider.[67]

In 2010 the full force of the worldwide banking crisis hit Greece and led to a memorandum for financial support by the EU, ECB and IMF. Social and economic turmoil prevailed over any legislative reform for broadcasting. While Greece is still in shock from the memorandum and austerity measures, on 11 June 2013 the Minister of Communications in a surprise move announced the immediate shutdown of ERT.[68] ERT at the time was economically healthy but was presented by the government as a corrupt business that cost the taxpayer money. An 'occupy ERT' movement rose immediately and ERT stared broadcasting what is considered by many its best information programme. Despite the outcry against the decision both locally and internationally the government did not budge and moved forward, slowly, to create the new 'uncorrupted' public broadcasting service by the name of NERIT.

The shutdown of ERT is a highly problematic issue for the modern media history of Greece. The decision was followed by an international tender, in 2014, for a digital signal provider and only DIGEA took part in it, making a private company that consists of quasi-legal broadcasters the sole digital provider of Greece. During the writing of this chapter, the new government of SYRIZA reopened ERT in a symbolic ceremony on 11 June 2015—exactly two years after it had closed down. Things are still in a state of flux.

An Overview of Content[69]

Greek television was shaped during the Junta regime. The regime had a very specific rationale on how to use television as a propaganda medium.[70] The specific goal of the Junta to promote the army as the lawful decision-maker alongside the ideology of nationalism was restrictive for new writers, and the majority of the programmes were theatrical plays, talk shows and quiz shows.[71]

---

[66] Oikonomou (2008).
[67] All information on the DIGEA website: www.digea.gr/en.
[68] *The Guardian* (2013); BBC (2013); *Euronews* (2013).
[69] On content—especially for fiction series—the Greek bibliography is limited; there are references to a hard to find book by Vasilis Georgiadis (1980) and a main source of information are the books by Valoukos and research by Koukoutsaki.
[70] Koukoutsaki in Vovou 2010.
[71] Valoukos (2008).

Despite the state control over television and the economic problems, during the period from 1974 to 1981, the ban on censorship brought back to Greece a number of artists who worked in television.[72] Foreign series—mostly soap operas and action-packed shows—were still present; notable examples are *Dallas* and *Dynasty* as well as *Charlie's Angels*, *Knight Rider* and *Kung Fu*, while Greek productions were mainly sentimental dramas with the exception of a few comedy shows.[73]

A notable first of the socialist era in Greek TV was the series *Lavreotika*, which is the first political series in Greek television[74] dealing with the birth of trade unions. With this series as a model, the majority of proposals for Greek productions were based on the triptych: socialism, village life, and women,[75] which was in accordance with the new socialist era. Another important series was the very successful *Minor of Dawn*, which received an extension in order to air more than 13 episodes—the absolute limit for any series of the period—and enabled the socialist government to use *rembetiko* music—urban Greek folk music—to appeal to the middle class and to gain popularity with musicians independent of their ideological orientation.[76]

During the years of the state monopoly (1970–89), the production trends of Greek television drama reflected the political interests of its state-controlled producers and broadcasters. The latter interfered directly or indirectly in the production by regulating the market, by imposing specific types of programmes, by authorising or banning specific contents.[77] Mirroring the government's specific ideology, Greek television drama of this period confirmed that every television system represented 'not only a people's culture, its customs and its language but also the point of view of the political system'.[78]

As far as the quality of the programmes after the deregulation is concerned, the private channels were fast to adopt shows and policies from the US. In addition, the deregulation of Greek television at the end of the 1980s marked a significant shift in the history of domestic drama, both in terms of quantity and genre production and the return to adventure and crime drama.[79] Besides the negative effects of private television,[80] we must also note a change towards a new generation of scriptwriters that led to a number of highly successful new series, including the first Greek soap operas.

During this period, there were a number of significant law-related shows. One notable series was the *Anatomy of a Crime* (ANT1, 1992), a show which lasted for three seasons and 72 episodes. Each episode was based on real events—usually

---

[72] Koukoutsaki (2010).
[73] Valoukos (2008).
[74] Koukoutsaki (2010).
[75] Valoukos (2008) and Koukoutsaki (2010).
[76] Valoukos (2008).
[77] Tsaliki (1997).
[78] Cazeneuve (1974) 46; Koukoutsaki (2003) 728.
[79] Koukoutsaki (2003) 728.
[80] Sorongas (2004). Commercialisation, aesthetic and cultural globalisation; soap operas, reality TV.

crimes of passion. ANT1 had another success with a comedy entitled *Sergeant Thanasis Papathanasis* (1990) which was based on the film/TV series *Officer on Duty*[81] and featured a beloved comedian Thanasis Vegos portraying the comedic situations of a kind sergeant. MEGA had minor success with a similar comedy series in 1996. MEGA was more successful in the field of soap operas and comedies. A satirical show which should be mentioned is *10 Small Mitsi*[82] with four full seasons and a number of special shows that lasted 11 years (1992–2003). Based on 10 different characters created by comedian Lakis Lazopoulos, among them a police sergeant, it was a satire on Modern Greek society. A success of ANT1 was the series *Vice Squad* with 116 episodes and which is actually the most successful Greek series based on the difficulties encountered by the police in fighting prostitution, drug trafficking and gambling. The competitive model of private stations explains the differences in programmes.[83] Both stations opted for exclusive deals with successful screenwriters, directors and production houses.[84]

Mega and ANT1 have been the major players in relation to Greek television series. The newer channels had difficulties in attracting viewers. Notable exceptions were imports like *CSI* introduced by SKAI to the Greek public and ALPHA's *Tenth Commandment* that broadcast 92 episodes in three years and was based on various court stories.

The fact that television stations have always been in charge of production has played a decisive role in the development of Greek television drama. Television drama has been used to function as an ideological medium of state propaganda, reproducing the discourse of its government-controlled broadcasters. In this context, Greek television drama was unable to find an autonomous language of expression and develop into a real cultural industry. Along with the lack of a coherent long-term strategy and specialisation,[85] the deregulation of Greek television did not change the situation; production remained a strongly concentrated sector, dependent on its broadcasters' short-term commercial interests.[86]

The Contemporary Context of the Representation of Law in Greek TV Content

Based on our historical background, the function of the Greek TV system is deeply influenced by the political elites, ie, different regimes and governments that have

---

[81] Produced by Nikos Mastorakis for NIRB in 1972.

[82] In Greek the word for 'small' also indicates 'young of age', so the title makes a dual comment both on the size and maturity of characters.

[83] More on Papathanassopoulos (1997); Sorongas (2004); Panagiotopoulou (2004); and Koukoutsaki (2010).

[84] Valoukos (2008).

[85] Papathanassopoulos (1999); Papathanassopoulos (2005).

[86] Poulakidakos and Karoulas (2009).

come to power in Greece since the early 1960s. Among its main aims have been the promotion of national identity and regime propaganda and the dissemination of common values within this context.

Our focus in the current research is on the entertainment content of Greek TV and more specifically the content related to the representation of the various 'stages' of law enforcement, hence police and apprehension, lawyers and trials, prison and post-prison.

In order to depict the contemporary situation regarding the above-mentioned content category, we first examined the daily programmes of the biggest Greek free-to-view TV stations (NERIT, MEGA, ANT1, ALPHA, SKAI, STAR), to locate productions belonging to these categories. After that, we conducted a content analysis with the use of a coding frame[87] so as to analyse this material in terms of specific parameters.

First we examined parameters concerning the placement of the programmes in the programming of the TV stations, such as their genre (drama, comedy, reality-based programme, reality-based entertainment, documentary); the content category (police, law, prison); their duration, their country of production, their broadcast time (afternoon, evening, prime time, night); and whether the programme was a first broadcast or a repeat. At a second level, we tried to categorise and quantify specific basic 'internal' characteristics of the broadcasts, such as the number of male and female basic characters of the episodes of the broadcasts; the race of the protagonists (white, black, other and their combinations); if there are any negative representations of the institutions we focus on (police, court/justice, prison); and which social classes and genders appear mostly as 'villains' or 'victims'.

The month selected for the empirical research was November 2014. The coding unit for our content analysis was the episode of a series or any other kind of broadcast (eg, movie) and the elaboration of the data and production of the quantitative results was conducted with the use of SPSS 22 statistics. The total number of broadcasts analysed—all of them series episodes—was 159 (N= 159).

Regarding the genre of the programmes, our research demonstrated that all 159 programmes focusing on law institutions broadcast during November 2014 can be categorised as dramas. More specifically, these 159 episodes belong to 12 different series, namely 'The Good Wife', 'Blue Bloods', 'Covert Affairs', 'Without a Trace', 'NCIS', 'Life', 'Chase', 'Law and Order: Special Victim Unit', 'Silk', 'NCIS LA', 'Criminal Minds' and 'Policeman Bekas' Stories', the only Greek series during November 2014. In addition, the vast majority of the programmes (96,2%) belong to the category of 'police and detective', whereas only 3.8% of the programmes belong to the 'lawyer and court' category. This result is closely connected to the prevalence of the production and the wide popularity of police series mostly in the US, the country of origin for the majority (83%) of similar shows aired in

---

[87] Budd and Thorp et al (1967); Berelson (1971); Carley (1972); Krippendorf (2004); Kumar (2011).

Greece. A little more than one out of 10 episodes (13,2%) was from the only Greek series *'Policeman Bekas' Stories'*, whereas only 3.8% of the episodes (from *'Silk'*) come from the UK.

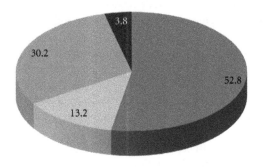

■STAR ▨ALPHA ▨SKAI ■NERIT

Figure 1: Channel broadcasting the programme

As far as the channel broadcasting the programme is concerned, STAR is responsible for more than half the broadcasts (52.8%), SKAI for about one-third of the broadcasts (30.2%), ALPHA for 13.2% and the public television channel, NERIT, broadcast only the 3.8% of the episodes in our research.

In addition, more than two-thirds of the broadcasts (76.7%) are first broadcasts. The success of the foreign police and crime series, and their significantly lower cost, compared with the high costs of a Greek production[88]—especially within the context of the economic crisis—urged the Greek channels to 'massively' introduce different series of the specific genre to their schedules.

Almost two-thirds of the broadcasts (71.1%) are aired during the night zone. This placement is due to their—in most cases—violent content and the restrictions posed by the Greek National Council for Radio and Television regarding the broadcast hours for violent scenes.

Moving to the 'internal' characteristics of the episodes, there is a pretty clear prevalence—concerning race—of white actors in the majority of the leading roles in the episodes (78%, Figure 2). Apart from that, there is a significant 17%, where all the leading roles are taken by white actors. On the other hand in only 4.4% of the cases does the casting seem balanced with equal representation of white and non-white characters.

---

[88] Poulakidakos, Karoulas (2009).

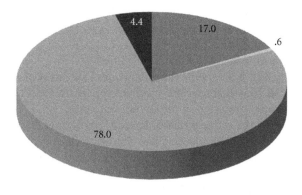

■ White   Other   ■ Combination (white majority) ■ Combination (balanced)

Figure 2: Race of the protagonists

In terms of gender, our research showed that the average number of male basic characters for each episode is significantly larger than the mean of female characters. An average of 10 male actors perfom as the main characters in the episodes, whereas the female characters are limited to less than seven (6.84, Figure 3).[89]

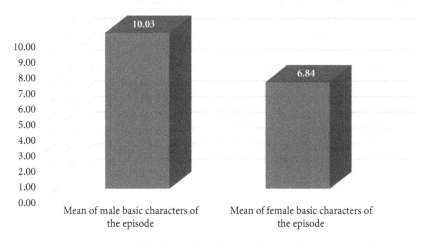

Figure 3: Average number of male and female actors (main roles) per episode

[89] In order to evaluate the statistical significance in the difference between the two means, we conducted a one-sample t-test, having as test value the male average (10.03). Our statistic test showed that the difference of means between male and female actors is significant at the 99% significance level (t- test p value =.000). Hence male actors appear significantly more compared to female actors in the basic roles of the episodes we analysed.

A not unexpected outcome revealed an overwhelmingly non-negative representation (98.1%) of police and justice. In the three cases (1.9%) in which a negative
representation of police took place, this negativity addressed issues of corruption
(one case) and incompetence (two cases) of the police.

The following results aim at providing a picture in terms of the different race,
gender and social class characteristics, as they appear on the TV screen, of the
'villains' and 'victims' characters in the episodes analysed.

In terms of race, the series scenario develops itself around white characters,
since in both cases—villains and victims—the white characters appear to be by
far the more dominant ones (90.6% of the villains and 86.8% of the victims).
The black characters, the second most represented race, appear in just 5% of the
episodes as villains and in almost 7% as victims (Figures 4a, 4b).

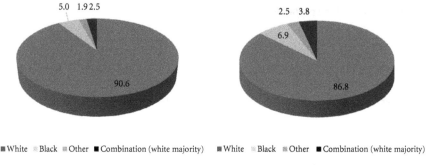

Figure 4a: Race of villains   **Figure 4b: Race of victims**

In terms of gender, the same discrimination (between villains and victims),
appears far less balanced. On one hand, when it comes to villains, the male characters outnumber the female since they reach an almost 87% of 'evil' appearances.
Women, on the contrary, incorporate the 'bad' characters in 13.2% of the episodes.
On the other hand, as far as the victims are concerned, the percentages are more
equally distributed, since men appear as victims in 55.3% and women in 44.7% of
the episodes (Figures 5a, 5b).

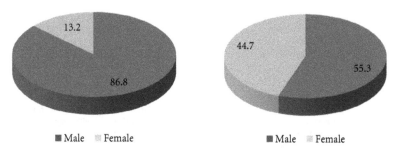

Figure 5a: Race of villains   **Figure 5b: Race of victims**

Last but not least comes the social-financial class of the villain and victim charac-ters of the episodes, as it becomes evident by the lifestyle of the specific character during a given episode. The majority of the villains (63.5%) belong to the work-ing class, since they appear as workers or employees. About one-third (32.1%) of the villains belong to the 'upper class', since they appear living a luxurious life-style. Pretty similar proportions appear in the victims' domain, since workers and employees are the majority of the victims as well (52.8%). The upper-class charac-ters 'serve' as victims in 27% of cases (Figures 6a, 6b).

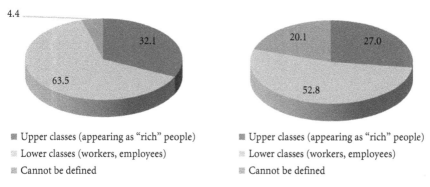

4.4

■ Upper classes (appearing as "rich" people)
▧ Lower classes (workers, employees)
▨ Cannot be defined

Figure 6a: Social class of villains

■ Upper classes (appearing as "rich" people)
▧ Lower classes (workers, employees)
▨ Cannot be defined

Figure 6b: Social class of victims

Discussion

The above-mentioned social, political and historical approach, along with the descriptive quantitative content analysis on contemporary law depiction in Greek TV, sought to provide an introductory approach to the political, ideological and financial schemes contributing to the development of television in Greece, as well as to demonstrate the traditional close ideological binding of the law content in Greek TV with its political and financial patrons.

The quantitative analysis of contemporary programmes demonstrated specific tendencies in terms of both structural characteristics of contemporary Greek TV law content (content category, origin, hours and channels of broadcast), as well as several content characteristics—predominantly in terms of race and gender—of the programmes under scrutiny. Of course, the descriptive analysis provided in the current chapter is far from being considered an exhaustive one, since it can be further elaborated so as to include more parameters seeking to address the issues raised by the content of law dedicated programmes.

10

Israel

ITAY RAVID

Introduction—*No* Lawyers in the Living Room[1]

This chapter will tell the story of the void. Not what is broadcast on Israeli TV but rather what is *left out*. The small Israeli television broadcasting market is comprised of three leading strands.[2] Two open-to-the-public strands (broadcast channels): a public channel (Channel 1) and commercial channels (Channels 2 and 10). Channel 2 is by far the most dominant of the three and receives the highest ratings.[3] The third strand, which reaches a substantial number of households, is subscription (paid) channels: cable (Hot) and satellite (Yes).[4] Audience-concentrated or topic-designated channels (such as a channel for Russian speakers, music channels, etc) are also part of the market, but are relatively marginal. Without underestimating the importance of either the subscription or designated channels, the current chapter will focus on the three most dominant channels that reach almost all Israeli households: Channels 1, 2 and 10. The subscription channels do deserve some mention as the main venue for importing foreign—mostly American—TV shows, and due to their legal commitment to broadcast original Israeli shows. Moreover, over the years their role as active participants in the evolving Israeli television market grew.[5] Therefore, I will briefly refer to these channels throughout the chapter.

---

[1] The title is a tribute to the book *Lawyers in Your Living Room!* Asimow, M (ed) (American Bar Association, 2009).

[2] The official report of the Israeli Council for Cable and Satellite TVs broadcasting (2011), see: www.moc.gov.il/sip_storage/FILES/5/3095.pdf (in Hebrew).

[3] Just to set an example, Channel 2 evening news receive an average of around 20–25% of viewers, Channel 10 evening news around 10–12% and Channel 1 evening news between 4% and 7%—see: www.ynet.co.il/articles/0,7340,L-4614537,00.html; www.ice.co.il/rating.

[4] Current data show that 60.8% of households in Israel that own TV have purchased cables and satellite services; 846,000 are connected to Hot and 635,000 to Yes. Sources: (A) The official Israeli Bureau of Statistics (CBS): Households that Purchased a Subscription for Culture, Entertainment and Sports Activities, by Selected Characteristics (2015): http://cbs.gov.il/reader/shnaton/templ_shnaton.html?num_tab=st09_05&CYear=2015; (B) 'Bezeq' group reports third quarter 2015 financial results; http://ir.bezeq.co.il/phoenix.zhtml?c=159870&p=irol-financialreports; (C) HOT Financial Report First Quarter 2015; http://www.hot.net.il//heb/About/investors/finance/2015/.

[5] Charlap (2011) marks 2004 as the year from which the subscription channels have become influential to the development of locally produced shows, dramas especially.

But first things first. The empirical analysis of the three leading channels throughout November 2014 confirmed prior beliefs about the Israeli TV market: law, its popular images, dominant narratives[6] and the ideological promise it holds for at least some modern Western societies,[7] does not receive much attention in Israeli TV in any of the three dimensions discussed in this book: apprehension (police focus); adjudication (lawyer focus); and disposal (prison/punishment focus).[8] In fact, throughout the month of November 2014 there was not even one show solely devoted to law, lawyers, or the legal system on *any of the channels*. Similarly, there was not even one show about prison or prisoners. Only *one* Israeli TV show about the police was broadcast on one of the channels,[9] bi-weekly reruns of an American police show in another,[10] and zero police shows on the biggest channel—Channel 2. Two episodes in two news magazine programmes, one on Channel 2 and the other on Channel 10, were devoted to stories that bear some legal components: a lawyer accused of criminal wrongdoing and the murder of a Palestinian child by Jewish-Israelis. Still, these are only two shows out of 12 broadcast that month.[11]

Based on this sample of TV shows, one might assume that popular legal culture, in its narrowest form: cultural artifacts, such as books, songs, movies, plays and TV shows about the law, lawyers or the legal system,[12] are rare commodities on the main channels in Israel. One would most probably be right.

Although not shocking, it is by no means a trivial conclusion. Most literature in the field of law and popular culture strongly adheres to the argument that popular culture serves as an inner window to the soul of society in which it functions, and reflects its values and fields of interest. As Steven D Stark rightly mentioned while discussing American television: 'If television is obsessed with crime and the law, it is because Americans are obsessed with them as well'.[13] Similarly, if television in Israel is *not* obsessed with crime and the law, the conclusion should be that Israelis are just not interested in these topics.

Yet, most Israelis would burst into laughter when hearing this proposition. In fact, there are few countries in the Western world whose courts are as busy as Israeli courts. An official report by the Israeli Judicial Authority shows that in 2015 around 762,055 cases were filed in Israeli courts, an overwhelming number considering the fact that Israel's population is only slightly more than 8 million people.[14]

---

[6] Ravid (2015) 68–73.

[7] Schachar (2007) 148–50.

[8] Clearly, we cannot claim that the November sample analyzed for the purposes of this book qualifies as a representative sample according to our accepted standards as social scientists. However, I argue, this sample in fact does capture quite accurately the lack of TV law in the census of shows broadcast in Israeli TV.

[9] The show *1-0-0* on Channel 10.

[10] CSI Miami and CSI Las Vegas on Channel 1.

[11] Eight that were broadcast on Channel 10, and four on Channel 2.

[12] Friedman (1989).

[13] Stark (1987) 233.

[14] The State of Israel, *The Judicial Authority Official Report for 2015* (in Hebrew, available at: http://elyon1.court.gov.il/heb/haba/dochot/doc/shnati2015.pdf.

Indeed, studies have found that the number of cases submitted to Israeli courts is substantially higher than in many other Western countries.[15] It is therefore axiomatic that courts are dominant institutions in Israeli public life. This is especially true with regard to the Israeli High Court of Justice that plays an important role in Israeli discourse and development.[16] Moreover, the ratio of lawyers-per-person in Israel is one of the highest in the world. Just in 2013 the numbers of lawyers in Israel reached a peak of one lawyer for every 150 people. For the sake of comparison, in the US, a country known for having one of the largest lawyer populations in the world (and one of the largest consumers of legally themed TV), the ratio of lawyer-to-person is only one for every 252 people.[17] All of these elements indicate that Israeli culture is extremely law centred.

The disparity between the ubiquitous nature of law in the daily lives of Israelis and the void in its representation on popular television channels is intriguing both at the internal and the external level. At the internal level, it is a way of understanding Israeli legal culture. At the external level, it challenges some of the basic premises of law and popular culture and thus deserves further exploration. Trying to unpack this disparity will be the focus of this chapter. But before heading deeper into the socio-legal discussion, an overview of the Israeli TV market is required.

The Israeli TV Market: Past, Present and Future

Like most pivotal moments in Israeli history, the beginning of Israeli TV is also closely connected to a war. In 1967, after the Six Day War, the Israeli government finally let go of its traditional objections to television in the young, presumably socialist, and no longer very fragile state of Israel, with the approval of the first (and at the time only) Israeli channel: the public channel (or Channel 1).[18] Although the law regulating the work of Channel 1 was enacted back in 1965,[19] it was only after the war, in 1968, that the channel was officially launched. This public channel, inspired by the British BBC model, was developed under the assumption that since broadcasting is a public good it needs to remain in the hands of the public, to be owned by it and service the needs of the whole population.[20] All of these

---

[15] For instance, a study conducted in 2004 comparing the burden on Israeli courts to courts in 16 countries, ranked Israel as the country with the highest ratio of cases per population and second highest in terms of burden on judges, See: Socialiano-Kenan et al, 'The Burden on Justice Systems—A Comparative Perspective' (The Center for Public Management and Policy, Haifa University, 2004). Can be viewed: pmpc.haifa.ac.il/images/nappa_and_more/Courts_burden_Final_report_5.07.pdf.

[16] Almog (2012) 41–42.

[17] L Shadmi-Shpitzer (26 May 2014), at: www.takdin.co.il/Pages/Article.aspx?artId=4603270.

[18] Caspi (2012) 76–77.

[19] Israel Broadcasting Authority Law, 5725-1965, *Sefer Ha-Chukkim* of 451, p 106 (hereafter: the law)

[20] Caspi (2005) 19–24.

elements were carved into the DNA of the channel and were clearly defined in the law itself, which stated, inter alia, that the broadcasting authority should allow broadcasting of educational, entertainment and informational shows in all fields of policy, society, economy, culture, science and art, for the purposes of reflecting the life of the Israeli State, its struggle, its creation and its achievements and more.[21] It was decided the channel would be free (or almost free)[22] of advertisements, in the hope of blocking external commercial pressures that might divert the channel from its original purpose.[23] The channel was funded by a yearly mandatory fee all Israeli citizens were required to pay.

The British BBC model provided the Israeli Parliament with the perfect solution: balancing between the need to regulate the new channel for the greater good, and the aspiration to avoid its over-politicisation.[24] Yet, the pure British model was slowly eroded in Israeli reality, with politicians and employees joining hands to meddle in the channel. These patterns, and the over-politicisation of Channel 1, has slowly but steadily contributed to its decay, and in 2014 a new law terminating the operation of the Israeli Broadcasting Authority was enacted, forming a new framework for the Israeli public broadcasting.[25] What the future holds for the Israeli public channel remains unclear. This issue is currently debated in Israeli politics.

It is important to understand that for almost three decades, from 1968 to 1993, Channel 1 was the *only* TV channel in Israel, the ultimate campfire of Israeli society. A survey conducted in 1990 revealed that 52.4% of the population watch Channel 1 every night between 9.00 pm and 10.00 pm, when the main news programme (*Mabat*) is on air.[26] One cannot overestimate the influence this channel had on Israeli culture, including the establishment of Israeli popular legal culture. The seeds of what we see today in terms of law and justice on the Israeli small screen were planted then.

A change in the monopoly of the public channel dates back to the early 1980s, with growing political, professional and economic pressures to open up the over-centralised Israeli TV market. In 1986 the existing law was amended[27] which allowed the entry of legal[28] cable TV to the Israeli market.[29] At first, the Israeli

---

[21] The channel should also promote good citizenship, tighten the connection with Jewish tradition and its values, spread knowledge, represent the lives of the Jews outside Israel, broadcast channels in Arabic for the Arabic-speaking Israelis and in order to promote peace and understanding with the neighbouring states.

[22] Sponsorships were allowed along the years, resulting in numerous legal proceedings challenging this decision.

[23] Caspi and Limor (1992) 118–19.

[24] Caspi (2005) 25–31.

[25] Public Broadcast Law, 5774-2014, *Sefer Ha-Chukkim* 2471, p 178.

[26] Caspi and Limor (1992) 120.

[27] Communications Law (Bezeq and Broadcasting) (Amendment No 4) 5747-1986, *Sefer Ha-Chukkim* 1192, p 224 (hereafter: Communications Law)

[28] The literature argues that one of the reasons which allowed the entry of the cable channels was the attempt to legally control the widespread phenomenon of pirate cable channels mushrooming in Israel in the1980s. See, eg, Caspi and Limor (1992) 127–28.

[29] Weiman (1996) 396.

regulator, the Council of Cable and Satellite TV Broadcasting,[30] decided to split Israel into 31 zones and declared a public tender in which 31 franchises were provided.[31] Over time, the 31 districts were consolidated into three companies and the franchise system was replaced by a licensing system, allowing the use of the cable platform to promote market competition and the entrance of new actors.[32] Indeed, in July 2000 a new company ('Yes') entered the multi-channelled television market, using a different platform: Israeli communications satellites. In 2006 the three existing cable companies merged into one company, known as 'Hot'.[33]

Both Yes and Hot are heavily regulated by the Council. Most channels on the cable and satellite platforms are foreign, though Hot and Yes both have several channels that broadcast locally produced shows. The licence owners are required by law to allocate at least 10% of their broadcasting time to local productions. They are also obliged to invest between 8% and 12% of the total income received from subscribers in producing or purchasing local productions, and 50% should be invested in either drama or documentary shows.[34] Commercials are not allowed.[35]

The penetration of cable TV to Israel was one of the fastest among Western societies, with over 40% of Israelis connecting to cables in areas where an appropriate infrastructure existed (mostly urban areas) within the first year.[36] By 2014, around 63% of Israeli households that owned a TV were connected to cable or satellite channels.

It is hard to assess to what extent these channels have contributed to the development of original legally themed shows. On the one hand, in terms of quantity they did not mark a significant rise in the production of such shows. On the other hand, especially in recent years, production quality was improved and a few legally themed drama series (mostly police dramas) were produced.[37] Moreover, over the years these channels have become the main—and almost only—platform for imported English-spoken shows, many of which are legally themed.

Major changes stemmed from the enactment of the Second Authority for Television and Radio Law.[38] The Authority is an independent statutory agency that

---

[30] Overseen by the Minister of Communications (hereafter: the Council)

[31] Caspi and Limor (1992) 128–29.

[32] The official report of the Council of Cable and Satellite TV Broadcasting from 2001, see: www.moc.gov.il/sip_storage/FILES/2/1032.pdf.

[33] Hot is 99.9% held by Cool Holdings, a company owned by Patrick Drahi, who also owns the European Altice SA cable TV group. Yes is 49.9% owned by Bezeq (the main Israeli telecommunication company) and 50.1% by Eurocom.

[34] Hamer (2012) 155. See also the official report of the Council of Cable and Satellite TV Broadcasting from 2012: www.moc.gov.il/sip_storage/FILES/5/3435.pdf.

[35] Part 7, Article (6)(24) of the Communications Law. The Council also regulates the content of adults, children's and sports shows.

[36] Weiman (1996) 394.

[37] As will be discussed later, although these channels have hardly produced shows focusing on law and lawyers, they were somewhat responsible for the increasing number of lawyers as—often minor—characters in *non-legal* shows.

[38] Second Authority for Television and Radio Law, 5750-1990, *Sefer Ha-Chukkim* 1304, p 59 (hereafter: Second Authority Law).

constitutes a normative mixture of economic-commercial and social-cultural regulatory purposes. Overall, Israel has designed a regulatory regime with relatively high ethical principles,[39] and thus defines a broad set of 'forbidden' broadcasts such as racist or discriminatory, unsuitable for children and more. The Second Authority monitors the content of broadcasts, the content of advertisements and any deviations from the allotted broadcasting time, as defined by the Second Authority Law. In terms of content, the franchise holders are required to broadcast local productions in 40–50% of the total broadcasting time.[40] In addition, 65% of the time should be devoted to productions bought by the franchise holder, rather than produced by the franchise holder or by another group it owns; 15% of the bought local production should be produced in the Israeli periphery.[41] Moreover, the law demands that each year a certain part of local shows' broadcasting time is dedicated to what is termed 'Elite' genre—ie, locally produced shows that are either documentaries, dramas or special shows. The financial commitment to broadcasting these shows is substantively higher than broadcasting foreign shows or entertainment such as reality shows.[42]

Since Channel 2 entered Israeli television, it has steadily and increasingly gained more viewers who abandoned the public channel. Only one year after Channel 2 was launched, in May 1994, its main news broadcast was more popular than *Mabat*, the main news broadcast of Channel 1, and its most solid show for over two decades. This change symbolised the demise of the Channel 1 era. Today Channel 2 is the most popular channel in Israel, at peak viewing times attracting up to 45% of the Israeli population to the small screen.

In 2002 a new commercial channel, Channel 10, entered the small Israeli television market. The purpose of establishing another commercial channel was well emphasised in the discussions preceding its arrival: breaking Channel 2's monopoly and providing an alternative to the Israeli audience in the hope of lowering the unreasonable advertisement fees demanded by Channel 2.[43] Like Channel 2, Channel 10 is also regulated by the Second Authority for Radio and Television, and abides by the same rules. Some argue that Channel 10 did not keep its promise to bring innovative and thought provoking TV and in recent years it has been struggling financially.[44]

Despite the relatively small size of the Israeli market, then, the political setting, economic pressures and rapid changes over the years have created a complex regulatory regime, unique in its political component among Western countries,

---

[39] Yadin (2014) 6–7.

[40] Hamer (2012) 154; local productions are defined as shows in which at least 75% of the creators and technical team members are Israeli citizens who reside in Israel, and which were originally produced for an Israeli audience (59(b) of the Second Authority Law).

[41] Rule 1, 11(a), 14—The Rules of the Second Authority for Television and Radio (Broadcasting by Franchise Owner) 2009; www.rashut2.org.il/editor/UpLoadLow/b-116.pdf.

[42] Yadin (2014) 10.

[43] ibid, 7.

[44] ibid, 21.

regulating television broadcasts through independent, professional agencies.[45] The struggle between maintaining high quality, educational and culturally rich products and the understanding that television is after all a business, is evident throughout Israel's short television history and its adopted legal regime.

TV Law in Israel: An Overview

Generally speaking law as a main theme is far from dominant in local Israeli shows, especially drama and comedy. In fact, very few Israeli law-related shows have entered the pantheon of modern Israeli culture. When Channel 1 was the only channel, Israeli dramas were a rare commodity, mostly due to financial limitations. Even the relatively limited number of dramas created did their best to avoid controversial issues, and for the most part focused on the new Zionist imagery, war stories and universal topics.[46] No drama series focusing on law and lawyers, police, prisons or prisoners seem to have been created during those years. There were some one-off productions, such as *Kastner's Trial* (1994), telling the true story of Israel Kastner who saved Jews in Hungary during the days of the Nazi regime using controversial means, and *Siton* (1995) following a lawyer and his daily life struggles.

In comedies, a generally minor area of broadcasting, one could sporadically find lawyer characters, but not as protagonists. For instance, in one of the leading Israeli sitcoms of all time, *Close Relatives* (*Krovim Krovim*) (broadcast between 1983 and 1986), a lawyer appeared in only one of the episodes. While there were no Israeli legally themed shows, Channel 1 did expose Israelis to foreign, mostly British and American legal shows, some of which were influential like *LA Law*, *Hill Street Blues*, or *Law and Order*. These days, however, foreign shows are hardly imported by either the public or commercial channels. Aside from the above-mentioned genres, over the years two other types of legally related shows were broadcast on Channel 1: (i) documentaries or magazine-like shows; and (ii) low-budget educational shows where lawyers or experts discussed legal topics, mostly not broadcast during prime time.

The domination of Channel 2 and to some extent the subscription channels has brought meaningful changes in the development of original Israeli productions between the years 1995 and 2004, mostly in the drama genre.[47] '[S]uddenly', as Alper and Amir point out, 'the screen is piling up with innovative, groovy, and well performed shows that are broadcast during peak hours'.[48] Apart from the quality

---

[45] Yizhar Tal and Dina Ivry-Omer, Regulation of Electronic Communications Services in Israel: The Need to Establish a Communications Authority, Israeli Democracy Institute Policy Papers Series (2009) 11 (in Hebrew). Available online: www.idi.org.il/media/277043/pp_76.pdf
[46] Charlap (2011) 34–36.
[47] ibid, 38.
[48] Alper and Amir (2012).

of the production, during those years it was probably the first time that Israeli shows lasted longer than one season.[49] Despite this positive wave of creativity, only a few shows produced by Channel 2 were law related, and even those did not survive long or gain much attention. For instance, one of the first shows ever produced in Israel on lawyers was *Franco and Spector* (2003). It followed a small Israeli law firm through two of its associates. One of its leading narratives was exposing the disparities between law and justice in the Israeli legal system. The show had 12 episodes and lasted only one season. Although shows focusing on law or lawyers were hardly produced, these years planted the seeds for a later phenomenon of lawyers appearing as characters in non-legally themed shows.[50]

Police dramas, also a rare breed on Israeli TV, received slightly more attention with several attempts to produce original Israeli police dramas. The first was *Yarkon District* (*Merchav Yarkon*) (1997) that was praised by critics but lasted only five episodes. In 1999 Channel 2 also broadcast a doc-reality inspired by the American series *Cops* (and with the same title), following police officers in their daily routine. As part of Channel 10's attempts to bring more sophisticated police dramas to Israeli TV, in 2002 it started broadcasting *Case Closed* (*Tik Sagoor*), one of the most expensive Israeli shows ever produced. The show was cancelled after three episodes. It should be noted that in 1995 Channel 1 broadcast the show *Criminal Reporter* (1995) (*Katav Plili*), one of its rare attempts to engage with criminal-related shows.

Prison dramas were also rare on Israeli TV, with one main exception; *Zinzana* (2000), which was broadcast on Channel 2 and told the story of prisoners in men's and women's prisons. The show gained popularity especially in its first season, and lasted three seasons. Although the launch of the commercial channels also revived the comedy genre, legally themed comedies were still uncommon. Throughout these years (1995–2004) the commercial channels kept importing shows from English-speaking countries (mostly the US), and shows like *Ally MacBeal, the practice* and *Oz* became part of Israeli culture.

The year 2004 marked the beginning of another era in Israeli TV, with the subscription channels providing more sophisticated and ambitious Israeli dramas.[51] This era, that Charlap considers the Israeli 'Television after TV' era, continues to the present. Despite this important change, the lack of original shows focusing on law or lawyers is still evident, with only *one* local show from that genre, *Such a Wonderful Divorce* (2010) (*Gerushim Niflaim*), a production of Yes principally about a law firm practising family law. On the other hand, the trend of including lawyers as characters in non-legally themed shows has significantly expanded.[52]

---

[49] Charlap (2011) 39.
[50] This was the case in the first Israeli soap opera broadcast on Channel 2—*Ramat Aviv G* (1995) with the lawyer Beni Peled, in *The Brown Girls* (2002) (*Bnot Brown*) with Eli Menashe as the capitalist lawyer, and *The Bourgeoisie* (2000) ('*H' Burganim*) introducing Israel, the not-so-honest lawyer.
[51] Charlap (2011) 42.
[52] Channel 2 introduced us to Amal, a female lawyer in the comic drama *An Arab's Work* (2007) (*Avoda Aravit*), and to Eti Ben-David, another female lawyer, in the drama *Until the Wedding* (2008)

Police dramas, on the other hand, received slightly more attention since 2004. In 2008 Channel 10 tried its luck again with a police drama called *The Naked Truth* (*Ha'emet Ha'eroma*). Once again, the show was quickly cancelled. The same happened with *Marziano's Dignity* (2011) (*H'kavod Shell Marziano*), another attempt to produce an Israeli-style crime drama, which lasted only five episodes. In 2007 Hot started broadcasting the Mafia-style crime drama *The Arbitrator* (*Ha'borer*), which became extremely popular. The show had four seasons, an impressive achievement among Israeli dramas. In 2009, also on Hot, the mystery, *Twin Peaks*-inspired Israeli drama *Pillars of Smoke* (2009) (*Timrot Ashan*) aired. This show followed a policewoman investigating a mysterious crime in one of the most expensive Israeli shows ever produced. Since 2012 there has been a slight increase in the prevalence of Israeli police dramas, with *The Special Unit* (*Ha'meyuchedet*) on Channel 2, *1-0-0* on Channel 10, the daily crime drama *Noy-York* (2012) on Yes, *Head* Injuries (2013) (*Ptzuim Barosh*), *Virgins* (*Betulut*) (aired during the last week of November 2014), and The Principle of Exchange (*Ikaron Ha'hachlafa*) (2016) on HOT. The third season of *1-0-0* was the only police show broadcast during November 2014. While the number of original Israeli police dramas does seem to increase over time, other originally produced legal shows remain absent from the Israeli small screen.

In terms of foreign content, for many years now both Channels 2 and 10 have not imported foreign shows. In contrast, Hot and Yes are constantly competing with each other to import popular American shows, some of which are legally themed such as *The Good Wife*, *Suits*, *Orange is the New Black*, among others.[53]

It should be mentioned that as on Channel 1, law could also be seen on Channels 2 and 10 through individual documentaries and news magazines, which once in a while focused on a law-related story. An example is the docu-reality *The Crackers* (*Hamefatzhim*) (2007), broadcast on Channel 2, which explored crimes the police could not solve, and *Sirens* (2013)—a Channel 1 magazine programme about criminal cases. All channels also continue broadcasting several low-budget shows, mostly during late mornings, in which legal scholars or lawyers discuss legal issues (such as *Legal Question* (2014) (*She'ela Mishpatit*) on Channel 2, or *The Juries* (*Hamushba'im*) (2012) on Channel 1. The subscription channels also broadcast legally themed documentaries, many of which are foreign. A few rare exceptions

(*Ad H'chatuna Ze Ya'avor*). A male lawyer with criminal tendencies was part of the cast in the (unsuccessful) comedy *70 Million Reasons for Wealth* (2014) (*70 Million Sibot Le'osher*). Channel 10 also introduced us to a few lawyers: in the drama *Alenbi* (2012) we got acquainted with Elad the lawyer of the protagonist—the owner of a strip club; in the comedy *Friends* (2013) (*H'averot*) we met Vered the lawyer; and recently in the mini-series *Suspect* (2015) (*Hashuda*) we met another female lawyer, Daphna, this time the protagonist of the thriller. This trend hasn't skipped the subscription channels either. Hot included a few lawyers in their locally produced shows: Elisha Ben-David in *Parashat H'ashavua* (2006); Talia from the second season of *In Treatment* (2008) (*Betipul*); Shir from *Asfur* (2010); and the minor character of Shachar as an American lawyer in the comedy *Relax* (2012) (*Tanuchi*). Yes had also introduced us to Mira, also a female lawyer, in the drama *Strike* (2012) (*Shvita*).

[53] Just as an example, in November 2014 Yes broadcast *The Good Wife*, *Suits*, *Oz*, *Castle*, *Elementary*, *Prime Suspect*, *The Closer*, *NCIS*, *Breaking Bad* and *Dexter* among others.

are two recent Yes documentary series, broadcast in November 2014: *Files from the Public Defender* (*Tikim Me'hasanegoria*), which provides a rare behind the scenes look at the Israeli Public Defender's office, and *Men of Law* (*Anshe'i Hachok*), a docu-reality on police work in Israel that was first broadcast in 2010.

To sum up, this brief overview confirms the surprisingly low number of legally themed shows produced in Israel over the years, especially by the public channels. One could count on the fingers of one hand the number of dramas or comedies devoted to lawyers, judges and prisons, and on a bit more than two hands police dramas (though this genre seems to be on the rise). These are clearly small numbers. Besides these shows, all channels broadcast a legal story once in a while as part of an investigative report in news magazines, or show a documentary related to these issues. Moreover, a steady stream of imported, mostly American, TV shows has flowed into Israeli TV, at the beginning through Channel 1, and later through subscription and commercial channels.

The empirical data from November 2014, despite its non-representatives, thus tells a pretty accurate story about law on Israeli TV: on all three main channels, there was not even one show solely devoted to law, lawyers, the legal system, prison or prisoners. Only one Israeli show about the police was broadcast on one of these channels,[54] bi-weekly reruns of an American police show on another,[55] and no police shows on the biggest channel—Channel 2. Two investigative reports in two news magazine programmes, one on Channel 2 and one on Channel 10, were devoted to stories that had legal components.

The subscription channels kept providing a constant flow of foreign, mostly American legally themed shows and a very limited number of original Israeli shows—as mentioned earlier—*Virgins* on Hot 3, *Files from the Public Defender* on Yes Doco and reruns of the docu-reality *Men of Law*.

These data provide a good foundation to discuss two interesting riddles: first, why the number of Israeli-produced legally themed shows is so small; second, and more generally, why legally themed shows, both local and foreign, are almost entirely absent from the three main Israeli broadcast channels.

Explaining the Void

Israeli television is not the only cultural arena neglecting law, lawyers and legal processes. This is also the case in other cultural arenas, such as Israeli cinema and literature,[56] both culturally flourishing fields.[57] As discussed, especially since 2004, the local television industry has also gone through a creativity boom, financial

---

[54] *1-0-0* on Channel 10.
[55] CSI Miami and CSI Las Vegas on Channel 1.
[56] Almog (2012) 41.
[57] ibid.

development and expansion. Despite these developments, the law—and especially law, lawyers and legal processes as a core theme—has yet to penetrate Israeli popular culture. This reality is especially interesting for two reasons. First, the dominance of law in the daily lives of Israelis. As mentioned, Israelis are 'Courtophiles' as evident by the number of cases handled by Israeli courts and the Israeli lawyer-per-person ratio. This approach towards law dominates the Jewish tradition, according to which the law is an autonomous system that can be applied in all instances of daily life. Second, the extent of the exposure Israeli courts—and particularly the Supreme Court—receive in the media, and the important role the Court plays in Israeli society.[58]

In the past, if asked to explain this void, one would likely provide a simple financial explanation: local productions, and especially dramas, are expensive to produce and the small and limited Israeli market simply cannot afford sophisticated legal dramas. It makes much more sense financially to import these shows from the US. Although this explanation still has some merit, there is no doubt that Israeli television has evolved not only artistically, but also financially, and in recent years some highly sophisticated and relatively expensive shows have been produced. Yet very few of those were lawyer/court-focused. This implies that there is a deeper explanation for the lack of legally themed Israeli produced shows, one that is embedded in Israeli culture and society. In her book, Almog attempts to answer these questions when discussing the absence of the law in Israeli cinema. Building on her explanations, as well as some of Schachar's, I wish to apply Almog's analysis to the TV context, and expand it by providing further explanations of my own for this cultural void.[59]

The first explanation provided by Almog is the lack of visualisation of the legal process in the Israeli—and maybe even the Jewish—tradition. Despite the fact that Israel is a common law country, none of the visual elements used in the English legal process have been imported to the Israeli legal system (such as wigs and other customs). Israeli judges and lawyers wear a simple black robe in court, and there are no other unique visual symbolic elements.[60] The lack of visual symbols minimises the symbolic side of law, which is often the source of its attractiveness for the visual arts—both film and television.

In my view, it is not only the lack of visualisation that makes the Israeli legal process unattractive for producers. There are also the structure and procedures of the system. For example, the fact that Israel is not a jury system takes the edge of the potential dramatisation of the legal process. Instead, in Israel professional judges are the sole authority deciding legal cases–a less sensational process indeed. Many American films and television shows devoted to legal processes consider the

---

[58] ibid, 41–42; Bogoch and Holzman-Gazit (2008) 54–55.
[59] Clearly, TV and film are two different media and although they are becoming less and less distinguishable, they still bear some distinctions that deserve attention (see for example: Niles and Mezey (2005) 167–168). For the purposes of this chapter, especially given the fact that law is absent from both Israeli TV and film, the differences between these media are of marginal importance.
[60] Almog (2012) 42–43.

jury system to be a valuable thematic tool in creating the drama that makes courts so intriguing for viewers around the world.[61] It is not only that the jury's mere presence that is missing in the Israeli legal process, but also that additional procedural characteristics are missing, such as attorneys' attempts to influence juries, closing arguments, the personal stories behind each juror and the like. Therefore, the structure and procedure of the Israeli legal process lack an attractive dramatic component, turning it into a less appealing institution as far as narratives are concerned.[62]

The second explanation provided by Almog, and supported by Schachar, relates to the difference between the role of law and courts in American and Israeli legal cultures. According to Schachar, the American court is pivotal to American culture, which considers the trial a main element in the redemption of the nation and the achievement of justice. The American collective finds within itself legal heroes—lawyers and juries—in order to turn into a better, more just, nation. A fair fight between parties, as occurs in the legal process, is the way to bring redemption.[63] This ethos, Schachar implies, was never adopted by the Israeli—nor by the Jewish—tradition. Almog adds another layer by suggesting that it is not only that Israelis did not adopt the American legal ethos, but also that for Israeli culture, collective redemption and courage were mostly found in war zones, where brave soldiers and commanders sacrificed their lives for the greater good. While war commanders and warriors won glory in Israeli society, lawyers and judges did not.[64] Therefore, both Almog and Schachar agree that law has not received an important role in the narrative of the Israeli nation, and has not penetrated Israeli popular culture. As much as I tend to agree with Almog's view of the essence of Israeli heroism in the first decades of the Israeli state, I believe the myths behind war heroes and commanders have been drastically eroded over the years, and nowadays I would be surprised if they still represent the ideal Israeli hero.[65] Whether lawyers will replace them is a different question, which I discuss below.

Besides these explanations, Schachar also discusses the role of American popular culture in Israeli culture, suggesting that the consumption of American legal shows by Israelis might have satisfied the Israeli need for law in popular culture. Not being fully convinced by this explanation, I also find it to be more descriptive than explanatory since it fails to provide the core answer—why the need is fulfilled only when it comes to law. As we know, there are many other fields in which the Israeli audience is exposed to American products, exposure that does not prevent

---

[61] Clover (1998) 98, 100–01.

[62] Almog [(2014) 969] claims that jurors contribute to the public appeal of the legal proceeding. I agree, and further suggest above that they have a greater role in explaining the meaningful presence of the Anglo-American court dramas on TV, by adding dramatic procedural components and complex legal narratives that make good stories which attract viewers.

[63] Schachar (2007) 155.

[64] Almog (2012) 44.

[65] Although in recent years, at least based on discussions and debates in the media, one might discern a wave of nostalgia is sweeping through Israeli society, resulting in a semi-revival of the Israeli hero-soldier myth.

the production of original Israeli dramas on these topics. Could his argument only be true when it comes to law, and if so, what makes law so unique?

I would like to offer another explanation for the lack of legally themed products in Israeli popular culture, one that expands and deepens Almog and Schechar's path. I would suggest law is missing from Israeli popular culture due to its overall demystification in the eyes of the Israeli public. As mentioned, the Israeli legal system is quite lacking in mystified elements—such as visual symbols or potentially dramatic structure or procedures. It is not only that these elements, however, are missing. It is also that in general, law in Israel is understood by most people to be an extremely instrumental tool, a mechanism, well used by almost everyone to simply solve problems—which at times succeeds and other times fails.[66] Law does not save the nation. Law does not provide moral myths for children to grow up on. Law solves problems. As Almog mentions, this instrumentality of Israeli law in the eyes of Israeli culture can explain the presence of the law in documentary films as opposed to its absence in fiction films. The same can be said about the small screen; where law as the core theme, if found, is more likely to be present in documentaries, news, news magazines and investigative reports. Moreover, on the rare occasions where Israeli dramas are law focused, it will most likely be in dramas based on true stories of Israeli history.

The demystification of the law is also related to the geographic and cultural characteristics of Israel. Israel is a small country, where social ties are densely woven between most members of society. That means that lawyers or judges are not distant and mythic figures. They can be your best friends, have served with you in the military, or be your relatives or neighbours. Under these conditions it is hard to maintain distance between the legal figures and the public—an essential element in creating myths. Moreover, besides lacking many of the dramatic elements so salient in the American process, the Israeli legal system and process is also known for being relatively informal. The daily encounter of Israelis with courts, especially trial courts, and the informal interactions within the system and between judges and lawyers, all affect the overall conception of law and the legal system, making it an extremely 'earthy' institution.

Without claiming that lawyers and judges have replaced soldiers as the national heroes, I do believe the penetration of law into the everyday lives of Israelis in recent decades, and the massive use of the Israeli Supreme Court by politicians, NGOs, parties from the Left and the Right, high-income and low-income families, religious and secular, Jews and Arabs have transformed the status of Israeli lawyers and judges.[67] They may not be the heroic figures one might see in American popular culture, but it is clear that lawyers and judges do take a more active role in the development of Israeli civil society. Lawyers and judges are promoting major legal

---

[66] See also Almog (2012) 46.
[67] Bogoch and Holzman-Gazit (2008) 67–68, 77 report on the increase of petitions filed to the Supreme Court and the varied interest groups submitting them.

changes that potentially affect the core values of the Israeli nation.[68] This reality might affect, even in the near future, the perception of Israeli lawyers and judges in the eyes of the public, thus potentially turning them into more appealing subjects for popular culture. As noted, this process has already started and in recent years lawyer characters—especially female—in non-legal shows are seen more often on the small screen. I expect this trend to continue. Soon enough, I believe, Israelis will be seeing a lot more lawyers in their living rooms.

---

[68] On the role of the Supreme Court in promoting these changes, see Dotan and Hofnung (2001) 8–10.

11

Italy

FERDINANDO SPINA

Numerous fault lines in Italian society are directly linked to the themes of law and justice—think of the long-running struggle between the state and the most famous organised crime networks, the Mafia, Camorra and 'Ndrangheta. However, questions in the social-legal sphere have multiplied: considering the always topical issue of urban crime blamed on foreign immigration; the growing sensitivity and opposition to gendered violence and the murder of women; and last, the conflict between politicians and the judiciary, with their three-decades-old reciprocal erosion of each other's legitimacy.

Nowadays, these highly topical issues are more 'televised' than ever. The legal representations in films and on television are considered to be 'Cultural Barometers',[1] which reflect the 'Cultural Zeitgeist'[2] and can be used to interpret society's values and opinions on law and justice. In the next few pages we will look briefly at the evolution of these representations in Italian television programming, excluding the news.

History and Development of Television

Italians love television so much, more than any other means of communication or any other cultural industry. In 2013 Italy had the highest level of television viewing in Europe (261' per person per day) and the third in the world.[3]

Regular television programming in Italy did not begin until 3 January 1954 from RAI (Radiotelevisione Italiana), the national state broadcaster.[4] In its early

---

[1] Sherwin (2004) 102.

[2] Robson (2005) 39.

[3] OFCOM, 'International Communications Market Report' (2014): stakeholdersofcomorguk/binaries/research/cmr/cmr14/icmr/ICMR_2014.pdf, 161.

[4] On the history of the Italian media system, see generally: Abruzzese and Borrelli (2000); Colombo (1999); Forgacs (1990); Forgacs and Lumley (1996); Gavrila and Morcellini (2015); Grasso (2002), (2004); Hibberd (2008); Menduni (1996); Morcellini (2005); Monteleone (1992), (2014); Ortoleva and Di Marco (2004); Padovani (2007); Sorice (1998).

years, television's cultural model was that of the BBC, centred on the need to educate, inform and entertain.[5] Throughout the period of its monopoly (that is, up until about the mid-1970s), the RAI's programming maintained a certain balance between the three functions. This phase is commonly considered, and not without some nostalgia, to be the golden age of Italian television.

The 1970s saw the definitive transformation of the television system; 1972 saw the arrival of Italy's first private local television channel. In 1975 the Parliament passed Law 103/1975, the first law specifically addressing the broadcasting sector. However, the Constitutional Court issued some rulings (225 and 226/1974, 202/1976) that undermined the whole basis of the public monopoly then in force. In this way the stage was set for the development of a chaotic and fragmented television system, with no unified regulation, no antitrust rules and no overall consensus about what the television system should look like.[6]

In the early 1980s at the national level there were only three private networks that belonged to the building magnate, media tycoon and then Prime Minister in three governments, Silvio Berlusconi.[7] This uncertain phase was given a regulatory framework by Law 223/1990, which legitimised the existing duopoly of RAI and Mediaset (Berlusconi's group), preventing any real competition in the sector. To date, the serious problems that have characterised Italian television as a whole—the close links with politicians, the conflicts of interest, the economic and industrial fragility—have not gone away.

Obviously, some important developments have taken place, above all thanks to technological innovation, such as the switch to digital terrestrial (DTTV) in 2012, and the rise of subscription-based satellite television. Today, the number of viewers on an average day of the month exceeds 11 million: the average audience share for free digital terrestrial is 83.6% of the total, with satellite television accounting for the rest.[8] Generalist channels jointly account for more than 70% of the total audience, but their popularity has fallen steadily.

In economic terms, the broadcasting sector accounts for 0.55% of GDP. It is characterised by excessive concentration, with the three corporate groups, Sky Italia, RAI and Mediaset, still collectively holding 90% of television resources. In 2013 advertising accounted for 41% of revenues, and thus remains television's main source of funding. This has undoubtedly resulted in a substantial similarity between the programming of the public service networks and that of the private networks.

---

[5] Reith (1924).

[6] Richeri and Balbi (2015).

[7] For an account of the 'Berlusconi era', see Padovani (2015).

[8] In March 2014. On these and the following data, see AGCOM (Communications Authority) *Annual Report* (2014): wwwagcomit/annual-report.

Law and Justice on Italian TV

The following—highly selective—description includes those programmes deemed to be emblematic of the evolution of the social meanings attributed to law and its representatives.[9] The main focus will be on the dramas, which in Italy are called 'fiction', without neglecting important reality-based programmes and documentaries on the theme, although they are not particularly numerous.

Police Dramas[10]

Despite being inspired by foreign models, Italy's production of police dramas is not without originality and innovation. Highly successful in the early years were series such as *Giallo Club. Invito al poliziesco* (*Thriller Club. Invitation to the Crime Story*, Rai 1, 1959–61) and *Le inchieste del commissario Maigret* (*The Cases of Inspector Maigret*, Rai 1, 1964–72), which spawned a long line of high quality TV adaptations of the classics of detective fiction.

In the 1970s, political and social tensions led to violence, with the emergence of terrorism and a steep rise in the overall crime rate.[11] One of the responses to this climate on the part of public television was the series *Qui squadra mobile* (*Flying Squad Here*, Rai 1, 1973–76). In the same period, to meet public television's need to provide entertainment which was now becoming more important than its educational function, increasing use was made of American police series, which enjoyed great success among the public.

Nevertheless, this was also the period of the most successful drama in the history of Italian television, *La Piovra* (*The Octopus: The Power of the Mafia*, Rai 1, 1984–2001).[12] It represented, and at the same time forged, Italians' most widely held cultural perceptions regarding the Mafia, the state and the police. Indeed, from this series onwards, the theme of the Mafia, which had previously been tackled only episodically, became central in television.[13]

The late 1980s had seen the arrival of docu-fiction programmes, describing the everyday duties of police officers. In the early 1990s, Italian police dramas began to proliferate, with series that sought to imitate (or more frequently to distinguish themselves from) American models. *Il maresciallo Rocca* (*Marshal Rocca*, Rai 2

---

[9] Very helpful in this regard are the accounts in Buonanno (2012), (2013); Pezzini (1997); Valentini (2012); and, for each programme, the information in Grasso (2002), (2004).

[10] In Italy, there are five separate national police forces providing law enforcement, including the State Police and the Carabinieri.

[11] Melossi (1997).

[12] See Buonanno (1996), (2012); Giomi (2010).

[13] On the representation of the Mafia, see generally Buonanno (2012) ch 6; Dino (2009); Morcellini (1986).

and Rai 1, 1996–2005), was the most successful Italian television drama since *La Piovra*.[14] *Il commissario Montalbano* (*Inspector Montalbano*, Rai 2 and Rai 1, 1999–) is the heir to the famous police dramas of television's earliest years, with which it shares its literary origins, overall quality and success among the public, both in Italy and abroad.[15] The end of the 1990s brought other interesting developments for Italian police dramas, including their first female leads, as in *Distretto di polizia* (*Police District*, Canale 5, 2000–12).

Trials, Judges and Lawyers

Real Trials and Programmes Based on the Trial Formula

According to Buonanno,[16] at least 35 legal or courtroom dramas were broadcast from the 1960s to the 1980s, and this is probably a conservative estimate. Most of these legal dramas, which were highly popular with the public, were based on famous trials of the past or present, and concerned private events but also political crimes. In this way they provided a critical view of the idea of justice, although the observations were without direct references to contemporary Italian justice.

Conversely, some programmes sought to enrich the drama series model with debates and investigations. Outstanding examples of this genre are *Teatro Inchiesta* (*Investigation Theatre*, Rai 2, 1966–73), *Processi a porte aperte* (*Open Court*, Rai 1, 1968) and *Di fronte alla legge* (*Before the Law*, Rai 1, 1967–74).

The formula of presenting investigations as courtroom dramas ran out of steam in the early 1970s, and was not taken up again systematically in subsequent years. In the mid-1980s, there was the rise of documentary-style television, or as it was called in Italy, 'TV-verità' (Truth TV), which sought to go beyond television's reassuring, fictional account, and tackle concrete problems as well as society's dark side.[17]

With *Un giorno in pretura* (*A Day in Court*, Rai 3, 1988–) recordings of real trials were broadcast without comment, showing the actual functioning of the law courts.[18] The key moment, for both the programme and the political history of the Republic, was the broadcast from 1993 to 1994 of the trials arising from the 'Mani pulite' (Clean Hands) investigations, in which high-ranking politicians, civil servants and businessmen were interrogated by the public prosecutor Di Pietro regarding allegations of bribery and corruption.[19]

---

[14] See Buonanno (2000).

[15] See Bechelloni (2010); Marrone (2003); Rinaldi (2012); Valentini (2012).

[16] Buonanno (2013).

[17] Cavicchioli and Pezzini (1993).

[18] Italian regulation of television coverage of courtroom trials is very liberal. Court hearings are public and, with the consent of the parties and after evaluation by the judge, cameras are also allowed in the court.

[19] Giglioli, Cavicchioli and Fele (1997).

The 'trial' formula on television began to shed its more formal characteristics, as in *Forum* (Canale 5, 1985–), Italy's first arbitration-style reality court show, which has so far presented 17,230 cases with about 40,050 participants.[20]

Judges

The development of the representations of judges on Italian television seems to reflect the evolution of the relationship between the judiciary and society. Until the late 1960s, there were very few dramas involving judges, and in any case they did not touch on their function in society or on the social problem of justice. This lack of interest was mirrored in cinema. How can the limited number of legal dramas, both in the cinema and on television, be explained? The notion that the adversarial procedure has a far greater dramatic and narrative potential than the inquisitorial system certainly has some force.[21] However, in *Il giudice sullo schermo* (*The Judge on the Screen*) (1973), probably the first major work in law and film, Tomeo suggests a cultural explanation. He discussed the apparently unbridgeable gulf between Italian society and the agent of the law: an attitude rooted in mistrust and fatalistic resignation according to which the law is merely the emanation of power and not an instrument of justice.[22]

In 1960s and 1970s, the judiciary underwent a profound transformation, becoming more open to social problems and taking on—at least in some quarters—an explicitly progressive political role.[23] Television recorded this transformation, presenting the profile of a 'problematic' judge, to use the words of Tomeo, in programmes like *La parola ai giudici* (*The Judges' Point of View*, Rai 1, 1973), and dramas like *Dedicato a un pretore* (*Dedicated to a Prosecutor*, Rai 1, 1973) and *Diario di un giudice* (*Diary of a Judge*, Rai 1, 1978).

Subsequently, the figure of the problematic judge did not enjoy great success on television. Many years later, *Un cane sciolto* (*An Unleashed Dog*, Rai 1, 1990–92) represented a 'credible magistrate', succeeding in the end in defending the rights of individuals and the community. This takes us to the beginning of the 1990s. Televised trials were a ritual that legitimised the entire judiciary. This was reinforced by the dramatic attacks of 1992 on two judges who had been the symbol of the struggle against the Mafia, Giovanni Falcone and Paolo Borsellino.

From then on, almost always in the framework of the Mafia genre and stereotypical representation bordering on hagiography and myth-making, television presented an unabashed figure of the 'judge-as-hero'.[24]

---

[20] See Forum Official Website: www.video.mediaset.it/news/forum/361/forum-story.shtml.

[21] See, generally, Drexler (2001); Garapon (2010); Machura and Ulbrich (2001b); on the case of Italy in particular, see Vitiello (2013).

[22] On this research by Tomeo, see Febbrajo (1992); Olgiati (2001); Raiteri (1992).

[23] See Moriondo (1969); Luminati (2007); Treves (1972).

[24] Eg, *Sospetti* (*Suspicions*, Rai 2 and Rai 1, 2000 and 2002); *Paolo Borsellino* (Canale 5, 2004); *Giovanni Falcone* (Rai 1, 2006); *Borsellino—I 57 giorni* (*Borsellino—The 57 days*, Rai 1, 2012).

Lawyers

It should be pointed out at the outset that the number of Italian dramas about lawyers barely reaches double figures, and they are also recent, beginning in the 1990s. This appears surprising considering that Italy has the highest number of lawyers in Europe.[25] It is even more unexpected, given the number of foreign legal television series broadcast in Italy, a sign of their fascination among the Italian public. It is difficult to give an explanation for this lack of interest, but it could be argued that Tomeo's hypotheses are also useful in the case of the under-representation of lawyers: a negative view of the profession is rooted in popular culture and elsewhere.

The first lawyer to appear on television was *Perry Mason* (Rai 1, 1959–67). The public was fascinated by his 'American-ness': the American system of justice appeared to be completely different from the Italian one, being not only more entertaining but also more just.

Not until the 1990s did an Italian lawyer become the lead character in a television series. Lawyer-centred dramas share certain traits: legal procedures receive less attention than descriptions of characters and the investigative phase; the lawyer's professional and private lives are intertwined; the family is a constant theme, both in the lawyer's cases and as a problem because of the difficulty of reconciling family and professional commitments. The latter theme is highlighted especially in dramas which have a woman lawyer as the main character like *L'avvocato delle donne* (*The Women's Lawyer*, Rai 2, 1997). The female lawyer shows determination and a solid commitment to the cause of justice, unlike her male antagonists (colleagues or counterparts), who are frequently depicted as cynical careerists.

The male leads in these dramas belie the negative stereotypes usually attributed to lawyers, such as careerism, thirst for power, greed.[26] *L'avvocato Porta* (*Porta the Lawyer*, Canale 5, 1997–2000) is disorganised and penniless, because he only defends poor and marginalised clients. The lawyer Tasca (*Un caso di coscienza* (*A Question of Conscience*, Rai 2 and Rai 1, 2003–13) is the 'Robin Hood of the courtroom'.

The television lawyer remains an idealised and idealist figure, dedicated to defending the poor and defenceless, not interested in money or their career, a person unburdened by either success or power—in short, a lawyer that does not exist.

---

[25] In 2012, Italy had 226,202 practising lawyers, the highest number in Europe, with a ratio of 379.9 per 100,000 inhabitants (European average 161.4): CEPEJ, 'Report on "European judicial systems—edition 2014 (2012 data): efficiency and quality of justice"': wwwcoeint/t/dghl/cooperation/ cepej/evaluation/2014/Rapport_2014_En.pdf, 378.

[26] CENSIS (2009).

Prison

The dramatic state of Italian prisons has frequently been on the agendas of politicians and the media.[27] In the last few years, even television has shown a greater interest in prisons. This has gone some way to compensating for a certain neglect that has characterised the history of Italian television.

Prison has mostly been used as a backdrop in police, crime and legal series, while the classic theme of wrongful imprisonment as a consequence of a miscarriage of justice is present in other melodramas. Two programmes—in which real detainees participated in various ways—have sought to tackle life in prison directly by means of comedy.[28] Two recent and successful series—*Romanzo Criminale* (*Crime Novel*, Sky Cinema 1, 2008–10) and *Gomorra* (*Gomorrah*, Sky Atlantic, 2014–) show prison in a raw and realistic way, similar to American prison dramas.

Lastly, prisons have also been covered in documentaries, as in *Storie maledette* (*Cursed Tales*, Rai 3, 1994–). The years 2004 to 2008 saw a whole genre of prison-set programmes which sought to show the reality of detention.[29] This interest in prison, limited to a period of a few years and based on the same type of product, proved to be a fad. However, it showed the public's interest in the theme, helping to generate a climate that led in 2006 to an early-release order for 28,586 detainees.[30]

Empirical Report

In order to measure the current representation of law and justice on television, programmes were classified on the basis of five categories: dramas, comedies, reality-based programmes (formal reality TV), reality-based entertainment (informal reality TV) and documentaries.[31] Films made for cinema were not considered. The top 21 national digital free television channels, which accounted for 74.98% of audience share in the period of reference, November 2014, were analysed.[32] These include the seven most important generalist channels, which together accounted for 63.14% of viewers (sorted by average audience: Rai 1,

---

[27] In 2013, the total number of inmates was 64,835, with an incarceration rate of 109 per 100,000 population (European mean 136.3). The prison density per 100 places was 148.4, the highest ever recorded: Council of Europe, 'Annual Penal Statistics Space I—Prison Populations Survey 2013' (2015): wpunilch/space/files/2015/02/SPACE-I-2013-English.pdf, 42.

[28] *Belli dentro* (*Beautiful Inside*, Canale 5, 2005–12); and *Cugino e cugino* (*Cousin and Cousin*, Rai 1, 2011).

[29] Among others, *Rebibbia G8* (Rai 3, 2004); and *Altrove* (*Elsewhere*, Italia 1, 2006).

[30] ISTAT, 'Prisoners in the Italian Penal Institutions' (2012): www.istat.it/en/archive/78654.

[31] On the distinction between formal and informal reality shows, see Robson (2007) 349. For the definition of documentary, we refer to Machura and Ulbrich (2001b) 119.

[32] Author's calculations based on Auditel data.

Canale 5, Rai 3, Rai 2, Italia 1, Rete 4 and La7) and 14 thematic channels with content that was potentially of interest to the study.[33] Two free-to-air digital channels entirely dedicated to crime and legal genres, Giallo and Top Crime (which together accounted for 1.88%) were not analysed, in order to avoid skewing the data from the 'normal' programming. The programmes were identified using the published television guides *Tv Sorrisi e Canzoni* and *Di Più TV*, and their actual broadcast was verified with reference to data from Auditel, an independent company that measures television audiences in Italy. The study analysed programmes broadcast from 7.00 am to midnight.[34]

In total, 59 programme titles were identified, corresponding to a total of 741 episodes with an overall duration of 771 hours, ie, 32 whole days of programming on crime, the police and justice.[35] Many of the series were repeats, with a low broadcasting profile, broadcast in the early morning or afternoon, or shown on minor digital channels, in order to fill the schedules with archive material.

The programming followed a fairly constant pattern over the month (Figure 1).

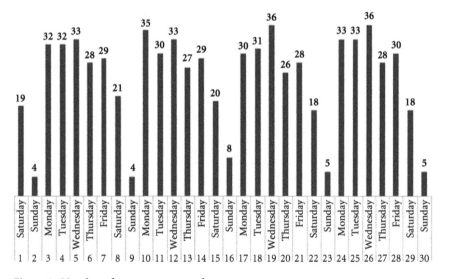

Figure 1: Number of programmes per day
These genres are widely shown every day of the week except Sunday (Figure 2).

---

[33] According to AGCOM *Annual Report* (2014): wwwagcomit/annual-report, 122 there are 38 major free channels, excluding local stations and channels available only via satellite. Of these, 15 were excluded from the analysis as they were thematic channels whose content was not relevant to the study (sport, children's, news, music, etc).
[34] Note that the television guides consulted do not cover the overnight period (midnight to 7:00 am).
[35] Commercial time has not been subtracted.

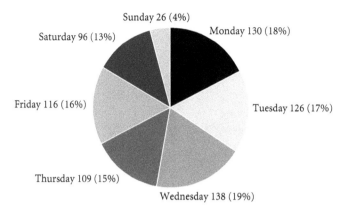

Figure 2: Number of programmes by day of the week

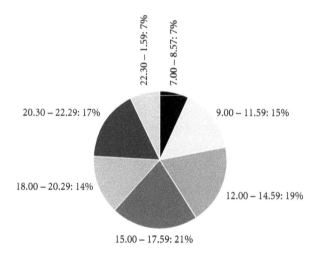

Figure 3: Distribution of programmes by time of day

It was found that of the 21 channels analysed, only 11 had programmes that fell within the categories of interest (Figure 4). Of these, three channels alone (Rete 4, Italia 1 and Rai 2) accounted for almost 60% of the programmes. Today as in the past, it is above all commercial TV that provides this genre of programme to Italian viewers.

By a wide margin, the dominant category of programme is drama (Figure 5).

Obviously, making a clear distinction between programmes on the basis of genre or format is difficult, and this is especially true of Italian television, which shows a strong tendency to hybridisation of genres.

All the comedy, reality and documentary programmes identified are Italian made. In contrast, the TV series are mainly imported (84%) (Figure 6).

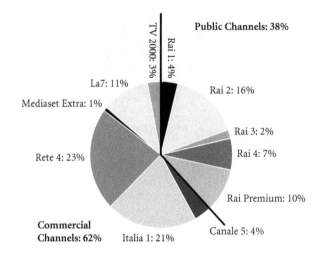

Figure 4: Distribution of programmes by channel

Figure 5: Distribution of programmes by genre

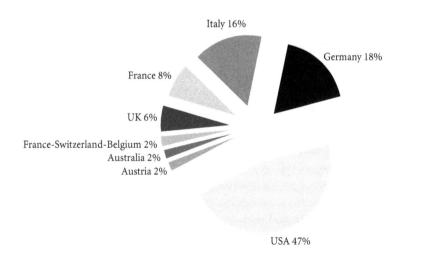

Figure 6: Distribution of dramas by country

The reality-based programmes, reality-based entertainment shows and documentary were all presented by women, except one that was presented by a man and a woman. The main characters in the TV series are mostly male (46%) rather than female (21%), while about a third of the series have main characters of both genders (33%).

Table 1 shows the 10 most popular programmes on crime, law and justice in November 2014. Note that programmes with just one episode a week always have more viewers than the average for the network.

Police and Detective Material

Undoubtedly, mystery, detectives and police are the most common themes, accounting for 88% of the sample: 48 dramas, one comedy, two reality-based programmes and one documentary.

More than two-thirds of the TV series are centred on official police forces. These lie along a continuum that runs from the figure of the individual policeman to an entire investigative team. *Squadra Antimafia 6* and *Le mani dentro la città*[36] are both series about the Mafia, but whereas the first is set—in keeping with tradition—in Sicily, the second is innovatively set in Milan, strengthening in the collective imagination the impression that organised crime is no longer an exclusively southern problem. *Squadra Antimafia* is now in its sixth season, liked by the critics and young viewers. Highly interesting and innovative is the presence of two female characters in the opposing (and traditionally male) roles of the head of the police team and the powerful Mafia boss.[37]

Highly popular is the classic figure of the amateur detective: these include the evergreen *Murder, She Wrote*,[38] which has been broadcast in Italy without interruption since 1988 and has an average audience share of 6%, despite the episodes now all being repeats. Also in this category is the TV miniseries *Una pallottola nel cuore*: the comic side of the series, also a classic ingredient, is guaranteed by the skills of the lead actor, Gigi Proietti, who also played the very popular *Il Maresciallo Rocca*. A comic representation of the Carabinieri is also provided by the only comedy identified in the month of November, the series *Carabinieri*.[39]

The two reality-based programmes, *Chi l'ha visto* and *Quarto Grado?* are 'infotainment', focusing on crime and investigations, a very successful genre in Italy, of which numerous examples have been produced by all the generalist networks.[40]

---

[36] Hands Inside the City (Canale 5, 2014 repeat).
[37] Buonanno (2014).
[38] CBS (1984–96) repeat.
[39] Canale 5 and Rete 4 (2002–08) repeat.
[40] On 5 November, *Chi l'ha visto* was the most watched programme on the Rai networks.

Table 1: Most popular programmes

	Name	Programme	Genre	Country	Channel	Scheduled	Time	Episodes × Running Time	Share	Viewers
1	Una pallottola nel cuore (A Bullet in the Heart)	D	Investigation	Italy	Rai 1	Sun and Mon	9.15 pm	3 × 1h 40'	21.44 (+1.59)	5,576,000
2	Squadra antimafia 6 (Anti-Mafia Squad 6)	D	Police/Mafia	Italy	Canale 5	Mon	9.10 pm	2 × 1h 40'	18.53 (+1.53)	4,728,000
3	Forum	RE	Courtroom show	Italy	Canale 5	From Mon to Sat	11.00 am	23 × 2h	16.50	1,413,087
4	Chi l'ha visto? (Who Saw It?)	RP	Investigation	Italy	Rai 3	Wed	9.05 pm	4 × 2h 50'	14.75 (+7.59)	3,395,250
5	Torto o ragione? Il verdetto finale (Right or Wrong? The Final Verdict)	RE	Courtroom show	Italy	Rai 1	From Mon to Fri	2.40 pm	20 × 1h 10'	12.35	1,620,650
6	Hawaii Five-0[41]	D	Police procedural	USA	Rai 2	Sun	9.45 pm	2 × 42'	9.26 (+2.30)	2,278,000

(continued)

[41] CBS (2010–) 4th season (2013).

Table 1: *(Continued)*

	Name	Programme	Genre	Country	Channel	Scheduled	Time	Episodes × Running Time	Share	Viewers
7	*NCIS Los Angeles*[42]	D	Police procedural	USA	Rai 2	Sun	9.45 pm	2 × 41'	9.24 (+2.28)	2,482,500
8	*Quarto grado (Fourth Degree)*	RP	Investigation	Italy	Rete 4	Fri	9.15 pm	4 × 3h	8.90 (+4.44)	1,905,750
9	*Un giorno in pretura (A Day in Court)*	RP	Courtroom show	Italy	Rai 3	Sat	00.00 am	5 × 1h 40'	8.79 (+2.11)	725,200
10	*Castle*[43]	D	Police procedural	USA	Rai 2	Sat	9.05 pm	7 × 45'	8.63 (+1.67)	2,181,429

Programme: D = drama; RE = reality-based entertainment show; RP: reality-based programme.

Share: the average number of share for each episode of the programme (in brackets, only for programmes with just one episode a week, the difference with the average share of the network).

Viewers: the average number of viewers for each episode of the programme.

[42] CBS (2009–) 5th season (2014).
[43] ABC (2009–) 6th season (2013).

These programmes show a full-blown trial-by-media of murder cases that have caught the public's attention, with the participation of the lawyers of the people involved, family members, experts, criminologists and even defendants and witnesses.

Lastly, we find the documentary *Amore Criminale* (*Criminal Love*, Rai 3, 2007–), which is dedicated exclusively to the highly topical theme in modern Italy of violence against women.

Lawyer-Focused and Court-Focused Material

Only 7 programmes out of 59 (12%) have the trial, with its judges, lawyers, plaintiffs and defendants, as the central theme. They include three series, two shown as repeats and one on its first showing, *The Good Wife*.[44] The latter series is one of the few legal dramas broadcast on a generalist television channel in the last few years, although the genre is much more common on free thematic channels and pay TV, drawing extensively on American productions.

Un giorno in pretura (*A Day in Court*) is currently the only reality courtroom programme on Italian television. It is also one of its most long-lived programmes. The three reality-based entertainment shows, accounting for a daily total of almost five hours, are *Forum*, its spin-off *Lo sportello di Forum* (*Forum Office*) and *Torto o ragione? Il verdetto finale* (*Right or Wrong? The Final Verdict*). As shown in Table 1, these programmes enjoy a consistently high number of viewers: mainly female, elderly, of limited education and low income.[45]

Prison and Post-Prison Material

As already mentioned, television pays little attention to prison. This is confirmed by the research, which found no dramas, reality-based programmes or any other genre dedicated to this theme in November. Outside our sample, just two cases may be cited. The first is the episode of the investigative programme *Report* (Rai 3, 30 November), focusing on the return of detainees to the world of work. The second is a thematic evening's programming (Laeffe, 19 November) dedicated entirely to prison, including the play *Urge: dietro le sbarre* (*Urgent: Behind Bars*) by A Bergonzoni, followed by the documentary *Meno male è lunedì* (*Thank Goodness it's Monday*) by F Vendemmiati on the return to the world of work of a group of detainees.

---

[44] CBS (2009–) 5th season (2013) aired on Rai 2.
[45] Gianotti (2012) 83.

Analysis

Looking at the data in Table 1, it seems clear that viewers of generalist channels are drawn to Italian dramas and programmes. This may help to reassure those who fear that Italians' opinion and knowledge of law and their attitude to it—in short, their 'legal culture'—to the extent that it is possible to speak of national legal cultures[46]—is forged entirely from the massive importation of legal movies and dramas from foreign countries. Obviously, this is not to deny that American products continue to enjoy great success and provide models for Italian programmes. Nor is it intended to dismiss the effects of foreign series on domestic legal culture. It is however fundamental to recognise the importance of cultural proximity and the products of local cultural industries in the preferences of national audiences.[47]

For example, in our small study, *Squadra Antimafia* and *Una pallottola nel cuore* (*A Bullet in the Heart*) plainly represent continuity, albeit with innovative elements, with two significant and distinctive themes of Italian TV production, the Mafia and the police. The Mafia is everywhere in Italian dramas, and not just in police series. Indeed, by means of this uninterrupted and compelling narrative, Mafia-style criminal organisations are blamed for all the most widespread forms of illegality and injustice in the country, from corruption to drugs, from poor politics to environmental pollution, conversely legitimising and absolving institutions and citizens. Moreover, and this is also true of cinema, it is possible to see a certain tendency to mythologise Mafia bosses, which in the past was avoided[48] but is evident today in series such as *Il capo dei capi* (*Boss of Bosses*, Canale 5, 2007), *Romanzo Criminale* and *Gomorra*.

The most successful police and legal dramas of the last few years indicate that a distinctively Italian way of representing the law has now become consolidated. Whereas Tomeo[49] observed that it was not possible to represent the social distance between the legal system and the citizens without recourse to either comedy or heroism, in more recent times this limited choice has become more nuanced, with more flexible and hybrid narrative styles. We have also seen the arrival of heroes who, following Buonanno[50] could be termed 'mimetic', who exemplify, often with self-deprecation, the characteristics of the common man.

Considering the cop shows, it would be difficult to imitate an absolute hero like Cattani in *La Piovra*. However, the public always love a detective, even one who does not wear a uniform, who instead of a gun uses a psychological magnifying glass to read the miseries of the human soul, as in the very popular series *Don Matteo* (Rai 1, 2000–). There is often a touch of comedy. The backdrop is usually a

---

[46] Nelken (2006), (2012).
[47] See Straubhaar (2007); Buonanno (2008), (2012).
[48] Canova (2011).
[49] Tomeo (1973).
[50] Buonanno (2012).

tightly-knit provincial community (everybody knows each other), where the basic assets of the Italian way of life (the family, the beautiful towns and landscape, good food) help people to face the troubles of everyday life or to resign themselves to them.

Indeed, the series, especially those of the generalist channels, tend to avoid tackling the social and ethical contradictions of the present, even when they provide the inspiration for their plots. They also avoid looking too closely at the police's limits. This avoidance is partly due to the numerous period dramas whose representations of law men contribute to their melodramatic, stereotypical and often exculpatory reading of Italy's recent history. This perpetuates the reassuring and consolatory message of the classic police novel[51] and legal television series in general.[52]

This is exemplified by the evolution of the female figures, which has had variable results.[53] On one hand, gendered stereotypes have not been abandoned; in fact in some ways police dramas have sharpened them. On the other hand, the success of the 'tough heroines' has helped to normalise the idea of women playing a central role, though this may not yet be the case in reality. The optimism inherent in television's current treatment of law and order issues should also be seen in relation to the public's fear of crime: while the Italian news media 'ethnicise' the problem by attributing it mainly to illegal immigrants,[54] Italian television series resolve the problems of ethnic integration by means of anti-discrimination measures and social solidarity, but also via the politically correct and 'charitable' acts of individuals and institutions.

As for lawyers, Italians appear to be better served by television than their American colleagues. Indeed, while in the US television and cinema reflect a process of disillusionment with the profession,[55] and a process of this kind also seems to be happening in British series,[56] in Italian dramas it is the lawyer who is called on to (successfully) tackle delicate social issues such as sexual assault, immigration, violence in prison and miscarriages of justice. In addition, lawyers seem to have the 'gift of judicial ubiquity', since they cover all the roles associated with justice: investigator, defender of the innocent, accuser of the guilty and even judge, given that their version of the facts anticipates or completely replaces the formal ruling or sentence. For this reason, Buonanno is right when she says that Perry Mason still inhabits Italian television.[57]

Regarding the judge, television has seen the gradual eclipse of the 'problematic judge', who laboriously expresses the contradictions of his or her role, in favour of the 'hero judge', with whom those contradictions could never be associated.

---

[51] Andrini (2009).
[52] Villez (2010).
[53] Buonanno (2012), (2014); Giomi (2012).
[54] Binotto and Martino (2005); Maneri (2012).
[55] Leonard (1988); Sherwin (1996); Rafter (2000).
[56] Robson (2007a).
[57] Buonanno (2013) 133.

Almost always the adversary or the martyr of the Mafia, the judge is a lone hero, comforted only by his family, a few friends and his bodyguards, tenaciously searching for the truth in a society that is too often resigned, cynical or corrupt.[58] The TV judge always works within a judicial system in crisis, but the impression is that the issue of how to 'do justice' has become simplified and deprived of significance over the years, mirroring the decline of television's educational function.

In this sense, even the aesthetics of TV-verità and reality-based programmes do nothing to raise the level of realism in the representation of law. The authority of television judges is purely fictional: they apply the norms in force in a ritual manner, transferring them from the legal domain to that of morality and common sense.[59] Partly because of this, even lay figures on television feel justified in 'laying down the law' and issuing rulings and verdicts as if they were judges or jurists, without making any effort to understand the *ratio iuris*.

Prison, despite the rare but praiseworthy attempts by authors and television channels to talk about what happens inside prisons, remains a dark and obscure place, in the sense that the social meaning and cultural significance of punishment is never highlighted or questioned.

In conclusion, it can be argued that the Italian dramas and shows provide a rather poor representation of the procedures and principles underpinning law and justice. Despite the wide-ranging and diversified nature of the programming, very little space is reserved for law in a formal sense: codes, procedures, juridical reasoning. There is little attempt to tackle the complexity of the relations between the legal system and the social system, while the reading of social reality and crime that is offered to the public by means of the people, institutions and rituals of the law as represented on television is excessively black-and-white.

This is not new: the media's representation of law serves its own purposes and is expressed in its own language, leading to oversimplification and manipulation of legal events.[60] But what happens when television's 'juridical weakness' is combined, albeit in a contradictory way, with the juridical weakness of Italian society, ie, with the weakness of the state and the ruling class, the widespread collective and individual lawlessness and the excessively broad discretionary powers of the bureaucracy, to name but a few of the features highlighted by the jurist and constitutional judge Sabino Cassese?[61] In such a context, do the risks of 'Justice out of Court'[62] not become even greater, in turn raising questions for democratic institutions? Does the transformation of crime shows and dramas into 'parallel prosecutors'[63] (in the eyes of the citizens just as legitimate as the real courts if not more so) not increase dissatisfaction with the legal system? Does the policeman

---

[58] On the Italian cultural roots of the 'hero as a martyr', see Montanari (1995).

[59] As noted by Machura (2012) regarding television judges in Germany.

[60] Nobles and Schiff (2000), (2013).

[61] Cassese (2014).

[62] Garapon (1996a), (1996b).

[63] A Grasso, 'Se il talk sui delitti si trasforma in una Procura parallela' *Corriere della sera* (10 November 2014) 47.

who is 'one of us' and the heroic judge *reassure* us regarding the functioning of the institutions or the opposite? That is, by exalting the individual over the procedure, do they not devalue those institutions? Do the foreign examples channelled by compelling and spectacular TV series not seem to be more just and effective than those of the Italian legal tradition, fuelling a widespread but unthinking demand for imitation?[64]

If the argument of this study regarding the current Italian context is plausible, ie, that there is a resonance between representation on television and legal culture, both characterised by poor knowledge of—and disillusionment with—the concept of law, then answering these questions and the many others facing scholars of Law and Television—both in itself and in comparative terms—is a key challenge.

---

[64] To give an example, in the home country of Cesare Beccaria there are those who invoke the return of the death penalty on the model of certain American states in order to deter violent criminals.

12

Poland

ZOFIA ZAWADZKA

TV and its Development in Poland

The Origins of Television and its Development

Poland is proud of its outstanding scientists who contributed significantly to the development of television. In 1878 the Polish researcher Jan Ochorowicz presented a project of long-distance transmitting optic pictures using selenium cells in the periodical *Kosmos*.[1] In January 1884 Paul Nipkow, a technological university student from Lębork in Pomerania, submitted an application for registration of an 'electronic telescope' to the Berlin Patent Office. His idea, consisting of transmitting a picture broken into points of light by a spinning shield with appropriately placed holes, is regarded as the beginning of television and Nipkow himself as the father of television. Another Polish scientist, Jan Szczepanik, together with the Austrian Ludwig Kleinberg, in 1897, submitted to the Patent Office of the United Kingdom, and the following year also to that of the United States, an electric device to reproduce and broadcast images. Another invention in this field was presented to press in 1898 by Kazimierz Prószyński. These projects, however, remained purely theoretical solutions.[2]

Practical solutions emerged in the late-1920s. In 1929 Stefan Manczarski obtained a patent for 'the television broadcast of images through wire and wireless'. From 1935 systematic research work was conducted in the State Telecommunications Institute in Warsaw.[3] Polish television was the result of these works. Poland was one of only a few countries in the world which launched broadcasting regular television programmes with its own television equipment.[4] In 1938 the Experimental Television Station was launched. On 5 October of that year it broadcast the film *Barbara Radziwiłłówna*. At that time there were but only around 10

---

[1] Wajdowicz (1964) 31.
[2] Kozieł (2003) 13–14.
[3] ibid, 14.
[4] Miszczak (1971) 163.

television sets in the whole country.[5] There were plans to start a regular broadcast of a TV programme from 1940 to 1942, but the outbreak of the Second World War thwarted the implementation of those plans.[6]

The first regular broadcast of a television programme was preceded by test broadcasts which started from 17 October 1952. On Saturday 25 October 1952 an inaugural programme was broadcast and since that date a Polish television service can be said to have existed.[7] The first broadcast programme was received through both a television and a radio set because the sound from the TV studio was broadcast by the radio station Warszawa II on medium wave. The audio transmitter was not launched until mid-January 1953 and from that moment on a television set alone was enough to receive a TV programme.[8]

The first regular TV station in Poland commenced broadcasting on 30 April 1956. TV programmes were transmitted on Fridays at 5.00 pm and lasted half-an-hour. The programme was initially watched on 24 imported Leningrad sets with screens measuring 12 by 18 centimetres, which were installed in common rooms and clubs. From 10 November 1954 the broadcasting of programmes still only took place once a week for two hours. On 1 April 1955 the transmission was twice a week: on Tuesdays and Fridays, and from 1955 onwards the joint broadcast time was around 100 hours a month.[9] The frequency of broadcasts was gradually extended until it reached five times a week in May 1956.

Also the number of TV set owners gradually grew. In 1953 the first batch of 80 Leningrad television sets was imported. By 1955 there were already 10,000 of them on sale. At the turn of 1956 the production of the first Polish TV set, Wisła, began and in 1957 the production of a more modern set Belweder commenced. At the end of 1956 more than 20,000 people owned a TV set. The following year obligatory registration of TV sets was introduced and their owners were obliged to pay a subscription.[10] In the period from 1960 to 1965 the number of TV subscribers grew from 425,900 to 1,871,000, which led to a more extensive supply of television sets and growing range of relay stations covering 63% of the area of the country.[11] At the beginning of the 1960s the potential permanent audience (subscribers and members of their households) was estimated as 4 million, with a further 2 million occasional viewers, mainly children. In the late 1960s, when the number of registered sets was 3.5 million, three-quarters of Poles over 15 years of age or 16 million people could sit in front of a TV set at the same time.[12]

On 30 April 1956, a ceremonial opening of the Warsaw Television Centre took place, which inaugurated the era of professional television. During the first decade

[5] Kozieł (2003) 14.
[6] Miszczak (1971) 13.
[7] ibid, 163.
[8] ibid, 164.
[9] ibid.
[10] Kozieł (2003) 20.
[11] ibid, 56.
[12] ibid.

of television in Poland, in the period from 1952 to 1962, studio centres were founded in other Polish cities. They had operated on a transitional and temporary basis until proper television centres were built. The second TV channel started broadcasting on 2 October 1970.[13]

During the first period of television the schedules included mainly theatre and films, which amounted to 80% of airtime. The situation gradually changed. By the end of 1956 television was being broadcast six days a week, four hours a day, of which 25% was filled with features and short films; 17% public affairs and news; 12% dramas; 11% shows for children and young people; while the remaining airtime was dedicated to instructional and educational programmes as well as numerous breaks resulting from technical faults.[14] Relatively soon commercials appeared on Polish television. In August 1956 commercial shows were introduced to the TV schedules, amounting to 15 minutes a week.[15]

It is worth noting that the Committee for Radio 'Polskie Radio', and then from 2 December 1960, the Committee of Radio and Television 'Polskie Radio i Telewizja', were in charge of television, and initially had the status of government departments. Thus, they were an element of the structures of power and, consequently, television was a political arm of the Polish United Workers' Party. Television played three roles: it was a protector of political and ideological purity as well as maintaining Polish culture, along with providing education and entertainment.[16] Television was also an instrument of propaganda and subject to censorship. An ideological message was included not only in news, political and historical programmes but also in numerous artistic programmes through an appropriately selected repertoire of the Television Theatre, films and entertainment programmes addressed at the 'working class'. Local artistic production was favoured over Western shows along with that of 'fraternal socialist countries'.

Until 1989 Polish television operated as a monopoly totally dependent on the state and providing information and propaganda policies determined by the government. In this way television was a politically significant element in the communist system. The information policy was centred on a propaganda function and lacked credibility. Political control and censorship resulted in limited information of international affairs. Nevertheless, it is important to emphasise that the standard of Polish television programmes at that time was high, especially shows of high culture, feature films, series and television theatres.[17]

The change of political system in Poland resulting from the collapse of communism in 1989 started a process of political, economic and social change. Along with democratic reforms many principles and structures found in Western European democratic countries were adopted, including especially the principle of freedom of speech and the mass media system. One of the first legislative acts in Poland

---

[13] Miszczak (1971) 15.
[14] Kozieł (2003) 21.
[15] ibid, 23.
[16] ibid, 7.
[17] Doktorowicz (2011) 42.

after 1989 was the abolition of censorship. On the basis of European models and the principle of the free market, a pluralistic media market was inaugurated. In 1992 legislation on radio and television was enacted, under which a system of public media was established, simultaneously opening the market for commercial broadcasters. Polish public service television emerged as the result of the transformation of state television in the period from 1989 to 1992.

Changes in the way the media operates over recent years stemmed from the rapid development of information technology. Technological developments and easy access to the media produced a great deal of sensationalist broadcasting in place of actual concrete news.[18] Despite this tendency, shows gradually started to appear particularly on private commercial channels, which did have a strong public interest theme.

Nowadays, the position of the public media is very difficult. The fundamental principles, for which they were created, have been lost. This has happened principally because of the takeover of the media by political parties. In addition, there has been a lack of understanding of the media in the Polish political arena. This threatens their very existence. This would be against the rules of the European Union, which requires Member States to provide conditions for public media to operate as protectors of European culture, national cultures and social affairs. This is the issue which is at the heart of the ongoing dispute between the Polish Law and Justice Party's programme of change and the European Commission. The law, which was passed in January 2016 and allows the government significant control over the media in the name of 'supporting traditional Polish values', is thought to pose a 'systemic threat to the rule of law'.[19]

The Right to Broadcast Television Programmes

A comprehensive law which regulates radio and television is the Radio and Television Act of 29 December 1992.[20] The body with responsibility for radio and television is the National Broadcasting Council (NBC, Krajowa Rada Radiofonii i Telewizji). Its job is to protect freedom of speech, the independence of providers of media services and the interests of recipients as well as to ensure open and varied radio and television services.[21]

The right to broadcast television programmes was granted to individuals, legal entities and partnerships on condition of obtaining a licence, which is granted for 10 years by the Chairman of the NBC on the basis of the National Council's resolution. The decision to grant or refuse a licence is final and there is no right

---

[18] Bielawski (2011) 29.
[19] *The Guardian* (12 January 2016): www.theguardian.com/world/2016/jan/12/european-commission-to-debate-polands-cointroversial-new-laws.
[20] Consolidated text: DzU of 2011, No 23, item 226 as amended; (hereafter AR&TV).
[21] Art 6, para 1, AR&TV.

of appeal. The licence may also be withdrawn. A fee is charged for granting the licence for disseminating a television programme and depends on various factors: the method of disseminating the programme; the time of commercials; the number of inhabitants covered by the programme; and the standard of the terrestrial digital television. The licence fee goes to the government.

In accordance with article 36 of the Radio and Television Act, in deciding whether to grant licences, the following factors are taken into account:

— The degree of the compatibility of the intended programme activity with the goals of television.
— The possibility of the applicant financing the service.
— The anticipated share in the shows produced by the broadcaster or on a commission basis, or else produced in cooperation with other broadcasters.
— The anticipated share of shows originally produced in the Polish language and European shows in the television programme service, as well as previous observance of radio communication and mass media regulations.

After looking at these factors, the licence will not be granted if dissemination of programmes by the applicant could result in a threat to the interests of national culture, or if there is any threat to national security or commercially sensitive information, or if the applicant might gain a dominant mass media position in a particular territory.

In the case of television programmes disseminated exclusively using ICT, only an entry into the register of such programmes kept by the Chairman of NBC is required. The register is public and the entry therein takes place on application.

The right to broadcast television programmes without the necessity of gaining a licence or an entry into the register, is granted to the branches of public television which act exclusively as a company wholly owned by the State Treasury, 'Telewizja Polska SA'. There are 16 of these.

Responsibilities of Television and the Content of Programmes

In terms of article 1, paragraph 1of the legislation the tasks of television include:

— Delivering information.
— Sharing values of culture and art.
— Facilitating the use of education, sport and achievements in science.
— Spreading civil education.
— Delivering entertainment.
— Supporting national audiovisual productivity.

In addition, in terms of article 15, broadcasters of television programmes are to allot at least 33% of the quarterly airtime for shows made originally in the Polish language, excluding information services, commercials, telesales, sports broadcasting, text messages and game shows. Moreover, broadcasters are required to dedicate over 50% of the quarterly airtime to European shows, excluding news services, commercials, telesales, sports broadcasting, text messages and game shows. The NBC may, however, determine a lower share in the television schedules, for specialised programmes, where there are not enough shows produced originally in the Polish language and European shows, as well as for programmes disseminated in ICT systems only.

An important task of the radio and television legislation is to provide guidance on the content of shows and other broadcasts.[22] First, they cannot advocate breaking the law, immorality or any actions against the public interest. They are specifically prohibited from hate speech or incitement to hatred or discrimination on the grounds of race, disability, sex, religion or nationality. They cannot support any action threatening health, security or threats to the natural environment. In addition, shows and other broadcasts must respect viewers' religious convictions, in particular the Christian system of values. Minors are particularly protected from the negative influence of television broadcasts. The Act specifies that it is forbidden to disseminate material threatening the physical, mental or moral development of minors, especially anything with pornographic or violent content. There is a watershed. Adult programmes, which contain scenes or content which could have a negative influence on the proper physical, mental or moral development of minors, may be shown between 11.00 pm and 6.00 am only.

Public Television

Public television was tasked with a particular responsibility of accomplishing public service goals. Thus, public television is expected to offer both the whole society, as well as its constituent parts, diverse programming and other services. The news, culture, entertainment, education and sport, must be impartial, balanced and independent, and from a variety of sources. It also should be innovative, of high quality and ethical. The pursuit of these public service goals for public television involves:

1. Creating and disseminating nationwide programmes, regional programmes, programme in the Polish language and other languages for viewers abroad as well as other programmes to meet the democratic, social and cultural needs of local communities.
2. Creating and disseminating those programmes for which a licence has been obtained.
3. Building and using radio and television stations.
4. Disseminating text messages.
5. Working on new technologies of creating and disseminating radio and television programmes.

[22] Art 18.

6. Activity involving production, services and trade connected with audiovisual creativity, including export and import.
7. Supporting artistic, literary and scientific creativity as well as educational and sporting activities.
8. Propagating knowledge about the Polish language.
9. Taking into consideration the needs of national and ethnic minorities as well as communities using a regional language, including broadcasting news programmes in the languages of national and ethnic minorities as well as a regional language.
10. Creating and publishing educational programmes for the Polish diaspora and Poles living abroad.
11. Securing access to programmes and other services for people with visual or hearing disabilities.
12. Propagating media education.

Programmes and other services of public television must also be responsible in their language and protect the good name of public television as well as meet certain requirements concerning the content. Programmes should:

— Honestly show the whole diversity of events at home and abroad.
— Favour free forming of citizens' views and public opinion.
— Enable citizens and their organisations to participate in public life through presenting diverse views as well as exercising the right to control and social criticism.
— Serve the development of culture, science and education, with particular emphasis on Polish intellectual and artistic achievements.
— Respect the Christian system of values, assuming as the foundation the universal principles of ethics.
— Strengthen the family, form pro-health attitudes, propagate sports, media education and combat antisocial activities.

Financing TV in Poland

The public media were founded to be part the structure of a democratic state and they are expected to fulfil tasks defined as public service goals. It is for this reason that in Poland a rule of double financing the public media has been adopted: both from subscription fees and from income from broadcasting commercials.

The income of the company Telewizja Polska SA comes from subscription fees, interests for delay in their payment and penalties for using unregistered television sets, from commercial rights in shows, from commercials and programmes sponsored as well as from other sources. The income of the company may also receive state subsidies. By contrast, commercial stations operate according to the same rules as any other commercial enterprise.

The issue of subscription fees is regulated by the Act of 21 April 2005 on subscription fees.[23] Subscription fees are charged for using radio and television receivers in order to enable the public service goals to be achieved by public radio and television. The Act introduces a presumption that a person who possesses a radio or television receiver capable of immediate reception of the broadcast, and who uses this receiver, consequently is obliged to pay the subscription fee.

Law and Justice on TV in Poland in 2014

Empirical Report

The analysis of programmes broadcast on Polish television in November 2014 covered 33 channels of public and commercial television. The research confirmed that the topic of justice-related material is very popular. There are a considerable number of series and films dedicated to such issues. It seems that, especially looking at series, the subject of justice is most prominent. It is even more popular than the other area frequently encountered: medicine.

In November 2014 the airtime of all films and series presenting problems of the judicial system was 2,325 hours or 96.8 days. Among all the issues, police and detective material enjoys the highest popularity. The airtime of films and series on police and detective material in November 2014 was 2,025.9 hours, or 84.4 days. The second place was occupied by lawyer and court material which in November took 282.3 hours, or 11.7 days. On the other hand, prison and post-prison material attracted the least interest: a mere 17.1 hours over the month.

It is important to note the enormous number of American productions broadcast on Polish TV. Films and series have interesting, gripping plots and unexpected twists and probably this is why they enjoy high viewership and popularity. They are, however, based on a completely different legal system, which affects how the Polish justice system is perceived: both at the stage of investigation and crime detection as well as in a courtroom. Only public television (jointly seven channels under analysis) show mainly series produced in Poland. In the police and detective material category we find eight Polish series and only three American. Moreover, in the lawyer and court-focused category the material broadcast was only Polish: albeit a single title.

The programmes in November 2014 dedicated separately to police and detective material, lawyer and court-focused material, and prison and post-prison material is presented in the three tables below, additionally divided into particular weeks of the month of November; categories of programme: movies and series; and genres: dramas, comedies, reality, reality entertainment and documentaries.

---

[23] Consolidated text: DzU of 2014, item 1204 as amended.

Table 1: Police and detective material on Polish TV

		Dramas	Comedies	Reality	Reality-based Entertainment	Documentaries	
WEEK 1 (3–9 Nov)	Movies	835	1175	0	0	0	2010
	Series	21240	1465	780	0	2410	25895
	Total	**22075**	**2640**	**780**	**0**	**2410**	**27905**
WEEK 2 (10–16 Nov)	Movies	1775	1015	0	0	0	2790
	Series	24030	905	600	0	2300	27835
	Total	**25805**	**1920**	**600**	**0**	**2300**	**30625**
WEEK 3 (17–23 Nov)	Movies	1624	630	0	0	0	2254
	Series	25425	930	780	0	2830	29965
	Total	**27049**	**1560**	**780**	**0**	**2830**	**32219**
WEEK 4 (24–30 Nov)	Movies	1970	700	0	0	0	2670
	Series	24000	1080	720	0	2335	28135
	Total	**25970**	**1780**	**720**	**0**	**2335**	**30805**

Table 2: Lawyer and court focused material on Polish TV

		Dramas	Comedies	Reality	Reality-based Entertainment	Documentaries	
WEEK 1 (3–9 Nov)	Movies	0	0	0	0	0	0
	Series	2300	0	0	1800	0	4100
	Total	**2300**	**0**	**0**	**1800**	**0**	**4100**
WEEK 2 (10–16 Nov)	Movies	0	0	0	0	0	0
	Series	2450	0	0	1320	0	3770
	Total	**2450**	**0**	**0**	**1320**	**0**	**3770**
WEEK 3 (17–23 Nov)	Movies	259	0	0	0	0	259
	Series	1965	0	0	1800	0	3765
	Total	**2224**	**0**	**0**	**1800**	**0**	**4024**
Week 4 (24–30 Nov)	Movies	515	90	0	0	0	605
	Series	2520	120	0	1800	0	4440
	Total	**3035**	**210**	**0**	**1800**	**0**	**5045**

Table 3: Prison and post-prison material on Polish TV

		Dramas	Comedies	Reality	Reality-based Entertainment	Documentaries	
WEEK 1 (3–9 Nov)	Movies	135	0	0	0	0	135
	Series	60	0	0	0	0	60
	Total	195	0	0	0	0	195
WEEK 2 (10–16 Nov)	Movies	145	0	0	0	0	145
	Series	60	0	0	0	0	60
	Total	205	0	0	0	0	205
WEEK 3 (17–23 Nov)	Movies	0	0	0	0	0	0
	Series	60	0	0	0	0	60
	Total	60	0	0	0	0	60
WEEK 4 (24–30 Nov)	Movies	300	0	0	0	210	510
	Series	60	0	0	0	0	60
	Total	360	0	0	0	210	570

Summary and Analysis of the Material

Police and Detective Material

The category of police and detective material includes shows devoted to the activities of police and other law enforcement agencies, detectives, specialised agencies such as FBI or CIA, assisted by coroners and medical examiners.

Polish police and detective material made up 10% of all shows on this matter; 62% were American productions; and 28% other foreign productions. As for police and detective series, Polish ones made up 31%, American 60% (40 different titles) and the remaining, other foreign, mainly German and British, productions a mere 9%. Over the whole month of November 2014 American police and detective series provided 37 hours of material per day. Most of the American series (97%) were dramas.

Within the category of Polish police and detective series it is possible to distinguish 23 titles. The largest group includes dramas, 57%, half of which involved one series: *Ojciec Mateusz* (*Father Mateusz*). Documentary or rather quasi-documentary series constituted 29% of Polish series. Their plots are based on true stories and investigations, though these shows were directed and particular roles were played by actors. Comedies made up 6% of Polish police and detective series: one title *13 posterunek*; reality 8%: also one title *STOP Drogówka*. Reality shows consist of actions carried out by real policemen previously recorded and then edited into the form of an episode.

Significant Emerging Themes

The issues which Polish police and detective series usually embrace involve problems which are not characterised by any special theme. They show offences ranging from murders to petty thefts. It is, however, worth noting that, from time to time, in single episodes, problems of greater importance are touched upon, these being, for example, racial, ethnic or religious discrimination. It seems that it is the response of producers and creators of series to certain events that can be observed in Polish life. There is inevitably a time delay because of the necessity of preparing the script. Series are expected to play an educational role aiming at changing social attitudes and behaviour. It is particularly noticeable in the Polish series *Ojciec Mateusz* produced on the commission of the public television channel TVP1. This series illustrates the implementation of the public service goals imposed on television of conducting media education and forming public opinion through creating proper social attitudes. The characteristic theme—being also a kind of novelty—is stalking. It is an offence which has been punishable since June 2011 under the Polish Criminal Code and which is finding its way into Polish TV series.

Lawyer and Court-Focused Material

Over the whole month of November 2014 television showed six lawyer and court films, of which one was a Polish production, one foreign other than American, and the remaining four came from the US.

Furthermore, the ratio of Polish lawyer and court-focused series to American series shows an advantage of the home-produced material. In November 2014 television broadcast 142 hours of Polish series and 126 hours of American series. This difference is a result of the greater number of reality entertainment shows (112 hours out of a total of 142 hours). There are, however, only two titles: *Sędzia Anna Maria Wesołowska* (2006–11) (*Judge Anna Maria Wesołowska*) and *Sąd rodzinny* (2008–11) (*Family Court*). As for drama, in November 2014, 28 hours of Polish series were broadcast and they were mostly two titles: *Magda M* and *Prawo Agaty* (*Agata's Right*). At the same time there were five times as many American dramas. What is worth noting is the fact that besides American series, there were no other foreign productions.

Significant Emerging Themes

As far as Polish lawyer and court series are concerned, one can observe a greater variety of themes and references to socially important or morally ambiguous issues. Besides the subjects which can be called ordinary, connected with drug-related crimes, building accidents, human trafficking and family affairs, there also appeared important social problems. A good example of this was the plot of one episode of a series. Here, a parent applied to court for the consent to a blood trans-fusion for a minor child in the situation where the other of the parents, a Jehovah's witness, refused to give consent on the grounds of religion. Another important issue, from the perspective of a Polish society with strongly conservative views, was a long-time partner's demanding before the court the right to bury his late partner. In terms of Polish law this right is granted to the immediate family only. This is important inasmuch as the theme of homosexual relationships and grant-ing partners certain rights is not often undertaken in Polish productions and tends to be avoided. Another significant theme that runs through several consecutive episodes of some series is the issue of corruption in various institutions, especially in the courts, the health service or business. It seems that they reflect the corrup-tion encountered in the media.

Prison and Post-Prison Material

Prison and post-prison material encompassed one American series *Prison Break*, one Polish documentary and three American movies: *Escape from Alcatraz*, *The Shawshank Redemption* and *Stone* with Robert De Niro playing the main character.

Law, Crime and Justice on Polish Television

The first Polish crime series *Kapitan Sowa na tropie* (*Captain Sowa on the Trail*) had its premiere on Christmas Day 1965.[24] Ten years later, in autumn 1976, came the premiere of what was advertised as a Polish version of *The Saint*, the series *07 zgłoś się* (*07 Come In*). During the years from 1976 to 1987 three seasons of this series were produced.[25]

After the events of 1989, the first good crime series, Ekstradycja (*Extradition*) did not appear until 1995 and showed a chief constable who struggled single-handedly with a drug trafficking gang and in the subsequent seasons with the Russian Mafia and corruption at the highest level of power.[26] The plot of the first Polish crime series was also based on the character of an amateur detec-tive, usually a reporter, who conducted his own investigation (eg, the series *SOS*, (*S.O.S.*)1974; and *Życie na gorąco*, (*Life Heated*) 1979). There appeared also a

---

[24] Wajda (2005) 247.
[25] ibid, 247–48.
[26] ibid, 248–49.

first series with a courtroom lawyer/barrister as a main character, who proved the innocence of his clients pointing at the real criminals (the series *Zdaniem obrony* (*According to Defence*) 1984–86).[27] Crime series also referred to the inter-war period (eg, *Temida*, (*Themis*) 1985–87; *Na kłopoty ... Bednarski*, (*For Trouble ... Bednarski*) 1986–88).

After 2000, new series appeared, as a result of competition between particular TV stations. Some of them were foreign series. Some were Polish series under foreign licence (eg, the series *Tak czy nie?* (*Yes or No?*) 2003 under Swedish licence) whilst others were Polish productions (eg, *Fala zbrodni*, (*Outbreak of Crimes*) 2003–05).

New formats also appeared, for example, a crime-documentary series *W11—wydział śledczy* (*W11—Investigation Department*), in which real policemen investigate staged crimes. The format of these series is similar to reality shows but with a flagrant 'lack of naturalness and inept acting'.[28] The series *Kryminalni* (*The Criminal Investigators*) (2004–08) enjoyed great success. Each part involved a separate puzzle to be solved. Also series such as *Glina (The Cop)* (2004) and *Oficer* (*The Officer*) (2004–05), produced by film directors, had good casts and interesting scripts.

In the lawyer and court-focused category the way was prepared by American series, especially the series *Ally McBeal* (1997–2002) which enjoyed high viewing figures. The dominance of American series on Polish television distorted the way society perceives the operation of justice in Poland. The Polish legal system based on the system of statutory codes differs considerably from the common law system based on precedent, where the lawyer's expertise thereupon often determines the court's decision. This gives a wide range of possibilities to the screenwriter.

There were attempts at changing this situation through reality entertainment series *Sędzia Anna Maria Wesołowska* and *Sąd rodzinny* set in a courtroom with all procedures and conventions adopted by Polish courts on a daily basis, and adaptation of authentic court proceedings.

What strikes any observer of these Polish series relating to law and justice is the stereotyping of certain occupations: police, courtroom lawyers/barristers and public prosecutors. Policemen are presented in Polish series in two ways: either as professionals and fearless tough guys, or as losers, helpless people, often obese who make sense of the disclosed facts rather slowly. The former way of presenting an image of policemen is similar to the image of the police in American police and detective series. American series present intriguing criminal puzzles, swift-paced actions and interesting main characters. In addition, series characters have the most up to date forensic equipment, which allows them to establish the culprit and to work out a particular case within a few days on the basis of a drop of blood,

---

[27] ibid, 249.
[28] ibid, 253.

a part of a hair, or a shoe imprint from the crime scene. A similar way of present-ing the actions of the police is sometimes adopted by Polish crime series, affecting (unfortunately erroneously) public images concerning criminal proceedings. This leads to a clash between our view of the police's actions developed on the basis of the television compared with reality. The high viewership of crime series, none-theless, leads to creating a positive image of police.

Another model, presenting policemen as losers, seems more frequent and is presented not only in comedy series but also in dramas. The character of a police-man is created as an image of a middle-aged man with a belly, not very fit, and, in addition, with low intellectual potential. The main characters, policemen, are empty-headed, lost and awkward. They have to be pushed in to every action with an additional impulse to act. The police often need help from outside. As an exam-ple we can point at the series *Ojciec Mateusz* produced on commission of the pub-lic television channel TVP1, based on a cult Italian format *Don Matteo*. In Poland the series is set in Sandomierz and its surroundings. Each episode tells a separate story, which is unravelled with the help of the title character, Father Mateusz who possesses a unique detective talent. It is Father Mateusz's assistance that renders the actions of the police effective.

In Polish lawyer and court series major roles are played by women. It is they who are the main characters of series. Female barristers in series are sensitive to human needs and problems, empathic, understanding and compassionate. The female lawyers, however, are women of different temperaments and pri-orities. What they have in common, nevertheless, is that men always stay in the shadow of women in gowns. The first Polish shows presenting barrister's work was *Magda M* (2005–07). The series showed the world young and educated law-yers who, though focused on pursuing their personal ambitions, notice that life is not confined to a professional career and financial success. The title character, Magda Miłowicz is a single lawyer in her thirties, who is successful in the court-room but in her private life she experiences ups and downs in love, longing for the love of her life—a fellow lawyer. The series shows a wide range of issues, characters and social problems, but at its heart there are the emotional conflicts of the main characters: two barristers.

Magda's successor, Agata Przybysz, is a heroine of the show *Prawo Agaty* (2012–). She is representative of a new generation of female lawyers: strong, funny, inde-pendent, consistent and firm. The creators of the series managed to find interest-ing court cases, in which the title character is not always successful. In contrast to the heroine of the show *Magda M*, Agata is dedicated to her job and career, as a result of which her private life recedes into the background. It is not until the next season that the main character begins struggle with her private problems: becomes pregnant and due to this fact becomes more emotional.

On the other hand, the role of the 'manipulative female' in Polish productions is usually assigned to public prosecutors, also played by women. Such a figure is

Public Prosecutor Maria Okońska in the show *Prawo Agaty*, cold Laura Curyło in the show *O mnie się nie martw* (*Don't Worry About Me*), or Public Prosecutor Iga Dobosz in the series *Wataha* (*The Border*). The female prosecutor comes across as being under control and perfectly prepared. Her goal is always to lead to conviction.

13

Spain

ANJA LOUIS

Introduction

A central mechanism through which law rules is popular culture. Most people learn what they know (or think they know) about law from popular culture, often without realising they are receiving a popular legal education.[1] Both law and visual culture are dominant discourses constituting an imagined community, which creates meaning through storytelling and performance. As will become clear in the following survey of television law shows in Spain, all shows invite a judgemental viewing process and encourage their viewers to participate actively in finding justice.[2] Televisual judgement offers jurisprudential commentary of its on-screen legal system.

Analysis of the on-screen construction of law will focus on a few key issues: gender, sexual orientation, corruption, justice and popular legal education. The latter is particularly interesting in the context of Spain, since the medium was used as a means of propaganda (1956–75), as a primary educator of democratic values (1975–89) and as creator of a social debate (1990 onwards).[3] If we consider television one of the most influential agents of value construction, then law shows can be considered a powerful tool to guide viewers through the moral climate of their time. TV shows of the 1980s, in particular, are often referred to as 'mythical', attesting not only to their nostalgic value, but also to the importance of a collective process of 'working through' social issues.[4] Furthermore, TV consumption is key to socialisation, providing collective memories and generational identities.

---

[1] See Macaulay (1987); Friedman (1989); and Sherwin (2000).
[2] Silbey (2001).
[3] See Palacio (2006).
[4] For further details on the concept of 'working through', see Ellis (1982).

Television in Spain

Television in Spain was launched relatively late compared with its European counterparts: on 28 October 1956 TVE (Televisión Española) broadcast its first programmes. Television bore witness to a fast-changing society from dictatorship
to democracy and has been an important means of political, social and moral
education. In the first phase TVE, the public television monopoly, was part of the
state apparatus without independent legal status and dictated by 'an erratic yet
tangible' censorship.[5] This mouthpiece of the government had two prime functions: reinforcing social and moral values at a symbolic level; and keeping the
population obedient, ignorant of politics, while entertained through sport and
popular imports.[6] From the mid-1960s onwards, however, the failure of separate
economic development led the Franco Regime to implement a new economic
policy, based on the creation of a market economy and the liberalisation of trade
and foreign investment. Ideologically driven publicity campaigns represented the
new lifestyles of the 1960s and hegemonic values of urban life, as Spanish society
was moving from a rural to an industrialised consumer society. Between 1965 and
1975 Spain witnessed a dictatorship 'where its citizen's lack of freedom ran parallel
to the initial creation of a mass-consumer society'.[7]

Since Franco's death in 1975 television has reinvented itself in a continuous process. The democratic project of the transition, enacted by the 1978 Constitution,[8]
ensured the rule of law and basic human rights. Shortly thereafter, the fundamental role of television was first defined in the Statute of Radio and Television (1980)
which confirmed the role of RTVE (Radio Televisión Española) as a state-run,
essential public service maintaining the constitutionally enshrined political values
of pluralism, freedom of speech and information, including education, linguistic
and cultural diversity.[9] Guaranteed objectivity, while ensuring a balanced democratic debate, and access to different genres of programming to satisfy the wid-
est audience, were also stipulated. However, given that the state had the power
to allocate broadcasting rights, appoint the board and director general of RTVE,
the information was hardly ever unbiased. The hybrid financial model—unique
in Europe—blends government subsidies and advertising revenues; to this day
there is no TV licensing system.[10] By 1983 the socialist government under Felipe
González promoted the constitutionally enshrined principle of regionalism in

---

[5] Palacio (2006) 16.
[6] See Palacio (2005).
[7] For an excellent article on early Spanish television, see Palacio (2005).
[8] Spanish Constitution (1978).
[9] Ley 4/1980, de 10 de enero, de Estatuto de la Radio y la Televisión (1980).
[10] See Brevini (2013) 78, where she argues that 'the total subordination of PSB in Spain to the
advertising industry and the absence of a cultural policy for public television ... has given rise to the
extreme commercialization of TVE'.

the Third Channel Law (1983)[11] which permitted the *autonomías* (self-governing regions) to each establish their own publicly funded channel to provide services in other languages (Basque, Catalan, Galician). Shortly thereafter, still under socialist leadership, Spain received a Private TV Law (1988)[12] which regulated the establishment of Antena 3, Telecinco and its first subscription broadcaster CanalPlus. These private channels finance themselves exclusively from advertising revenues.

In 2006 the socialist Zapatero Government radically reformed public television in an attempt to reorganise its structures and model of funding that enables it to fulfil its public service function. Public television was still accountable to Parliament, but would also be overseen by an independent audiovisual authority assuring TVE's independence, neutrality and objectivity. The Corporation still had many of the duties laid down in the original 1980 law.[13] For TVE the competition with other channels resulted in both a financial crisis (due to lost advertising revenue) and loss of audience share: from 1990 to 2006 TVE1's share decreased from 52% to 18.2%.[14] The battle for audience share, then, is split into four broadly equal rivals: TVE1, FORTA (the consortium of subsidised regional channels), Antena 3 and Telecinco.[15] Finally, in 2010 a General Act on Audiovisual Communication was approved.[16] This takes cultural and linguistic diversity (Article 5) further, in that it requires television service providers to allocate at least 51% of their annual broadcasting time to European productions (50% in any of the co-official languages) and apportions at least 5% of the total revenue to pre-financing the production of European films.[17]

Historical Overview

Police Dramas

Police dramas are without doubt one of the most important genres on television, both in representing social issues and reflecting ideological changes. The public perception of the preservation of order in a country haunted by fascism makes the viewing of crime dramas in Spain interestingly ambivalent. Viewer reception is influenced by both cognition and affect, just as justice is often guided by reason

---

[11] Ley 46/1983, de 26 de diciembre, reguladora del Tercer Canal de Televisión (1983).

[12] Ley 10/1988, de 3 de mayo, de Televisión Privada (1988).

[13] See *Compendium: Cultural Policies and Trends in Europe* (2014), where it states that TVE had to promote: 'territorial cohesion; linguistic and cultural diversity; social integration of minorities; knowledge of the arts, science, history and culture. Furthermore, it has an obligation to develop multimedia material in the languages of Spain, as a contribution to the development of Spanish and European culture industries'.

[14] Brevini (2013) 78.

[15] Contreras and Palacio (2001) 91.

[16] General Act on Audiovisual Communication (7/2010 Act).

[17] *Compendium: Cultural Policies and Trends in Europe* (2014).

and emotion. Noticeable shifts occur between each of the noted phases: in phase one there are non-political crimes during the dictatorship; in phase two one of the mythical police dramas, *Central Brigade*, deals with the clash of the old and new Spain in the transition to democracy; while phase three, when crime drama is at its peak, gives us a large variety of different formats, genres and subject matters. Some themes are so universal that they are represented in all police dramas: corruption and the abuse of police power. Although quantitatively more prevalent in recent shows, there is enough evidence in *Central Brigade* to suggest that it is an ongoing issue that haunts every police force. The structure of crime dramas usually keeps to the classic 5-part structure: opening hook, exposition, obstacles, resolution and final catch/cliffhanger.[18] In order to differentiate between studio-shot sitcoms and action-based crime dramas, the latter often display a series of production practices: sophisticated plotlines, multiple locations and special effects.[19] Production practices become increasingly sophisticated over the three phases of television history. The typical array of police characters ranges from macho men, sticklers for procedure, sensitive cops, to the joker and corrupt cops; there is something for everyone in the viewer identification process. In all quality drama shows continuing narrative threads in the subplots lend regular characters unexpected traits and make them fully rounded individuals. The mix of narrative strands usually combines deep-level plotlines and surface stories that are concluded by the end of the episode. These patterns of repetitiveness inscribe themselves in our memory after only a few viewings and give us a sense of connection and continuity. Staple scenes at the police station and exterior locations for the public duty of law enforcement are intertwined with scenes in the local bar (where Spanish co-workers socialise daily) and police officers' private flats. Every show deals differently with the distribution of public and private locations, depending on how much the private lives are an integral part of the storytelling.

Brigada Central (1989–92, TVE)

Brigada central/Central Brigade (1989–92), is an iconic police show directed by Pedro Masó, starring Imanol Arias and depicting an elite police squad dealing with organised crime. Comisario Manuel Flores (Imanol Arias) is of gypsy origin, a maverick with existential angst. He positions himself in an intercultural space par excellence: both rejecting his cultural heritage while also deliberately ignoring the methods of an old-fashioned and fascist police system. His moral ostracism and bohemian lifestyle are reminiscent of Ramón, the left-wing lawyer, in *Wedding Rings* (see below). Yet unlike Ramón, who is highly critical of the law, Flores never questions the law or fails to enforce it. He and his fellow officers display high moral standards, particularly juxtaposed to corrupt police officers. In almost every episode corrupt colleagues are eliminated, while our heroes fight on despite huge

---

[18] Smith (2007) 63.
[19] Barroso García (2002) 294–95.

personal sacrifice, thus clearly demonstrating the gulf between moral rectitude and the corrupt system of the past.

Petra Delicado (1999, Telecinco)

Petra Delicado is the first female superintendent.[20] Attractive and self-confident Delicado (Ana Belén) is a complex representation of a career woman and, as her name suggests, she is both strong and delicate in everything she does. Sensitive in her manner of solving cases, she can also be harsh, stern and decisive in the rough macho world of a police station. Her unconventional methods are notorious. Every episode has its fair share of complications and obstacles that Delicado and her assistant Sergeant Garzón (Santiago Segura) have to overcome. In the course of the series she starts a romantic relationship with Garzón which gets increasingly complicated as their private and professional lives overlap.

El comisario/The Superintendent (1999–2009, Telecinco)

By 1999 Spanish TV drama was at a peak. This was partly due to the competitive market of private networks, which produced groundbreaking local dramas. Two of these groundbreaking shows were police dramas which tried to achieve a cultural immediacy that only home-produced shows can render. Both shows (*The Superintendent* and *Policías*) had consultants from the National Police Agency to help them with legal procedures and police jargon, which resulted in public acknowledgement from the Agency in recognition of the contribution to its public image. Spain had come a long way from being a police state to a country in which the police were respected and it seems that these cultural constructions, particularly in *The Superintendent*, played a part in that.

The long-running *The Superintendent* is set in the small fictitious police station of San Fernando, Madrid. Comisario Castilla (Tito Valverde) and his officers handle a vast array of cases, which—Telecinco claims—are based on true stories; they are certainly about contemporary social issues: sexual harassment, street violence, drugs, violence in old people's homes, human trafficking, Latin American crime gangs, and property speculation.[21] The implicit values and politics of the show are liberal (due process, individual rights and rehabilitation). But unlike any of the other police shows before or after *The Superintendent*, the representation is based on normal daily life in the police force of a liberal European democracy. What is most striking in *The Superintendent* is the likeability of the police officers. Charlie and Pope, the two main inspectors solving any given case, are dressed so casually that they seem a pair of punks. Their casual dress sense makes them visually immediately identifiable as personifying liberal politics. They straddle the difficult

---

[20] The TV series is based on the novels of Alicia Giménez Bartlett, one of Spain's most popular crime writers.

[21] For excellent close readings of *The Superintendent* and *Policías*, see Smith (2007).

lines between the law, private moral dilemmas and public operation of justice. This goes hand in hand with the amount of screen time given to the private issues of the officers. Not only does it render them into human beings with almost as many problems as their suspects, but it also explains their liberal approach to law enforcement. To take a few examples at random: Pope dates a prostitute; the son of a police officer hangs out with drug dealers; the comisario's love interest is a female judge, and his daughter is critically injured in an explosion aimed at him. These relationships are a high-wire act, but the officers always err on the side of (liberal definitions of) justice. This is mirrored in an 'intimate televisual style and a sensibility based on affect [...] and the dignity of the individual'.[22] It is also reinforced in staple scenes in the reception area of the very busy police station mixing the main case with casual perpetrators of minor misdemeanours. Even in those minor scenes we are made aware of its subtly liberal politics, and no viewer would mind ending up in the police station of San Fernando.

Policías, en el corazón de la calle/Police on the Street (2000–03, Antena 3)

One of the most popular,[23] if short-lived, crime series, *Police on the Street* is set in a police station in Madrid. Arguably one of the most important, and action-packed, Spanish quality police dramas, the show is run by towering Chief Superintendent Héctor Ferrer (Josep Maria Pou).[24] The format of each season relies on a prime antagonist combined with several secondary plotlines; recurrent themes include police corruption and antisocial personality disorders. Although *Policías* is billed as dealing with the private lives of the police officers, this is less prominent than in other dramas (*The Superintendent, Paco's Men*). Instead we get a fair share of action in exterior locations; and our heroes routinely risk their lives in the line of duty. As in *Central Brigade*, the personal sacrifice is huge, which is particularly developed in the Carlos Gándara storyline, whose own life and that of his loved ones is endangered regularly. The world view is conservative: law enforcement as maintaining the social order, yet without the moral absolutism of a blockbuster film; thanks to the scriptwriters the baddies usually have redeeming features and the police officers are not exactly saints. Women are conspicuous by their absence, the main female police officer, feisty Lucía Ramos, was killed off after the first series. Although all the episodes' titles are lines from poems recited by one of the police officers in each episode, there is nothing particularly poetic about the series. Police work is represented as gloomy and intense; action scenes are frequently filmed with a shoulder-held camera. Both the aesthetics and the fast-paced narratives convey the frenetic environment of the police on the beat. A recurring feature adding cultural immediacy involves scenes in their local bar, where well-known pop groups play gigs (Amaral, Café Quijano, Fangoria).

---

[22] Smith (2007) 55.
[23] See viewers' comments on the 'Transgresión continua' blog.
[24] Pou was regularly nominated for best actor awards for the role.

Los hombres de Paco (2005–10, Antena 3) Paco's Men

Los hombres de Paco/Paco's Men is one of the most successful crime comedies in Spain. It is set in San Antonio, a fictitious underprivileged neighbourhood in Madrid, where the police station is run by Comisario Lorenzo Castro Riquelme (Juan Diego), who thinks little of his chaotic colleagues—the archetypal angry superintendent who is constantly dismayed by his staff's mediocrity. Inspector Paco Miranda Ramos and 'his men' have a haphazard and surreal way of solving crimes; in fact, the solution of the crime is often by accident rather than design. Police procedures are not followed; interrogations are controlled by the suspects rather than the investigating officers; police officers are scared of their prisoners— a perfect caricature of the national police. Webs of relationships are taken to an extreme, mocking the stereotype of nepotism. *Paco's Men* is an excellent example of a professional dramatic comedy, set in the workplace, but full of personal melodramatic narratives. As is customary in a dramatic comedy, melodramatic elements seamlessly meld into humorous scenes to rescue the viewer from too much emotional turmoil. One staple of creating humour is the constant meddling in other people's affairs, and here humour and melodrama are beautifully intertwined.

Serious issues are brought in casually and allow for the treatment of social issues in a light-hearted context. *Paco's Men* is particularly noted for its treatment of homosexuality. In the second series Quique, one of the police officers, is 'helped' in the process of coming out. Despite farcical exaggeration the viewer learns about cultural sensitivity, namely how very difficult both sides find this: the coming out in a macho environment and the genuine acceptance of such an act. In a magnificent scene (season 2, episode 5) in the changing room (the interspace between public and private), a straight cop starts dancing provocatively to a Boney M song with the genuine intention of declaring his acceptance of gay culture. Quique is delighted and both put on an *impromptu* gay strip show. In seasons six to eight *Paco's Men* found international fame with its storyline of a lesbian relationship and marriage between officer Pepa Miranda Ramos, Paco's sister, and forensic scientist Silvia Castro León, Don Lorenzo's daughter. When Silvia was assassinated in season eight, such was the outcry that there was an international campaign in more than 50 countries to save the character from being killed off.[25]

Los misterios de Laura/The Mysteries of Laura (2009–, TVE)

The Mysteries of Laura is a wonderfully light-hearted crime comedy with Spanish humour at its best. Laura Lebrel[26] (María Pujalte), a police officer with a chaotic life and absent-minded personality does not seem intelligent enough to solve crimes. Yet despite her inimitable scatterbrained style Laura solves each

---

[25] For further details, see Ramos Pérez and Fernández Casadevante (2012).
[26] Lebrel means hound in Spanish.

mystery with Sherlock Holmes-style attention to detail. Relationships loom large in this series, both professional and private, and give it the feel of a family drama. Martín Maresca (Oriol Tarrasól) is Laura's sidekick, 10 years her junior, an eternal charmer, who deeply cares about his boss and might even be in love with her. The fact that the immediate superior is her ex-husband (Fernando Guillén Cuervo) complicates matters of office politics. Laura's main antagonist, Lydia Martínez, is the exact opposite of our heroine: she is methodical, analytical and relies on scientific evidence. Laura relies on sheer intuition to get through the vicissitudes of their cases, but the light bulb moment—which leads to the most unlikely link of seemingly spurious evidence—is usually brought about by an off-the-record conversation between mother and daughter while both women cook dinner. Female intuition is literally written into the format, both in the form of professional success as well as a source for ridicule. Yet identity construction is also achieved through comparison: cold, intelligent and scientific Lydia should be the winner of all unspoken professional duels with Laura, but very much to our pleasure she is not. Intuition and old-style detective work win over reason and modern forensic science. However, Laura has always found her master in her incomparable mother, for it is she who always drives the detective work forward. The mother's function is that of an innocent bystander outside the police station, who approaches the mystery with nosy nonchalance and is, thus, the closest to the viewer's own position, when we watch the series trying to guess what is going to happen next. The prize-winning series was premiered on 27 July 2009 and was an instant success. Italy, Russia, Holland and most recently, the American network NBC adapted the series.

Lawyer Shows

Spanish television can boast some excellent lawyer shows. A popular legal education is more obviously present than in crime shows; viewer reception is influenced by both reason and emotion. The nature of justice is an overarching question running through all shows, as is the lawyers' behaviour, which is judged by us with a mixture of reason and emotion. Furthermore, the judicial system is on trial when delivering doubtful forms of justice. Noticeable shifts occur in the representation of gender, sexual orientation and popular legal education, dealt with in more detail below. Lola in *Wedding Rings* is a career woman without any feminist agenda; Eva in *Public Defender* is politically feminist and socialist, while Mapi in the second series of *Public Defender* is a bossy corporate lawyer who happens to be a woman. By the 2000s there is wide variety of female lawyer roles. Sexual orientation is discussed in *Wedding Rings*, while more convincingly foregrounded at case and collegial level in *Public Defender 2*. The popular legal education moves from the quasi 'educational shows' of the 1980s to a more subtle education in the public debate of social issues in the 2000s. The structure of lawyer shows usually keeps to the classic five-part structure. Staple scenes take place in the lawyer's offices, the courtroom, at the local bar and in the characters' private spaces. The typical array of lawyers ranges from rookie lawyers, veteran partners, idealist heroes and corruptible villains, and anything in between to allow for more complex characters; there is something for everyone in the viewer identification process. The shows usually focus on the private lives of the lawyers to lend them a multitude of traits; as in crime shows the unresolved private stories give us a sense of continuity. Office politics are prevalent themes in all shows, often involving a love triangle between colleagues and/or jealous rivalries that complicate the work environment.

The Mythical 1980s

The process of democratisation during the transition from dictatorship to democracy rested very much on the shoulders of a new generation. What better way to celebrate lawyers than with series set in one of the most challenging times of recent Spanish history, in which democracy was in the making and law was instrumental, both real and imagined, in major social changes of the time. The TV shows *Wedding Rings* (1984) and *Public Defender* (1986) convincingly capture this *Zeitgeist* of change. They represent stories of hero lawyers as personifications of progress and active agents of social change. Television was used to erode Francoist values; the pedagogical value of television shows was exploited when democracy needed to be imagined and democratic values taught through narratives of private lives.

Anillos de oro/Wedding Rings (1984, TVE)[27]

In this highly acclaimed and award-winning TV show Lola Martínez Luque (Ana Diosdado) and Ramón San Juan (Imanol Arias) specialise in divorce cases. The focus on divorce attests to the anxiety about the breakdown of marriages and their consequences for the family as the most basic structural unit of society. Law, however, is conspicuous by its absence. Lola's bourgeois family life and Ramón's bohemian lifestyle feature heavily in each episode making their own private lives a case study and an integral part of the ongoing debate about divorce. The series uses an assortment of cases as a careful mix of injustices in which neither gender is blamed for their supposedly egotistical desires of filing for divorce. In each case, the viewer empathises with the spouse who wishes to leave, and this empathy—through storytelling—gives the viewer indirect educational value. Personalised emotive accounts of claimants lend themselves to melodramatic narratives of family life and law. Arguably, cultural narratives are in conflict in the Lola character: she can be read as vacillating between a self-confident mother-of-three/divorce lawyer

---

[27] For a close reading of *Wedding Rings*, see Louis (2012).

superwoman and a middle-aged back-to-work-type mum, constantly on the verge of a nervous breakdown. *Wedding Rings* is also the first lawyer show to deal openly with homosexuality, but given the historical time, the issue is marriage as a cover-up for homosexuality, so the exact opposite of coming out.

Turno de oficio/Public Defender (Season 1: 1986, TVE)

Another excellent case study is *Public Defender*. Three hero lawyers who take it in turns to fight for justice: the veteran Juan Luis Funes (Juan Galiardo), the rookie Cosme Fernández (Juan Echanove) and the feminist Eva García (Carmen Elías). The cases are anything from petty crimes of the socially disadvantaged to medical negligence, rape, domestic violence, and miscarriages of justice. The cases are not particularly well developed, we learn more from the three lawyers' conversations with each other than through an analysis of the cases. Particularly in the conversations between Cosme (who is a child of democracy) and Funes (who had seen how law was perverted under Franco) the viewers learn about the usefulness of a public defender's role, and basic legal concepts (habeas corpus, the presumption of innocence, due process, individual rights). All these conversations run through the series like a jurisprudential commentary of its on-screen legal system. The cognitive viewing process, then, is two-fold at the level of law: popular jurisprudence as well as receiving a popular legal education, as the viewer follows the cases' storylines week after week.

There are a sufficient number of scenes to give it a legal aesthetic, but staple scenes also take place in the lawyers' flats and, above all, in bars and restaurants. Private lives make them fully rounded characters, particularly when these social justice lawyers of the first hours of democracy themselves are in trouble with the law. Various Francoist voices also run through the series like an ongoing political commentary, reminding us that not everybody sees the point of public defenders, legal representation and the right to a fair trial. *Public Defender* invites the viewer to take sides on the (social) justice spectrum from conservative 'law and order' to a more liberal approach of a democracy based on basic human rights for offenders and their rehabilitation. It is in cases with overpowering feelings of disgust that the legal system is most tested, and where the contemporary viewers' political colours are likely to emerge. As is customary with feminist issues, these are dealt with at two levels: within the cases covered as well as the public performance and private life of the female lawyer. Eva García is young, self-confident and outspokenly feminist. Despite being an excellent lawyer she suffers the macho treatment of her colleagues and clients. She is idealistic about the new Spain and cares deeply for her clients, be it in domestic violence cases or miscarriages of justice; the judges commend her for her tenacity and remind us of the importance of a liberal legal system—a pertinent reminder that Franco's subjects did not expect law to deliver justice.

Turno de oficio (diez años después)/Public Defender (Ten Years Later) (1996, TVE)

Due to its huge success the show returns 10 years' later: Funes, even older and now clearly alcohol dependent, is sidelined by his colleagues as well as the narrative, and serves more as a wise guy in the background. The main storyline is driven by Cosme, who returns to Madrid as a *juez instructor*[28] and becomes a 'judge-cum-detective'. His passion for social justice has not changed and in the careful questioning of the numerous suspects he is always at pains not only to find the truth but also to treat the criminals with the utmost respect. Staple scenes are set in his office when he interrogates the suspects with his inimitable teddy-bear approach. Crimes range from drug-related crimes, juvenile delinquency and hate crimes against homosexuals, to international law around asylum seekers and the international drugs trade. The murder of a homosexual is mirrored in a subplot (episode 4), when Cosme realises that his forensic specialist is gay. Cosme's non-judgemental attitude towards gays personifies blind justice and has the signalling function of liberal politics amongst his colleagues. One ongoing narrative thread is the corruption not only in the police force but also amongst judges. His incorruptibility makes him likeable in his fight for (social) justice and against corruption. Here he clashes with Funes, who is initially delighted to have direct access to a judge to further his own cases, only to find that he had underestimated his friend's rectitude. Nevertheless, they remain friends and still incessantly talk about law, whisky and women.

Eva García's storyline brings in a very international dimension: she returns to Madrid after 10 years as a human rights lawyer in El Salvador. Completely burnt out, all the old-time feminist wants is to get married. Little is left of her feminism or human rights lawyering. This is juxtaposed with Mapi, who represents female lawyers of the mid-1990s. She is young, middle class, careerist and money driven. What she lacks in legal skills, she makes up for in her fervour to teach old lawyers new tricks; and predictably falls in love with her boss Funes. What then is the representation of lawyers in the 1996 version of *Public Defender*? Neither Mapi nor Eva are particularly inspiring role models for lawyers, yet neither is Funes with his alcoholism and dubious desire to corrupt his best friend, the judge. Long gone are the idealist days of the young democracy that was Spain in the 1980s. Only Cosme still fights crime and a corrupt legal system with quixotic stubbornness.

Al filo de la ley/At the Edge of Law (2005, RTVE)

One year after José Luis Rodríguez Zapatero (PSOE—Spanish Socialist Workers' Party) was elected Prime Minister, TVE launched one of the most interesting law

---

[28] The investigating judge is different from the judge conducting the public hearing, the former having wide powers to clarify the circumstances of an offence; see Merino-Blanco (1996) 174.

shows in recent history. *At the Edge of Law* is set in the law firm Álvarez & Associates in Madrid. The senior partner, Gonzalo Álvarez (Emilio Gutiérrez Caba), has a young and dynamic team consisting of the handsome Álex Villar (Leonardo Sbaraglia), his girlfriend Patricia Muñoz (Fanny Gautier) and his ex-girlfriend Elena Castro (Natalia Verbeke)—a triangle full of sexual tension that keeps us entertained throughout the series. The series is billed as dealing 'with current and controversial issues of our society, such as domestic violence, drugs trade, racist attacks, labour disputes, [...] stories based on headline news about marginalised people'.[29] The format usually consists of two cases: while the main cases are of social urgency,[30] the second cases are usually of a lesser offence[31] and might bring in humorous elements as comic relief to lighten up the sombre mood of the main case. The main cases are show trials of the new socialist administration that wanted to improve the dire social situation that the previous Conservative government left. A case in point is gender violence. Three months after coming to power the Socialist government presented the first draft of the Comprehensive Law of Protective Measures against Gender-based Violence (2004). Legal changes had been informed by feminist associations and angry public debate. The way in which legal, media and cultural discourses work together to condemn gender violence is superbly dealt with in one of the episodes when Álex and Elena defend a woman who is accused of murdering her violent husband. The judge blatantly sides with the prosecution, and the defence's case seems to crumble, until in a dramatic turn we go from domestic violence to child abuse and it transpires that the son shot his father. The strength of this episode, and the series, lies in its bringing together of the socio-political agenda of the Socialist government, public opinion and the function of lawyers as beacons of justice. In this sense the series is reminiscent of the 1980s with its hero lawyers.

LEX (2008, Antena 3)

LEX is the law firm of the three partners Daniela León, Mario Estrada and Gonzalo Xifré, another lawyer trio, and another example of a female lawyer being the capable, decent and serious one, while Estrada and Xifré happily bend rules and make the law work for their clients. The format is best described as an *esperpento*, a genre that represents reality in grotesque exaggerations to criticise society. LEX is a wonderful example of a law comedy which plays with popular stereotypes about law and lawyers. Reminiscent of *Ally McBeal* in its absurd assortment of cases, legal arguments are nevertheless regularly used to discuss various social issues. A mirroring between the issues in legal cases and private lives usually reinforces a

---

[29] *Al filo de la ley* TVE webpage.

[30] Miscarriage of justice against a Moroccan immigrant; medical negligence; rape; mobbing in schools; corruption in politics, the judicial system and the real estate sector; sexual harassment; forced marriages.

[31] Misappropriation of a lottery win; marriage swindlers; hit-and-run driver; insurance fraud; embezzlement of funds in an old people's home; petty street crime; abandonment of the elderly.

character's dramatic impact. Visually most striking is the highly sexualised work environment; lawyers and secretaries regularly flirt and/or have romantic interludes with each other. Apart from Dani, who as a partner wears expensive suits, all women in the office show very low cleavage; reinforced by both Estrada and Xifré constantly making sexualised remarks about their secretaries and clients. One of the recurring themes is the good/bad lawyer dichotomy and the perennial question: what is justice? True to the genre of comedy the case work usually ends happily with justice being done, but the methods and professional ethics are highly questionable. In a beautiful intertextual nod to American films Estrada blames idealist representations of justice in popular culture, rather than questioning his own dubious, and at times illegal, behaviour. His desire to win every case is mainly fuelled by money. His courtroom performances are a masterpiece in unconventional methods. The cases range from drugs-related crimes, health and safety and grievous bodily harm, to sexual harassment, domestic violence, medical negligence and attempted murder. What makes these cases grotesque is the extreme to which the narrative, both of the client and the resulting legal representation, takes them. Playing with stereotypes trivialises serious issues and yet we cannot help but be amused by the star performances of the *trio infernale*. This highly entertaining legal *esperpento* ultimately questions our own assumptions about lawyers and the law/justice dichotomy. Maybe some viewers have their worst prejudices confirmed in this series, while a gentler viewer might realise that this series holds up a mirror and shows us that justice cannot always be reached by entirely legal means.

Prison Dramas

There has been one Spanish prison drama entitled *La fuga/The Escape* (2012, Telecinco). It is set in the mid-twenty-first century and combines the formula of a romantic thriller and a prison drama. Ana (María Valverde) and Daniel (Aitor Luna) are newlyweds, when Daniel is imprisoned by a global dictatorship that rules the world, its natural resources and its people with an iron hand. Both are part of a resistance movement that fights for freedom and basic human rights. The whole series is driven by Ana trying to get her husband back: she infiltrates the prison as an officer in the hope of helping her husband escape. In an interesting role reversal the female lead is the active hero while her husband plays a more passive part as a prison inmate. The huge success of the series might be due to its uncomfortably realist mood.

Empirical Study versus Historical Overview

The empirical study covered November 2014: channels included in the study were the six main national freeview channels (TVE1, TVE2, Antena 3, Cuatro, Telecinco,

La Sexta) and one subscription channel (Canal+). This was based on share of total viewing[32] and the TV guide of the liberal daily newspaper *El País*. Virtually 100% of the sample was police shows (of a total 338 episodes/programmes). The sample was 99.5% imported programmes from Canada (6.5%: *Crime Stories*), Germany (16%: *Alarm for Cobra 11*; *The Last Cop*), Italy (11%: *One Step from Heaven*; *Inspector Montalbano*), Sweden (1%: *The Fjällbacka Murders*) and the US (65%: *Body of Evidence*; *Castle*; *CSI*; *Fargo*; *Forensic Files*; *White Collar*). The one notable exception was the home-produced feature-length documentary *Seré asesinado/I Will Be Murdered*. By far the largest category is crime dramas (65%), followed by documentaries (32%) and comedy dramas (3%). The vast majority of programmes were shown on Cuatro (52%) and La Sexta (31%); TVE2 aired 11% of programmes and Canal+ 5%. Half of the programmes were shown in the morning slot (6.00 am to 2.00 pm), followed by an almost equal split between the afternoon/evening slot (2.00 pm to 10.00 pm) and the night slot (10.00 pm to 6.00 am), 26% and 24% respectively. Forensic science documentaries were aired every day (morning or night slots), suggesting a *CSI* effect in viewer preferences of content.

The historical overview suggests a fair amount of quality shows on a par with other countries. Particularly in the 2000s law shows were at their peak and in general Spain boasted huge home-grown success stories, achieving higher ratings than US imports.[33] Furthermore, Spain used to be one of the biggest producers of series drama in Europe, overtaking France and Germany, while also selling original formats abroad.[34] The empirical study, however, returns a result of almost 100% imports. This might suggest that since Spain's recent economic crisis television had to resort to the much cheaper importation rather than production of TV shows. Concurrently, 'creating virtue out of necessity', it also encouraged producers to start securing international business again.[35] This research presents two stories: Spanish television reaching global recognition and exporting its shows, while—at least in the empirical study—the exact opposite is the case. More research is needed; fruitful directions could be comparative case studies in content analysis of Spanish formats exported abroad.

Content-wise there was only one noteworthy programme in the sample: *Seré asesinado/I Will Be Murdered* (TVE, 2013) a Spanish feature-length, award-winning documentary about a Guatemalan lawyer allegedly murdered by the then president Álvaro Colom Caballeros. Shortly before his death in 2009, Rodrigo Rosenberg produced a video of himself starting: 'If you're watching this video, it's because the president of the country has killed me'.[36] With the government on public trial, special prosecutor Carlos Castresana, head of the International

---

[32] For statistics of audience share, please see Formula TV (2015).
[33] Vaca Berdayes (2004) 60.
[34] Smith (2003) 14.
[35] Pablos (2013).
[36] For the English translation of the full video statement, see Rosenberg (2009).

Commission against Impunity in Guatemala, began to investigate the case. The documentary mainly follows Castresana and Rosenberg's son, Eduardo, in their attempt to make sense of the evidence. The portrayal of the honorable lawyer Rosenberg is sustained for a long time, mainly because the conspiracy theory has all the ingredients the viewer expects from a Central American political scandal involving corruption. The viewer only becomes suspicious when we learn that Rosenberg had a secret affair with a business woman entangled in the allegations. Castresana, who is Spanish and hence deemed neutral, explains dispassionately that he could not find any evidence of corruption. His conclusion is 'stranger than fiction': Rosenberg was so distraught by his lover's death that he had convinced himself she had been killed by the government, but knew his case would not hold up in court. In a bizarre ending Rosenberg orchestrated his own suicide, hiring a hitman to kill him in broad daylight, thus implicating the government in a scandal.

It is apposite to finish this chapter with a documentary about a stranger-than-fiction reality, not only because it is a reminder of the blurred boundaries between fact and fiction, but also because, at the time of writing, a similar case has made headlines in Argentina.[37] The pop-educated viewer might want Rosenberg to be the honourable lawyer who dies a martyr and brings down a corrupt Latin American government. Our popular legal education might have created this imagined community of hero lawyers who fight for justice. The documentary encourages its viewers to participate actively in televisual judgement, brilliantly manipulated by the editing and cross-cutting of the various strands of evidence and points of view. Very much to our chagrin, then, after 67 (of 90) minutes we realise that prosecutor Castresana belongs to the same community of lawyers, his professional ethics cannot let him collude in a conspiracy theory. Yet the lack of conclusive evidence is no hindrance for our legal imagination and our sense of justice to pit two honourable lawyers against each other—the truth of Castresana's verdict is still questioned today.[38]

[37] For further details, see online newspaper reports about the death of public prosecutor Alberto Nisman, such as that in *The Guardian* (3 February 2015).

[38] For further details, see the following blog at: candidatos2011gua.blogspot.co.uk/2011/04/ases-inato-del-abogado-rodrigo-rosemberg.html.

14

Switzerland

LUKAS MUSUMECI AND FABIAN ODERMATT

In 2018, it will be 60 years since the establishing of television in Switzerland. Highly controversial at the time of its introduction, TV has now become a most popular entertainment and information medium. Compared, however, with other European countries, Switzerland ranks last in terms of TV consumption, with 42% of the people watching less than an hour a day.[1] Still, it is hard to imagine Swiss everyday life without TV. As anywhere else, technological developments left neither broadcasting nor reception untouched.[2] The convergence of technologies and media combined with online services enable it to turn telephones into TV sets, thus emancipating TV from a specific device, from space and also from time. These developments and the attempts of politics—often lagging behind technology—to catch up by adjusting regulation, stimulated an intense and sometimes emotional public political debate. This debate culminated most recently in one of the tightest decisions in a popular referendum indicating the importance Swiss people attribute to TV.

We structure our report in two major parts. The first part describes the Swiss television landscape including its historical development and the current legal regulation. In the second part, we turn to an analysis of law and justice on Swiss TV, based on an empirical enquiry of TV shows in November 2014.

Swiss TV and its Development

Structure of the Swiss TV Market

With a population of 8.2 million, the TV market in Switzerland is relatively small. Moreover, this market is not coherent. It is divided by three of the four national

---

[1] Federal Statistical Office based on the European Social Survey: www.bfs.admin.ch/bfs/portal/de/index/themen/16/03.html.
[2] On digitalisation and its effects on broadcasting in Switzerland, see Scherrer (2012).

languages: German, French and Italian. Hence, there are three even smaller sub-markets on the linguistic-regional level, each of which competes with considerably bigger foreign markets. The main competitors for Swiss broadcasters are therefore found in the neighbouring countries Germany, France and Italy. As a result, domestic broadcasters obtain an audience share of around 40%.[3] This market structure has consequences for broadcasters as well as for the legislator. An international-ised market reduces the possibility to regulate through domestic legislation. As for the broadcasters, the structure favours a strong public broadcaster while it makes life difficult for private ones. The public service Swiss Broadcasting Corporation (SRG) enjoys more than a 30% audience share. Domestic private programme ser-vices only obtain around 7%.[4] Even though the potential to raise funds through advertising and sponsorship on the local and regional level is often small, private broadcasters have proved to be pretty successful in this regard. One reason is that they mainly broadcast regional and local news, which keeps costs moderate. Fur-thermore, most of them are part of a bigger media company and thus get cross-financing from other products such as radio and newspapers.[5] Some broadcasters also receive public funding from reception fees.

Life is toughest for private broadcasters on the linguistic-regional level. There, they face strong competitors working under better circumstances: the publicly funded SRG and foreign broadcasters that are either publicly funded or get pri-vate funding on a distinctly bigger advertising market. Most linguistic-regional programme services are narrowcast, covering for example sports,[6] music videos,[7] or children's and youth TV.[8] The first two ambitious projects to establish com-prehensive private broadcasting on the linguistic-regional level, Tele 24 and TV3 have failed.[9] After TV3 closed down, another private project, however, success-fully adapted to the difficult conditions focusing on popular series and films. Since 2006, TV3+ has broadcast in-house produced reality shows and US series in the German-speaking part. It remains as the only comprehensive linguistic-regional programme service.

Historical Development

Switzerland does not belong to the broadcasting pioneer countries. The Fed-eral Council, ie, the federal government, addressing the legal and economic circumstances underlying broadcasting, renounced claims by the francophone

---

[3] See the official data on TV usage in Switzerland at: www.mediapulse.ch.
[4] Mediapulse, Jahresbericht 2014, Band 1: Allgemeine Daten, 26: www.mediapulse.ch.
[5] eg, TeleZüri and Tele Bern both belong to the AZ Medien Group.
[6] Swiss Sport TV.
[7] TVM3 or VIVA Schweiz.
[8] Joiz and Nickelodeon Schweiz.
[9] See Künzler (2012) 69–73.

pioneers for a liberal, US-like system and decided not to leave broadcasting to market forces, but to regulate it, following the British model.[10] Broadcasting as well as receiving radio programme services required a government licence. Reception fees were used for the financing of programme services. While government then opposed a monopoly system, it restricted the number of broadcasting licences, permitting only four programme services in the beginning.

The first programme services were broadcast by local corporations.[11] In 1931, the seven local corporations merged into the Swiss Broadcasting Corporation (SRG), based on the model of the BBC. The SRG received the exclusive licence for radio broadcasting, hence holding a de facto monopoly position. This licence subjected the distribution of fees to a variety of conditions. In other words, it put in place a public service broadcast remit. Radio was supposed to be a public service that informs, educates and entertains the people.[12] Up until today, the SRG has remained the public service broadcaster. It held its radio monopoly until 1983, and the TV monopoly as late as 1991.

Television started in 1953, at least provisionally. After trial broadcasts in Lausanne, Basel and Zürich, the SRG started their first official programme service in Zürich, still as an experiment. On five evenings a week, a one-hour programme was broadcast. Highlights of that period were broadcastings of the 1954 Football World Cup in Switzerland, and the 1956 Eurovision Song Contest held in Lugano. Still, while TV was received with open arms in the French and Italian speaking part, opposition emerged in the German region.[13] In this climate, the proposal of government and Parliament to introduce a constitutional provision on radio and TV failed in the popular referendum in March 1957.[14] However, in this same year, TV grew considerably in popularity.[15] The Federal Council negotiated a new licence arrangement with the SRG and its opponents. This licence entered into force on 1 January 1958 and covered the whole country. Finally, TV was permanently established in Switzerland. The SRG broadcast one programme service for the German-speaking part and one for the French-speaking part. In the Italian-speaking part, they transmitted the German and the French programme service, dubbed with commentaries in Italian, before the first Italian programme service was broadcast in 1961.

In its early years, the story of TV was one of growth and success. The number of TV sets in Swiss households rose from 129,000 in 1960 to 1 million in 1968.[16] Two milestones occurred within that period: the introduction of commercial TV

---

[10] Schade (2000a) 23; Schade (2000b) 25–26; and Schade (2015).
[11] Schade (2000b) 32–37.
[12] ibid, 49–51.
[13] Ehnimb-Bertini (2000) 175.
[14] See ibid, 184–85.
[15] The number of TV sets rose within one year from 19,971 up to 31,3741.
[16] Vallotton (2006) 43–33.

in 1965[17] and the launch of colour TV three years later. At that time, the broadcasting regime, including the monopoly position of the SRG achieved broad acceptance.[18] The wind changed in the late 1960s. Technological progress,[19] economic changes[20] as well as controversies on political control over and political orientation of TV[21] brought pressure upon the SRG monopoly.

On 2 December 1984, the constitutional provision codifying the general outline of the broadcasting regime was approved in a popular referendum. Based on this constitutional authority to regulate broadcasting, in 1991 Parliament adopted the Federal Act on Radio and Television which finally ended the SRG monopoly and allowed market access for private broadcasters. This was in due course revised in April 2007, with further changes in 2009 and 2015.

The Central Features of Swiss TV Legislation

Performance Obligations

The Federal Constitution lays down the public service remit of the broadcasting system requiring it to 'contribute to education and cultural development, to the free shaping of opinion and to entertainment … (with) … events (presented) accurately and allow a diversity of opinions to be expressed appropriately'.[22]

The Constitution does not prescribe a model in which the public serviced remit has to be realised. It only excludes programmes broadcast by the state itself. The implementation is regulated in the Federal Act on Radio and Television. The Act provides for a moderated dual system. The public service SRG bears the main responsibility to fulfil the public service remit,[23] receives a licence and the major part of the collected reception fees. Currently, the SRG runs 17 radio and seven TV programme services. However, there are also two kinds of private broadcasters meeting the constitutional goals and requiring a licence. First, broadcasters can apply for a licence for local-regional programme services that provide comprehensive information about their area. If they cannot get adequate financing there, they may get funding from reception fees revenue (known as a fee-splitting licence).[24] Second, private programme services that contribute significantly to the fulfilment of the constitutional public service remit in a linguistic region can get a licence, but without fee-splitting.[25] Broadcasters are entitled to broadcast licensed

---

[17] Aziz and Piattini (2006) 156–57.

[18] Schneider (2006) 84–87.

[19] Müller (2006) 217–29.

[20] Schade (2006) 296–97, 306–13 and 347–55.

[21] Vallotton (2006) 63–76; Schneider (2006) 90–101 and 112–14.

[22] Art 93(2).

[23] Art 24(1) Radio and TV Act.

[24] ibid, Arts 38(1)(a) and 43(1)(a).

[25] ibid, Art 43(1)(b).

programme services in their respective area.[26] Currently, there are 13 local-regional TV programme services with a mandate, including fee-splitting, but no licensed linguistic-regional ones. Thus, while the SRG fulfils the public service remit in respect of the linguistic-regional and the national level, private broadcasters fulfil it at the local-regional level. In order to protect the latter, the SRG is not allowed to broadcast local-regional programme services.

The Radio and TV Act lays down the public service remit for the SRG.[27] As a result, the SRG must provide the whole population with radio and TV programmes and promote understanding, cohesion and exchange between the different parts of the country, its linguistic communities, cultures and social groups, including Swiss citizens living abroad. To reach these goals, the SRG must contribute to free public debate, cultural diversity and the reinforcement of the country's cultural values, public education and entertainment. Additionally, the licence provides that the SRG programmes have to satisfy high quality and ethical standards. The relevant quality criteria are credibility, responsibility, relevancy and journalistic professionalism.[28]

The programme public service remit for the licensed private broadcasters is specified in their licence. The standard provisions in all current licences require them to broadcast on a daily basis a regional programme service that provides information about relevant local and regional political, economic and social events and that contributes to the cultural life of their respective area of coverage.[29]

Finally, there are private broadcasters whose programme services are not licensed, who do not contribute to the constitutional public service remit and therefore get neither financing from reception fees nor privileged access to frequencies. These broadcasters profit from a simplified access to the market as they do not have to go through the lengthy and complex licensing procedure and thus do not have to pay a licensing fee. Currently there are 139 private broadcasters without mandate and licence.

Content Requirements and Supervision

The minimal content requirements as laid down in articles 4–8 of the Radio and TV Act cover all programme services.

Whether editorial programmes comply with these requirements is dealt with by content supervision. In order to protect broadcasters from government influence on their programmes, Parliament established an independent supervision regime outside the central administration. It provides for a two-step procedure before two specially created authorities: a mediation procedure before the Ombudsman[30] and subsequently a complaints procedure before the Independent Complaints Authority.

---

[26] ibid, Art 38(2).

[27] ibid, Art 24.

[28] Art 3(1) SRG Licence of 28 November 2007, at: www.srgssr.ch/fileadmin/pdfs/ Konzession_srg_281109_de.pdf.

[29] See as an example Art 5(1) Tele M1 Licence of 31 October 2001: www.bakom.admin.ch/rtv_files/61_2.pdf.

[30] Art 92(1) Radio and TV Act.

Financing

The Radio and TV Act provides for two kinds of financing: public financing through reception fees on the one hand; private financing through advertising and sponsorship on the other. Reception fees must be paid by every household, notwithstanding the actual or potential broadcasting consumption. They are the main source of funding for the SRG and the SRG receives the major part of revenue from such fees. Private broadcasters with a fee-splitting licence receive 4–6% of the revenue from reception fees,[31] covering not more than 70% of their operating costs.[32]

All types of broadcasters, including the SRG,[33] are allowed to raise funds through advertising and sponsorship. Private financing for the public service broadcaster runs somewhat counter to a dual system.[34] The SRG is provided with that option, because the total revenue of reception fees is not regarded as sufficient to allow survival against competition from broadcasters from the big neighbouring markets.[35] Therefore, in addition some SRG-specific advertising restrictions have been reduced to meet European minimal standards, so the SRG does not suffer from a disadvantage in the advertising market compared with its foreign competitors.

Current Issues

At the core of current debates is the privileged position of the SRG along with its goals. What should be the precise content of the goals? How much sport and how much entertainment is part of the public service and should be paid with funds from reception fees? There was also criticism that the SRG had been allowed to obtain money through advertising and sponsorship while at the same time receiving reception fees, thus competing with private broadcasters within an already limited advertising market. For summer 2016, Parliament announced an extensive and comprehensive debate on these issues based on a report it commissioned from the Federal Media Commission.

Law and Justice on Swiss TV

We start with the empirical report of shows on Swiss TV in relation to law and justice. Then we analyse the empirical data focusing on Swiss productions, as well as looking beyond the period of the detailed study.

---

[31] ibid, Art 40 (1).
[32] ibid, Art 40(1) in conjunction with Art 39 Radio and TV Ordinance.
[33] In contrast, the SRG must not broadcast advertising in their radio programme services: Art 14(1) Radio and TV Act.
[34] Dumermuth (2006) 253.
[35] Nobel and Weber (2007) 446.

Empirical Report

The relevant period for the empirical report is November 2014. We cover the biggest of the three linguistic-regional markets: the German-speaking one, excluding pay TV. This includes shows on the SRG programme services SRF 1 and SRF 2, as well as the local-regional private programme services with public service goals. Regarding private programme services without such a public service remit, we covered 3+ and StarTV. We left out the other private programme services, because their very narrow goals exclude shows about law and justice. It is important to keep in mind that the empirical report does not necessarily reflect what people in German-speaking Switzerland actually watch, since about 60% of audience viewing is of foreign programme services.

We classify the data adopting the approach used in this volume. The first dimension refers to the location of the material within the legal process (police and detective; lawyer and court; prison and post-prison), the second to genre (drama; comedy; reality; documentaries). Further, we indicate the country of production and the programme service that broadcast the respective show.

Table 1: Shows relating to law and justice on Swiss TV

Police and detective material	Drama: series	Drama: movies
WEEK 1 (3–9 Nov)	**German (3)** *Heiter bis tödlich: Alles Klara* (SRF 1) *Kommissar Rex* (SRF 1) *Der Kriminalist* (*The Criminalist*; Germany/ Switzerland, SRF 1) **Austrian (1)** *SOKO Wien* (SRF 2) **US (5)** *Magnum* (SRF 2) *The Mentalist* (3+) *Navy CIS* (3+) *NCIS Los Angeles* (3+) *Hawaii Five-0* (3+) **Canadian (1)** *The Border* (StarTV) **Scandinavian (2)** *Kommissarin Lund—Das Verbrechen* (*Forbrydelsen*; Denmark, SRF 1) *Die Brücke I—Transit in den Tod* (*Bron/Broen*; Denmark/Sweden, SRF 1)	**US (1)** *Disturbia—Auch Killer haben Nachbarn* (*Disturbia*;[36] SRF 2) **Italian (1)** *Engel des Bösen—Die Geschichte eines Staatsfeindes* (*Vallanzasca—Gli angeli del male*; Italy/France/ Romania, SRF 2)

(continued)

---

[36] We indicate the original title if it is not identical to the German one.

Table 1: *(Continued)*

Police and detective material	Drama: series	Drama: movies
WEEK 2 (10–16 Nov)	The same as week 1 plus **German (1)** *Tatort* (SRF 1)	**US (1)** *Taking Lives—Für Dein Leben würde er töten* (*Taking Lives*; USA/Australia/Canada, SRF 2)
WEEK 3 (17–23 Nov)	Same as week 2 plus **Australian (1)** *Top of the Lake: Am Rand des Universums* (*Top of the Lake*; Australia/USA/GB, SRF 1) **Italian (1)** *Allein gegen die Mafia* (*La Piovra*; StarTV)	None
WEEK 4 (24–30 Nov)	Same as week 3 plus: **German (1)** *Der Alte* (SRF 1)	**US (2)** *Ein Mann für gewisse Stunden* (*American Gigolo*, SRF 1) *Suspect Zero* (StarTV)
Total	**16**	**5**

Lawyer and court-focused material	Drama: movies
WEEK 1 (3–9 Nov)	**US (1)** *Zwielicht* (*Primal Fear*, SRF 2)
WEEK 2 (10–16 Nov)	No shows in this category
WEEK 3 (17–23 Nov)	**US (1)** *Der Exorzismus von Emily Rose* (*The Exorcism of Emily Rose*, StarTV)
WEEK 4 (24–30 Nov)	No shows in this category
Total	**2**

(continued)

Table 1: *(Continued)*

Prison and post-prison material	Drama: movies	Comedies	Documentaries
WEEK 1 (3–9 Nov)	US (1) *Lockout* (USA/France, SRF 2)	German (1) *Stufe Drei* (Shortmovie, SRF 2)	Swiss (2) *Reporter: Drei Knast-Tränen für Jerry—Ein Basler Totentanz über die Liebe* (SRF 1) *Dok: Schweizer im Stasi-Knast* (SRF 1)
WEEK 2 (10–16 Nov)	No shows in this category		
WEEK 3 (17–23 Nov)	US (1) *Con Air* (SRF 2)	No shows in this category	No shows in this category
WEEK 4 (24–30 Nov)	**British (1)** *Boy A* (SRF 1)		
Total	**3**	**1**	**2**

Analysis

Preliminary Remarks

We found a total of 29 shows relating to law and justice, counting series as one. As far as the four parameters were concerned, we found the following:

— More than two-thirds of the shows (21) concern police and detective material. Only two fall within the category of lawyer and court-focused material, and with six comprising prison and post-prison material. We say more on this uneven distribution below.

— Regarding the type of show, the distribution is even more one-sided. There are 26 dramas, one comedy and two documentaries. There were no shows belonging to the reality genre. The dramas split up into 10 movies and 16 series, the latter all falling within the category of police and detective material, while the two documentaries both concern prison material.

— These two findings combined, we note a clear dominance of dramas concerning detective and police material.

— Almost half of the shows were produced in the US (13). Germany ranks second (6), followed by Scandinavia, Italy and Switzerland (2), as well as Austria, Australia, Canada and the UK (1).

— The two Swiss shows are the only documentaries covered. They both concern prison material.

— There were no Swiss series or movies, be it drama or comedy, with a law and justice theme in addition to there being no Swiss shows containing police or court material.
— Two-thirds of the shows covered were broadcast by the SRG programme services SRF 1 and SRF 2. Star TV and 3+ broadcast four shows each. There were no shows broadcast by any private local-regional programme service with a public service remit.
— We also note that all 29 shows relate to criminal law or criminal procedure law, none to civil, constitutional, administrative or public international law.

The small number of Swiss productions is not surprising, given the rather modest output of the Swiss film industry[37] on the one hand and the few in-house productions of Swiss programme services on the other. This is the reality of a small movie and TV market with 5 million potential German-speaking viewers. The SRG, with roughly 90% of reception fee revenues plus funding through advertising and sponsorship, enjoys the biggest financial resources and financial security of all broadcasters. Therefore, SRG programme services are also the only ones to produce in-house dramas. The total absence of private programme services with a public service remit is not surprising due to their broadcasting profile. Following their remit, they focus on local-regional news, talk shows and reports and neither produce nor import dramas or comedies, most probably due to lack of finances.

Police and Detective Material

As noted, the vast majority of shows are police and detective shows. This can be explained by their basic conception that makes them better apt for cinematic adaptation than the other two categories examined. At the beginning of a (criminal) investigation, much is uncertain, be it the relevant facts and circumstances or the trustworthiness of certain witnesses. It is difficult to tell truth from lies. Finding the truth, discovering what has happened within the context of an investigation corresponds widely with the dramaturgy of a movie with the arrest of the perpetrator as the dramatic climax. Notwithstanding these dramaturgy-specific explanations, a historical perspective reveals a general Swiss preference for detective and police stories, dating back to the early days of radio broadcasting.[38] Examples include the movie adaptations of the *Wachmeister Studer* (*Constable Studer*) novels by Swiss author Friedrich Glauser, *Es geschah am hellichten Tag* (*It Happened in Broad Daylight*),[39] scripted by Friedrich Dürrenmatt, or *Polizischt Wäckerli* (*Policeman Wäckerli*).[40]

A new representative of this genre is the award-winning cop movie *Strähl*[41] which depicts the work and life of a police officer investigating drugs law in a

---

[37] www.swissfilms.ch—also available in English.
[38] Mäusli (2000) 218–19.
[39] Switzerland/Spain (1958).
[40] Switzerland (1955).
[41] Switzerland (2004).

particularly tough and uncompromising way. Herbert Strähl, the main character, a substance addict himself, takes the law into his own hands as a Swiss version of Abel Ferrara's *Bad Lieutenant*.

The TV series *Der Bestatter* (*The Undertaker*) shows police work less gloomily over three series between 2013 and 2015. Luc Conrad once was an inspector in the cantonal police and is now the head of a small funeral parlour. In his new job, he is confronted with mysterious fatalities that seem to have a criminal background. Of course he tries to solve the cases. The highly successful series combines horseplay with entertaining detective stories. With regard to this concept it seems evident that the focus lies more on good punchlines than on an accurate depiction of legal realities. Another recent representative of Swiss police and detective material is the adaptation of the *Kommissär Hunkeler* novels by Hansjörg Schneider, a loose series of six TV movies produced between 2004 and 2012, starring the late, great Swiss actor Mathias Gnädinger. The movies are classical whodunits following down-to-earth and, in a loveable way, grumpy and stubborn Inspector Peter Hunkeler solving murder cases. Set in Basel and its surroundings, local colour is an important part of the movies.

With regard to the empirical report, we can add some remarks on the police series *Tatort* (*Crime Scene*). *Tatort* is a German language police television series developed by the German television channel ARD and co-produced by ARD, ORF and SRG. The first episode was broadcast on 29 November 1970. Ever since, the series has been on air, which makes it the longest-running crime series on German-speaking TV.[42] It is broadcast simultaneously on ARD's main programme service Das Erste, Austrian ORF 1 and Swiss SRF 1, every Sunday at prime time. The feature length episodes amount to stand-alone police stories where different police teams solve murder mysteries in their respective cities.[43] Also the genre of the episodes shifts and varies from classic whodunit, film noir, mystery, crime comedy, thriller, spy movie or action, with some cities being used for a certain genre.[44] The peculiarities of the cities, their customs and dialects, local celebrities or political and economic issues are an important aspect of the series sometimes making the city the main character of an episode. Besides local colour, socio-political aspects are another important feature of the series. The episodes address issues such as corruption,[45] drugs,[46] prostitution,[47] neo-Nazi groups[48] or migration.[49] Often the

---

[42] Himmelman, M, 'German Viewers Love Their Detectives on Tatort', *New York Times* (New York, 26 September 2009): www.nytimes.com/2009/08/27/arts/television/27abroad.html?_r=0.

[43] As of June 2015, there are 20 investigator teams, 18 in German cities, one in Vienna and one in Lucerne.

[44] The episodes set in Münster, Weimar and Saabrücken, for example, are crime comedies.

[45] 'Deckname Kideon' ('Code name Kideon') broadcast 4 January 2015.

[46] 'Der Himmel über Kiel' ('The sky over Kiel') broadcast 25 January 2015.

[47] 'Angezählt' ('Down for the count') broadcast 15 September 2013.

[48] 'Hydra' ('Hydra') broadcast 11 January 2015.

[49] Migration is one of the most prominent political issues addressed in the history of *Tatort*. See, eg 'Tod im U-Bahnschacht' ('Death in the subway tunnel') broadcast 9 November 1975 or the controversial episode 'Wem Ehre gebührt' ('Honour to whom honour is due') broadcast 23 December 2007, leading to protests by the Alevist community.

investigators have to enter a certain social milieu in order to solve the episode's mystery. Popular *Tatort* settings include business and financial circles, politics, the gritty milieu of the underclass, or red-light districts and organised crime. The focus on a very limited environment offers close insights into milieus, which are usually hidden from the audience's attention.

The SRG joined the production pool from 1990 to 2001 and again in 2011. The Swiss episodes are produced as bilingual versions: in standard German for ARD and ORF and in Swiss–German dialect for the SRG. The first Swiss episode, 'Howalds Fall' ('Howald's Case') was broadcast on 16 April 1990. Back then it was the most expensive SRG in-house production and up to now one of the most radical *Tatort* episodes. Currently, the Swiss episodes are set in Lucerne. According to the series' concept, there are references to local customs, for example, the Lucerne carnival.[50] Recent episodes addressed issues such as intersexuality,[51] whistle-blowing[52] and migration.[53]

Due to these social aspects, *Tatort* has drawn academic attention, especially in the fields of sociology, philosophy and literary studies.[54] Meanwhile, legal scholars have also become increasingly interested in the series.[55] Some recently broadcast episodes addressed controversial legal issues.[56] However, the investigation methods as shown in the series are often beyond any legal reality, with breaches of law by the investigators being neither discussed nor criticised. In this respect, an episode has been accused of engaging in 'propaganda against the rule of law' and of anti-justice tendencies.[57] Indeed, from a rule of law point of view, it seems dangerous that the series regularly justifies these breaches of law, be it the violation of procedural rules or even police brutality, by your favourite investigator successfully catching the perpetrator.[58] The question is even more relevant if we assume that the *Tatort* series has a huge influence on how people see the actual domestic legal system.[59]

---

[50] 'Schmutziger Donnerstag' ('Dirty Thursday'—the day, carnival starts in Lucerne) broadcast 10 February 2013.

[51] 'Skalpell' ('Scalpel') broadcast 28 May 2012.

[52] 'Verfolgt' ('Tracked') broadcast 7 September 2014.

[53] 'Schutzlos' ('Without Protection') broadcast 5 July 2015.

[54] See, eg, Hißnauer, Scherrer and Stockinger (2014); and Eilenberger (2014).

[55] See, eg, the not always serious episode reviews by Swiss legal scholars and practitioners 'Tatort —Experten rezensieren den Fernsehkrimi' ('Tatort reviewed by Experts') on the website of legal publishing house Schulthess: www.schulthess.com/portal/aktuell/tatort.

[56] eg, the episode 'Machtlos' ('Helpless') broadcast on 6 January 2013, impressively addresses the conflict area between the interest in establishing the truth on the one hand and the right to refuse to testify of the accused on the other.

[57] Müller (2014). The review refers to the episode 'Ohnmacht' ('Powerlessness') broadcast 11 May 2014.

[58] The episode 'Macht und Ohnmacht' ('Power and powerlessness') broadcast 1 April 2013, is a welcome exception since it not only critically addresses police brutality, but also the popular justification that the police are the good guys in the end.

[59] See also below, 'Concluding Remarks'.

Lawyer and Court-Focused Material

There are almost no Swiss productions, be it series, feature films or documentaries that focus on attorney work. One exception is an episode of the SRF in-house documentary series *Reporter*, 'Von Gangstern, Huren und weissen Westen' ('Of Gangsters, Whores and Clean Slates').[60] It portrays the defence lawyer Valentin Landmann, nationally famous for being a red-light district attorney, representing prostitutes as well as the Hell's Angels. The same holds true for productions focusing on court proceedings. There is no such thing as a Swiss courtroom drama. On the one hand this might be because although court proceedings are in general conducted in public, audio and video recordings are not permitted. Accordingly, no such thing as the American courtroom TV could have evolved. Swiss court proceedings, on the other hand, contain few dramaturgically exciting components which would be apt for cinematic adaptation. First, in Swiss criminal proceedings there is the inquisitorial principle. The principle obliges 'criminal justice authorities to investigate *ex officio* all the circumstances relevant to the assessment of the criminal act and the accused',[61] which leads to a simplification of defence work, as compared with defence work in the US. Further, the investigation by the public prosecutor is of considerably higher significance than in the Anglo-American procedural laws. Judges decide based on the files and the evidence as gathered in the investigation proceedings. The examination hearings in the main proceedings are restricted to a re-examination of the evidence gathered by the public prosecutor in the investigation. Therefore, the Swiss main proceedings, as well as the (defence) attorney work are considerably less suitable for cinematic adaptation, than the adversarial Anglo-American court proceedings. Hence, it is not surprising that the only two shows falling within this category in the reporting period are US feature movies. *Primal Fear* (1996) is an exemplary representative of the American courtroom drama while *The Exorcism of Emily Rose* (2005) combines elements of both courtroom drama and horror movie.[62]

Prison and Post-Prison Material

Within the reporting period, we found two Swiss documentaries that fall within prison and post-prison material. *Schweizer im Stasi-Knast* (*Swiss Citizens in Stasiprison*) tells the story of a Swiss citizen who tried to smuggle his girlfriend out of the German Democratic Republic (GDR) in the 1970s. They were arrested and were sentenced to several years in prison. The documentary does not only address the protagonists' time in prison, but takes a closer look at the repressive system of the GDR as a whole, such as observation by the Stasi and its

---

[60] Broadcast 3 May 2006.
[61] Art 6, Swiss Criminal Procedure Code.
[62] For a short analysis of this movie with references to the true events the movie is based on, see Greenfield, Osborn and Robson (2010) 194–96.

interrogation techniques, everyday life within the system and the resistance to it. *Drei Knast-Tränen für Jerry* (*Three Prison Tears for Jerry*) portrays a terminally ill inmate in custody after imprisonment whose wish to die in freedom has been denied by the authorities. The movie accompanies him and his relatives in his last days and discusses the issue of human dignity and imprisonment.

In recent years, there have been several noteworthy Swiss documentaries with a focus on the execution of sentences and disciplinary measures. The emergence of documentaries with a prison theme corresponds with the emergence of law and order issues on the political agenda, particularly in popular referendums.[63] Examples of Swiss prison documentaries include the feature length movies *Faustrecht* (*Fist Law*),[64] a long-time observation of teenagers in juvenile detention, *Vol special* (*Special Flight*),[65] addressing the issue of detention and deportation of illegal immigrants and *Thorberg*,[66] portraying the fate of several inmates in the high-security facility of the same name. These movies have in common that they deal with the nature and purpose of punishment and disciplinary measures. They point to the problem areas of the so-called dualist-vicarious Swiss criminal law system.[67] The audience inevitably gets confronted with the question whether a punishment is meant to compensate for the wrong done or whether the purpose of criminal law should rather be to rehabilitate the offender, preventing recidivism. Thus, at the end of *Faustrecht*, a considerable part of the audience might hope for the two delinquent teenagers to get probation again, notwithstanding their quite serious crimes. Most of the documentaries mentioned through their direct relation to those immediately affected punishment, seem to take a stance which prefers rehabilitation rather than retribution.[68] Finally, it seems that documentaries are particularly suitable to show the fates of individual inmates. Thus, they can provide realistic insights into everyday life in prison, a world unknown to the general public.

In contrast to documentaries, dramas therefore seem to be less apt.[69] The static nature of everyday prison life, ruled by routines, contains much less dramaturgical components than, for example, criminal investigations. Prison movies, as well as

---

[63] They have included: introduction of lifelong custody after imprisonment for certain offenders with restricted possibility for review (2004); abolition of statutory time bars for certain sexual offences (2008); mandatory deportation of foreign offenders for certain crimes (2010); mandatory and lifelong exclusion from certain professions for people sentenced for a sexual offence with minors (2014).

[64] Switzerland (2006) directed by Bernhard Weber and Robi Müller.

[65] Switzerland (2011) directed by Fernand Melgar.

[66] Switzerland (2012) directed by Dieter Fahrer. In order to experience everyday life in prison, Fahrer spent 200 days and several nights locked up in Thorberg.

[67] 'Dualist' refers to the possibility for a judge to combine (repressive) punishment with (preventive) disciplinary measures. 'Vicarious' means that in this case the disciplinary measure can suspend the punishment and is operated first. Should the measure prove to be unsuccessful, punishment is then implemented.

[68] Except the gritty and melancholic ending of the movie *Thorberg* which shows a prisoner who has to undergo psychiatric therapy for an unlimited time.

[69] For what prison dramas can contribute to the perception of prison, see Wilson and O'Sullivan (2004) 14–15.

series, such as *Oz, Prison Break* and *Orange is the New Black* often need dramatisations. Rather than realistically representing prison life, which is what most of these movies do not intend, they discuss capital punishment or tell stories about violence, sexual abuse, escape, corruption or resistance against an oppressive system. This is also true for the probably best-known and latest Swiss prison movie, *Chicken Mexicaine*.[70] The movie tells the story of a felon who tries to get out of prison in order to see his daughter again. After an unsuccessful attempt to escape, he finds a way to blackmail the prison director. Furthermore, the prison theme related exploitation movies *Gefangene Frauen* (*Caged Women*), *Frauengefängnis* (*Barbed Wire Dolls*) and *Frauen für Zellenblock 9* (*Women in Cellblock 9*), produced by the notorious and bustling Swiss producer Erwin C Dietrich, deserve an honourable mention.[71]

Regarding the empirical report, the action movies *Con Air* and *Lockout* as well as the comedy *Stufe Drei* (*Level Three*), with its story of a young man sentenced to social service in an institution for the mentally handicapped and making friends with the residents, rather indirectly addresses issues of sentencing and imprisonment. *Boy A*, however, empathically describes the difficulties of a teenage murderer to integrate into society after release.

Concluding Remarks

At the outset of this contribution, we provided an overview on the specifics of the Swiss TV market, how TV in Switzerland has developed and how TV is regulated today. We pointed out that a small market is separated into three partial markets, each of which is competing with considerably bigger foreign markets. Foreign programme services get up to 60% audience shares in Switzerland. Under these economic circumstances a moderate dual system has evolved with the SRG as public service broadcaster, fulfilling the public service remit to inform, educate and entertain the people. In return, the SRG is mainly financed through public funds. Besides the SRG, there is not much space for private programme services, at least not on the linguistic-regional level, where 3+ is the only comprehensive private programme service (not only in the German-speaking part). The rest are all narrowcast.

The empirical report mirrors the market structure. There are only a few broadcast services that, due to their broadcasting profile and their financial resources, have the potential to produce or broadcast shows in relation to law and justice. Further, the SRG programme services are the only ones with the potential for producing in-house movies and series. Thus, there are few shows with a law and justice topic and even fewer respective Swiss productions. As a consequence, depictions

---

[70] Switzerland (2007) directed by Armin Biehler and starring Bruno Cathommen.
[71] Eppenberger and Stapfer (2006) 5–10.

of the Swiss legal system are very rare and they are strikingly under-represented as compared with depictions of foreign legal systems. This under-representation is aggravated even if we include the German and the Austrian market, where there are hardly any Swiss productions. In other words: when Swiss people see law on TV, they see US or German law most of the time. This raises the question of the way this influences how people see the domestic legal system. Does it rather promote or prevent a realistic perception, or does it not have an effect at all? It is up to future research to answer this question.

15

United States of America

CHRISTINE A CORCOS

Since the start of television broadcasting in the United States after the Second World War, audience interest in programmes about lawyers, police and the legal system has been extremely high.[1] A fair number of these programmes had already been popular radio programmes of the period, including *Dragnet* and *Perry Mason*. These programmes easily made the transition to the nascent television networks, and similar programmes followed suit.

After the Second World War, television evolved into the nation's major broadcast medium. In 1945 there were 12 authorised television channels and by the late 1950s, licences had been granted to 395 VHF and 96 UHF stations.[2] UHF remained a less popular alternative than VHF until cable technology became more lucrative and more widespread in the early 1980s. In addition, changes in Federal Communications Commission (FCC) rules allowed cable providers to transmit their programming via satellite to other cable systems, allowing the cable infrastructure as a whole to develop more fully.

In 1984, the United States Congress passed the Cable Communications Policy Act[3] and in 1992 the Cable Television Consumer Protection and Competition Act,[4] both of which addressed the increasing importance and competition of the cable industry in the marketplace. The 1992 Act also includes the 'must carry' rules, upheld in two important US Supreme Court cases.[5] Under these rules, cable companies must transmit locally over-the-air stations if they request transmission.[6] The Telecommunications Act 1996 also includes provisions applicable to the television industry.[7] For example, it requires that television set manufacturers

---

[1] See generally Stark (1987).
[2] VHF stands for 'very high frequency' and UHF stands for 'ultrahigh frequency'. KPMG Consulting, History of the Broadcast License Application Process: Final Report, November 2000 (prepared for the Federal Communications Commission) at: transition.fcc.gov/opportunity/meb_study/broadcast_lic_study_pt1.pdf).
[3] 47 USC §521 (2015).
[4] ibid, §533.
[5] *Turner Broadcasting v FCC*, 512 US 622 (1994) (Turner I); *Turner Broadcasting v FCC*, 520 US 180 (1997) (Turner II).
[6] www.fcc.gov/encyclopedia/evolution-cable-television.
[7] Codified throughout Title 47 of the USC.

incorporate V chips into their TV sets in order to regulate the broadcast of objectionable content. It also encourages broadcasters to develop a ratings system.[8]

The FCC has authority to regulate indecent language and material[9] and therefore channels programming considered indecent between 10.00 pm and 6.00 am to protect children from exposure to such broadcasts.[10] Both the FCC and the Federal Trade Commission (FTC) administer various regulations concerning advertising on television. Such regulations may cover beverage and food advertisements, political advertisements, cigarette advertisements, drug advertisements, and many other products, depending on the type of complaint.[11] The FCC also handles complaints dealing with loud commercials[12] and with advertisements on children's programmes.[13] Finally, on 12 June 2009, US over-the-air-broadcasters ceased sending analogue signals and switched over to digital signals, in accordance with law.[14]

Legal Dramas

Perhaps the quintessential courtroom drama in US television history is *Perry Mason*, which ran on the CBS television network from 1957 to 1966 and starred Raymond Burr as the archetypal attorney who never loses a murder case. His faithful secretary Della Street (Barbara Hale) and favourite private investigator Paul Drake (William Hopper) assisted him with all his cases. CBS based the series

---

[8] See Letter to Secretary William Caton: transition.fcc.gov/Bureaus/Cable/Public_Notices/1997/fc97034a.pdf. The 1934 Telecommunications Act and other legislation which regulate broadcast media are codified at 47 USC §151 passim (2014). FCC rules are available in the Code of Federal Regulations at 47 CFR 0-199 (parts 102-199 reserved). The FCC website is available at www.fcc.gov/.

[9] FCC licensees are those stations, both commercial and non-profit, that hold licences granted by the agency.

The FCC gives application, filing and renewal requirements for licences beginning at 47 CFR 73.612 (2014), including the requirement that licencees agree to administer their stations in accordance with the best interests of the community they serve. See 47 CFR §73.1001-4280.

The Supreme Court upheld the FCC's authority to regulate indecent programming in *Federal Communications Commission v Pacifica Foundation* (438 US 726 (1978)). It overturned the FCC's 'fleeting expletives' policy in *FCC v Fox TV Stations, Inc*, 132 S. Ct. 2307 (2012)). To date, the agency has not promulgated a new policy. Obscenity is a different matter. The obscenity test is laid out in *Miller v California*, 413 US 15 (1973). The First Amendment does not protect material deemed obscene, but in order for material to be deemed obscene that material must first fail the following test: '(a) whether "the average person, applying contemporary community standards" would find that the work, taken as a whole, appeals to the prurient interest…(b) whether the work depicts or describes, in a patently offensive way, sexual conduct specifically defined by the applicable state law; and (c) whether the work, taken as a whole, lacks serious literary, artistic, political, or scientific value.' Miller, at 24.

[10] *Action for Children's Television v Federal Communications Commission*, 58 F 3d 654 (DC Cir, 1995).

[11] See, eg, 47 CFR 73.4055 (2015) (FCC regulations prohibiting cigarette advertising based on prohibition in 15 USC 1335 (2015)) and 16 CFR 408 (2015) (FTC regulations).

[12] The Commercial Advertisement Loudness Mitigation (CALM) Act (47 USC §621 (2015)).

[13] For standards for children's TV programming, see 47 USC §303a (2015).

[14] www.fcc.gov/guides/dtv-and-over-air-viewers-along-us-borders.

on the extremely popular novels by attorney Erle Stanley Gardner, who served as consultant to the show.[15] The series became famous for the ways in which Mason demonstrated the innocence of his client. He would catch witnesses in lies and inconsistencies on the stand, he would reconstruct scenarios in the courtroom (with or without the permission of the judge and much to the consternation of the prosecutor) and he would magically find solutions to overwhelming problems that his clients would present to him. These skills made him invincible in the courtroom.[16] Throughout the years, the Perry Mason character came to represent the American popular culture attorney as tenacious, honest, ethical and above all, successful. *Perry Mason* is still the ultimate symbol in a legal representative, not just in US popular culture, but in real life.[17]

Other influential lawyer shows followed, including *The Defenders* (1961–65), another CBS show, which starred EG Marshall and Robert Reed, and whose storylines focused primarily on questions of social justice (civil rights, abortion, euthanasia). In 1963, the first of the combined police procedural/legal dramas made its debut. While *Arrest and Trial* starring Ben Gazzara and Chuck Connors ran for only one year on ABC, it introduced the format in which viewers saw the commission of the crime, investigation by the police and arrest in the first half of the episode, and then the trial and verdict in the second half, thus bringing the legal process to its conclusion. Dick Wolf adapted this format for his popular and long-running franchise, *Law & Order*, in the 1990s.

Legal dramas continued to grow in popularity from the 1960s onwards, and tended to fall into certain categories. One category is the classic courtroom drama, exemplified by *Perry Mason* and *The Defenders* in the 1960s, *Owen Marshall, Counselor at Law* in the 1970s and *Matlock* in the 1980s to 1990s, which focused on the activities of the defence attorney who takes the case of a client, usually innocent, against whom the state brings its immense power in order to secure a conviction. In the early history of the television legal drama, many of these series focused on one main character. In later decades, legal dramas often became ensemble shows, as in *LA Law, Law & Order, the practice,* and *Boston Legal.* These shows tend to emphasise the personal flaws and ethical concerns of the characters as much as the difficult or interesting legal cases the characters take on for their clients. The increasing complexity of the ethical and moral dilemmas presented in these legal shows parallels the complexity of personal and moral relationships presented in police and detective dramas of the same period (discussed below). In these legal and courtroom shows, lawyers often become involved with colleagues, opposing counsel, clients, judges and witnesses, raising questions about the fairness or ethics of the justice system.[18]

---

[15] A few films during the 1930s had been made, usually featuring actor Warren William.

[16] In 1985, Burr and Hale returned in a series of made-for-TV *Perry Mason* films; the Paul Drake role was taken by the actor William Katt (Hale's real life son) as Paul Drake, Jr.

[17] On the influence of the show see generally Bounds (1996).

[18] On *LA Law,* as well as *Moonlighting* and a number of David E Kelley shows such as *Picket Fences,* see Thompson (1996).

Other categories of legal shows that have emerged over the past 50 years include the legal comedy (*The Tony Randall Show, Night Court, Bad Judge, Bent*). Of these, only *Night Court* (NBC, 1984–92) was successful, because of the quirky characters, the odd twists in plotting and the compassionate nature of its protagonist, Judge Harold T Stone, a judge and amateur magician, whose manner reflected his interest in the spirit rather than the letter of the law. The Judge Stone character exemplified the kind of judge that audiences hope to encounter in the courtroom: kind but firm, a judge who listens and realises that the defendants and victims who appear in his court could easily switch roles. Other shows such as *Bad Judge* and *Bent* feature judges or lawyers with ethical or personal problems intended to appeal to audience sympathies. Such shows raise questions about the behaviour of attorneys and judges both in the minds of viewers and in the minds of lawyers, law professors and law students, and some scholars have examined the role that such shows can play in legal education.[19] A version of the legal comedy is the police comedy. Here, the most important is *Barney Miller*, a comedy which aired on ABC from 1975 to 1982. *Barney Miller* was set in a New York precinct house and was an ensemble comedy which included a diverse group of police officers. It emphasised relationships among the characters, who truly cared about one another, and about the people, both suspects and victims, who came to the station. *Barney Miller* and shows like it changed the emphasis from pure procedure to the issues that US society was considering at the time.

The next important legal drama was the NBC series *LA Law* (1986–94), created by Steven Bochco and Terry Louise Fisher. The show's famous first episode began with the death of the managing partner, setting a tone for the series that featured episodes highlighting stories current in the media, or featuring social issues. In 1990, Dick Wolf's series *Law & Order* premiered on NBC, and ran for 20 years, tying with the classic western series *Gunsmoke* as the longest-running series on US television. *Law & Order*, set in New York City, combined elements of the police procedural and the legal drama. The first half of each episode featured a crime, an investigation by the police department and an arrest; the second, the prosecution of the arrestee by the district attorney and his team. The prosecutor won often, but not always. Sometimes the outcome demonstrated unforeseen consequences or unresolved legal issues. Wolf developed four US spin-offs of the original series.[20]

The David E Kelley series *Ally McBeal* (starring Calista Flockhart as McBeal), broadcast on ABC (1997–2002), introduced new elements into the classic legal drama, including a young female lawyer at the centre of the show, and the extensive use of music and fantasy sequences to underline plot points and express the characters' moods, thoughts and emotions. The writers often used emerging trends in the law to develop interesting, provocative storylines including episodes

---

[19] Menkel-Meadow (2001).
[20] *Law & Order: Special Victims Unit; Law & Order: Criminal Intent; Law & Order: Trial By Jury;* and *Law & Order: LA.* Various versions of the series have been adapted for the UK, France and Russia.

involving sex discrimination and harassment, organ transplants and mental ill-ness. Feminists raised objections to the depiction of McBeal as an attorney, calling her ineffective, overly interested in marriage to the detriment of her career, and unprofessional in her behaviour. *Time* magazine put her on its 29 June 1998 cover, together with feminist icons Susan B Anthony, Betty Friedan and Gloria Steinem. In spite of these objections, she seems to have had an enduring effect on popular culture.[21]

Other legal dramas that made their mark in popular culture include the David E Kelley productions *the practice* (ABC, 1997–2004), which explored ethical issues in the practice of law for the underprivileged and *Boston Legal* (ABC, 2004–08), a spin-off from *the practice*, which focused on civil law. The USA network comedy *Suits* (USA, 2011–) was set in the world of corporate law. The twist in *Suits* was that a partner in the New York law firm hired a clever young man to work as an associate who never graduated from law school but who manages to function bril-liantly as an attorney.

Some legal dramas have explored the idea of following one case throughout an entire season. Steven Bochco premiered this idea with his show *Murder One* (1995–97) on the ABC network. In each season, the story arc involved one major trial and, per episode, one or two smaller stories. Other shows that repeated this pattern include *Damages*, which premiered on the cable channel FX in 2007, and moved to DirecTV in 2010, concluding in 2012, and *How To Get Away With Murder*, which began its run on ABC in 2014.

Finally, in a recognisable category of its own are legal dramas and comedies that feature minority lawyers: women, persons of colour and other minorities.[22] Among these, a continuing theme is the disastrous lack of personal and profes-sional success of female pop culture lawyers as demonstrated in shows such as *Ally McBeal*, *The Good Wife* (CBS, 2009–), *Drop Dead Diva* (Lifetime, 2009–14) and *How To Get Away With Murder*. All of the main characters in these shows struggle with balancing the demands of personal life and professional responsibilities. The general pop culture image of women lawyers continues to be one of personal and/or professional failure, as exemplified by the unhappy marriage of Alicia Florrick in *The Good Wife*, the ethical problems of Patty Hewes in *Damages*, the unhappy love life of Jane Bingum in *Drop Dead Diva*, and the plethora of women lawyers in *Ally McBeal* who make bad personal and professional choices.[23]

---

[21] On the impact of the character and the show generally, see Smith (2007).

[22] On minorities as lawyers and as defendants see Tamborini et al (2000). Taunya Loyell Banks has studied the over-representation of female and minority lawyers in the reality TV courtroom. See Banks (2009) 309.

[23] See Klein (1997–98).

Police Dramas

Police dramas have been staples since the early days of broadcasting. One of the first popular dramas was *Dragnet*, a half-hour show airing first on NBC and then on ABC, and starring Jack Webb. *Dragnet* originated on radio and moved to television in 1951, running until 1959.[24] The police officers, played by Webb and Ben Alexander, were famous for asking witnesses for 'Just the facts'. The series emphasised crisp dialogue, matter-of-fact police procedure and arrest of the suspect. *Dragnet* returned in a revived format in 1967, starring Webb and Harry Morgan, and ran until 1970. Other police procedurals, which featured federal and state law enforcement, included *Highway Patrol* (1955–59), made with the assistance of the California Highway Patrol; *The Untouchables* (ABC, 1959–63), set in the 1930s, which emphasised the work of the FBI; *The FBI* (ABC, 1965–74), which based its episodes on actual FBI files; and *CHiPs*- (1977–83), which featured the adventures of two California Highway Patrol motorcycle officers. In particular, *The Untouchables*, with its emphasis on the incorruptibility of the FBI officers, served as a template for later shows such as *The FBI, SWAT* and other 'cop agency' shows. Such shows emphasised the honest and straightforward operations and procedures of law enforcement and its personnel.

Raymond Burr, the star of *Perry Mason*, returned in the police procedural *Ironside* (NBC, 1967–75), in which the main character, a former police commissioner, is confined to a wheelchair after surviving an assassination attempt. *Ironside* and another long-running police drama, *Kojak* (CBS, 1973–78) represented a wave of law enforcement shows in which the main character was not just a police officer but also a member of a minority (the disabled) or ethnic group. Debuting in 1984, the NBC series *Miami Vice* (1984–90) was set in Miami, Florida, and featured vice detectives Sonny Crockett (played by Don Johnson) and Ricardo Tubbs (played by Philip Michael Thomas). The driving beat of the music, the two main characters' flashy wardrobes and the exotic setting contrasted with the storylines which featured stories of criminals and drug lords.

The detective series *Columbo* debuted in 1968 as part of the NBC Mystery Movie series.[25] It starred Peter Falk and represented an 'inverted mystery', in which the viewer knows who commits the crime, and then watches the detective solve the crime, based both on observation and deduction. Lieutenant Columbo had certain little personality quirks that aided in detection, such as his tendency to return to ask the killer 'Just one more thing' after an interview was presumably completed in an effort to put pressure on him or her, his seeming inability to

---

[24] *Dragnet* was famous for its opening lines, 'Ladies and gentlemen: the story you are about to hear is true. Only the names have been changed to protect the innocent'.

[25] It ran on NBC from 1968 to 1978, and then on ABC as the *Columbo* mystery movie from 1989 to 2003.

handle firearms, his unwillingness to replace his ageing Peugeot with a reliable vehicle, and his plethora of relatives, who always seemed to play a role in endless shaggy-dog stories, which nevertheless had something to do with the solution to the murder. The show influenced the rise of such detective dramas as *Monk* (2002–09), in which the detective protagonist's obsessive compulsive behaviour led to his suspension from the San Francisco Police Department. In spite of that, Adrian Monk remained a consultant to the SFPD, and demonstrated crime-solving skills far above those of any other detective of his day.[26]

In 1981, MTM Productions introduced the highly acclaimed *Hill Street Blues* (NBC 1981–87).[27] Almost every episode began in the station house, with the watch commander giving the officers a briefing, and ending with the line, 'Let's be careful out there'. The episodes invariably included a number of storylines, some extending over several episodes, which focused on the characters' personal and professional lives. The episodes, written by Steven Bochco and Michael Kozoll, emphasised characters from the lower socio-economic strata of the unnamed city in which *Hill Street Blues* was set. The show influenced later police dramas such as *NYPD Blue*. *Hill Street Blues*, with its emphasis on gritty reality, contrasts sharply with the later Bochco vehicle *LA Law*. Although both were filmed in Los Angeles, *Hill Street Blues* takes place in an unnamed city, in which the problems that the police encounter are universal; the issues that the LA lawyers deal with, although socially relevant, are to some extent linked to southern California, as exemplified by Arnie Becker's lucrative divorce practice.

Other police dramas include the more particularised *JAG* (NBC, 1995–2005), which follows the work of the Judge Advocate General's office; *NCIS* (CBS, 2003–) which dramatises the work of the Naval Criminal Investigative Service; and *CSI* (2000–), which focuses on the work of the Crime Scene Investigative Unit in Las Vegas. One of the concerns that prosecutors have raised concerning shows like *CSI* is that members of the public now expect that real-life prosecutors will present forensic evidence in every criminal case, just as the fictional prosecutors and crime scene teams obtain on television. Prosecutors complain that the 'CSI effect' makes obtaining convictions more difficult in cases in which forensic evidence is limited or non-existent.[28]

The private investigator genre has also been perennially popular, beginning with such series as *Richard Diamond*, *Moonlighting*, *The Rockford Files*, and *Murder, She Wrote*, and continuing with the newest adaption of the Sherlock Holmes story, *Elementary*. A popular series like *Ghost Whisperer* also represents the 'amateur sleuth'

---

[26] *Columbo* and *Monk* both bear resemblances to Arthur Conan Doyle's iconic Sherlock Holmes character, but because they are members of the police force, are devoted to the letter of the law as well as to the spirit. On police procedure in *Columbo*, see Corcos (1992–93).

[27] Daniel J Travanti starred as Captain Frank Furillo and Veronica Hamel as his girlfriend, attorney Joyce Davenport.

[28] Scholars have examined the 'CSI effect' at some length. See, eg, Schweitzer and Saks (2007); and Shelton et al (2006).

type of detective show, with the added component of the paranormal, indicating the rising interest of US audiences in such phenomena. Such other long running shows as *Psych* (USA) and *The Mentalist* (CBS), take the opposite approach, positing that the paranormal does not exist, but that techniques used by fortune-tellers and psychics can help in crime detection. The main character in *Psych* pretends to be psychic while working on cases for the Santa Barbara Police Department, and the main character in *The Mentalist* was once a psychic, but has given up that occupation, admitted he was a fraud, and is now working as a consultant for the 'CBI', a California investigative agency. US television concerns itself relatively little with prison and post-prison drama or comedy.[29] *The Rockford Files* featured an ex-convict as the protagonist, the television series *Hardcastle and McCormick* paired a judge and an ex-convict, and the HBO cult hit *Oz* is set in a prison.[30]

Finally, it should be mentioned that the time from the 1950s through the 1970s formed the heyday of the western series, some of which, like the long-running *Gunsmoke* (CBS, 1955–75), were effectively police procedurals in cowboy boots. The protagonist, Marshall Matt Dillon, represented law and order in the period bringing justice to what had been the 'Wild West'. Such shows allowed the audience to explore the legends and myths of the founding of the United States after the Civil War period. Other popular 'law and order' westerns included *The Lone Ranger* (originally a radio programme), which aired from 1949 to 1957, and the Disney series *Zorro* (1957–59). *The Wild, Wild West* (1965–69) featured two secret service agents who brought federal law and order to the western part of the US after the Civil War. Similarly, many science fiction shows often posit legal regimes of the future, based on an evolving legal structure such as that of the United Nations (*Star Trek*), or some other philosophical or legal organisation after the collapse of a society resembling that of earth (*Battlestar Galactica*, *Firefly*). Using science fiction tropes, these shows explore contemporary social, religious, legal and moral issues.[31]

Reality Shows

Legal reality shows began on radio in the 1930s with such courtroom-based series as *The Court of Human Relations* (1934–39). Reality shows are as almost as old as broadcast television. Beginning with series such as *They Stand Accused* (1949–55),

---

[29] McNeely (1995) 9.

[30] On prison films and television see Wilson and O'Sullivan (2004); and Rapping (2003) 71–99.

[31] On *Battlestar Galactica* see for example, S Kapica, '"What a Glorious Moment in Jurisprudence": Rhetoric, Law, and Battlestar Galatica' (2012) *Law and the Humanities* 1, online: lch.sagepub.com/content/early/2012/12/12/1743872112466720.abstract.

on which actual court cases were re-enacted, the networks offered a fairly large variety of programmes that showed viewers aspects of the legal system from investigation to trial to incarceration. In the late 1950s and early 1960s half-hour programmes such as *Traffic Court, Divorce Court,* and *Day in Court* allowed viewers to see both civil and criminal courts in session. In 1981 *The People's Court* made its debut with retired judge Joseph Wapner presiding, and showed the audience the workings of the small claims court. Judge Wapner took pains to explain the law to the litigants; the show was popular for its educational approach. Eventually, a plethora of 'judge' shows hit the airwaves, each headed by a judge with his or her own particular personality; these included the popular *Judge Judy* as well as a number of other shows headed by retired judges. Many of these newer shows demonstrate a very different attitude towards the dispensation of justice, in which the judges demonstrate a no-nonsense attitude, often castigating the parties for their behaviour.[32]

Other legal reality shows included the wide variety of programs available on TruTV (formerly CourtTV), a network previously devoted to legal reality programming.[33] This network has broadcast or currently broadcasts specialty programming on forensic investigation (*Forensic Files*); paranormal investigation (*Haunting Evidence*); and hidden camera and 'stupid criminal' video (*World's Dumbest ...*). *Cold Case Files* (A&E Network) is a type of show which introduces the audience to unsolved cases both to educate it about police work and to encourage it to assist in solving the crime (if it is still unsolved).

Yet another popular type of show is the documentary. *Dateline NBC*, for example, usually concerns itself with crime stories and has in the past been somewhat controversial. In 2004, the programme began airing a special series called *To Catch a Predator*; the producers decoyed men into believing that they would be meeting sexual (underage) partners; these men then found themselves face to face with the programme host, Chris Hansen. Critics objected that the show blurred the line between reporting and complicity with law enforcement.

While proponents of courtroom-based reality television and televised court trials argue that these programmes have educational value for viewers, and audiences certainly find them interesting and entertaining, some researchers question whether viewers actually understand more about the justice system after viewing them.[34]

---

[32] See Kohm (2006).

[33] TruTV no longer broadcasts any legal programming. See Rodney Ho, 'TruTV Ends "In Session" Cutting Vestiges of Court TV' AJC.com (26 September 2013) at: www.accessatlanta.com/weblogs/radio-tv-talk/2013/sep/26/trutv-ends-session-cutting-all-ties-court-tv/.

[34] Paul (1997–98).

Scripted Shows with Lawyer Characters

Lawyer characters have also been very popular choices on scripted shows, particularly comedies. That the legal profession should be so heavily represented among TV characters reflects both the very high proportion of lawyers in US society today and the continuing concern that the public has with law and the legal regime. The comedy show *Hazel* (NBC, 1961–65, CBS, 1965–66) featured George Baxter as a corporate attorney although the main character was the family maid Hazel. The popular sitcom *The Cosby Show* revolved around an upper middle class African-American family in which the mother was a partner in a law firm. Marshall Eriksen, one of the five main characters on *How I Met Your Mother* (CBS, 2005–14), was first a law student, then an environmental lawyer turned corporate lawyer. Others include Jackie Chiles, Jerry's lawyer in *Seinfeld* (NBC, 1989–98) and Lionel Hutz, the lawyer in the animated comedy *The Simpsons* (Fox, 1989–) whose firm is called 'I Can't Believe It's a Law Firm'. The niche comedy *Arrested Development*[35] featured the eccentric Bluth family, represented by the delightfully awful Barry Zuckerkorn (Henry Winkler), whose spectacularly bad advice threatened to destroy them. The comedy *Will and Grace* followed the friendship of New York-based attorney Will Truman and interior designer Grace Adler; although relatively few storylines focused on Will's law practice, his legal skills often assisted him in dealing with Grace and their friends. More recently, lawyers have served as guest characters on shows such as *Two and a Half Men*, *The Big Bang Theory*, *My Wife and Kids*, and *Everybody Loves Raymond*.

Television Films with Legal Themes

Many network offerings include made-for-television movies based on historical or current cases. The thriller *See How They Run* (1964) is generally considered to be the first made for television film. *The Legend of Lizzie Borden* (1975), a docudrama dramatising the Borden murders; *Helter Skelter* (1976), based on prosecutor Vincent Bugliosi's book about the murders of Sharon Tate and others carried out by the Charles Manson family; and many other legal-related docudramas have aired over the decades, including such 'ripped from the headlines' fare as *Fatal Vision* (1984) (the murders of the MacDonald family); *The Deliberate Stranger* (1986), a TV movie based on the life and crimes of the serial killer Ted Bundy; *The OJ Simpson Story* (1995); and a number of other TV films dramatising high-profile cases.[36]

---

[35] (Fox, 2003–06; Netflix, 26 May 2013–).
[36] These include *Barbarians at the Gate* (1993), a TV movie based on the takeover of RJR Nabisco; *The Positively True Adventures of the Alleged Texas Cheerleader-Murdering Mom* (1993); two TV movies

Law and Justice on TV in the United States in 2014

I examined the basic cable offerings from Comcast, the leading cable provider in the United States, for the period from 1 to 30 November 2014.[37] Other, smaller cable providers (Charter, Cox, ATT) offer essentially the same palette of network choices as Comcast. I did not examine the offerings available through premium subscriptions (HBO, Cinemax, STARZ) because these offerings are available to a relatively small number of subscribers. In this chapter, I divide US television programming material into the categories and subcategories as listed in the table below:

Table 1: Shows relating to law and justice on American TV

1. Police and detective material	Dramas	Comedies	Reality	Reality-based entertainment	Documentaries	
WEEK 1 (1–2 Nov)	122		37.5		4	163.5
WEEK 2 (3–9 Nov)	360	.5	173.5		12	546
WEEK 3 (10–16 Nov)	476	5	194.5		1	676.5
WEEK 4 (Nov 17–23)	353	4.25	131		1	489.25
WEEK 5 (24– 30 Nov)	397	6.5	185		9	
Total	1708	16.25	721.5		27	

(continued)

based on the story of Carolyn Warmus (*A Murderous Affair* and *The Danger of Love*, both 1992); three docudramas based on the attempted murder carried out by teenager Amy Fisher (*Lethal Lolita* (1992), *Casualties of Love* (1993), and *The Amy Fisher Story* (1993)); and *Indictment: The McMartin Trial* (1995).

[37] In February, 2014, Comcast had announced that it was planning to acquire Time Warner Cable for more than $45 billion in stock, a deal that would require assent from the Federal Communications Commission and probably change the FCC's outlook towards net neutrality. At least one member of the US Senate expressed concern over the proposed merger. Senator Al Franken issued a statement saying that it 'could compromise the open nature of the Internet' because the new, more

Table 1: *(Continued)*

1. Lawyer and court-focused material						
	Dramas	Comedies	Reality	Reality-based Entertainment	Documentaries	
WEEK 1 (1–2 Nov)	59	1.5	32		4	96.5
WEEK 2 (3–9 Nov)	122	3.5	148.5		12	286
WEEK 3 (10–16 Nov)	158	4.5	157			319.5
WEEK 4 (17–23 Nov)	114	1	87.5			202.5
WEEK 5 (24–30 Nov)	135	3	146.5		8	292.5
Total	588	13.5	571.5		24	
2. Prison and post-prison material						
	Dramas	Comedies	Reality	Reality-based Entertainment	Documentaries	
WEEK 1 (1–2 Nov)			18.5			18.5
WEEK 2 (3–9 Nov)	8		35.5	5		48.5
WEEK 3 (10–16 Nov)	10	10.75	54	2		76.75

(continued)

dominant company could squeeze out competition from smaller stakeholders and from streaming sites such as Netflix and Hulu which rely on Comcast to deliver their product. See Chris Welch, 'Sen Al Franken: Comcast buying Time Warner Cable could threaten "open nature" of internet' *The Verge* (19 March 2014) at: www.theverge.com/2014/3/19/5526820/al-franken-says-comcast-buying-twc-threatens-open-nature-internet. Comcast and Time Warner eventually called off the merger in April 2015. See Alex Sherman, Gerry Smith and Todd Shields, 'Comcast Plans to Drop Time-Warner Deal' *Bloomberg Business* (22 April 2015) at: www.bloomberg.com/news/articles/2015-04-23/comcast-said-planning-to-withdraw-offer-for-time-warner-cable.

Table 1: *(Continued)*

WEEK 4 (17–23 Nov)	7	6.75	56.5	1			71.25
WEEK 5 (24–30 Nov)	5	6	84				95
Total	**30**	**23.5**	**248.5**			**8**	

Table compiled by Kirbie Watson

Summary and Analysis of Material Findings

Police and Detective Material

Police and detective material dominated network programming. Scripted police dramas dominated by approximately 3:1 over reality (unscripted) shows that featured comparable content. Popular shows included the scripted *CSI* and reality programmes such as *Forensic Files*, both of which emphasise the workings of independent teams that support the investigation of crime and the notion that science has no agenda, thus leading to a fair result at the conclusion of a trial. Reality investigative shows such as *The First 48* highlight the work of law enforcement, again catering to the interests of viewers in the work of police rather than lawyers, although the media covering the case do spend on-air time interviewing lawyers, as well as police officers, witnesses and suspects. Such shows tend to suggest that once law enforcement has focused on a particular suspect or theory of the case, that approach is likely to be the correct approach.

Currently airing shows (*Blue Bloods*, for example) have already reached the necessary critical mass of episodes and/or popularity needed in order for studios to make syndication deals.[38] The insatiable appetite of the constantly proliferating niche cable networks also means that these networks are always looking for content, either among shows that are on air now, or among shows that have aired within the past 10 to 40 years (for example, *Hawaii 5-0*). This is true not just in the police and detective genre but also in the lawyer and court material genre and in the prison and post-prison genre, although this last area is the least popular genre of legally themed television material in the US.

---

[38] While the number of episodes necessary to make a syndication package economically viable can vary, it is generally accepted to be between 88 and 100, that is, about four seasons. However, streaming services such as Hulu and Netflix are very interested in acquiring niche shows that have shorter runs or seasons, and a built-in fan base and will purchase the rights to such shows; these shows would not be candidates for syndication on legacy networks or cable networks. See M James, 'Non-hit TV Shows Get a Lifeline on the Web' *LA Times* (11 December 2011) at: articles.latimes.com/2011/dec/31/business/la-fi-ct-comedy-syndication-20111231.

Nearly 100% of the source material was US in origin. One notable exception is the show *Da Vinci's Inquest* (Canadian). Other imports are the shows aired on PBS or niche networks, which, depending on the area of the country, include series such as *Murdoch Mysteries* (Canadian) and *Sherlock* (UK). NBC Universal owns the Spanish language cable network Telemundo, which produces both telenovelas and reality programming that feature police and detective shows (for example, *Pablo Escobar: El Patrón del Mal*). Legal themes feature on telenovelas as well (for example, *Correa de innocents*).

Police officer characters, like lawyer characters, appear in scripted shows that are not necessarily 'police and detective' shows (for example, *Mike & Molly*). Audiences seem comfortable with shows that present police officers balancing personal and professional relationships (*Blue Bloods, Chicago PD*) and ultimately the main characters on the shows resolve those questions in favour of loyalty to the legal system and to the department.

Lawyer and Court-Focused Material

Both scripted and reality programming in the lawyer and court-focused category were next in the popularity category, but were significantly less popular than police and detective shows. Again, US producers created nearly 100% of such material.

Scripted, reality and reality entertainment programmes reflected the increased and continued interest in minority and ethnic characters, suggesting that creators of such programmes are reacting to viewer interest in such characters (*Drop Dead Diva, The Good Wife*). The reality shows aired included court-based shows such as *Judge Mathis*, which features a male African-American judge; and *Divorce Court*, which features a female African-American judge. Among scripted shows, popular themes included the inclusion of women lawyers (*Sex and the City*); ethnic, minority and gay lawyers (*Modern Family*); and lawyers as types of characters rather than as protagonists in legal dramas (*How I Met Your Mother*). Lawyers also played supporting or guest roles in scripted police dramas (*Criminal Minds*).

Prison and Post-Prison Material

US audiences are least interested in prison and post-prison material, and their lack of interest seems to be an historical one. Shows in this category seem to appeal to a niche audience; these shows air on cable networks (see for example *Pit Bulls and Parolees, Prison Wives*) and they are almost exclusively reality or reality entertainment shows. The origin of the shows suggests that viewer interest may originate in the actual personalities or lives of the individuals who appear on the shows, rather than an interest in the issues. That is, there may be some moral, ethical or intellectual barrier that interferes with viewers' ability to engage with scripted shows about prison, prison reform or punishment. Viewers may be more interested in issues of actual arrest, sentencing, punishment, post-conviction and suffering than in considering the abstract issues that writers might present in a scripted show. Some reality shows (*Dog the Bounty Hunter*) emphasise the use of private parties to assist law enforcement with their work, an aspect of the legal regime that viewers might not be familiar with. Again, virtually all material comes from US producers.

Most if not all prison and post-prison material locates within the lower socioeconomic classes and within certain ethnic and racial minorities, because most of the programmes are reality or reality-based programmes. The individuals who appear on the shows, either because they are inmates or members of their families, or because they are crime victims, are likely to be members of ethnic, racial and sexual minorities (although not exclusively so).

Finally, several niche cable networks (RetroTV, MyTV, WGN) offer a number of syndicated 'golden age' police, detective and legal dramas including *Hawaii 5-0, The X-Files*, and *Perry Mason* to various US markets. In addition, cable companies are slowly losing subscribers to streaming services (for example, Netflix, Hulu) as well as to newly launched services owned by legacy networks.[39]

Access to streaming services allows viewers to watch content when and where they want, since streaming is available to them on many wireless devices. In addition, some streaming services are also becoming 'networks' themselves. Netflix and Amazon are either commissioning or creating content. Netflix commissioned a fourth season of the cult favourite *Arrested Development*, which has featured lawyer characters,[40] and Amazon, through its video arm, now creates and airs its own television series.[41]

Many if not all cable services offer 'on-demand' services that provide access to recent episodes of popular series, but rights-holders control access to those episodes. As cable costs continue to rise, and as content becomes available through streaming services and the networks' own sites, viewers may opt to purchase only basic cable services and supplement their entertainment choices with streaming services, or drop cable completely and watch over-the-air channels using HD antennas.

Broadcast and cable networks plan to offer more scripted and reality show programming for the 2016 season, reflecting the fact that audiences continue to enjoy and respond to such programming.[42] In addition, a new aspect of law and

---

[39] See, eg CBS All-Access at: www.cbs.com/all-access/; and L Moraski, 'CBS Launches Expansive Digital Streaming Service' CBS News (16 October 2014) at: www.cbsnews.com/news/cbs-launches-digital-subscription-service-cbs-all-access/.

[40] Todd Leopold, '*Stay Tuned for More "Arrested Development"*' CNN (6 August 2014) at: www.cnn.com/2014/08/06/showbiz/tv/netflix-more-arrested-development/.

[41] Angela Moscaritolo, 'Get Ready to Binge Watch: Amazon Oks More Original Series' *PC Mag* (18 February 2015) at: www.pcmag.com/article2/0,2817,2476978,00.asp.

[42] Lesley Goldberg, 'TV Pilots 2016: The Complete Guide' *The Hollywood Reporter* (3 December 2015) at: www.hollywoodreporter.com/live-feed/tv-pilots-2016-complete-guide-845373.

justice programming is making its mark. Alternative networks such as Netflix offer viewers the opportunity to experience and question the justice system in radical new ways through streaming series such as the multi-part documentary *Making a Murderer*.[43] *Making a Murderer* focuses on the stories of Steven Avery and his nephew Brendan Dassey, who implicated Avery in a murder charge. Popular reaction has called for President Obama to pardon Steven Avery. Reality podcasts such as *Serial*[44] encourage viewers to revisit trials and question whether justice has been done. Indeed, through its presentation of the case of convicted murderer Adnan Syed, *Serial* may have assisted Syed in obtaining a new trial.[45] HBO's *The Jinx* follows the story of real estate heir Robert Durst, suspected of several murders. During filming, the documentarians happened upon what appears to be Durst's confession, creating excitement but also ethical and legal concerns.[46] Thus, to feed the audience's desire for law-related programming, creators are now offering new kinds of programming to add to the scripted programme, the traditional documentary and the reality show. Viewers are now more and more likely to find interesting, provocative or thoughtful law programming on any number of platforms in the US entertainment market.

[43] See: Adde Morfoot, '"Making a Murderer" Filmmakers Eye Second Installment of Netflix Series' *Variety* (26 February 2016) at: variety.com/2016/tv/news/making-a-murderer-steven-avery-season-two-new-episodes-netflix-1201716194/; Mike Hale, '*Making a Murderer*: True Crime on Netflix' *New York Times* (16 December 2015) at: www.nytimes.com/2015/12/17/arts/television/review-making-a-murderer-true-crime-on-netflix.html?_r=1; and Leslie Messer, 'White House Responds to Petition for Steven Avery of *Making a Murderer*' ABC News (7 January 2016) at: abcnews.go.com/Entertainment/white-house-responds-petition-steven-avery-making-murderer/story?id=36153350.

[44] serialpodcast.org.

[45] Mariam Khan, 'Hearing For Adnan Syed of "Serial" is "Hard To See" For Victim's Family As Case Goes On' ABC News (8 February 2016) at: abcnews.go.com/US/hearing-adnan-syed-serial-hard-victims-family-case/story?id=36780927.

[46] Jonathan Mahler, 'Irresistible TV, but Durst Film Tests Ethics, Too' *New York Times* (17 March 2015) A1.

BIBLIOGRAPHY

Abruzzese, A and Borrelli, D, *L'industria culturale: Tracce e immagini di un privilegio* (Rome, Carocci, 2000).

Almog, S, *Law and Film* (Srigim-Leon, Nevo, 2012).

Almog S, Where there is no Need to Screen Local Justice: Law and Film in Israel, p. 959–973, in *Law, Culture and Visual Studies*, Wagner A, Sherwin R. K. (eds) (New-York, NY, Springer, 2014)

Anastasiadis, G, *Thessaloniki through the Newspapers* (Thessaloniki, Ekfrasi, 1994) 133–145.

Andrini, S, 'Estetica del giallo' (2009) 1(1) *Sociologia* 89.

Annan Committee, *The Future of Broadcasting* (Chair Lord Annan) (Cmnd 6753, 1976–77).

Anthierens, J, *Tien jaar Vlaamse televisie (Ten Years of Flemish Television)* (Hasselt, Heideland, 1965).

Aristodemou, M, *Law and Literature* (Oxford, Oxford University Press, 2000).

Asimow, M (ed), *Lawyers in Your Living Room! Law on Television* (Chicago, IL, ABA Press, 2009).

Asimow, M, Brown, K and Papke, D (eds), *Law and Popular Culture: International Perspectives* (Cambridge, Cambridge Scholars Publishing, 2014).

Asimow, M, Greenfield, S and Guillermo, J et al, 'Perceptions of Lawyers: A Transnational Study of Student Views on the Image of Law and Lawyers' (2005) 12 *International Journal of the Legal Profession* 407.

Asimow, M and Mader, S, *Law and Popular Culture: A Course Book* (New York, Peter Lang, 2004).

Aziz, S-H and Piattini, M (2000) 'Servicio pubblico o il respeto delle minoranze' in Mäusli, T and Steigmeier, A (eds) (2006)

Bal, N, *De mens is wat hij doet: BRT memoires (Man is What He Does: BRT Memoirs)* (Leuven, Kritak, 1985).

Banarjee, I, 'Cultural Autonomy and Globalization' in A Goonasekera, C Hamelink and V Iyer (eds), *Cultural Rights in a Global World* (New York, Eastern Universities Press, 2003).

Banks, TL, 'Judging the Judges: Daytime Television's Integrated Reality Court Bench' in M Asimow (ed), *Lawyers in Your Living Room! Law on Television* (Chicago, IL, ABA Press, 2009).

Barroso García, J, *Realización de los géneros televisivos (Production of TV Genres)* (Madrid, Síntesis, 2002).

Barthes, R, 'L'Effet de réel' (1968) 11 *Communications* 84.

—— *Littérature et réalité* (1st edn, 1968) (Paris, Seuil, 1982).

Bechelloni, G, 'Il programma dell'anno. Il commissario Montalbano. La vampa d'agosto: Un eroe mediatico tra letteratura e realtà' in M Buonanno (ed), *Se vent'anni sembran pochi: La fiction italiana, l'Italia nella fiction anni XX–XXI* (Rome, RAI-ERI, 2010).

Berelson, B, *Content Analysis in Communication Research* (New York, Hafner Publishing Company, 1971).

Bergman, P, 'A Third Rapist? Television Portrayals of Rape Evidence Rules' in P Robson and J Silbey (eds), *Law and Justice on the Small Screen* (Oxford, Hart Publishing, 2012).

Bielawski, P, 'Media publiczne—potencjalny fundament demokracji w Polsce' in P Bielawski and A Ostrowski (eds), *Media publiczne. System medialny w Polsce—pytania i dezyderaty* (Poznań-Opole, Wydawnictwo Naukowe Scriptorium, 2011).

Bielby, P, *Australian TV—The First 25 Years* (Melbourne, Cinema, 1981).

Billedbladet 44, 30 October 2014—77th year; *Her & Nu* week 45, 5 November 2014; *Her & Nu* week 46, 12 November 2014; *Her & Nu* week 47, 19 November 2014; *Her & Nu* week 48, 26 November 2014.

Binotto, M and Martino, V (eds), *Fuoriluogo: L'immigrazione e i media italiani* (Cosenza, Pellegrini, Rai-Eri, 2005).

Black, DA, *Law in Film: Resonance and Representation* (Urbana, IL, University of Illinois Press, 1999).

Blue, WR, 'The Politics of Lope's *Fuenteovejuna*' (1991) 59(3) *Hispanic Review* 295.

Blumler, JG, 'Public Service Broadcasting Before the Commercial Deluge' in J Blumler (ed), *Television and the Public Interest: Vulnerable Values in West-European Broadcasting* (London, Sage Publications, 1992).

Boesch, I and Hungerbühler, R (2006) 'Anspruchsvoll und Massentauglich: Der Spagat der SRG in der Kultur' in Mäusli, T and Steigmeier, A (eds) (2006)

Bogoch, B and Holzman-Gazit, Y, 'Mutual Bonds—Media Frames and the Israeli High Court of Justice' (2008) 33(1) *Law & Social Inquiry* 53.

Böhnke, M, 'Myth and Law in the Films of John Ford' in S Machura and P Robson (eds), *Law and Film* (Oxford, Blackwell, 2001).

Bounds, JD, *Perry Mason: The Authorship and Reproduction of a Popular Hero* (New York, Greenwood Publishing Group, 1996).

Boyd-Barrett, O, *The International News Agencies* (London, Constable, 1980).

—— 'Media Imperialism: Towards an International Framework for the Analysis of Media Systems' in J Curran, M Gurevitch and J Woollacott (eds), *Mass Communication and Society* (London, Edward Arnold, 1977).

Brauck, M, 'Die Reality-Falle' (2009) 43 *Der Spiegel* 86.

Brevini, B, *Public Service Broadcasting Online: A Comparative European Study of PSB 2.0* (London, Palgrave, 2013).

Briggs, A (1979) *The History of Broadcasting in the United Kingdom (vol 4): Sound and Vision (1945–1955)* (Oxford, Oxford University Press)

Brinton, S, 'Regulating Diversity: Culture and Identity in Canadian Television' (Thesis, National Library of Canada, Ottawa, 2001).

Broadcasting Committee Report (Chair Lord Beveridge) (Cmd 8116, 1951).

BROADCASTING, *Copy of Royal Charter for the continuance of the British Broadcasting Corporation* (Department for Culture, Media and Sport) (Cm 6925, 2006).

Brochand, C and Mousseau, J, *L'Aventure de la Télévision* (Paris, Nathan, 1987).

Brunsdon, C and Spigel, L (eds), *Feminist Television Criticism: A Reader* (Maidenhead, Open University Press, 2008).

Budd, RW and Thorp, RK et al, *Content Analysis of Communications* (New York, Macmillan, 1967).

Buonanno, M, 'Donne al comando fra action e melodramma: Il caso di Squadra antimafia' in M Buonanno (ed), *Il prisma dei generi: Immagini di donne in TV* (Milan, Franco Angeli, 2014).

—— 'Il sistema opaco: La giustizia nella fiction italiana' in G Vitiello (ed), *In nome della legge: la giustizia nel cinema Italiano* (Soveria Mannelli, Rubbettino, 2013).

—— *Italian TV Drama and Beyond: Stories from the Soil, Stories from the Sea* (Bristol, Intellect Books, 2012).

—— *The Age of Television: Experiences and Theories* (Bristol, Intellect Books, 2008).

—— 'Il Maresciallo Rocca: The Italian Way to the TV Police Series' in H Newcomb (ed), *Television: The Critical View* (Oxford, Oxford University Press, 2000).

—— *La piovra: La crriera politica di una fiction popolare* (Genoa, Costa & Nolan, 1996).

Buxton, D, *From the Avengers to Miami Vice: Form and Ideology in Television Series.* (Manchester, Manchester University Press, 1990).

Canova, G, 'La (dis)onorata società: La rappresentazione delle mafie nel cinema italiano' (2011) 7 *Quaderni del CSCI: Rivista annuale di cinema italiano* 145.

Carley, TF, *Content Analysis: A Technique for Systematic Inference from Communications* (Winnipeg, University of Manitoba Press, 1972).

Caspi, D, *Beyond the Mirror—The Media Map in Israel* (BS University, Bialik Publishing, 2012).

—— *Due to Technical Difficulties—The Fall of the Israeli Broadcasting Authority* (Tel Aviv, Tulips Publishing, 2005).

Caspi, D and Limor, Y, *The Mediators: The Mass Media in Israel 1948–1990* (Tel Aviv, Am-Oved Publishing, 1992).

Cassese, S, *Governare gli italiani: Storia dello Stato* (Bologna, Il Mulino, 2014).

Cavicchioli, S and Pezzini, I, *La Tv-verità: Da finestra sul mondo a panopticon* (Rome, RAI-ERI, 1993).

Cazeneuve, J, *L'homme téléspectateur (Homo Telespectator)* (Paris, Denoël/Gonthier 1974).

CENSIS, 'Comunicare il futuro: Il ruolo sociale dell'Avvocatura italiana' (2009) 9 *Note & Commenti.*

Chambliss, W and Seidman R, *Law, Order and Power* (Reading, MA, Addison-Wesley, 1971).

Charlap, I, 'Drama in Three Parts (and Prologue): Histography of the Israeli Drama in Television' (2011) 6 *Media Frames* 29.

Clark, D and Samuelson, S, *50 Years: Celebrating a Half-century of Australian Television* (Sydney, Random House, 2006).

Clover, C, 'Law and the Order of Popular Culture' in A Sarat and TR Kearns, *Law in the Domains of Culture* (Ann Arbor, MI, University of Michigan Press, 1998).

—— *Men, Woman and Chainsaws* (Princeton, NJ, Princeton University Press, 1992).

Cohen, J, 'Defining Identification: A Theoretical Look at the Identification of Audiences with Media Characters' (2001) 4(3) *Mass Communication and Society* 245.

Colombo, F, *La cultura sottile: Media e industria culturale in Italia dall'Ottocento agli anni Novanta* (Milan, Bompiani, 1999).

Contreras, JM and Palacio, M, *La programación de televisión (Television Programming)* (Madrid, Síntesis, 2001).

Cooke, L (2003) British Television Drama: A History (London, BFI)

Corcos, C A, 'Columbo Goes to Law School: Or, Some Thoughts on the Uses of Television in the Teaching of Law' (1992–93) 13 *Loyola Los Angeles Entertainment Law Journal* 499.

Crawford Committee, *Report of the Broadcasting Committee, 1925* (Chair the Earl of Crawford and Balcarres) (Cmd 2599, 1926).

Culture, Media and Sport Committee (2015)—4th Report *Future of the BBC* HC 315.

Cunningham, S and Turner, G (eds), *The Media and Communications in Australia*, 3rd edn (Sydney, Allen & Unwin, 2010).

Curthoys, A, 'Television before Television' (1991) 4(2) *Continuum: Journal of Media & Cultural Studies* 152.

Custers, K, and Van den Bulck, J 'The Cultivation of Fear of Sexual Violence in Women: Processes and Moderators of the Relationship between Television and Fear' (2012) 40(1) *Communication Research* 96.

Dagtoglou, P, *Broadcasting and the Constitution* (in Greek) (Athens, Sakkoulas, 1989).

Dailly, J and Davidson, R, *The Law of Superheroes* (New York, Gotham Books, 2012).

Dampasis, G, *In the Time of Television* (in Greek) (Athens, Kastaniotis, 2002).

De Bens, E and de Smaele, H, 'The Inflow of American Television Fiction on European Broadcasting Channels Revisited' (2001) 16(1) *European Journal of Communication* 51.

De Sola Pool, I 'The Changing Flow of Television' (1977) 27(2) *Journal of Communication* 139.

Delavaud, G, 'Television and Culture According to Jean D'Arcy: The Culture Project of 1950s French Television' (2012) 7 *Critical Studies in Television* 1.

Department of National Heritage, *The Future of the BBC: A Consultation Document* (Green Paper, Cmnd 2098, 1992).

Department of Trade and Industry and Department of Culture, Media and Sport, *A New Future For Communications* (London, Cm 5010, 2000).

Dhoest, A, 'The National Everyday in Contemporary European Television Fiction: The Flemish Case' (2007) 2(2) *Critical Studies in Television* 60.

—— *De verbeelde gemeenschap: 50 Jaar Vlaamse tv-fictie en de constructie van een nationale identiteit (Imagined Community: 50 Years of Flemish TV Fiction and the Construction of a National Identity)* (Leuven, Universitaire Pers, 2004).

Dino, A, 'Un racconto allo specchio: La costruzione del mito mafioso attraverso le sue immagini' (2009) 4(3) *Studi sulla questione criminale* 57.

Doktorowicz, K, 'Polski system mediów publicznych—jak to się stało?' in P Bielawski and A Ostrowski (eds), *Media publiczne. System medialny w Polsce—pytania i dezyderaty* (Poznań-Opole, Wydawnictwo Naukowe Scriptorium, 2011).

Dotan, Y and Hofnung, M, 'Interest Groups in the Israeli High Court of Justice: Measuring Success in Litigation and Out-of-Court Settlements' (2001) 23(1) *Law & Policy* 1.

Drack, M T (ed) (2000) *Radio und Fernsehen in der Schweiz, Geschichte der Schweizerischen Rundspruchgesellschaft SRG bis 1958* (Baden: hier + Jetzt)

Drexler, P, 'The German Courtroom Film During the Nazi Period: Ideology, Aesthetics, Historical Context' (2001) 28(1) *Journal of Law and Society* 64.

Dumermuth, M (2006) 'Die Revision des Radio- und Fernsehgesetzes und das duale System' 125 *Zeitschrift für Schweizerisches Recht* 229.

—— (2007) 'Rundfunkregulierung: Alte und neue Herausforderungen' in Jarren, O and Donges, P (eds) (2007).

Dupangne, M and Waterman, D, 'Determinants of US Television Imports in Western Europe' (1998) 42(2) *Journal of Broadcasting & Electronic Media* 208.

Egger, T, (2000) 'Das Schweizer Radio auf dem Weg in die Nachkriegszeit: 1942–1949' in: Drack, M T (ed) (2000).

Ehnimb-Bertini, (2000) 'Jahre des Wachstums' in Drack, M T (ed) (2000).

Ellis, J, *Visible Fictions: Cinema, Television, Video* (Abingdon, Routledge, 1982).

Eppenberger, B and Stapfer, D (2006) *Mädchen, Machos und Moneten. Die unglaubliche Geschichte des Schweizer Kinounternehmers* (Erwin C Dietrich, Zurich).

Erickson, H, *Encyclopedia of Television Law Shows: Factual and Fictional Series About Judges, Lawyers and the Courtroom 1948–2009* (Jefferson, NC, McFarland & Company, 2009).

European Audiovisual Observatory (1999) Statistical Yearbook.

FCC v Fox TV Stations, Inc, 132 S Ct 2307 (2012).

Federal Communications Commission v Pacifica Foundation, 438 US 726 (1978).

Febbrajo, A, 'Ideologie della magistratura e società italiana' in A Giasanti (ed), *Giustizia e conflitto sociale: In ricordo di Vincenzo Tomeo* (Milan, Giuffrè, 1992).

Febbrajo, A and Harste, G (eds), *Law and Intersystemic Communication: Understanding 'Structural Coupling'* (Farnham, Ashgate, 2013).

Fernández Casadevante, JL, and Ramos Pérez, A, 'La presencia de la minorías religiosas en las series de ficción nacional' ('The Presence of Religious Minorities in National TV Series') (2012) *Documentos del Observatorio del Pluralismo Religioso en España* 2.

Forgacs, D, *Italian Culture in the Industrial Era, 1880–1980* (Manchester, Manchester University Press, 1990).

Forgacs, D and Lumley, R (eds), *Italian Cultural Studies: An Introduction* (Oxford, Oxford University Press, 1996).

Franklin, B (ed), *Law and Popular Culture: A Reader* (London, Routledge, 2001).

Freeman, M (ed), *Law and Popular Culture* (Oxford, University Press, 2005).

—— (ed), *Law and Sociology* (Oxford, University Press, 2006).

Friedman, LM, 'Law, Lawyers, and Popular Culture' (1989) 98 *Yale Law Journal* 1579.

Garapon, A, 'Foreword' in B Villez, *Television and the Legal System* (New York, Routledge, 2010).

—— 'Justice Out of Court: The Dangers of Trial by Media' (1996a) in D Nelken (ed), *Law as Communication* (Aldershot, Dartmouth, 1996).

—— *Le gardien des promesses: Le juge et la démocratie* (1996b) (Paris, Odile Jacob, 1996).

Gavrila, M and Morcellini, M, 'RAI Narrates Italy: Current Affairs, Television Information and Changing Times' (2015) 3(1–2) *Journal of Italian Cinema & Media Studies* 81.

Gest J *The Lawyer in Literature* (London, Sweet &Maxwell, 1913).

Gianotti, M, *La Tv al tempo del web 2.0* (Rome, Armando, 2012).

Giglioli, PP, Cavicchioli, S and Fele, G, *Rituali di Degradazione: Anatomia del processo Cusani* (Bologna, Il Mulino, 1997).

Giomi, E, 'Donne armate: sessismo e democrazia nelle fiction poliziesche' in A Simone (ed), *Sessismo democratico: L'uso strumentale delle donne nel neoliberismo* (Milan, Mimesis, 2012).

—— 'Public and Private, Global and Local in Italian Crime Drama: The Case of La Piovra' in M Ardizzoni and C Ferrari (eds), *Beyond Monopoly: Globalization and Contemporary Italian Media* (Lanham, MD, Rowman & Littlefield, 2010).

Grasso, A, *Storia della televisione italiana* (Milan, Garzanti, 2004).

—— (ed), *Enciclopedia della televisione* (Milano, Garzanti, 2002).

Green, MC and Brock, TC, 'The Role of Transportation in the Persuasiveness of Public Narratives' (2000) 79(5) *Journal of Personality and Social Psychology* 701.

Greenfield, S, Osborn, G and Robson, P (2010, 2nd edn) *Film and the Law: The Cinema of Justice* (Oxford: Hart).

Greenfield, S, Osborn, G and Robson, P, *Film and the Law* (London, Cavendish Publishing, 2001).

Grossey, R, *Groot lexicon van de tv series uit de spetterende jaren 70 (Lexicon of TV Series from the Rousing 70s)* (Antwerp, Standaard Uitgeverij, 1997).

—— *Groot lexicon van de tv series uit de fabuleuze Jaren 50–60 (Lexicon of TV Series from the Fabulous 50–60s)* (Antwerp, Standaard Uitgeverij, 1995).

Hamer, Y, 'Law, Culture and Minorities: Content Related Restriction in the Israeli TV and Radio' (2012) 14 *Mishpat U'mimshal* 149.

Hannerz, U, *Cultural Complexity* (New York, Columbia University Press, 1992).

Hemmer, K, (1998) *Fernsehen: Ein neues Medium zwischen Faszination und Ablehnung* (Bern: Universität Bern).

Heretakis, M, *Media, Advertisement, Consumption 1960–2000* (Thessaloniki, Studio University Press, 2010).

—— *Television and Advertisement: The Greek Case* (in Greek) (Athens, Sakkoulas, 1997).

Hermsdorf, D, *Glotze fatal* (Bochum, Filmdenken Verlag, 2010).

Hißnauer, C, Scherrer, S and Stockinger, C (2014) *Zwischen Serie und Werk: Fernseh- und Gesellschaftsgeschichte im "Tatort"* (Bielefeld: transcript).

Hibberd, M, *The Media in Italy: Press, Cinema and Broadcasting from Unification to Digital* (Maidenhead, Open University Press, 2008).

Hoog, E, *La télé Une histoire en direct* (Paris, Gallimard, 2010).

Hoskins, C and Mirus, R, 'Reasons for the US Dominance of the International Trade in Television Programmes' (1988) 10 *Media, Culture & Society* 499.

Hunt Committee, *Report of the Inquiry into Cable Expansion and Broadcasting Policy* (Chair Lord Hunt) (Cmnd 8679, 1981–82).

Idato, Michael 'Pick and mix' *The Sydney Morning Herald* (3 January 2008).

Jarvis, RM and Joseph, PR (eds), *Prime Time Law: Fictional Television as Legal Narrative* (Durham, NC, Carolina Academic Press, 1998).

Jarren, O and Donges, P (eds) (2007) *Ordnung durch Medienpolitik?* (Konstanz: UVK).

Johnson, C and Turnock, R, 'Introduction: Approaching the Histories of ITV' in C Johnson and R Turnock (eds), *Independent Television Over Fifty Years* (Maidenhead, Open University Press, 2005a).

—— 'From Start-Up to Consolidation: Institutions, Regions and Regulation over the History of ITV' in C Johnson and R Turnock (eds), *Independent Television Over Fifty Years* (Maidenhead, Open University Press, 2005b).

Karter, G, *Greek Radio and Television* (in Greek) (Athens, Kastaniotis, 2004).

—— *Historics of Television* (in Greek) (Athens, Tehniki Eklogi, 1979).

Kastoras, SD, 'Greek Television. A Descriptive Study of its Programming and Production as an Approach to Human Communication' (PhD Thesis, University of Southern California, 1978).

Kohl, C, *Das Zeugenhaus* (Munich, Goldmann, 2005).

Klein, D, 'Ally McBeal and Her Sisters' (1997–98) 18 *Loyola Los Angeles Entertainment Law Journal* 259.

Knight Foundation, 'Decoding the Net Neutrality Debate' at: www.knightfoundation.org/features/netneutrality/.

Kohm, SA, 'The People's Law Versus Judge Judy Justice: Two Models of Law in American Reality-Based Court TV' (2006) 40 *Law & Society Review* 693.

Komninou, M, *From Forum to Spectacle* (in Greek) (Athens, Papazisis, 2002).

Koukoutsaki, A, 'Greek Television Drama: Production Policies and Genre Diversification' (2003) 25 *Media, Culture & Society* 715.

Koukoutsaki, M, 'Greek Fiction Programmes: Diachronic Evolution and Production Trends' in *Vovou I, The World of Television* (in Greek), (Athens, Herodotus, 2010).

Kountouri, F, 'The Communication Dimension of Politics. The Configuration of the Partisan Field under the Predominance of Mass Media in the Public Sphere' (in Greek) (2010) 35 *Greek Review of Political Research* 57.

Kozieł, A, *Za chwilę dalszy ciąg programmu … Telewizja Polska czterech dekad 1952–1989* (Warszaw, Oficyna Wydawnicza ASPRA-JR, 2003).

Krippendorf, K, *Content Analysis. An Introduction to its Methodology*, 2nd edn (London, Sage Publications, 2004).

Kumar, R, *Research Methodology. A Step-by-Step Guide for Beginners* (London, Sage Publications, 2011).

Künzler, M (2012) 'Die Abschaffung des Monopols: Die SRG im Umfeld neuer Privatradio und Privatfernsehsender', in Mäusli, T, Steigmeier, A and Vallotton, F (eds) (2012).

Lange, A, *Fiction on European TV Channels, 2006–2013* (Strasbourg, European Audiovisual Observatory (Council of Europe, 2014)).

Leandros, N, *Party Manipulation and Financial Bankruptcy. The Case of Public TV and Radio Broadcasting in Greece* (in Greek) (Athens, Sakis Karagiorgas Foundation, 1996).

Leonard, DP, 'Perry Mason to Kurt Walheim: The Pursuit of Justice in Contemporary Film and Television' (1988) 12 *Legal Studies Forum* 377.

Leysen, B, *Gedenkboek Bert Leysen* [Festshrift Bert Leysen](Leuven, Story-Scientia, 1969).

Louis, A (2012) 'Television Divorce in Post-Franco Spain: *Anillos de oro*' ('*Wedding Rings*')' in P Robson and J Silbey (eds), *Law and Justice on the Small Screen* (Oxford, Hart Publishing, 2012).

Lowe, GF and Nissen, CS (eds), *Small Among Giants: Television Broadcasting in Smaller Countries* (Göteborg, Nordicom, 2011).

Luck, P, *50 Years of Australian TV—An Insider's View 1956–2006* (Sydney, New Holland, 2006).

Luminati, M, *Priester der Themis: Richterliches Selbstverständnis in Italien nach 1945* (Frankfurt am Main, Vittorio Klostermann, 2007).

Macaulay, S 'Images of Law in Everyday Life: The Lessons of School, Entertainment, and Spectator Sports' (1987) 21 *Law & Society Review* 185.

Machura, S, 'Television Judges in Germany' in P Robson and J Silbey (eds), *Law and Justice on the Small Screen* (Oxford, Hart Publishing, 2012).

—— 'Law and Cinema Movement' in C Picart (ed), *Framing Law and Crime* (New York, Rowman & Littlefield, 2016) (2016a).

—— 'Und die Moral von der Geschicht: Rechtspolitische Botschaften in Rechtsfilmen und Fernsehserien' in F Stuermer and P Meier (eds), *Recht populär* (Baden-Baden, Nomos, 2016) (2016b).

Machura, S and Robson, P (eds), *Law and Film* (Oxford, Blackwell, 2001).

Machura, S and Ulbrich, S, 'Law in Film: Globalizing the Hollywood Courtroom Drama' in S Machura and P Robson (eds), *Law and Film* (Oxford, Blackwell, 2001) (2001a).

—— 'Law in Film: Globalizing the Hollywood Courtroom Drama' 2001 28(1) *Journal of Law and Society* 117 (2001b).

Maneri, M, 'L'immigrazione nei media: La traduzione di pratiche di controllo nel linguaggio in cui viviamo' (2012) 1(1) *ANUAC* 24.

Marder, N, 'Judging Reality Television Judges' in P Robson and J Silbey (eds), *Law and Justice on the Small Screen* (Oxford, Hart Publishing, 2012).

Marrone, G, *Montalbano: Affermazioni e trasformazioni di un eroe mediatico* (Rome, RAI-ERI, 2003).

Mäusli, T, (2000) 'Radiohören' in Drack, M T (ed) (2000).

Mäusli, T and Steigmeier, A (eds) (2006) *Radio und Fernsehen in der Schweiz: Geschichte der Schweizerischen Radio- und Fernsehgesellschaft SRG 1958–1983* (Baden: hier + jetzt).

Mäusli, T, Steigmeier, A and Vallotton, F (eds) (2012) *Radio und Fernsehen in der Schweiz: Geschichte der Schweizerischen Radio- und Fernsehgesellschaft SRG 1983–2011* (Baden: hier + jetzt).

McNeely, CL, 'Perceptions of the Criminal Justice System: Television Imagery and Public Knowledge in the United States' (1995) 3 *Journal of Criminal Justice and Popular Culture* 1.

Melossi, D, 'Andamento economico, incarcerazione, omicidi e allarme sociale in Italia: 1863–1994' in L Violante (ed), *Storia d'Italia. Annali 12: La criminalità* (Turin, Einaudi, 1997).

Menduni, E, *La più amata dagli italiani: La televisione tra politica e telecomunicazioni* (Bologna, Il Mulino, 1996).

Menkel-Meadow, C, 'Legal Negotiation in Popular Culture: What Are We Bargaining For?' in M Freeman (ed), *Law and Popular Culture* (Oxford, Oxford University Press, 2004).

—— 'Can They Do That? Legal Ethics in Popular Culture: Of Characters and Acts' (Georgetown Public Law Research Paper No 288803, 2001).

Merino-Blanco, E, *The Spanish Legal System* (London, Sweet & Maxwell, 1996).

Miller v California, 413 US 15 (1973).

Miszczak, S, *Radiofonia i telewizja w świecie 1920–1970* (Warszawa, Wydawnictwa Radia i Telewizji, 1971).

Montanari, A, *Eroi immaginari: L'identità nazionale nei romanzi, film, telefilm, polizieschi* (Naples, Liguori, 1995).

Monteleone, F, *La chiamavamo radiotelevisione: Saggi e interventi dagli anni novanta a oggi* (Venice, Marsilio, 2014).

——*Storia della radio e della televisione in Italia: Società, politica, strategie, programmi, 1922–1992* (Venice, Marsilio, 1992).

Moran, L, Christie, I, Sandon, E and Loizidou, EL (eds), *Law's Moving Image* (London, Cavendish Publishing, 2004).

Morcellini, M (ed), *Il mediaevo italiano: Industria culturale, TV e tecnologie tra XX e XXI secolo* (Rome, Carocci, 2005).

——*Mafia a dispense: Stili della rappresentazione televisiva* (Rome, RAI-ERI, 1986).

Moriondo, E, 'The Value System and Professional Organization of Italian Judges' in V Aubert (ed), *Sociology of Law: Selected Readings* (Harmondsworth, Penguin, 1969).

Müller, H E (2014) *Propaganda gegen den Rechtsstaat*, 2014, http://blog.beck.de/2014/05/14/ der-tatort-am-vergangenen-sonntag-propaganda-gegen-den-rechtsstaat.

Müller, R (2006) 'Technik zwischen Programm, Kultur und Politik', in Mäusli, T and Steigmeier, A (eds) (2006).

Murphy, P 'Sea Change: Re-Inventing Rural and Regional Australia' (March 2002) *Transformations* 1.

Murray, C, 'Silent on the Set: Cultural Diversity and Race in English Canadian TV Drama' prepared for the Strategic Research and Analysis (SRA) (Strategic Policy and Research, Department of Canadian Heritage, 2002).

Nelken, D, 'Using Legal Culture: Purposes and Problems' in D Nelken (ed), *Using Legal Culture* (London, Wildy, Simmonds & Hill, 2012).

——'Rethinking Legal Culture' in M Freeman, (ed), *Law and Sociology* (Oxford, Oxford University Press, 2006).

Niles, M, and Mezey, N, 'Screening the Law; Ideology and Law in American Popular Culture' (2005), 28(2) *Columbia Journal of Law & The Arts* 91.

Nobel, P and Weber, R H (2007) *Rundfunkrecht* (Bern: Stämpfli).

Nobles, R and Schiff, D, 'Structural Coupling Between the Systems of Law and the Media: The Contrasting Examples of Criminal Conviction and Criminal Appeal' in A Febbrajo and G Harste (eds), *Law and Intersystemic Communication: Understanding 'Structural Coupling'* (Farnham, Ashgate, 2013).

——*Understanding Miscarriages of Justice: Law, the Media and the Inevitability of Crisis* (Oxford, Oxford University Press, 2000).

Office of Communications (2005) Ofcom Review of Public Service Television Broadcasting Phase 3—Competition for Quality 8 February:www.ofcom.org.uk/consult/condocs/psb3/psb3.pdf.

Oikonomou, A, 'The Institutional Framework of Terrestrial Digital Television' (in Greek) Presentation at E-Business Forum (Athens, 2008).

Olgiati, V, 'La "positività" del diritto positivo nel pensiero di Vincenzo Tomeo' (2001) 31(2) *Materiali per una storia della cultura giuridica* 441.

Ortoleva, P and Di Marco, MT, *Luci del teleschermo: Televisione e cultura in Italia* (Milan, Electa, 2004).

Osborn, G, 'Borders and Boundaries: Locating the Law in Film' (2001) 28 *Journal of Law and Society* 164.

Pablos, E de (2013) 'Spains producers go global'. Available at: http://tbivision.com/features/2013/10/drama-as-spains-producers-go-global/171201/ [Accessed 21 July 2016]

Padovani, C, '"Berlusconi's Italy": The Media Between Structure and Agency' (2015) 20(1) *Modern Italy* 41.

——*A Fatal Attraction: Public Television and Politics in Italy* (Lanham, MD, Rowman & Littlefield, 2007).

Palacio, M, 'Early Spanish Television and the Paradoxes of a Dictator General' (2005) 25(4) *Historical Journal of Film, Radio and Television* 599.

——'La television pública española (TVE) en la era de José Luis Rodríguez Zapatero' (2007) 1 *Journal of Spanish Cultural Studies* 71.

——*Las cosas que hemos visto: 50 años y más de TVE* (*Things We've Seen: 50 Years of TVE*) (Madrid, RTVE Institute, 2006).

Panagiotopoulou, R, 'Media in Greece Today' (in Greek) (2010) *Communication Issues* 10.

——*Television Outside the Walls* (in Greek) (Athens, Kastaniotis, 2004).

Papathanassopoulos, S, *Television in the 21st Century* (in Greek) (Athens, Kastaniotis, 2005).

——'The Effects of Media Commercialization on Journalism and Politics in Greece' (1999) 3(4) *The Communication Review* 379.

——*The Power of Television. The Rational of the Medium and the Market* (in Greek) (Athens, Kastaniotis, 1997).

——*Deregulating Television* (in Greek) (Athens, Kastaniotis, 1993).

——'Broadcasting, Politics and the State in Socialist Greece' (1990) 12 *Media, Culture & Society* 387 (1990a).

——'Public Service Broadcasting and Deregulatory Pressures in Europe' (1990) 16 *Journal of Information Science* 113 (1990b).

Papatheodorou, FMD and Machin, D, 'The Umbilical Cord That Was Never Cut. The Post-Dictatorial Intimacy between the Political Elite and the Mass Media in Greece and Spain' (2003) 18 *European Journal of Communication* 31.

Paul, AM, 'Turning the Camera on Court TV: Does Televising Trials Teach Us Anything About the Real Law?' (1997–98) 58 *Ohio State Law Journal* 655.

Peacock Committee, *Report of the Committee on Financing the BBC* (Cmnd 9824, 1986).

Penney, S, 'Mass Torts, Mass Culture: Canadian Mass Tort Law and Hollywood Narrative Film' (2004) 30 *Queen's Law Journal* 205.

Peponis, A, *1961–1981 Facts and Persons* (in Greek) (Athens, Livanis, 2002).

Pezzini, I, 'La figura criminale nella letteratura, nel cinema e in televisione' in L Violante (ed), *Storia d'Italia. Annali 12: La criminalità* (Turin, Einaudi, 1997).

Pfau, M, Mullen, LJ, Diedrich, T and Garrow K 'Television Viewing and Public Perceptions of Attorneys' (1995) 21 *Human Communications Research* 307.

Philippopoulos-Mihalopoulos, A, *Spatial Justice: Body, Lawscape, Atmosphere* (Abingdon, Routledge, 2015).

Pilkington Committee, *Report of the Broadcasting Committee* (Cmnd 1753, 1961–62).

Pineau, G, 'La Justice saisie par la télévision' (January–February 2003) 107 *Dossiers de l'audiovisuel* 69.

Podlas, K, 'Impact of Television On Cross Examination and Juror "Truth"' (2009) 14 *Widener Law Review* 483.

——'Guilty on All Counts: Law and Order's Impact on Public Perceptions of Law and Order' (2008) 18 *Seton Hall Journal of Sports and Entertainment Law* 1.

Porsdam, H, *Legally Speaking. Contemporary American Culture and the Law* (Amherst, MA, University of Massachusetts Press, 1999).

Poulakidakos, S and Karoulas, G, 'Multilateralism and Concentration of Greek Television Productions' (Research conducted for the Institute of Applied Communication of Cyprus, 2009).

Powelz, M 'Haus der Verdammten' (14 November 2014) 47 *Gong* 15.

Quinet, E, *Philosophie de l'histoire de France* (Paris, Payot, 1857) (republished 2009).

Rafter, N, *Shots in the Mirror. Crime Films and Society*, 2nd edn (Oxford, Oxford University Press, 2006).

Raiteri, M, 'Rappresentazione del giudice e realtà della magistratura' in A Giasanti (ed), *Giustizia e conflitto sociale: In ricordo di Vincenzo Tomeo* (Milan, Giuffrè, 1992).

Ramiro Avilés, M, Rivaya, B and Barranco Avilés, M, *Derechos, Cine, Literatura y Cómics. Cómo y por qué* (Valencia, Tirant lo Blanch, 2014).

Rapping, E, *Law and Justice As Seen on TV* (New York, New York University Press, 2003).

Ravid, I, 'Watch & Learn: Illegal Behavior and Obedience to Legal Norms Through the Eyes of Israeli and American Popular Culture' 2015 4(1) *Berkeley Journal of Entertainment and Sports Law* 38.

Reith, JCW, *Broadcast over Britain* (London, Hodder & Stoughton, 1924).

Richeri, G and Balbi, G, 'The Final Days of the RAI Hegemony: On the Sociocultural Reasons Behind the Fall of the Public Monopoly' (2015) 3(1–2) *Journal of Italian Cinema & Media Studies* 63.

Rinaldi, L, *Andrea Camilleri: A Companion to the Mystery Fiction* (Jefferson, NC, McFarland & Co, 2012).

Robson, P, 'Lawyers and the Legal System on TV: The British Experience' (2007a) 2(4) *International Journal of Law in Context* 333.

—— 'Developments in Law and Popular Culture: The Case of the TV lawyer' (2007b) (in Representations of Justice (eds Masson A and O'Connor K (Brussels, P.I.E. Peter Lang).

—— (2006) The Justice Films of Sidney Lumet (2006) (in (eds) Greenfield S and Osborn G (Abingdon, Routledge).

——'Law and Film Studies: Autonomy and Theory' in M Freeman (ed), *Law and Popular Culture* (Oxford, Oxford University Press, 2005).

——*Housing and the Judiciary* (Glasgow, University of Strathclyde, 1979).

Robson, P, Osborn, G and and Greenfield, S 'The Impact of Film and Television on Perceptions of Law and Justice: Towards a Realisable Methodology' in A Wagner and R Sherwin (eds), *Law, Culture and Visual Studies* (Dordrecht, Springer, 2014).

Robson, P and Silbey, J (eds), *Law and Justice on the Small Screen* (Oxford, Hart Publishing, 2012).

Rosenberg, R (2009) 'Document left by Rodrigo Rosenberg'. Available at: http://www. guate360.com/blog/2009/05/11/document-left-by-rodrigo-rosenberg-marzano- guatemala/ [Accessed on 21 July 2016].

Rosenthal, A (ed), *Why Docudrama? Fact-Fiction on Film and TV* (Carbondale, IL, Southern Illinois University Press, 1999).

Ruppen Coutaz, R (2012) 'Les ripostes de la SSR à la liberalisation du marché de l'audiovisuel: Vers une redéfinition de son mandat de service public' in Mäusli, T, Steigmeier, A and Vallotton, F (eds) (2012).

Saeys, F, 'Statuut, organisatie en financiering van de openbare televisieomroep in Vlaanderen' ('Status, Organization and Financing of Public Television in Flanders') in A Dhoest and H Van den Bulck (eds), *Publieke televisie in Vlaanderen: Een geschiedenis* (Gent, Academia Press, 2007).

Salzmann, V and Dunwoody, P, 'Prime Time Lies: Do Portrayals of Lawyers Influence How People Think about the Legal Profession?' (2005) 58 *Southern Methodist University Law Review* 411.

Sarat, A, Douglas, L and Umphrey, M (eds), *Law on the Screen* (Stanford, CT, Stanford University Press, 2005).

Sauvage, M and Veyrat-Masson, I, *Histoire de la television française* (Paris, Nouveau Monde, 2012).

Saxer, U and Ganz-Blättler, U (1998) *Fernsehen DRS, Werden und Wandel einer Institution: Ein Beitrag zur Medienhistographie als Institutionengeschichte* (Zürich: Institut für Publizistikwissenschaft und Medienforschung der Universität Zürich).

Savelsberg, JJ, 'Knowledge, Domination and Criminal Punishment Revisited' (1999) 1 *Punishment and Society* 45.

Scannell, P and Cardiff, D, *A Social History of British Broadcasting, Volume One 1922–1939: Serving the Nation* (Cambridge, Basil Blackwell, 1991).

Schachar, Y, 'When Faust Takes a Lawyer—On the Relationship Between Culture and Law' (2007) 3 *Din U'dvarim* 147.

Schade, E (2000a) 'Wenig radiotechnischer Pioniergeist vor 1922' in Drack, M T (ed) (2000).

—— (2000b) 'Das Scheitern des Lokalrundfunks: 1923–1931' in Drack, M T (ed) (2000).

—— (2006) 'Die SRG auf dem Weg zur forschungsbasierten Programmgestaltung' in Mäusli, T and Steigmeier, A (eds) (2006).

—— (2015) 'Versöhnung der Zerstrittenen' *Neue Zürcher Zeitung* 19 May 2015.

Scherrer, A (2012) 'Die Digitalisierung: Schrittmacher und Sparpotenzial', in Mäusli, T, Steigmeier, A and Vallotton, F (eds) (2012).

Schiller, HI, *Communication and Cultural Domination* (New York, International Arts and Sciences Press, 1976).

Schneider, T (2006) 'Vom SRG-"Monopol" zum marktorientierten Rundfunk' in Mäusli, T and Steigmeier, A (eds) (2006).

Schulz, JL, '*Fairly Legal*: A Canadian Perspective on the Creation of a Primetime Mediator' in M Asimow, K Brown and D Papke (eds), *Law and Popular Culture: International Perspectives* (Cambridge, Cambridge Scholars Press, 2014).

——'Canada: ADR and *The Associates*' in P Robson and J Silbey (eds), *Law and Justice on the Small Screen* (Oxford, Hart Publishing, 2012).

——'Settlement and Mediation in Canadian Legal Television' (2011) 1 *Journal of Arbitration and Mediation* 77.

——'girls club Does Not Exist' in M Asimow (ed), *Lawyers in Your Living Room! Law on Television* (Chicago, IL, ABA Press, 2009).

——'Law & Film: Where are the Mediators?' (2008) 58 *University of Toronto Law Journal* 233.

Schweitzer, NJ and Saks, MJ, 'The CSI Effect: Popular Fiction About Forensic Science Affects the Public's Expectations About Real Forensic Science' (2007) 47 *Jurimetrics* 359.

Sendall, B, *Independent Television in Britain: Volume 2, Expansion and Change 1958–1968* (London, Macmillan, 1983).

Sharp, C, 'Justice with a Vengeance—Retributive Desire in Popular Imagination' in M Asimow, K Brown and D Papke (eds), *Law and Popular Culture: International Perspectives* (Cambridge, Cambridge Scholars Publishing, 2014).

——'The "Extreme Makeover" Effect of Law School: Students Being Transformed by Stories' (2005) 12 *Texas Wesleyan Law Review* 233.

Sharp, C and Leiboff, M (eds), *Cultural Legal Studies: Law's Popular Cultures and the Metamporhosis of Law* (Abingdon, Routledge, 2016).

Shelton, DE et al, 'A Study of Juror Expectations and Demands Concerning Scientific Evidence: Does the "CSI Effect" Exist?' (2006) 9 *Vanderbilt Journal of Entertainment and Technology Law* 330.

Sherman, A, McCracken, J, and Lee, E, Comcast Agrees to Buy Time-Warner for $45.2 Billion, http://www.bloomberg.com/news/articles/2014-02-12/comcast-said-to-agree-to-pay-159-a-share-for-time-warner-cable.

Sherwin, RK, 'Introduction: Law, Culture and Visual Studies' in A Wagner and R Sherwin (eds), *Law, Culture and Visual Studies* (Dordrecht, Springer, 2014) xxxiii-xli.

——'Law in Popular Culture' in A Sarat (ed), *The Blackwell Companion to Law and Society* (Malden, Blackwell, 2004).

——*When Law Goes Pop: The Vanishing Line between Law and Popular Culture* (Chicago, University of Chicago Press, 2000).

——'Cape Fear: Law's Inversion and Cathartic Justice' (1996) 30 *University of San Francisco Law Review* 1023.

Silbey, J, 'Patterns of Courtroom Justice' in S Machura and P Robson (eds), *Law and Film* (Oxford, Blackwell, 2001).

Sims, JR, 'Politicians and Media Owners in Greek Radio: Pluralism as Diaplokí' (2003) 10(2) *Journal of Radio Studies* 202.

Siune, K and Hultén, O, 'Does Public Service Broadcasting have a Future?' in D McQuail and K Siune (eds), *Media Policy. Convergence, Concentration and Commerce* (London, Sage Publications, 1998).

Skolnick, J, *Justice Without Trial* (New York, John Wesley, 1965).

Slotten, HR, *Radio and Television Regulation: Broadcast Technology in the United States, 1920–1960* (Baltimore, MD, The Johns Hopkins University Press, 2000).

Smith, A (ed), *Television: An International History*, 2nd edn (Oxford, Oxford University Press, 1998).

Smith, GM, *Beautiful TV: The Art and Argument of Ally McBeal* (Austin, TX, University of Texas Press, 2007).

Smith, PJ, *Contemporary Spanish Culture: TV Fashion, Art and Film* (Cambridge, Polity, 2003).

——'Crime Scenes: Police Drama on Spanish Television' (2007) 1 *Journal of Spanish Cultural Studies* 55.

——*Television in Spain: from Franco to Almodóvar* (Woodbridge, Tamesis, 2006).

Sorice, M, *L'industria culturale in Italia* (Rome, Editori Riuniti, 1998).

Sorongas, E, *The Phenomenon of Reality TV* (in Greek) (Athens, Kastaniotis, 2004).

Spada, C, 'European Original Fiction: A National Resource and Different Ways of Self-representation' (2002) 2(2) *Canadian Journal of Communication* 197.

Stark, S, 'Perry Mason Meets Sonny Crockett: The History of Lawyers and the Police as Television Heroes' (1987) 42 *University of Miami Law Review* 229.

Straubhaar, JD, *World Television: From Global to Local* (London, Sage Publications, 2007).

——'Choosing National TV: Cultural Capital, Language, and Cultural Proximity in Brazil' in MG Elasmar (ed), *The Impact of International Television: A Paradigm Shift* (Mahwah, NJ, Lawrence Erlbaum Associates, 2003).

——'Beyond Media Imperialism: Asymmetrical Interdependence and Cultural Proximity' (1991) 8(1) *Critical Studies in Mass Communication* 39.

Stürmer, F and Meier, P (eds), *Recht populär* (Baden-Baden, Nomos, 2016).

Surette, R, Media, Crime and Criminal Justice: Images and Realities (1992 Introduction

Sykes Committee, *Broadcasting Committee Report* (Chair Sir Frederick Sykes) (Pacific Grove, Brooks/Cole Publishing, Cmd 1951, 1923).

Syvertsen, T, Enli, G, Mjøs, OJ, and Moe, H, *The Media Welfare State: Nordic Media in the Digital Era* (Ann Arbor, Michigan: The University of Michigan Press, 2014).

Tal, Z, and Ivry-Omer, D, Regulation of Electronic Communications Services in Israel: The Need to Establish a Communications Authority, Israeli Democracy Institute Policy Papers Series (2009) (in Hebrew). Available online: http://www.idi.org.il/media/277043/pp_76.pdf (2009).

Tamborini, R, Mastro, DE, Assad, RMC and Huang, RH, 'The Color of Crime and the Court: A Content Analysis of Minority Representation on Television' (2000) 77 *Journalism & Mass Communication Quarterly* 639.

Tasker, Y, 'Television Crime Drama and Homeland Security: From Law & Order to "Terror TV"' (2012) 51 *Cinema Journal* 44.

Tate, MA, 'Canada, Culture and Broadcasting: An Examination of the Cultural Components of Canada's Broadcasting Policies' (Thesis, Pennsylvania State University, College of Communications, 2000).

Terzic, M, 'Judge Judy: Constructions of "Justice with an Attitude"' in P Robson and J Silbey (eds), *Law and Justice on the Small Screen* (Oxford, Hart Publishing, 2012).

Thompson, RJ, *Television's Second Golden Age: From Hill Street Blues to ER* (New York, Continuum, 1996).

Thussu, DK (ed), *Media on the Move: Global Flow and Contra-Flow* (London, Routledge, 2007).

Thym, B, 'Kultivierung durch Gerichtsshows. Eine Studie unter Berücksichtigung von wahrgenommener Realitätsnähe, Nutzungsmotiven und persönlichen Erfahrungen' (Unpublished Master's dissertation, Ludwig-Maximilians-Universität Munich, 2003).

Tomeo, V, *Il giudice sullo schermo: Magistratura e polizia nel cinema italiano* (Bari, Laterza, 1973).

Tomlinson, J, *Globalisation and Culture* (Oxford, Polity Press, 1999).

Tracey, M, *The Decline and Fall of Public Service Broadcasting* (Oxford, Clarendon Press, 1998).

Treves, R, *Giustizia e giudici nella società italiana* (Rome, Laterza, 1972).

Tsaliki, L, 'The Role of Greek Television in the Construction of National Identity Since Broadcasting Deregulation' (PhD Thesis, University of Sussex, 1997).

Tsoukalas, K, *State, Society, Labor in Post War Greece* (in Greek) (Athens, Themelio, 2005).

Turnbull, S, *The TV Crime Drama* (Edinburgh, Edinburgh University Press, 2014).

Vaca Berdayes, R, *El ojo digital: Audiencias 1* (Madrid, Ex Libris, 2004).

Valentini, P, 'Whodonit? Rai Tv Fiction Production Between Detection and Giallo' (2012) 12(2) *Cinéma & Cie* 25.

Vallotton, F (2006) 'Anastasie ou Casandre: Le role de la radio-télévision dans la société helvétique', in Mäusli, T and Steigmeier, A (eds) (2006).

Valoukos, S, *History of Greek Television* (in Greek) (Athens, Aigokeros, 2008).

Van Casteren, A, *25 dozijn rode rozen. Een kwarteeuw Vlaamse televisie* (*25 Dozen Red Roses. A Quarter Century of Flemish Television*) (Gent, Het Volk, 1978).

Van den Bulck, H, 'The Last Yet Also the First Creative Act in Television? An Historical Analysis of PSB Scheduling Strategies and Tactics' (2009) 15(3) *Media History* 321.

——'Het beleid van publieke televisie: van hoogmis van de moderniteit naar postmodern sterk merk?' ('Public Television Policy: From High Mass of Modernity to Postmodern Strong Brand?') in A Dhoest and H Van den Bulck (eds), *Publieke televisie in Vlaanderen: een geschiedenis* (Gent, Academia Press, 2007).

——'Public Service Broadcasting and National Identity as a Project of Modernity' (2001) 23(1) *Media, Culture and Society* 53.

——*De rol van de publieke omroep in de moderniteit. Een analyse van de bijdrage van de Vlaamse publieke televisie tot de creatie van een nationale cultuur en identiteit* (*The Role of Public Service Broadcasting in Modernity: An Analysis of the Contribution of Flemish Public Television to the Creation of a National Culture and Identity*) (Leuven, CeCoWe, 2000).

Van den Bulck, H, Tambuyzer, S and Simons, N, 'Scheduling and Continuity Techniques in a Changing Television Landscape: A Case Study in Flanders' (2014) 5(1) *International Journal of Digital Television* 39.

Van den Bulck, J, 'The Selective Viewer Defining (Flemish) Viewer Types' (1995) 10(2) *European Journal of Communication* 147.

——'Television News Avoidance: Exploratory Results from a One-Year Follow-Up Study' (2006) 50(2) *Journal of Broadcasting & Electronic Media* 231.

Van Poecke, L and Van den Bulck, H (eds), *Culturele globalisering en lokale identiteit: Amerikanisering van de Europese media* (*Cultural Globalisation and Local Identity: Americanisation of European Media*) (Leuven, Garant, 1994).

Varis, T, 'International Flow of Television Programmes', Reports and Papers on Mass Communication, No 100 (Paris, UNESCO, 1985).

Veltroni, W, *I Programmi che hanno Cambiato l'Italia: Quarant'anni di Televisione* (Milan, Feltrinelli, 1992).

Villez, B, 'Engrenages: Antilegalism and French Realism' in M Asimow, K Brown and D Papke (eds), *Law and Popular Culture: International Perspectives* (Cambridge, Cambridge Scholars Publishing, 2014).

——*Television and the Legal System* (New York, Routledge, 2010).

Villiers, C, *The Spanish Legal Tradition* (Aldershot, Ashgate, 1999).

Vitiello, G, 'Indagini preliminari: Perché non esiste un coutroom drama italiano' in G Vitiello (ed), *In nome della legge: La giustizia nel cinema Italiano* (Soveria Mannelli, Rubbettino, 2013).

Vovou, I, *The World of Television* (in Greek) (Athens, Herodotus, 2010).

Wagner, A and Sherwin, R (eds) *Law, Culture and Visual Studies* (Dordrecht, Springer, 2014).

Wajda, K, 'Milicjant, glina i pani prokurator, czyli jak się zmieniał polski serial kryminalny' in W Godzic (ed), *30 najważniejszych programów TV w Polsce* (Warsaw, Wydawnictwo Trio TVN SA, 2005).

Wajdowicz, R, *Julian Ochorowicz jako prekursor telewizji i wynalazca w dziedzinie telefonii* (Wrocław, Zakład Narodowy im Ossolińskich, 1964).

Weil, S, *La Pesanteur et la grâce (Gravity and Grace)* (Librairie PLON, Paris, 1947).

Weiman, G, 'Connecting to Cables, A Study on the Effects of the Transition to Multi-channeled Television in Israel' (1996) 37(4) *Megamot* 394.

Wilson, D and O'Sullivan, S, *Images of Incarceration: Representations of Prison in Film and Television Drama* (Winchester, Waterside Press, 2004).

Yadin, S, 'Regulating the Commercial Television: The Second Authority Enforcement Model on Channel 10' (Jerusalem, Van Leer Jerusalem Institute, 2014).

US Regulations

16 CFR §408 (2015).

47 CFR §73.612 (2015).

47 CFR §73.1001–4280 (2015).

47 CFR §73.4055 (2015).

15 USC §1335 (2015).

47 U.S. C. §151 (2015).

47 USC §303 (2015).

47 USC §521 et seq.

47 USC §533 (2015).

INDEX OF TV SHOWS

1-0-0 (Channel 10, 2012). A successful police drama focusing on the professional and private lives of a detective in one of Israel's police stations. Israel.

5 Colonnes à la Une (Antenne 2). French TV report (magazine). Not all episodes, crimes or trials, but it is one of the first TV reports to explore the legal conditions of immigrants in Paris or deal with prostitution issues in the mid-1960s where French television tended to consider such topics as a social taboo. France, 1959–1968 (irregularly).

07 zgłoś się [07 Come In] (1976–87). Polish criminal series following the life of lieutenant Borewicz (Bronisław Cieślak), who is an unconventional and efficient investigator, working for the International Affairs Office. Poland.

13 posterunek [13th Precinct] (1997–98). A comedy series showing the day to day life of a group of helpless and unlucky policemen, working in a small precinct. Poland.

19-2 a French language police procedural which first aired on Télévision de Radio-Canada in 2011, Canada.

24 Hours in Police Custody (2014–). Series following a British police force in its day to day activities. Britain.

70 Million Reasons for Wealth [70 Million Sibot Le'osher] (Channel 2, 2014). This comedy, which was broadcasted for only a few months, tells the story of an insurance appraiser who wins the lottery.

87th Precinct (1961–1962) gritty policy series revolving around Manhattan's 87th precinct and focusing on neighbourhood crime and the personal lives of the policy officers. The series was based on the novels by Ed McBain. US, shown in Flanders.

Accused [Acusados] (Telecinco, 2009–10). An interesting variation of the normal lawyer show. Judge Rosa Ballester investigates a relatively harmless fire in a night club when the storyline quickly leads to corruption and murder. Spain.

Achtung Kontrolle! [Attention Control!] (Kabel 1, 2008–12; 2013–, 1052+ episodes). Reality show about the work of the traffic police, food controllers, customs official and other control personnel. Germany.

Ad H'chatuna [Until the Wedding] (Channel 2, 2008). A bitter romantic drama revolving around a couple preparing for their wedding and the obstacles they face. Israel.

Against the Wall (Lifetime, 2011). Police drama television series about a policewoman Abby Kowalski (Rachael Carpani), who starts a new career path at Chicago PD's Internal Affairs Division. This decision causes a split between her and her family members, who are also a part of the force. USA, shown in Poland.

Agatha Christie's Marple (2004–13). Later versions of the 'golden age' tales of the amateur detective Miss Marple (*qv*). Britain.

Agatha Christie's Poirot (2004–13). Amateur detective from the 'golden age' where the Belgian solves problems which defeat the police. Britain.

Aktenzeichen XY Ungelöst [*File Number XY Unsolved*]. This German forerunner of shows like America's *Most Wanted*, profiles cases involving the search for fugitives wanted for serious crimes with at least one murder case per episode. The factual circumstances of each case are re-enacted by lay persons. Dating back to 1967 the show is one of the longest running in German television history. The legendary status of the show stems from the fact that it helped solve some grave crimes that were formerly cold cases. Germany.

Aktionen. Danish 12-part documentary about major police actions. Each programme follows a major police action from start to end including planning and the actual action. Denmark.

Alarm 112. Danish documentary series and the equivalent to the *American Rescue 911*. We follow the first people to react when calling about an accident. Denmark.

Alarm for Cobra 11 [*Alerta Cobra*; original German title: *Alarm für Cobra 11*] (Cuatro, 2014). A long-running successful German export about the highway police: German highways are depicted as a thoroughfare for Europe's organised crime—making the show transnational by definition. Its transnationality can be observed in both content and format. Germany, shown in Spain.

Alenbi (Channel 10, 2012). A series based on a book written by Gadi Taub, which tells the story of a strip bar owner at the centre of Tel Aviv and the lives of the strippers working in his bar.

Alias Smith and Jones (1971–1973) western series about two outlaws, Hannibal Heyes and Kid Curry, who are offered amnesty if they can stay out of trouble for a year which them attempt under the aliases of Smith and Jones. US, shown in Flanders.

Alice Nevers, le Juge est une Femme (TF1, 1993). Centring on the work of Alice Nevers, a 'juge d'instruction' (examining magistrate). Most of episodes take place in Paris and its surroundings. It was formerly known as *Florence Larrieu, le juge est une femme*, and the series is composed of over 19 seasons and 72 episodes. France.

Ally McBeal (Fox, 1997–2002). Legal 'dramedy' focusing on the private lives and careers of associates and law partners at the Boston law firm of Cage and Fish. The show featured cutting-edge legal issues and a soundtrack that also drew attention for its use of music that recalled events in the episode. Many of the characters had theme songs as well. USA.

Der Alte [*The Senior*] (ZDF, 1977–). Long-running crime series centring on a seasoned veteran of the Munich police department (hence the title). Due to the longevity of this programme there were already several protagonists in the leading part while a few of the (younger) assistants stayed with the series. The plots focus mainly on a single murder case in the upper middle class of Bavarian society. Usually the case is solved by the cunning commissioner. Germany.

American Gigolo (1980). Feature movie about a Los Angeles male escort who is framed into a murder plot. USA.

Anatomy of a Crime [*Anatomia enos Egklimatos*] (ANT1, 1992–95, 72 episodes). Self-contained stories of real crimes, usually of passion, it presented the profile and the circumstances that led to the crime. It had a big audience and featured many new writers and directors. Greece.

An Arab's Work [*Avoda Aravit*] (Channel 2, 2007). A comedy drama focusing on the relationship between Jews and Arabs in modern Israel. Israel.

Annika Bengtzon (1998–). Book and film series about a crime reporter, created by the Swedish journalist and crime writer Liza Marklund. Sweden, shown in Denmark.

Anti-Mafia Squad [*Squadra antimafia*] (Canale 5, 2009–). Set in today's Palermo, this series focuses on the war between Mafia families for the leadership of *Cosa Nostra*. It innovatively features two women as the main characters: deputy chief of police Claudia Mares, who leads a special anti-Mafia squad, and young Rosy Abate, a member of one of the oldest criminal clans, who returns to Palermo after a long stay in the USA. Italy.

Anwälte im Einsatz [*Lawyers in Action*] (2013–). Documentary-style drama series set around a team of lawyers helping clients in cases of divorce, mobbing, disputes with neighbours and the like. The cast consists of real-life lawyers and other lay actors. Germany.

APTN Investigates Breach of Trust. The Aboriginal Peoples Television Network produces this show which investigates legal issues connected to Canada's first peoples. Canada.

The Arbitrator [*Ha'borer*] (2007–). A Mafia-style crime drama which became extremely popular. It tells the story of a law-abiding middle-class social worker who discovers that he is adopted. While searching for his biological father, he is dragged into the life of the head of an organised crime network in Israel, and his family. So far, the show has had four seasons, which is an impressive achievement among short-term Israeli dramas. Israel.

Are You the Assassin? [*Es usted el asesino?*] (TVE, 1967). A huge success, this is the story of the investigation into the assassination of a rich banker. Stretched over nine episodes viewers were kept hooked by the very slow solution of the crime. Spain.

Arrest and Trial (ABC, 1963–64). Ninety-minute crime drama that featured the arrest of a suspect in the first half of the show and prosecution of the case in the second half. It served as the model for Dick Wolf from *Law & Order* franchise of the 1990s. USA.

Arsène Lupin (ORTF, 1971–74). Series inspired by Maurice Leblanc's short stories. Lupin was known as a 'gentleman burglar', never caught by the police but happy to restore stolen goods to lovely women whose smiles would move him. France.

Asfur ('Hot', 2010) is one of the most popular TV shows in recent years, which tells the story of four good friends who live in a deserted bus at the margins of an industrial area in Jerusalem. Israel.

Aspe (2004–14). Police show, based on the books of Flemish crime writer Pieter Aspe, who appears in cameo roles throughout the 10 seasons. The stories feature Bruges City police. Made for VTM, a Flemish commercial TV channel, but some seasons were also broadcast by Dutch television. Belgium.

The Associates was an hour-long prime-time Canadian dramatic series that ran for two seasons on CTV, in 2001 and 2002. It featured five new associates in a large Toronto Bay Street law firm. Interestingly, *The Associates* was full of instances where lawyers chose to use alternative dispute resolution (ADR) processes such as negotiation, mediation and arbitration instead of litigation. Almost half of the first season's episodes had mediation-themed storylines and mediation was made to look as interesting and as exciting as courtroom work—something extremely rarely seen on television. Canada.

Audience privée (France 2, 2002). Two people confront each other in a civil dispute before a mediator who tries to find a settlement on the air. Could be considered the only reality programme on legal material in France. France.

Auf Streife [*On Patrol*] (2013–). Cameras following police officers and their cases. Germany.

Avocat des étrangers (Public Sénat, 2014). This series of documentaries broadcast on the channel, Public Sénat, emphasises the legal issues related to immigrants in France and in the rest of the world. France.

Avocats et Associés (France 2, 1998–2010). Drama series based on the personal and professional intrigues of lawyers in a small Parisian firm. Limited number of scenes in court. France.

Awaiting Judgment [*Visto para sentencia*] (TVE, 1971). A Perry Mason style series which focuses on both the investigation of the crime and the court proceedings. Set in a courtroom, the 12 episodes deal with a different case—based on true story—every week. Spain.

Axel Nort (1966). Flemish TV show, produced for the Public Broadcasting Channel and aimed at a young audience, about a detective called Axel Nort. Belgium.

Bad Judge (NBC, 2014–15). Unconventional California state trial judge tries to balance her reckless private life and her uncompromising stand on the bench. USA.

Barney Miller (ABC, 1975–82). Comedy set in a Manhattan precinct, featuring police officers and their personal and professional relationships. USA.

Beautiful Inside [*Belli dentro*] (Canale 5, 2005–12). This sitcom, one of the few in Italy, was the first Italian production to represent everyday life in prison by means of comedy. The programme, starring well-known television comedians, was conceived by real-life detainees in San Vittore prison in Milan. Italy.

Beauty and the Beast (CBS, 2012–). The show follows the life of a NYPD detective Catherine Chandler (Kristin Kreuk) who falls in love with an ex-soldier Vincent Keller (Jay Ryan). He is hiding from the secret government organisation that experimented on him and changed him into a super-soldier beast. USA, shown in Poland.

Before the Law [*Di fronte alla legge*] (Rai 1, 1967–74). This series dropped the reference to famous trials but not the procedure, which it used to structure the comparison between opposing ideas and positions on cases of contemporary relevance. Italy.

Bent (NBC, 2012). An Associate at a California firm tries to put her life back together after divorce. USA.

Bergerac (1981–91). Detective series set on Jersey dealing with non-Jersey residents shown originally on BBC1. Britain.

Der Bestatter [*The Undertaker*] (2012–). A former police inspector who now runs a small funeral parlour solves murder cases. Highly successful crime comedy. Switzerland.

Betipul [*In Treatment*] (HOT, 2008). This successful and inventive series had a daily broadcast, and revolved around a psychologist and his weekly sessions with patients, as well as his sessions with his own therapist. The series was sold to HBO and broadcasted in the USA. Israel.

Betrugsfälle [*Cases of Betrayal*] (2010–13). 310 episodes. Different kinds of betrayal form the subject of this RTL series, not always criminal by nature. Germany.

Bex and Blanche (1993). Flemish TV show on the commercial channel VTM about a police detective who was also an anti-hero. Cancelled after one season despite high ratings because of high production costs. Belgium.

The Bill (1984–2010) soap-like series following the work and lives of the police in an inner-city London police station, covering a wide range of issues. Britain, shown in Denmark.

Billable Hours was a Canadian comedy series that aired on the pay-per-view Showcase channel from 2006 to 2008. It was set in a Toronto law firm and focused on three young lawyers struggling to balance their expectations of life with the difficult realities of building a career in law. The show was accompanied by a 10-part webisode series entitled *Billable Minutes*. *Billable Hours* also aired in Australia on ABC2. Canada.

The Blacklist (NBC, 2013–). One of the FBI's most wanted, Raymond Reddington (James Spader), turns himself in and offers to help catch dangerous criminals from the blacklist. His only condition is that he gets to work with a young FBI profiler Elizabeth Keen (Megan Boone). USA, shown in Poland.

Bloc Operation Coslada Zero [*El bloke Coslada Cero*] (TVE, 2009). Docu-drama about police corruption in Coslada, Madrid. In 2008 a corruption network was discovered which resulted in one of the biggest investigations into police corruption. Spain.

Blue Bloods (SKAI, 2012–2014) the life of a family of dedicated police officers (the Reagans), whose opinions on delivering justice vary. The only thing they all have in common is their willingness to deliver justice. USA, shown in Greece.

Blue Heelers (1993–2006). Long-running, popular police drama. Depicted the lives of police officers in Mount Thomas, a fictional town in rural Victoria. Australia.

Blue Murder (1995). Two-part true-crime miniseries, depicting the controversial relationship between successful NSW Detective Roger 'the Dodger' Rogerson, and underworld figures such as Neddy Smith. Australia.

Blue Murder (2003–9). Police detective series showing the professional and personal life of single mother of four dealing with serious crime in a northern city over five series and 19 episodes on ITV1 prime time. Britain.

Body of Evidence [*Las pruebas del crimen*] (La Sexta, 2014). Crime series focusing on the cases of Florida Department of Law Enforcement criminal personality profiler, Dayle L Hinman. USA, shown in Spain.

Body of Proof (2011–13). American medical drama set in Philadelphia from ABC featuring ex-neuro-surgeon and now Medical Examiner (Coroner) Dr Megan Hunt over three series and 42 episodes as she tries to balance her new professional life after a car crash, a patient dying while she was operating, and her problems with her estranged daughter. USA.

Bones (FOX, 2005–). A forensic anthropologist Dr Temperence Brennan (Emily Deschanel) and a FBI special agent Seeley Booth (David Boreanaz) team up to solve years-old crimes based on the examination of human remains. USA, shown in Denmark, Poland, etc.

The Border (CBC, 2008–10). Set in Toronto in a paranoid post-9/11 world concerned with one topic—the border, with its security crises, terrorist infiltrations, cross-border police actions, and trafficking in everything from enriched uranium to abducted children. Canada.

Border Security: Australia's Front Line (Seven, 2004–). Follows the work of the Australian Customs and Border Protection, the Australian Quarantine and Inspection Service and the Department of Immigration and Citizenship enforcing these areas of law principally around Sydney and Melbourne over 14 series from Seven Network. Spin-off from *Border Security: Canada's Front Line*. Australia.

Border Security: Canada's Front Line (2012–). The original, this show follows the work of the men and women who protect Canada's borders. On the National Geographic channel, documentary/reality. Canada.

Borsellino—The 57 Days [Borsellino—I 57 giorni] (Rai 1, 2012). The 57 days between the deaths of Judges Giovanni Falcone and Paolo Borsellino. During this time Borsellino, a friend and colleague of Falcone, realises his destiny and comes to terms with his life and affections. He is a man devoted to both his family and to his duty and tries feverishly to complete his investigations against the Mafia before he is killed. The drama was broadcast on 22 May 2012 to mark the twentieth anniversary of the murder of Judge Falcone. Italy.

Boston Legal (ABC, 2004–08). Spin-off of David E Kelley drama *the practice* featuring the character of Alan Shore, who had previously been a character in *the practice*, and who then became a partner at the firm of Crane, Poole, and Schmidt. *Boston Legal* had the Kelley hallmarks of quirky characters and cutting-edge legal themes. USA.

The Bourgeoisie [H'Burganim] (Channel 2 & 'Yes', 2000) focuses on the lives of a middle-class group of friends living in Tel Aviv at the beginning of the new millennium. Israel.

Boulevard du Palais (France 2, 1999–). Police drama based on the collaboration of an examining magistrate and a commander in the criminal police force. France.

Boy A (2007). Feature movie, empathically describing the difficulties of a teenage murderer to integrate into society after release. Britain.

Boyd QC (1958–64). British barrister, with the assistance of his clerk, defends clients and solves crimes in a weekly half-hour show on prime-time commercial ITV. Britain.

Breaking Bad (AMC, 2008). An American crime drama tracing the transformation of Walter White (Bryan Cranston) from a high school Chemistry teacher diagnosed with cancer to a violent manufacturer and seller of methamphetamine in the city of Albuquerque, New Mexico. This show is regarded by some to be one of best television show ever created. USA.

The Bridge (FX, 2014). When a body is found on a bridge between American El Paso and Mexican Juarez, two detectives Sonya Cross (Diane Kruger) and Marco Ruiz (Demián Bichir), start to work together in order to catch the serial killer. USA, shown in Poland.

The Bridge (2011–). Detective series following an investigation of a dead body found on a bridge between Sweden and Denmark. Joint Sweden and Denmark, shown in Poland as *Bron*.

Brigade Navarro (TF1, 2007–9). Spin-off of the police drama centred around Navarro (see below) who has now been promoted to a higher position. France.

Britcam: Emergency on Our Streets (2014). The lives of those in the emergency services, such as ambulance staff and including police and fine enforcers or bailiffs. Britain.

Brooklyn Nine-Nine (2013–). Comedy following the work of a fictional New York police precinct over two seasons and 41 episodes to date. USA.

The Brown Girls [*Bnot Brown*] (Channel 2, 2002). A mini-series based on a popular book written by Irit Linor. The series followed the story of the Brown family from the mid-eighties to the beginning of the nineties, and through their story dealt with the decline of the Israeli Moshav. Israel.

A Bullet in the Heart [*Una pallottola nel cuore*] (Rai 1, 2014). TV miniseries whose main character is a crime journalist nearing retirement who, having rediscovered the ethical duty of telling the truth, takes up a cold case and manages to solve it with intuition and enthusiasm. In typical Italian style, the criminal case is accompanied by developments in the main character's personal and family life. Italy.

Campus PD (2009–12). A reality series where viewers feel as if they are riding along with the men and women who keep the peace when college life gets out of control. USA.

Candice Renoir (France 2, 2013). Police drama centred on a police commander and mother of four. France.

Carla Cametti PD (2009). Follows female Italian-Australian police detective, with relatives in the Mafia, who investigates her own family. Australia.

Carson's Law (1983–84). Set in the 1920s featuring progressive lawyer and mother of three Jennifer Carson. The series combined a focus on both Carson's cases and personal life, and she constantly fights prejudice in the male-dominated legal world. Australia.

Case Closed [Tik Sagoor] (Channel 10, 2002). A police drama focused on a police station in Be'er Sheva, the biggest city in the southern part of Israel. It was one of the most expensive Israeli shows ever produced, but was cancelled after three episodes. Israel.

The Cases of Inspector Maigret [*Le inchieste del commissario Maigret*] (Rai 1, 1964–72). A highly popular series based on Belgian novelist George Simenon's detective Jules Maigret. Despite his foreign origins, the main character, played by Italian actor Gino Cervi, seemed fully Italian, like 'a provincial officer of the

Carabinieri, respectful of the law, paternal and sympathetic' (in the words of an Italian television critic of that time). Italy.

Castle (2009–). American ABC series in which unusual crimes are solved when a crime writer is shadowing a female homicide detective in New York. Mystery novelist Rick Castle teams up with NYPD detective Kate Beckett to solve cases. His writer's intuition and her creative detective work make them solve the most difficult cases. USA, shown in Britain, Canada and Spain.

CATS Eyes (1985–87). Maggie Forbes from *The Gentle Touch* (*qv*) works ostensibly for a private detective agency which is in fact a front for the Home Office for three series and 30 episodes on Saturday night prime time. Britain.

Centraal Station (1974–79). Co-production of the Dutch KRO channel and Flemish Public Television about the railway police and crimes and cases centred around trains and railway stations. The cast was part Flemish, part Dutch. Joint Netherlands and Belgium.

Central Brigade [*Brigada central*] (TVE, 1989–92). *Central Brigade* depicts an elite police squad dealing with organised crime. Spain.

Chase (STAR, 2014). Annie Frost is a charming and sexy sheriff! Her difficult childhood left her with traumas and nightmares. Her father was a cruel criminal and she is now chasing the most dangerous fugitives in the U.S. Her sharp mind helps her being one step ahead of the criminals. USA, shown in Greece.

Chérif (France 2, 2013–). Police drama centred on a police inspector using original methods. France.

Chicken Mexicaine [*Chicken Mexican Style*] (2007). Feature movie about a felon who, in order to get out of prison to see his daughter, blackmails the prison director. Switzerland.

CHiPs (NBC, 1977–83). Action show featuring the exploits of two California Highway Patrol officers, Ponch and Jon, played by Erik Estrada and Larry Wilcox. Many episodes had comedic elements. USA.

City Homicide (2007–11). A drama series following a team of homicide detectives in Melbourne. Australia.

The Client (1995–96). Lawyer series based on the John Grisham book and film centred on the work of a single woman practitioner. USA.

Close Relatives [*Krovim Krovim*] (Channel 1, 1983) is the first Israeli sitcom and of the most culturally influential TV series in the history of Israel. It tells the story of three families—all related to each other—living in an apartment building in Tel Aviv. Israel.

Close to Home (also called Juste Cause in France, 2005-7). Fiction series about a young female prosecutor having to balance family life and a strong ethical commitment to her work. USA.

The Closer (TNT, 2005). An American police television drama focusing on Chief Brenda Leigh Johnson (Kyra Sedgwick), who runs the Priority Homicide Division in LAPD and famous for her unorthodox style and methods of investigation. USA.

Cold Case Files (A&E, 1999–2008). Documentary-style TV show demonstrating the solution of 'cold case' or long unsolved crimes using newly developed forensic techniques. USA.

Cold Squad (1998–2005). A one-hour police crime drama about a team of Vancouver police officers in charge of investigating and solving cases that have been in the 'cold case' file—cases that that police gave up on because there were no leads. Canada.

Columbo (NBC, 1971–78; ABC, 1989–2003). Originally one of the NBC rotating Mystery Movies, the audience witnessed the guilty party commit the murder in the first few minutes of the show, and then watched as the eponymous Lieutenant Columbo discovered the identity of the perpetrator through observation and deduction. USA.

Commisaris Roos (1990–92). Two seasons, Flemish commercial television channel VTM, about a detective called Roos, in the style of similar German crime shows. Belgium.

Commissaire Cordier (TF1, 2005–08). Spin-off of the French police series *Les Cordier, Juge et Flic* (see below). In this spin-off, Commissaire Pierre Cordier is promoted Chief Commissaire. The series, which is composed of over three seasons and 12 episodes, focuses on the work of his police team. France.

Commissaire Magellan (France 3, 2009–). French police series created by Laurent Mondy, taking place in the imaginary city of Saignac, where Commissaire Magellan investigates various criminal cases. France.

Commissaire Maigret (1991–2005, Antenne 2 then France 2). Police series based on George Simenon's novels. The series focuses on the work of Commissaire Maigret, famous for his intelligence and composure. Each episode deals with a particular case. The series has lasted 14 seasons and is composed of 54 90-minute episodes. Co-produced by France, Belgium, Switzerland and the Czech Republic.

Commissaire Moulin (TF1, 1976–82; 1989–2008). This is the oldest French police drama which aired on the first channel. The series follows the adventures of light-hearted Jean-Paul Moulin, a police inspector and his team, as they solve crimes. France.

Common Law (USA, 2012). Wes Mitchell (Warren Kole) and Travis Marks (Michael Ealy) are two detectives working for the Los Angeles Police Department, who can't stand each other. In order to remedy the situation they are sent by their captain to couples therapy. USA, shown in Poland.

Con Air (1997). Feature movie about a paroled convict on board an inmate transport airplane that gets hijacked by its passengers. USA.

Conseils utiles et inutiles (ORTF, 1964–65). Talk show occasionally on legal subjects. France.

Continuum (2012–). Canadian science fiction series concerning a conflict between a group of terrorists from 2077 and a police officer. Canada, shown in Denmark.

Cop Shop (1977–83). Set in the fictional Riverside police station. Each episode combined cases handled by the police officers, with ongoing storylines regarding the officers' personal lives. Australia.

Cops (1989–). Cops was among the earliest reality-based law enforcement shows, and remains one of the most popular of the genre. Each week, a camera crew follows the activities of the officers of a different city's police department. Incidents range from routine traffic stops that evolve into charging the subjects with drug-related offences; domestic violence; high-speed chases; and stakeouts and raids. The success of *Cops* led to other similar programmes, such as *Cops Reloaded*. USA.

Cops (Channel 2, 1999). A docu-reality series inspired by the American series following cops in their daily routine. Israel.

Cops Reloaded. A spin-off of *Cops*. USA.

Covert Affairs (USA, 2010–). The show centres on a young CIA trainee Annie Walker (Piper Perabo) who is suddenly promoted to the CIA field agent. With the help of a co-worker Auggie Anderson (Christopher Gorham) Annie tries to settle in the world of bureaucracy, intrigue and excitement. USA, shown in Poland.

The Crackers [*Hamefatzhim*] (Channel 2, 2007). A documentary series exploring crimes the police could not solve. Israel.

Crash Investigation Unit (2008–11). A factual series following the Metropolitan Crash Investigation Unit as they work to uncover the causes of traffic accidents on major roads. Australia.

Crime Novel: The Series [*Romanzo criminale: La serie*] (Sky Cinema 1, 2008–10). Crime drama in 55-minute episodes based on the novel by the Italian judge Giancarlo De Cataldo. This successful series focuses on the true story of the Magliana Gang, an Italian criminal organisation based in Rome, active from the late-1970s until the early-1990s. Italy.

Crime Stories (1998–). Chronicles some of the most intriguing crimes in history. This investigative series takes the viewers behind the scenes, unveiling techniques used in solving the crime, exposing the emotion experience by those affected and the final resolution of the case. Police officers, family and friends of the victim, defence lawyer, and prosecutors all share their differing points of view regarding the crime and its consequences. Their first-hand accounts, coupled with dramatic re-enactments, news footage, clippings and photographs paint a comprehensive picture. Canada, shown in Spain.

Crimes en haute société (Paris Première, 2013–). This series of documentaries exclusively focuses on the assassination of rich people where money is the motive. France.

Crimes en série (France 2, 1998–2003). French police drama, broadcast simultaneously on France 2 in France and on La Une in Belgium. Thomas Berthier, father and caring husband, is in charge of the profilers' unit of the criminal brigade. His team often deals with cases the traditional police department is unable to solve. France.

Crime Watch (1984–). TV show which shows re-enacted crimes, CCTV footage, photos of suspects and asks the public to come forward with information of help to the police. Britain.

Criminal Love [Amore Criminale] (Rai 3, 2007–). Dedicated exclusively to the highly topical theme in Italy of violence against women, the programme reconstructs the stories in the style of a docudrama, accompanied by statements from family members, lawyers and police officers. Since the 2014 season, it has included statements from the victims themselves, with the aim of raising awareness among women who are potential targets of domestic violence. Italy.

Criminal Minds (2005–). A fictional drama that focuses on the cases of the FBI's Behavioural Analysis Unit (BAU), an elite group of profilers who analyse the nation's most dangerous serial killers and individual heinous crimes in an effort to anticipate their next moves before they strike again. USA.

Criminal Reporter [Katav Plili] (Channel 1, 1995). One of the few attempts of Channel 1 to engage with crime-related shows by telling the story of a criminal reporter. Israel.

Crossing Lines (Rai 2; NBC, 2013–). After being injured on the job, a former NYPD officer Carl Hickman (William Fichtner) is recruited by the International Criminal Court special crime unit. The new department is based in The Hague and set up to investigate a variety of criminal cases that cross over European borders. USA, shown in Poland.

Crownies (2011). Five young solicitors, recently graduated from law school, begin work at the Crown Prosecutor's office. Based on the real-life NSW Office of the Director of Public Prosecutions, this programme highlighted the moral dilemmas faced by these young men and women in the course of their work. Australia.

CSI: Crime Scene Investigation (CBS 2000–). Horatio Caine (David Caruso) leads a team of police department investigators solving the most odd and ghastly crimes using the most advanced forensic techniques and analysts. Spin-offs *CSI: Miami* (qv), *CSI: NY* (qv) and *CSI: Cyber*. CSI: Miami (CBS, 2002–12). USA.

Cursed Tales [*Storie maledette*] (Rai 3, 1994–). Common criminals convicted of high-profile crimes speak from inside prison and give their side of the story, which often contrasts with the version established at trial. Italy.

Dalziel and Pascoe (1996–2007). Police detective series focusing on murder, based on the Reginald Hill novels, featuring the blunt 'old style' boss and his more cerebral graduate assistant. Britain.

Damages (FX, 2007–10; Direct TV Audience Network, 2011–12). A legal drama focusing on the law firm of attorney Patty Hewes (Glenn Close) and her associates, and a nemesis, played by a notable guest star (the first season Ted Danson played this character, Arthur Frobisher). The show followed one story arc per season. The series was also famous for its use of parallel narratives and ethical ambiguities. USA.

Danni Lowinski (2012–13). Humorous courtroom drama, centred on lawyer Danni Lowinski, produced for Flemish commercial channel VTM, based on a German show of the same name. Germany, also shown in Belgium.

Dark Waters of Crime (2007–14). Docudrama showing events leading to investigations where water has played a role in covering up or committing a crime. Canada.

Dateline NBC (NBC, 1992–). Weekly news magazine show, often devoted to legal issues. Airs Fridays, and on Sundays except during American football season, and sometimes on Saturdays. Sometimes simply referred to as *Dateline*. USA.

Da Vinci's City Hall (CBC 2005–06). Dominic Da Vinci, former coroner and police officer in Vancouver, BC, starts his first term as the newly elected mayor of Vancouver. Canada.

Da Vinci's Inquest (CBC 1998–2005). A Vancouver cop turned coroner searches for truth and justice with the help of his friends. Only non-USA law show broadcast in USA in November 2014. Canada.

A Day in Court [*Un giorno in pretura*] (Rai 3, 1988–). Currently the only reality courtroom programme on Italian television. Recordings of real trials are selected and broadcast without comment, showing the actual functioning of the law courts. Italy.

Deadly Women (Discovery Channel, 2005–14). The show presents the cruellest crimes committed by women. Each episode focuses on a different theme explaining actions of those notorious female murderers. USA, shown in Poland.

Dedicated to a Prosecutor [*Dedicato a un pretore*] (Rai 1, 1973). Through the figure of a young woman magistrate, this drama tackled a significant dual shift in the Italian judiciary: on one hand, the judicial activism of young magistrates, oriented towards rebalancing social conflicts by means of legal rulings; on the other, the arrival of the first women members of the judiciary. Italy.

The Defenders (CBS, 1962–66). A legal drama featuring a father and son defence firm which handles controversial cases. Starred EG Marshall and Robert Reed. It had and continues to have, great influence in pop culture, and other shows of the period, including the *Dick van Dyke Show*. USA.

Défendez vous vos droits (Antenne 2, 1991–92). Talk show on legal issues. France.

De Ridder (2013–). Flemish crime show in which the central character is Helena De Ridder, a prosecutor. Produced for the Flemish public television channel Een (one), but also broadcast in the Netherlands. Belgium.

Derrick (1974–98). Title figure is a very polite and always correct police inspector who leads an unfailing team. At its time one of the most popular TV shows, exported to many countries. Germany.

The Detectives (2015). Three-part documentary series following the work of the Greater Manchester Police Serious Sexual Offences Unit. Britain.

Detektywi [*The Detectives*] (2005–12). A group of experienced police officers run a private investigation agency. They solve both serious criminal as well as missing persons cases. Each episode is based on facts and presents a different story. Poland.

Deux flics sur les docks (France 2, 2011–). Police drama based on the investigations of a team of plainclothes policemen. France.

Dexter (Showtime, 2006). An American crime-mystery drama following the life of Dexter Morgan (Michael C. Hall), a forensic technician in the Miami Metro Police Department who lives a parallel hidden life as a serial killer, hunting criminals that the justice system failed to put behind bars. USA.

Dharma & Greg (1997–2002). American sitcom about the couple Dharma (a yoga instructor) and Greg (a lawyer). USA. Shown in Denmark.

Diane, femme flic (TF1, 2003–10). Police drama based on a police chief and mother. France.

Diary of a Judge [*Diario di un giudice*] (Rai 1, 1978). The drama was centred on the unsuccessful struggle of a magistrate against an intensely hierarchical judiciary that is indifferent to social problems and against a law seen as the tool of injustice and inequality. The drama was adapted from the book of the same name by Judge Dante Troisi (1955). Because of this book, Troisi underwent disciplinary proceedings for having undermined the prestige of the judiciary. Italy.

Dicte (TV2, 2013–). A Danish drama series about a crime reporter returning to her home town of Aarhus following a divorce. The series is based on Danish author Elsebeth Egholm's series of novels about the titular character. It is distributed in Denmark on TV2. Original release was 7 January 2013 and so far two seasons (20 episodes) have been aired. Denmark.

Disturbia (2007). This feature movie is a reinterpretation of Alfred Hitchcock's *Rear Window*. A teenager under house arrest with ankle monitor becomes convinced his neighbour is a serial killer. USA.

Division 4 (1969–75). A police drama set in Yarra Central, a fictional inner Melbourne suburb with a broad demographic. The show depicted various cases handled by police. Australia.

Dixon of Dock Green (1955–68). Long-running police series set in a London police station focusing on minor crime and the daily problems of an ordinary police officer and those in a local police station. Britain.

The Docket, a half-hour Canadian legal affairs show produced in Halifax in 2003 which aired nationally on CBC Newsworld. The show had a documentary plus panel format that aimed to document the effects of legislation on ordinary Canadians. Canada.

The Doctor Blake Mysteries (ABC, 2013–). Mystery solving with a medical doctor in 1950s Australia in the town of Ballarat in Victoria—over three series and 28 episodes so far. Australia.

Dog and Beth: On the Hunt (2013–15). The further adventures of Dog the Bounty Hunter (*qv*) focusing on assisting bail bondsmen track down criminals. USA.

Dog Patrol (2014–). Series focusing on the work of the Animal Control Officers based in South Auckland. New Zealand.

Dog the Bounty Hunter (A&E, 2004–12). A bounty hunter's experiences set in Hawaii and Colorado tracking Duane 'Dog' Chapman. USA.

Don Matteo (Rai 1, 2000–). A very successful series which features a Catholic parish priest in the beautiful medieval town of Gubbio who brilliantly solves mysteries and crimes that the local police struggle to understand. This is due to his prodigious intuition but also because, being a clergyman, he is free from the formal constraints imposed by the law. Italy.

DR2 Undersøger: 'Mistænkt på livstid' [*DR2 Investigates:* 'Suspect Serving Life Imprisonment'] (DR2, 2013). Episode in the Danish documentary series *DR2 Undersøger* where journalists investigate various matters in detail. Denmark.

Dragnet (NBC 1951–59, 1967–70, 1989–91 and 2003–04). Los Angeles police procedural detective series over 448 episodes and 16 series for NBC. *Dragnet* was originally a radio series, brought to TV by Jack Webb, who played the lead, Sergeant Joe Friday, a dedicated Los Angeles detective. The show emphasised law and order, the simple mechanics of investigation of a reported crime and apprehension of a suspect. Webb's emphasis on clipped dialogue ('just the facts, ma'am') and the show's predictable format have made it as much a part of US law and TV pop culture as *Perry Mason*. USA.

Drei Knast-Tränen für Jerry [*Three Prison Tears for Jerry*] (2014). Part of the documentary series *Reporter*. Portrays a terminally ill inmate in custody after imprisonment whose wish to die in freedom has been denied by the authorities. The movie accompanies him and his relatives in his last days and discusses the issue of human dignity in imprisonment. Switzerland.

Drop Dead Diva (Lifetime, 2009–14). A young overweight attorney comes back from the dead with the soul of an attractive, thin, model inside her. The show confronts stereotypes about image, body type and the legal profession. USA.

Due South (1994–99). The cases of a cynical American police detective and an upright Royal Canadian Mounted Police constable in the city of Chicago. Dramedy, created by Paul Haggis and starring Paul Gross. Canada.

East West 101 (2007). Crime drama set in Sydney's multicultural western suburbs, with a focus on race relations surrounding the police force. Australia.

The Edge of Law [*Al filo de la ley*] (RTVE, 2005). Set in the law firm Álvarez & Associates in Madrid. A young and dynamic team deals with controversial issues such as domestic violence, drugs trade, racist attacks and labour disputes. Spain.

Ehen vor Gericht [*Marriages at Court*] (1970–2000). Series about divorce cases, filmed in a studio with expert interviews, discussion elements and re-enactment of court scenes. Germany.

Eigen Kweek [*For Personal Use*] (VRT, 2013–). Flemish crime comedy about a family of farmers who start an illegal cannabis plantation to deal with debts. Belgium.

Ein Fall für zwei [*A Case for Two*] (1981–). Friday night crime slot of the second national TV channel. Instead of police work the series presents a duo of posh lawyer and working-class private eye, who solve the crime, usually a murder case, with a combination of brain and muscle. The series runs a little faster than the contemporary police shows, focusing more on action and offering a dose of humour. Germany.

Ekstradycja [*Extradition*] (1995–1999). The show follows both professional and private life of a police officer Olgierd Halski (Marek Kondrat), who has to stand everyday against the drug dealers, Russian mobs and corruption among Polish state officials. Poland.

Elementary (CBS, 2012–). The show presents a modern take on a Sherlock Holmes story. The detective (Jonny Lee Miller) and his therapist Joan Watson (Lucy Liu) help NYPD solve the most difficult crime mysteries. USA, shown in Poland.

Endeavour (ITV1, 2012–). Police detective series set in Oxford, England, following the career of Endeavour Morse (later of Inspector Morse *qv*) when he has just started as a detective constable in the mid-1960s with an irascible boss. Britain.

Engrenages (Canal +, 2005–). Examines the French justice system from the points of view of prosecutors, defence attorneys and police officers; involves the viewer in gritty and personal stories. Set in Paris, the show follows the lives and work of police officers in the criminal brigade and the lawyers and judges who work at the Palais de Justice. *Engrenages* is known as one of the most realistic series aired and produced in France. Anne Landois, the presenter of the series consults a team of judges and lawyers in order to assure the high degree of realism in the reconstruction of the legal process. The series has so far lasted five seasons and 52 episodes. France. Shown as *Spiral* in Britain.

Enigmes (sometimes called *A chacun sa vérité*) (RTF, 1956). Dramatisation of famous unsolved criminal cases after which a panel of historians discussed possible solutions to the enigmas. France.

En votre âme et conscience (RTF and ORTF, 1956–69). Programme presented by Pierre Dumayet in which each episode began with the reconstitution of a past case. Arguments for the defence were then given once again, so that the viewers could vote as a jury. France.

Es geschah am hellichten Tag [*It Happened in Broad Daylight*] (1958). Police Lieutenant Dr. Matthäi traces a child murderer. Swiss movie classic with remarkable cast, scripted by Friedrich Dürrenmatt. Switzerland/Spain.

The Escape [*La fuga*] (Telecinco, 2012). Set in the mid-twenty-first century, this show combines the formula of a romantic thriller and a prison drama. Daniel is imprisoned by a global dictatorship that rules the world, its natural resources and its people. The whole series is driven by Ana trying to get her husband back: she infiltrates the prison as an officer in the hope of helping her husband escape. Spain.

The Exorcism of Emily Rose (2005). Feature movie combining elements of both court room drama and horror movie. USA.

A Fact [*Uvda*] (Channel 2, 1993) is one of the leading Israeli newsmagazines, following 60 Minutes' reporter-centered investigation style. Israel.

Fairly Legal (USA, 2011–12). After her father's death Kate Reed (Sarah Shahi) decides to change her profession from an attorney at her father's firm to a mediator. She believes that justice can be found everywhere, not necessarily in the courthouse. USA, shown in Poland.

Fala zbrodni [*Outbreak of Crimes*] (2003–08). The show centres on a group of policemen from an organised crime unit. Viewers experience not only scenes showing brutal events and fights but also beginnings of true friendships and real love. Each episode follows a different set of events. Poland.

Family Matters with Justice Harvey Brownstone was a Canadian show that billed itself as the only TV show hosted by a real sitting Ontario provincial court family law judge. This was English Canada's *only* reality court TV show. It aired on CHCH TV, an independent Ontario channel and on CHEK TV, an independent British Columbia channel, from 2011 to 2013. *Family Matters* focused on the relationship between modern family issues, divorce and the justice system, and had an online legal Q&A which provided free legal information from lawyers and other legal professionals. Canada.

Fangekoret [*Prisoners' Choir*] (2012). Danish documentary about the prisoners' choir in the closed state prison Vridsløselille and their charismatic choir leader Louise Adrian. Denmark.

Fargo (Canal Plus, 2014). A US black comedy crime series inspired by the Coen brothers movie of the same name. USA.

Faustrecht [*Fist Law*] (2006). Documentary: long-time observation of two teenagers in juvenile detention. Switzerland.

Femmes de Loi (TF1, 2000–09). Series based on the collaboration of two women: an assistant prosecutor and a lieutenant in the criminal police force. Each episode carried a police investigation and prosecutorial activity although not always in court. France.

Files from the Public Defender [*Tikim Me'hasanegoria*] (Yes, 2014). A new documentary which tells the stories behind the work of the Israeli Public Defender's office. Israel.

The Fjällbacka Murders [*Los crimenes de Fjällbacka*; original Swedish title *Fjällbackamorden*] (Canal Plus, 2014). A Swedish crime series set in the seemingly tranquil small town of Fjällbacka. The protagonists are the police inspector and his crime-writing wife. Spain.

Flashpoint (CTV and CBS, 2008–12). A one-hour prime-time drama about the Strategic Response Unit or SRU, inspired by Toronto's Emergency Task Force. They are a handpicked team of elite cops but they're different from other SWAT teams, because their arsenal also includes a gift for words; a knowledge of human intuition; an instinct for when it's time to negotiate; 'There's always a solution'. Canada, shown in USA.

Flikken (1999–2009). 'Flik' is the Dutch word for 'cop' ('flic' in French). The show was set in Ghent and ran for 10 years. The series was also broadcast in the Netherlands, where Dutch versions of the franchise were made as *Flikken Maastricht* (set in the border town of Maastricht) and *Flikken Rotterdam*. Belgium.

Flying Squad Here [*Qui squadra mobile*] (Rai 1, 1973–76). A police action drama which offered a realistic glimpse of the daily work of the police and the investigative techniques they use, including the giant 'electronic brains' controlled by policemen wearing white coats. It had a political objective, which was to help overcome the mistrust of citizens towards the forces of law and order. Italy.

Forbrydelsen i virkeligheden (2014). Danish documentary series about how police and prosecutors work with various cases. Denmark.

Forensic Files (TLC, 1996–2000; Court TV, 2000–07; truTV, 2008–11). Documentary-style TV show emphasising the use of forensic techniques to solve crimes and other mysteries, including those relating to epidemics and accidental deaths. The original series which aired on TLC was called *Medical Detectives*. USA, shown in Spain as *Crimenes imperfectos*.

Fornemmelse for mord [*Sense of Murder*] (2002–). Danish documentary series about clairvoyants trying to solve murder cases. Denmark.

Forum (Canale 5, 1985–). Italy's first arbitration-based reality court show. The cases are based on small-scale civil litigation (effectively a small claims court). The tone of the disputes among participants is often heated; the presenter (always a woman) controls the pace of the proceedings. The studio audience expresses its verdict, but the final decision falls to the judge, who is a real magistrate. *Forum* maintains the ritual basis of a trial, with a judge whose function is to preside over the participants' undisciplined debate as if seeking to impose order on the confusion of daily experience. The programme's most famous judge, Santi Licheri, was a paternal figure: authoritative but not authoritarian, witty and sentimental, who loved to ritually cite aphorisms and brocards in Latin, which he then explained to the audience. Italy.

Fourth Degree [*Quarto Grado*] (Rete 4, 2010–). This reality-based programme is 'infotainment', focusing on crime and investigations and enacting a full-blown trial-by-media of murder cases that have caught the public's attention, with the participation of the lawyers of the people involved, family members, experts, criminologists and even defendants and witnesses. Italy.

Foyle's War (2002–15). Chief Inspector Christopher Foyle combats murder and other serious crime in war-torn rural Britain in the south coast town of Hastings during the Second World War with his reliable, war-wounded Sergeant Milner and additional input from the female driver seconded to him, Sam(antha). Britain.

Franco and Spector (Channel 2, 2003). Drama focusing on a small Israeli law firm and its associates. Through their private stories and the stories of their clients the show aspired to expose the gap between law and justice in Israeli society and the legal system. Israel.

Franklin and Bash (2011–14). American comedy featuring two young lawyers taking on challenging cases and the legal system. USA.

Frauen für Zellenblock 9 [*Women in Cellblock 9*]. Exploitation-movie about six women incarcerated by mercenaries somewhere in the South American jungles. Switzerland.

Frauengefängnis [*Barbed Wire Dolls*] (1976). Exploitation-movie about a woman serving time after murdering her father who wanted to rape her. Germany/Switzerland.

Fugitive, The (ToA, 1968). A doctor is accused of the murder of his wife and tries to find the true murderer, while being hunt by the police. USA, shown in Greece.

Gang Related (FOX, 2014–). Ryan Lopez (Ramon Rodriguez) is a member of a gang who works as a police detective in order to infiltrate the Gang Task Force. He leads a double life coping between being loyal to his gang family and his new friends in the police department. USA, shown in Poland.

Gefangene Frauen [*Caged Women*] (1980). Exploitation-movie about delinquent women who are shipped to an island prison run by a sadistic warden. Germany.

The Gentle Touch (ITV1, 1980–84). The first appearance of a London-based female detective, Detective Inspector Maggie Forbes, who led investigations into routine police work. The show covered social issues including racism, sexism and homophobia in its five series and 56 episodes for ITV1 prime time. Britain.

Get Christie Love (1974–1976) series about female undercover agent Christie Love working for the Los Angeles Police Department. Her undercover work is helped by her intelligence and skills, US, shown in Flanders, Belgium.

Ghost Whisperer (CBS, 2005–10). A drama featuring a protagonist who has the ability to see and talk to the dead. In various episodes she helps the authorities solve mysterious deaths or crimes. USA.

Gift ved første blik [*Married at first sight*] (2015). Six-part documentary about eight people (four couples) who voluntarily marry a person they have never met. Denmark.

Gilliams & De Bie (VTM, 1997). Flemish detective story for the commercial channel VTM. Belgium.

Giovanni Falcone (Rai 1, 2006). A miniseries about Judge Giovanni Falcone, murdered along with his police escort by the Mafia in 1992. It describes Falcone's investigation of the links between organised crime and politics, and his constant search for the truth. Italy.

The Glades (A&E, 2010–13). A Chicago police detective Jim Longworth (Matt Passmore) leaves for Florida after being shot in the backside by his captain. There he decides to join the state police department. USA, shown in Poland.

Glina [The Cop] (2003–08). A group of policemen from the Homicide Department in Warsaw police headquarters struggle with both criminal mysteries and daily life troubles that come as a part of their job description. Poland.

Going Straight (1978). The life of a post-release prisoner is covered, again principally for laughs in the sequel to the Ronnie Barker series *Porridge* (*qv*). Britain.

Gold Coast Cops (2014–). Day to day activities of the police officers in the Rapid Action & Patrols Group (RAP) on Queensland's Gold Coast. Australia.

Gomorrah: The Series [*Gomorra eo La serie*] (Sky Atlantic, 2014–). Based on Roberto Saviano's bestselling book, this publicly and critically acclaimed Italian crime drama depicts the brutal Neapolitan crime organisation the Camorra with unusual realism and toughness for Italian dramas. Italy.

Good Law [*De buena ley*] (Telecinco, 2009–14). Linguistically playing with the Spanish term for Italiafaithis (*de buena fe*) this court show deals with people whose behaviour is anything but in good faith. Spain.

The Good Wife (CBS, 2009–16). A politician's wife, Alicia Florrick, returns to her original training as a lawyer after her cheating politician husband, the disgraced

States Attorney is jailed for corruption. The series trace their relationship and her development as a lawyer focusing on individual cases as well as ongoing family themes and professional conflicts after her husband's release. USA.

Gotham (FOX, 2014–). A story about commissioner James Gordon (Ben McKenzie) who fights crime in Gotham City before Batman's arrival. USA, shown in Poland.

Grantchester (2015–). A young cleric helps his friend, a police detective, solve murders in rural Cambridgeshire. Britain.

Gunsmoke (CBS, 1955–75). Originally a radio drama, *Gunsmoke* was the quintessential western. It starred James Arness as Marshal Matt Dillon and ran for 20 seasons on CBS, with *Law & Order*, tying the record as the longest-running US TV show of all time. It centred on Dillon's release from prison and re-establishes his political career, eventually becoming governor and on his relationships with his friends. Many of the episodes dealt with serious subject matter, and in later years Burt Reynolds joined the cast as Quint Asper, son of a Native American mother and a Caucasian father. USA.

H'averot [*Friends*] (Channel 10, 2013). This situation comedy revolves around four female friends and their daily lives (no relation to the American comedy). Israel.

Hannibal (NBC, 2013–). Criminal profiler Will Graham (Hugh Dancy), who has unique ability to empathise with serial killers, runs the Behavioral Analysis Unit. He is being supervised by forensic psychiatrist Hannibal Lecter (Mads Mikkelsen). What he doesn't know is that his doctor is a serial killer himself. USA, shown in Poland.

Happy Valley (2014–). Catherine Cawood copes with her life as a divorced uniformed police sergeant, with a recovering drug-using sister and young child, in the rural north of England. Britain.

Hardcastle and McCormick (ABC, 1983–86). A legal buddy dramedy, featuring a tough retired judge who partners with a thief to catch up with malefactors who have evaded the law. USA.

Has anyone seen them? [*Chi l'ha visto?*] (Rai 3, 1989–). A historic example of the *TV-verità* (Truth TV) genre, which, because of its efforts to find missing persons or help people in various sorts of difficulty, is still considered (at least by its makers), a public service programme. However, over the years it has tended to focus increasingly on crime reports and the most notorious unsolved cases, using similar techniques to other TV shows, which has ensured its growing popularity. Italy.

Haunting Evidence (Court TV, 2006–08). Documentary-style series following three paranormal investigators who attempted to solve cold cases. USA.

Hawaii 5-0 (CBS, 2010–). Steve McGarrett (Alex O'Loughlin) returns home to Hawaii to catch his father's killer. Meanwhile he is offered by the governor the possibility to build his own task force (Hawaii-Five) as a special police unit. USA, shown in Poland.

Hazel (NBC, 1961–65; CBS 1965–66). Comedy about a practical and well-organised live-in maid who takes care of a successful lawyer and his family. USA.

Head Injuries [*Ptzuim Barosh*] ('Hot', 2013) tells the story of two good friends that served together in the Israeli army but followed different paths and reunite after a few years. Israel.

Heartbeat (ITV1, 1992–2010). Police drama set in North Yorkshire with an emphasis on the lives of the locals and the occasional incursions of crime into their lives in a rural 1960s setting over 18 series and 372 episodes from ITV1. Originally a vehicle for a popular soap star, the series spawned a 1960s set medical drama, *The Royal*. Britain.

Heiter bis tödlich: Alles Klara (2012–). Pre prime-time comedy-crime series about a police secretary solving murder mysteries. Germany, shown in Switzerland.

Heterdaad (1996–99). Flemish TV show for the public broadcasting channel. The title means 'Red handed'. Four seasons. High ratings. About detectives of the Gendarmerie. Belgium.

The High Chaperral (1967–1971) NBC produces law series about The Cannon family on the High Chaparral Ranch in Arizona Territory in 1870s. The family works to establish a cattle business but meets Indian opposition. USA, shown in Flanders, Belgium.

Highway Patrol (Syndicated, 1955–59). An action show generally based on the activities of the California Highway Patrol, made with the assistance of the agency until 1956, and starring Broderick Crawford. However, the show never mentions the CHP, nor do scripts normally mention towns or cities in California. Crawford ended each 30-minute episode with a safety tip. USA.

Highway Patrol (2009–). A factual series following the day to day activities of the Victoria Police Highway Patrol. Australia.

Hill Street Blues (NBC, 1981–87). A police drama which features the personal and professional lives of officers, set in an unnamed but large US city. Centred on the lives of the Captain, Frank Furillo, and his girlfriend, public defender Joyce Davenport. Famous for its storylines, which continued over several episodes, and for its willingness to confront contemporary issues, such as racism, police brutality and institutional corruption. Many of the storytelling and film techniques first used on the show, such as hand-held cameras, now seem like cliches because of the show's pervasive influence. USA.

Hinterland (S4C, 2013–). Detective Tom Mathias (Richard Harrington) moves to Aberystwyth in Wales, where he leads a local investigation unit. Together they solve crime mysteries from the area. Britain, shown in Poland and Germany (in 2016).

History's Courtroom, a 2002 docudrama on History Television. It explored landmark Canadian legal decisions in an effort to educate the public. Canada.

Hof van Assisen [Court of Assises]. Originally a series of one-off reconstructions or dramatisations of existing court cases, from 1965 onwards on Flemish public television. Later serialised as *Beschuldigde sta op* (*Defendant, Please Rise*) from 1971 to 1980. Resurrected using fictional stories in 1998. Belgium.

Homeland (2012–). Crime series revolving around CIA operations officer Carrie Mathison, who gets assigned to the Counter terrorism centre and who chases American soldier turned Al-Qaeda terrorist Nicholas Brody. USA, shown in Flanders, Belgium.

Homicide (1964–77). One of the earliest Australian police dramas, set at Russell Street Police Headquarters in Melbourne. While it followed a fictional homicide squad, many episodes were based on real cases. Australia.

How to Get Away with Murder (ABC, 2014–). A criminal law professor hires her most promising students to work in her law firm; they are caught up in a baffling murder in which most of the main characters in the series are suspects. USA.

Hot Bench (2014–). Reality TV series wherein a panel of three judges hear court cases, argue the merits of the case amongst themselves and render a verdict. USA.

How I Met Your Mother (CBS, 2005–14) American comedy about how one of the main characters, Ted, met the mother of his two children. One of the other four main characters Marshall Eriksen is a law student, becoming a lawyer and then judge later on. USA. Shown in Denmark.

I am the Law (1953). Gritty crime series about an NYPD detective operating in New York City in the early 50s. There were only 26 episodes made by Cosman Productions and Television Corporation of America. USA, shown in Flanders, Belgium.

Ice Crime, la nouvelle vague de polar scandinave (Canal+, 2014). Through the example of famous writers (Stieg Larson and Camilla Lackberg, for instance), this documentary tends to explain how Scandinavian writers succeeded in the rejuvenation of crime genre. France.

I Will Be Murdered [*Seré asesinado*] (TVE, 2013) is a Spanish feature-length, award-winning documentary about a Guatemalan corporate lawyer allegedly murdered by the then president Álvaro Colom Cabelleros. Spain.

Im Namen der Gerechtigkeit, Wir Kämpfen für Sie! [*In the Name of Justice, we will fight for you!*] (2013–15). Documentary-style drama series featuring various legal eagles in support of their clients. The series is set outside the court room so the jurists appear often more like community workers assisting people who in one way or another are in trouble with the law. Personnel consist of lay actors, with some also featured in *Richter Alexander Hold*. Germany.

In Gefahr: Ein Verhängnisvoller Moment (*In Danger: A Fatal Moment*, 2014–). Mockumentary-style crime fiction series centring on average people who by accident get involved in crime and usually are cleared due to the investigations of the police. The series is set in various cities in Germany and features an array of (lay) performers. Germany.

In Plain Sight (USA, 2008–12). Mary Shannon (Mary McCormack) works as a US Marshal relocating people in witness protection programmes. At the same time she also has to deal with issues in her personal life. USA, shown in Poland.

Inspector George Gently (BBC, 2007–). Conventional police detective series focusing on murder and set in northern England in the 1960s; over seven series thus far. Britain.

Inspector Montalbano [*Il commissario Montalbano*] (Rai 2 and Rai 1, 1999–). The television adaptations of Andrea Camilleri's novels, in which Italy's most popular detective is played by the athletic and good-looking actor Luca Zingaretti. Montalbano is an introverted character, sympathetic to the victims of crime and at times even to its perpetrators, in contrast to his cynical and careerist superiors; he has little time for either bureaucracy or firearms. The series' stories are complex and multifaceted, with minimum space given to family and personal relationships, although there are moments of comedy. Italy, also shown in Britain and Spain.

Inspector Morse (ITV1, 1987–93 and five specials 1995–2000). Police drama set in Oxford. It followed the murder-solving intellectual Inspector Morse and his plodding assistant, Sergeant Lewis and an irascible boss over 33 episodes and seven series and specials on ITV1 prime time. Two spin-offs: *Lewis* (*qv*) and *Endeavour* (*qv*). Britain.

Intelligence (CBC, 2005–07). Jimmy Reardon and Mary Spalding head their respective organisations, Mary as Director of the Organised Crime Unit, Jimmy the boss of his family's organised crime business. Unexpectedly, Mary successfully recruits Jimmy to act as her star individual in the OCU's underground intelligence network on organised crime. However, it's a two-way street as she needs to provide Jimmy with inside information on police knowledge of his businesses. Both Mary and Jimmy need to tread lightly in their relationship while they try and maintain a grip hold on their respective businesses. Canada.

Investigation Theatre [*Teatro Inchiesta*] (Rai 2, 1966–73). Inspired by the theatrical realism school, the numerous episodes of the series presented historic events, cases reported in the media and famous trials, exploiting the clear dramatic parallels between the stage and the courtroom. Italy.

The Investigator (TV ONE, 2009–12). Television New Zealand series by documentary-maker and author, Bryan Bruce looking at unsolved murders with a new case for each of the seven episodes. New Zealand.

Ironside (NBC, 1967–75). A police procedural, set in San Francisco, starring Raymond Burr as the paraplegic former Chief of Detectives, now specially appointed to solve particularly perplexing crimes. *Ironside* was the first series to feature a physically disabled character as protagonist. USA.

Ivanhoe (ITV 1958–1959, on French television 1959 with periodic reruns through 1995). The adventures of Walter Scott's valorous knight under the reign of the infamous Prince John. Britain.

JAG (NBC, 1995–96; CBS 1997–2005). A legal drama featuring the officers of the Judge Advocate General, who prosecute and defend crimes in the military. Many of the episodes involve contemporary events. USA.

Jake and the Fatman (CBS, 1987–92). The show follows local district attorney Jason Lochinvar 'Fatman' McCabe (William Conrad) who solves cases and catches bad guys with the help of a young investigator Jake Styles (Joe Penny). USA, shown in Poland.

Janet King (ABC, 2014). Eight-hour legal/political thriller, a spin-off of *Crownies* (2011). Follows the fiercely independent Janet King, previously introduced in *Crownies*, returning from maternity leave and immediately involved in an intense prosecution. Australia.

Jo (TF1, 2013–). Commander Jo Saint-Clair (Jean Reno) is a detective working for Parisian elite Criminal Brigade. His experience and intelligence help him to solve the most mysterious and challenging cases. France, shown in Poland.

Joey (NBC, 2004–06). American sitcom following the *Friends* character Joey Tribbiani's life in Los Angeles. Joey's neighbor and main love interest is the lawyer Alexis Garrett. USA. Shown in Denmark.

Judge John Deed (2001–07). Quixotic English High Court judge is at odds with the establishment and seeks to secure justice in his courtroom whilst conducting extra-forensic affairs aplenty. Britain.

Judge Judy (1996–). Syndicated reality small claims court TV show featuring retired Manhattan trial court judge Judith Sheindlin. Parties agree to Sheindlin's authority before appearing on the show. USA.

Judge Rinder (2014–). Afternoon show with a young gay barrister, Robert Rinder, deciding cases relying on legal principle much more than shows like *Judge Judy*. Britain.

The Judges' Point of View [*La parola ai giudici*] (Rai 1, 1973). The programme clearly presented the crisis in the Italian legal system by means of documentaries, interviews and debates, lively but not rhetorical, between the five judges who co-authored the programme. Italy.

Judging Amy (1999–2005). A divorced young female judge, back living with her interfering social worker mother, attempts to do justice in family court in Hartford, Connecticut. USA.

Julie Lescaut (TF1, 1992–2014). This French police drama details the investigations of detective Julie Lescaut and her team. Set in Paris, the series stresses the issues Julie Lescaut has to deal with, being a mother and a full-time detective. The series is composed of over 22 seasons and 101 episodes. France.

Juliet Bravo (1980–85). Second British series with a central character a female police officer. Here covering the everyday policing work of a police inspector, Jean Darblay (call sign Juliet Bravo), (replaced by Kate Longton in 1983) in charge of a small town police station in northern England over six series and 88 episodes. Britain.

The Juries [Hamushba'im] (The Educational Channel, 2012). The show is aiming to depict the 'behind the scenes' of the legal process, and exposes viewers to issues that are pivotal to Israeli society. Interestingly, the show exposes viewers to the work of jurors, despite the fact they do not exist in the actual Israeli legal system. Israel.

Justice (1971–74). Early breakthrough for a female barrister who confronts prejudice and seeks to make her way at the Bar in a north of London city and then in London over three prime-time series. The format involved her dealing with a case per week and starred a former British film star from the 1940s, Margaret Lockwood, and had some coverage of her post-divorce personal life. No other major roles for women lawyers on British TV for the ensuing 40 years. Britain.

Justice a Canadian French language half-hour legal issues show called that ran from 2004 to 2005 in Québec, with a view to bringing legal topics to the French-speaking public's attention. Canada.

K 11 Kommissare im Einsatz [K 11 Commissioners in Action] (2003–14). Reality-style show about the investigations of a group of police officers in Munich. The series features ex-policemen and lay actors in re-enactments of typical police procedure. The plots, usually murder cases, were fictitious. Germany.

Kapitan Sowa na tropie [Captain Sowa on the Trail] (1965). First Polish criminal TV show directed by Stanisław Bareja, centering on the character of Tomasz Sowa— the captain of Citizen's Militia played by Wiesław Gołas. Each episode focuses on a different case that Sowa and his assistant Albin are trying to solve. Poland.

Kartoteka [Criminal Record] (2014). It is a documentary series following the lives of a group of police officers working on difficult and brutal criminal cases. Each episode focuses on two seemingly different crimes that eventually together lead to finding a killer. Poland.

Kastner's Trial [Mishpat Kastner] (Channel 1, 1994). Tells the true story of Israel Kastner who saved Jews in Hungary during the days of the Nazi regime using controversial means. Israel.

Kate McShane (1975). Kate is an Irish-American lawyer who gets help from her dad, an ex-cop, and her brother, a priest and a law professor. USA.

Kavanagh QC (1995–2001). Blunt northern barrister combines a successful career defending a range of accused people with a tricky family life in a London chambers with other minor characters. Britain.

The Killing [Forbrydelsen] (2007–12). Danish police detective Sarah Lund investigates difficult cases with personal and political consequences. Denmark.

King (Showcase, 2011–12). A homicide detective, Jessica King (Amy Price-Francis) is promoted to be the head of the Major Crime Task Force. With an exquisite eye for detail and astute mind she tries to prove that she is the best cop in the city. USA, shown in Poland.

Kingdom (2007–09). A rural lawyer's practice in Norfolk with comic touches, some eccentric clients and a few serious issues over three series and 18 episodes. Britain.

Kojak (CBS, 1973–78). A police detective series set in New York over five seasons and 118 episodes for CBS. It opened with a fictional version of the case which established 'Miranda Rights'(*Miranda v Arizona* 384 US 436), featuring a Greek-American detective, played by Telly Savalas. USA.

De Kolderbrigade (1980). 'The Slapstick Police', comedy show, feature Flemish comedians, about a police station in Ghent, produced for the Flemish Public Broadcasting channel. Belgium.

Der Kommissar [*The Inspector*] (1969–76). Police procedural, focusing on the work of the inspector and his team. Germany.

Komisarz Alex [*Inspector Alex*] (2012–). Three police officers Marek Bromski (Jakub Wesołowski), Ryszard Puchała (Ireneusz Czop) and Michał Orlicz (Antoni Pawlicki) working in Łódź police headquarters solve crime mysteries with the help of a police dog Alex. It is a Polish version of a popular German–Austrian TV series *Kommissar Rex*. Poland.

Kommissär Hunkeler [*Inspector Hunkeler*] (2004–12). A loose series of six TV movies adapting the *Kommissär Hunkeler* novels by Swiss author Hansjörg Schneider. Classical whodunits following down-to-earth and, in a loveable way, grumpy and stubborn Inspector Peter Hunkeler solving murder cases. Set in Basel and its surroundings, local colour is an important part of the movies. Switzerland.

Kommissar Rex [*Inspector Rex*] (Sat. 1, 1994–2004). A German–Austrian TV series taking place in Vienna. The show follows police dog Rex and his partners. Together with the rest of the Vienna Kriminalpolizei homicide division they solve crimes in and around the city. Joint Germany and Austria, shown in Poland.

Krimi[5] (Kanal 5, 1999–). Danish documentary series exposing some of the recent shocking criminal problems/acts in Denmark. Denmark.

Der Kriminalist [*The Criminalist*] (2006–). Prime-time series about Bruno Schumann, inspector in a Berlin homicide squad. As a victimologist, he empathises with the victims in order to find the perpetrator. Germany, shown in Switzerland.

Kriminalreport Hessen (HR3, 2014–, 10+ episodes). Magazine-style programme featuring unsolved crimes in the Hessen region. Somewhat moulded after the pattern of *Aktenzeichen xy ungelöst*. Germany.

Kryminalni [*The Criminal Investigators*] (2004–08). A Polish criminal series created in a form of a puzzle showing multiple aspects of an investigation including scheme, false leads and suspicious behaviours. The show takes place in Warsaw and focuses on a life of the Commissar Andrzej Zawada (Marek Włodarczyk) from the Warsaw Homicide Department. Together with two police officers they fight crime on the streets of Warsaw. Poland.

La Commune (Canal+, 2007). French police series focusing on the rivalry between politicians, police investigators and inhabitants of *La Commune*, a neighbourhood sadly known for its high crime rate. France.

La Crim' (France 2, 1999–2006). Police drama centred on a team working for the criminal brigade of Paris. France.

LA Law (NBC 1986–94). A legal drama, set in Los Angeles, and featuring the personal and professional relationships of attorneys at the firm of Mackenzie, Brackman, Cheney, and Kuzak. One of the most popular characters was attorney Arnie Becker, whose promiscuous life became the subject of several storylines. Like many other shows created by Steven Bochco, the series used contemporary events to comment on current issues such as racial tensions, abortion, gay rights, politics and feminism as well as tensions within the legal profession itself. USA.

Langs de kade [*Along the Waterfront*] (1988–93). TV show produced for the Flemish Public Broadcasting channel about the Antwerp harbour police. Following the current American fashion it focused on the private lives of officers as much as on police work. Belgium.

The Last Cop [*El ultimo poli duro*; original German title: *Der letzte Bulle*] (Cuatro, 2014). Puts the police on the stand: Mick Brisgau, a Dirty-Harry-type police officer in Germany's tough Ruhr area, wakes up after 20 years in a coma. This plot device makes two worlds collide and part of the charm of the series is the constant bickering between Brisgau and his partner, Kringge, a young careerist who is a stickler for procedure. Germany, also shown in Spain.

Lavreotika (ERT, 1982, 13 episodes). The story of the miners' strike in Lavrio, their uprising against the attempts for half pay up until the army's attack and the bloodshed. Important series as it signals the new era after the fall of the conservative parties and the rise of PASOK in 1981. Greece.

Law & Order (NBC, 1990–2010). A combination of police procedural and legal drama, created by Dick Wolf, which follows a now-familiar pattern. In the first half of the show, detectives investigate a crime, usually a murder, and arrest a suspect, and in the second half, prosecutors and defence attorneys participate in the trial of the accused. This divided show descends from the 'Arrest & Trial' pattern. Wolf updated it by focusing on the prosecution. Most of the episodes derive in part from actual cases but the writers change fact patterns, usually by adding more serious crimes and changing venues. However, the show has been criticised for this 'ripped from the headlines tendency', and at least one person has sued for defamation. *Law & Order* gave rise to a number of spinoffs: *Law & Order: Criminal Intent*; *Law & Order: LA*; *Law & Order: Special Victims Unit*; and *Law & Order: Trial by Jury*. USA.

Law & Order: Criminal Intent (NBC, 2001–11). A police procedural from the *Law & Order* franchise, the show featured detectives from the Major Case Squad of New York City. The show featured few trials; most suspects confessed. USA.

Law & Order: LA (NBC, 2010–11). A police procedural and legal drama series from the *Law & Order* franchise, set in Los Angeles. Cancelled after one season. USA.

Law & Order: Special Victims Unit (NBC, 1999–). A police procedural, *Law & Order: SVU* is the first of the *Law & Order* spin-offs. It follows the *Law & Order* format in which during the first half of the show, detectives investigate the crime, which in this series is a sexual offence, and arrest a suspect; and during the second half of the show, the trial takes place. USA.

Law & Order: Trial by Jury (NBC, 2005–06). This *Law & Order* spin-off focused on the trial, and trial aspects of the legal process, examining trial strategies, jury selections and other, more unfamiliar procedures. USA.

Lebenslänglich: Mord, Kommissar Wilfings Kriminalfälle [*Life in Prison: Murder, Inspector Wilfing's Criminal Cases*] (2014–). Features the ex-commissioner of the Munich homicide division who presents real-life murder cases in this magazine-style programme. The show consists of re-enactments, voice-over narration and on-camera commentaries by commissioner Wilfing. Germany.

Legal Question [*She'elaMishpatit*] (Channel 2, 2014). A show where legal scholars or lawyers discuss legal issues. Israel.

Le JAP (TF1, 1992–96). Police drama on the activities of the *juge d'application des peines*. France.

Le petit guide de l'empoisonneur (Arte, 2014). This docu-fiction centres on the birth of forensic science. It reveals the evolution of scientific techniques helping the police in solving crimes. France.

Les Bleus, premiers pas dans la police (M6, 2006–10). Police drama based on new recruits, some dreaming of exciting investigations and others content to have job security. France.

Les 5 dernières minutes (RTF, then channel 1 ORTF, then Antenne 2, then France 2, 1956–96). Famous French police drama giving the answer to the crime enigma during the last five minutes of the show. The programme began as a game show with viewer participation to help determine the guilty party. Later the game aspect of the show was dropped. France.

Les Cordiers, Juge et Flic (TF1, 1992–2005). French police drama following the Cordier family. The father is a police chief, his son a *juge d'instruction* and his daughter an investigating journalist. The series is composed of over 12 seasons and 61 episodes. France.

Les dossiers Karl Zéro and Les faits Karl Zéro (2007–). Series of French documentaries presented and produced by Karl Zéro. Each episode focuses on an unsolved criminal case. Both legal and judicial processes are brought to the audience. France.

Les Petits Meurtres d'Agatha Christie (France 2, 2009–). French police series based on Agatha Christie's novels. The first season takes place in the 1930s while the second focuses on the 1950s. France.

Let Justice Be Done (1950). Early drama documentary examining the role of the Probation Service in England. Britain.

Lewis (ITV1, 2007–). Police detective series with Inspector Lewis now with his own assistant, intellectual Sergeant Hathaway, continuing to deal with Oxford's murders and an irascible female boss, over eight seasons and 30 episodes so far on ITV1 prime time. Britain.

LEX (Antena 3, 2008). This is the law firm of the three partners Daniela Leela Le with his own assistant, Xifr2. LEX is an example of a law comedy which plays with popular stereotypes about law and lawyers. Reminiscent of *Ally McBeal* in its absurd assortment of cases, legal arguments are nevertheless regularly used to discuss various social issues. Spain.

Lie to Me (FOX, 2009–11). Dr Cal Lightman's (Tim Roth) team specialises in reading people's mimic and body language. They help government agencies and private persons. USA, shown in Poland.

Life (STAR, 2014). Charlie Cruz is an eccentric police officer, accused for three murders he has not committed. A well set up trap puts him behind bars for twelve years. During those years Charlie loses his dignity, his self-esteem, his job, his wife, his friends. His attorney Constance Griffith, using DNA as evidence to get him out of prison and restore him in his previous police duties. Charlie wants to take advantage of his second life chance and uses his experience in prison to unveil the mystery of the crime that put him in prison. USA, shown in Greece.

Line number 300 [*Kav 300*]. (Channel 1, 1997). This miniseries tells a controversial story from the modern era of the Israeli State that shook up Israeli society its legal and its governmental institutions. Israel.

Lockout (2012). Science-fiction movie about a wrongly convicted men offered freedom in exchange for saving the president's daughter from on outer space prison. USA/France, shown in Switzerland.

Lommetyvens tricks [*Pickpockets' tricks*] (2013). Documentary about pickpockets' tricks. Denmark.

Longmire (A&E and Netflix, 2012–). Police series centring on a county sheriff based in Wyoming investigating major crimes in the area over four series and 33 episodes to date. USA.

Louis la Brocante (France 2, 1998–2014). This crime series follows the work of Louis Roman, an antique dealer who is also a private detective in his spare time. France.

Magda M (2005–07). A TV series focusing on a life of a brilliant lawyer Magda Miłowicz (Joanna Brodzik), who together with her friends tries to help innocent people and fight for justice in a court of law. Poland.

Magnum, PI (1980–88). Thomas Magnum an ex-navy captain and Vietnam special ops veteran enjoys life as a private investigator in Hawaii. USA, shown in Switzerland.

Maigret (1960–63). Paris detective series based on Simenon short stories. Britain.

Malanowski i partnerzy [*Malanowski and Partners*] (2008–). It is a documentary series showing all aspects of a private investigation agency work routine from following unfaithful spouses to fighting drug dealers and traffickers. The agency is run by detective Bronisław Malanowski (Bronisław Cieślak). Poland.

The Man from U.N.C.L.E. (1964–1968). Series revolving around two agents, Napoleon Solo and Illya Kuryakin, that work for the so-called United Network Command for Law Enforcement, and that fight criminal organisations using all kinds of gadgets. US, shown in Flanders.

Mannix (1967–1975). Violent detective series about Los Angeles based private investigator Joe Mannix. In the first season, Mannix works for detective agency Intertect, in the second season, Mannix starts his own agency with side kick Fair. USA, shown in Flanders, Belgium.

Maria Wern (2006–). Swedish TV series about police officer Maria Wern as she tries to solve crimes on the island of Gotland. Sweden, shown in Denmark.

Marshal Rocca [*Il Maresciallo Rocca*] (Rai 2 and Rai 1, 1996–2005). A crime series that brought to the screen the authentically Italian figure of the marshal of the Carabinieri, the most successful example of this type. Marshal Rocca, a widowed father of three, divides his time between his family and the Carabinieri police station where he is commander, in a typical small Italian town. He is modest, compassionate and witty, and fights crime with a sense of duty and truth, notwithstanding his constant disputes with the district attorney. Italy.

Marziano's Dignity [*H'kavod Shell Marziano*] (Channel 10, 2011). This series tells the story of two rival organised crime families. Israel.

Matlock (NBC and ABC 1986–95). Folksy Southern lawyer with a criminal defence practice in Atlanta, Georgia recreates the *Perry Mason* courtroom format with the real criminal being revealed in court in the final two minutes of each show over nine prime-time series. A weekly legal drama set in Atlanta featuring a defence attorney with a remarkable record of successes. Popular for Griffith's portrayal of the trustworthy and no-nonsense advocate who is ready to take on and defend his client, and at the end of the day relax with a glass of iced tea and his guitar. Matlock, like Perry Mason and Owen Marshall before him, is reliable, ethical, responsible and trustworthy. USA.

Matlock Police (1971–76). Drama focused on the personal lives of police officers working in the fictional country town of Matlock. Australia.

Medical Detectives [aka *Forensic Files*; *Murder Detectives*; *Mystery Detectives*] (1996–). Documentary-style series showing how forensic science is used to solve violent crimes, mysterious accidents and outbreaks of illness. Originally produced on the TLC Network and running to date to 400 episodes. USA.

Medium (NBC, 2005–09; CBS, 2009–11). A drama about a psychic (Patricia Arquette) who works for the district attorney's office in Phoenix, Arizona. Based on the story of real-life psychic Allison DuBois. USA.

Med politiets øjne: Bødler i statens tjeneste [*Executioners in the Service of the State*] (2009). Three-part Danish documentary series (DR) about the Danish policemen who in the aftermath of the Second World War executed 46 people for treason. Denmark.

Men of Law [*Anshe'i Hachok*] (Yes, 2010). A docu-reality on police work in Israel. Israel.

The Mentalist (CBS, 2008–15). A police procedural in which a former 'psychic' decides to work with the California Bureau of Investigation (a state agency akin to the Federal Bureau of Investigation—FBI) law enforcement after a serial killer murders his wife and child. Using his extraordinary powers of observation and his deductive powers, he solves crimes but is haunted by his inability to catch the serial killer. See also shows such as *Psych* and *Monk*, which make reference to *The Mentalist* in some of their episodes. USA.

Met voorbedachte rade (1981–86). Five seasons of about four shows, courtroom drama. The title means 'premeditated'. It was a continuation of *Defendant Please Rise* with fictional stories. Produced for the Flemish Public Broadcasting channel. Belgium.

Miami Vice (NBC, 1984–90). A police procedural set in Miami; the crimes are loosely based on actual events. The show also delved into political themes. The protagonist police officers wore high fashion and drove expensive cars; the show's soundtrack featured contemporary rock and other popular music. Beginning in the third season, the original producer, Michael Mann, turned over production to Dick Wolf, who later originated the *Law & Order* series. USA.

Midsomer Murders (1997–). British detective series set in the fictional heritage style county of Midsomer where DCI John Barnaby is in charge of solving murders with his consecutive side-kicks (Sgt Gavin Troy, Sgt Dan Scott, Sgt Ben Jones and Sgt Charlie Nelson). In 2011 Barnaby retires but is succeeded by his younger cousin Tom Barnaby. Britain, shown in Flanders, Belgium.

Mike & Molly (2010–). American sitcom about the police officer Mike and his wife Molly. USA, shown in Denmark.

Miss Fisher's Murder Mysteries (ABC, 2012–). The Australian show is based on Kerry Greenwood's novel. It centres on the professional and personal life of a private detective Phryne Fisher (Essie Davis). The action takes place in Melbourne in the 1920s. Australia, shown in Poland.

Miss Marple (1984–92). Amateur detective series featuring Agatha Christie's sleuth solving crimes that baffle the police in the 1950s. See also Agatha Christie's *Marple* (*qv*). Britain.

Missing (2003–06). Two FBI agents—one guided by reason, and another by intuition—looking for missing people in Washington DC. Joint Canada/USA production.

Mister Defender [*O Kirios Sinigoros*] (YENED, 1970–72). Two hundred and fifty-six 15-minute episodes, with a remake in 1990 on ANT1 with 18 episodes). The first Greek comedic series, it follows the life of an in debt attorney with illusions of grandeur and the comedic situations that arise. Greece.

Mongeville (France 3, 2013–). French police drama set in Bordeaux. The series follows the work of Antoine Mongeville, a former *juge d'instruction*, and Valentine Duteil from the judicial police. The show is so far composed of seven 90-minute episodes. France.

Monk (USA 2002–09). A police procedural centring on a former San Francisco detective who becomes a consultant after his wife is murdered. Adrian Monk has extraordinary deductive skills but his OCD hampers him in dealing with others. He also demonstrates critical thinking and an unwillingness to take what he sees for granted. Similar shows of this type include *The Mentalist* and *Psych*. The show's inclusion of humour tempers otherwise somewhat grisly subject matter. USA.

Montmartre du plaisir et du crime (Arte, 2005). This French documentary centres on the evolution of the Paris neighbourhood of Montmartre. Notorious for its rough reputation and its high crime rate, Montmartre has become a major art scene in the French capital. France.

Mordkommission Istanbul (2008–). German TV police procedural playing in Istanbul. Germany.

Motive (2013–). Crime drama. Each episode begins by revealing not only the victim, but the killer as well. It is not a 'whodunit', but a 'whydunit'—the question faced by spirited female Vancouver homicide detective Angie Flynn as she begins to piece together the clues from the crime. How are the victim and killer connected? What is the motive? Canada.

Motives & Murders (2012–14). Combining the thrill of a mystery with the visceral experience of true-crime drama, *Motives & Murders: Cracking the Case* returns to the scene of the most perplexing crimes and follows detectives as they unearth the clues that lead them to the killer. With news footage, interviews, and gripping re-enactments, the series explores the personal toll on the victim's family and friends, and also features the law enforcement agents who work tirelessly to track down the perpetrator and finally crack the case. Joint Canada/USA.

Motorway Patrol (2001–). Documentary series which follows the daily lives of police officers patrolling the motorways of New Zealand. New Zealand, shown in Britain.

Murder City (2004–06). British police detective series featuring a murder squad in and around London with two principal characters working both alone and together. Britain.

Murder One (ABC, 1995–97). A legal drama created by Steven Bochco, in which the law firm at the centre of the series took on a high-profile criminal case. The entire season followed the development and conclusion of that case. Various episodes dealt with other, unrelated cases which began and concluded within those episodes. USA.

Murder She Solved: True Crime (2010–13). An eight-episode, one-hour documentary series, tells the true stories of female crime solvers who, against all odds, have solved some of the most daunting murder cases in North America. Combining elements of mystery and intrigue, the series' unique visual style and riveting storytelling compels viewers to connect the dots as crime-solvers unravel the clues in their journey to solve the crime. Canada.

Murdoch Mysteries (2009–15). Period piece crime drama. In the 1890s Toronto, Canada, William Murdoch uses radical forensic techniques for the time, including fingerprinting and trace evidence, to solve some of the city's most gruesome murders. Canada.

The Mysteries of Laura [*Los misterios de Laura*] (TVE, 2009–). Laura Lebrel, a police officer with a chaotic life and absent-minded personality, does not seem intelligent enough to solve any crime. Nevertheless, she solves each mystery with Sherlock Holmes-style attention to detail. Italy, Russia, Holland and most recently, the American network NBC adapted the series. Spain.

Na kłopoty … Bednarski [*For Trouble … Bednarski*] (1986–1988). A private investiator Bednarski (Stefan Friedmann) solved criminal cases in the Free City of Gdańsk. Every episode tells a separate story and shows how the best detective in the city finds criminals. Poland.

Na krawędzi [*On the edge*] (2012–14). Marta Orpik vel Sajno (Urszula Grabowska) is a rape victim, who after years spent abroad, comes back to Poland to serve justice to her tormentors, dirty officers of the law. The show focuses on a private investigation led by the woman in order to reveal involvement in crime activities by police and justice department employees. Poland.

Na patrolu [*On Patrol*] (2014–). A documentary TV series showing everyday work of police officers, who are called to intervene in cases of street fights, child abuse, underage crime and sometimes thoughtless and risky teenagers' behaviour. Each episode follows two separate cases solved by one police patrol. Poland.

The Naked Truth [*Ha'emet Ha'eroma*] (Channel 10, 2008). This police drama focuses on the mystery behind the disappearance of a young girl. The show is fully filmed within the boundaries of a police station. Israel.

Narco-finance: les impunis (Arte, 2014). This documentary directed by Agnès Gattegno explores the excesses of modern capitalism. It explains how narco-trafficking has become a part of the global economy and how some traditional banks, such as HSBC, tend to participate in this financial system. France.

Nash Bridges (CBS, 1996–2001). Nash Bridges (Don Johnson) is a smart and brilliant detective working for San Francisco Police Department. Together with his partner Joe Dominguez (Cheech Marin) they fight crime in the city. Meanwhile Nash is struggling with personal issues—two ex-wives, teenage daughter and sick father. USA, shown in Poland.

Navarro (TF1, 1989–2007). This series centres on Commissaire Antoine Navarro, a single father raising his daughter Yolande. Set in Paris, the topics vary from one episode to another. France.

Navy NCIS (CBS, 2003–). A group of Navy Criminal Investigative Service employees solves challenging criminal mysteries related to the US Navy. The unit is led by special agent Jethro Gibbs (Mark Harmon), who has unique operation methods. USA, shown in Poland.

NCIS (CBS, 2003–). A police procedural spin-off from the CBS series *JAG*, focusing on the work of the Naval Criminal Investigative Service. The team investigates criminal offences punishable under the US Code of Military Justice. USA.

NCIS: Los Angeles (CBS, 2009–) is a spin-off of *Navy NCIS*. A team of special agents working undercover for NCIS Los Angeles investigates the most difficult and bizarre crime scenes. USA.

NCIS: New Orleans (2014–). Offshoot of the *NCIS* franchise centred on the Mississippi River and Texas panhandle looking at crimes, especially murders, connected with the naval military. USA.

Nestor Burma (Antenne 2, 1991–92; France 2, 1992–2003). French crime series focusing on Nestor Burma, a private detective. Originally based on Léo Malet's novels, the programme emphasises the hard-boiled dimension of the character and his humour. France.

New Street Law (BBC1, 2006–07). Courtroom drama centred on competing sets of chambers in Manchester and their individual barristers some with a radical anti-establishment edge and shown on BBC1. Britain.

New Tricks (2003–15). Police procedural series following the exploits of the Unsolved Crimes Squad (UCOS) staffed by three ex-police detectives and their feisty female boss. Britain.

Night Court (NBC, 1984–92). Judge Harold T Stone presides over law and mayhem in a Manhattan courtroom full of eccentric characters. Notable for the emphasis on star Harry Dean Anderson's use of magic tricks in some episodes. USA.

No Hiding Place (1959–66). Police procedural series centred on the work of Detective Chief Superintendent Tom Lockhart at Scotland Yard, with a one-hour format. Britain.

North Square (2000). Channel 4 series focusing on the courtroom work and personal battles of a group of six barristers—of both sexes and some ethnic diversity—operating in the context of the machinations of their chief clerk to obtain business for this new set of chambers in the northern city of Leeds. Britain.

Nowa [*The New One*] (2010–). Ada Mielcarz (Justyna Schneider) is a police academy graduate, who starts as a trainee in one of the best criminal investigation departments in Poland. She is assigned to Commissar Maciej Wolski's (Marcin Bosak) team. Her new boss believes that working in the police is a man's job, so in order to stay she has to work doubly hard to prove her worth. Poland.

Noy-York (Yes, 2012). The daily crime drama tells the story of the youngest son in an Israeli crime family that ran away from Israel and moved to New York. Israel.

Numb3rs (CBS, 2005–10). Don Eppes is an FBI Agent who, together with his brilliant mathematician brother Charlie Eppes, solves the most complicated cases that happen in Los Angeles. He investigates crime scenes and collects evidence while his brother uses equations to find dangerous criminals. USA, shown in Poland.

NYPD Blue (ABC 1993–2005). Crime drama tales created by David Milch and Steven Bochco, focusing on the personal and professional lives of the officers of a fictional Manhattan precinct. Critics and audiences viewed it as particularly realistic for its depiction of problems inherent in the lives of members of law enforcement, notably alcoholism, racism and violence. The series was criticised by some conservative groups for its depictions of nudity. USA.

The Octopus: The Power of the Mafia [*La Piovra*] (Rai 1, 1984–2001). This long-running and hugely successful series, set mostly in Sicily, describes the struggle of the honest elements in Italian society, represented by heroic 'servants of the state' such as police officers and judges, against the tentacles of the Mafia, which are increasingly intertwined with finance, politics and the state. The main character, Inspector Corardo Cattani, is 'passionate, sentimental, perhaps a bit of an anarchist, one who perceives the law and formal justice as strange and remote' (Buonanno (2012) 71). He is a tragic hero, who winds up dying in a hail of bullets in a famous scene, in which the small crowd that gathers around the corpse of the inspector is the perfect simulacrum of a civil society that is at once angry and resigned. Italy.

Oficer [*The Officer*] (2004–05). Kroszon—Tomasz Kruszyński (Borys Szyc) is a special forces officer who has to work under cover in order to investigate an organised crime organisation. Poland.

Ojciec Mateusz [*Father Mateusz*] (2008–). Extraordinary priest—Father Mateusz (Artur Żmijewski)—helps local police solve criminal cases in Sandomierz. It is a Polish version of the Italian TV series Don Matteo. Poland.

Omerta a French language police procedural produced by the CBC from 1996 to 1999. Canada.

O mnie się nie martw [*Don't worry about me*] (2014–). Iga Małecka (Joanna Kulig) is a 30-year-old women, mother of two children and a two time divorcee. She starts a new job in a law firm, where she meets very handsome attorney Marcin Kaszuba (Stefan Pawłowski). Together they try to help innocent and defenceless people fight for their rights. Poland.

Ond, ondere, ondest [*Mean, Meaner, Meanest*] (2014). Six-part Danish (DR3) reality programme about the psychological experiment whether power can make good men evil. Fifteen unknowing young men are locked in a prison in an old fortress. Five of them get the role of watcher and 10 become prisoners. Denmark.

One Step from Heaven [*A un paso del cielo*; original Italian title: *Un passo dal cielo*] (TVE2, 2014). An Italian crime comedy series set in the *Tre Cime* National Park in the Alps. Terence Hill plays a forest ranger helping the local police with their investigations. Spain.

Open Court [*Processi a porte aperte*] (Rai 1, 1968). This series used the structure of the criminal trial to authentically reconstruct cases while highlighting their controversial aspects. The programme concluded with the studio audience giving their own verdict, before learning that of the real court. Italy.

Operation Malaya [*Operación Malyaya*] (TVE, 2011). A cross-over of a police and lawyer show. Based on a true story set in Marbella, it deals with corruption in urban development. We follow Operation Malaya headed by an investigating judge and the two main police officers. Spain.

Orange is the New Black (Netflix, 2013–). Comedy drama set in a women's prison looking at the interactions and past lives of the inmates of the New York federal penitentiary; over two seasons and 26 episodes thus far. USA.

Out (1978). Comedy drama covering the post-prison life of a bank robber so featured in *Porridge* (*qv*). Britain.

Outlaws (2002). A cynical but good-hearted lawyer and his ethnic minority assistant attempt to run a business with legal aid clients accused of minor crimes in a northern magistrates' court. Britain.

Overruled! (2010–). Teen comedy, about the trials of Jared 'Coop' Cooper, a smooth-talking teen who puts his charm and principles to good use as a lawyer at Banting High's teen court. Students with school issues that can't be settled in the halls can have their case decided by a jury of their peers in the after-school court with funny representation from Coop Cooper—a guy who can cut the tension of any courtroom drama with his comedic courtroom theatrics. Canada.

Owen Marshall, Counselor at Law (ABC, 1971–74). A legal drama featuring Arthur Hill as defence attorney Owen Marshall. Depicts the defence attorney in the *Perry Mason* mould as trustworthy, ethical and reliable. USA.

Oz (HBO, 1997–2003). A TV drama set in a maximum security state prison, exploring the interactions of the guards and the inmates. One of the inmates, Augustus Hill, narrates the episodes. USA.

Paco's Men [*Los hombres de Paco*] (Antena 3, 2005–10). *Paco's Men* is one of the most successful crime comedies in Spain. It is set in San Antonio, a fictitious underprivileged neighbourhood in Madrid. Inspector Paco Miranda Ramos and his men have a haphazard and surreal way of solving crimes; in fact, the solution of the crime is often by accident rather than design. Spain.

Paradoks [*Paradox*] (2012–). The story centres on a police detective Marek Kaszowski (Bogusław Linda) and officer Joanna Majewska (Anna Grycewicz), who is assigned to join Kaszowski's unit in order to investigate her supervisor. While doing that she helps the team solve criminal mysteries. Poland.

Parashat H'ashavua (HOT, 2006). This ambitious series discusses the lives of Israeli families from different backgrounds at the backdrop of biblical references. Israel.

Paris, Enquêtes Criminelles (TF1, 2007–08). Created by Dick Wolf, this police series is an adaptation of *Law & Order: Criminal Intent. Paris, Enquêtes Criminelles* follows the investigations of two police detectives with very different methods of investigation. Vincent Revel is very intuitive, while his partner Claire Savigny is more logical. France.

The People's Court (syndicated, 1981–). Presided over by Joseph Wapner and successively by former New York City mayor Ed Koch and Judge Jerry Sheindlin, and now by Judge Marilyn Milian (since 2001). USA.

Perception (TNT, 2012–). Dr Daniel Pierce (Eric McCormack) is an eccentric neurobiologist suffering from schizophrenia. His knowledge and unique way of seeing things turn out to be of great use for the FBI. Together with agent Kate Moretti (Rachel Leigh Cook) they solve complex criminal cases. USA, shown in Poland.

Perry Mason (CBS, 1957–66). As the star of this iconic and long-running series, Raymond Burr became the epitome of the attorney who defends his client to the utmost, and virtually all his clients were innocent. The episodes were formulaic. Mason and his private detective Paul Drake investigated the case in each episode, and in the last few minutes, Mason unmasked the real killer. Mason famously won all but three criminal cases. USA.

The Persuaders (1971–1972). British series featuring affluent playboys and character opposites English Lord Brett Sinclair and American Danny Wilde. They are thrown together to investigate crimes which the police is unable to solve. Britain, shown in Flanders, Belgium.

Petits meurtres en famille (France 2, 2006–). Famous novels, such as *Hercule Poirot's Christmas*, originally published in 1938 are often transposed into episodes under this title. The series is over two seasons and 23 irregular episodes. France.

Petra Delicado [*Petra Delicado*] (Telecinco, 1999). The first female superintendent, Petra Delicado is a complex representation of a career woman who is harsh, stern and decisive in the rough macho world of a police station. Spain.

Petrocelli (1974–76). A small town defence lawyer replicating the *Perry Mason* format except that Petrocelli always finished with his suggestion as to what had really happened shown in fade-away reconstruction of the actual events as they played out and nailing the true criminal. USA

Phoenix (1992–93). Loosely based on the 1986 Russell Street bombing, this series follows the bombing of a Victorian State police headquarters. Australia.

Pillars of Smoke [*Timrot Ashan*] (Hot, 2009). A 'twin-peaks' inspired police drama telling the story of a policewoman investigating a mysterious crime in one of the most expensive Israeli shows ever produced. Israel.

PitBull (2005–08). Police officers from the homicide department in Warsaw fight crime on the streets of the city while struggling with obstacles and difficulties in their private lives. Poland.

Pit Bulls and Parolees (Animal Planet, 2009–). Reality TV show set in New Orleans. Tia Torres, founder of the Villalobos Rescue Center, rescues and re-homes pitbulls with the assistance of parolees and works to overcomes misunderstandings concerning the nature and behaviours of pitbulls. USA.

PJ (France 2, 1997–2009). French police drama taking place in the Tenth arrondissement of Paris, near the Canal Saint-Martin. *PJ* centres on the daily life of a *commissariat* with various team mates. Each episode follows the work of the team on burglary, car accidents and sometimes murders, but it basically represents the social diversity of a local police station's employees. *PJ* brings the audience a reflection on various topics such as homosexuality, ethnic and religious minorities or sexism. The series is composed of over 13 seasons and 146 episodes. France.

Police District [*Distretto di Polizia*] (Canale 5, 2000–12). The most successful police series produced by Italian commercial television. It follows the workings of a police station in Rome. The chief of the station, Giovanna Scalise, was the first female commanding officer in a police series. A lot of space is given to the private life and personal relationships of the team's members. Italy.

Police Interceptors (2008–). It follows the work of an 'intercept team' with high-speed car chases interspersed with light comedic moments off duty, or with harmless drunks and practical jokers over five seasons looking at the work of four different police authorities. Britain.

Police on the Street [*Policías, en el corazón de la calle*] (Antena 3, 2000–03). One of the most popular, if short-lived, crime series, *Police on the Street* is set in a police station in Madrid. The format of each season relies on a prime antagonist combined with several secondary plotlines; recurrent themes include police corruption and antisocial personality disorders. Spain.

Police State (1989). Film recreation of the events of the Fitzgerald Inquiry, also known as the 'Commission of Inquiry into Possible Illegal Activities and Associated Police Misconduct' into the Queensland police force. It resulted in the deposition of a premier, and the incarceration of three former ministers and a police commissioner. Australia.

Policeman Bekas' Stories [*Istories tou Ipastinomou Beka*] (Alpha, 2006). Self-contained police stories from the books of Giannis Maris, set forth in modern times (28 episodes). Greece.

Policjantki i policjanci [*Policewomen and Policemen*] (2014–). It is a dynamic and full of twists TV series showing the work of two police squads patrolling streets of Wroclaw. Each day those police officers have to deal with social misery, abuse problems, assaults and drunk drivers. Poland.

Politijagt [*Policehunt*] (Kanal 5, 2009–). Danish documentary series about the traffic police. Demark.

Politiskolen (TV2, 2014–). Documentary series about the Danish police academy. Denmark.

Polizeiruf 110 [*Police Call 110*] (DFF1, 1971–91 and 1993–, ARD, 247+ episodes). The East German counterpart of the *Tatort* series became the most successful crime series in the history of the DFF (East German State TV). A variety of officers of the People's Police investigated a sort of crime that officially shouldn't exist in a socialist state. Because of the social background, the realistic locations and cases often inspired by real-life events the older episodes are a fascinating time capsule offering a glimpse into the customs and circumstances of real existing socialism. It's also the only crime TV show of the GDR that survived the fall of the Berlin Wall and continues to this day, alternating with the *Tatort* entries on Sunday nights, adopting some of *Tatort's* aesthetics as well. Germany.

Polizischt Wäckerli [*Policeman Wäckerli*] (1955). Swiss movie classic about a village policeman. Portrays the rural lower middle class in Switzerland at that time. Switzerland.

Porridge (1974–77). Comedy set in a standard 1970s British prison which also reflects on the themes of prison hierarchy and the problems of labelling. Britain.

Post Mortem (RTL, 2007–). The German crime drama series focusing on a group of forensic experts led by Dr Daniel Koch (Hannes Jaenicke). They help solve the most complicated murder cases by meticulously analysing evidence left on a human body. Germany, shown in Poland.

the practice (ABC, 1997–2004). This David E Kelley legal comedy/drama focused on a law firm that took cases 'ripped from the headlines'. The characters in the show also had many personal and ethical conflicts, which often became concerns during the episodes. USA.

Prawo Agaty [*Agata's Right*] (2012–). A TV series following life of a 30-year-old attorney, who, after losing her job in a law firm, is forced to face the challenge of starting her own practice. Every day she has to fight both in the courtroom and in her private life. Poland.

Primal Fear (1996). Exemplary representative of the American court room drama about a famous attorney who defends an altar boy charged with murdering the Archbishop of Chicago. USA.

Prime Suspect (ITV, 2006). A British police television drama focusing on Jane Tennison (Helen Mirren), one of the first female Detective Chief Inspectors in London Police. Britain.

The Prince [*El príncipe*] (Telecinco, 2014). Set in the Prince Alfonso neighbourhood in Ceuta, close to the Moroccan border, this TV show tells the story of a Christian police officer's love affair with a young Muslim who is the sister of a well-known drug baron. Aimed at a young audience, this is a story of multicultural love, passion, police corruption and international crimes. Spain.

Prison Break (FOX, 2005–09). Lincoln Burrows (Dominic Purcell) is falsely convicted and sent to death row by a political conspiracy. His younger brother Michael Scofield (Wentworth Miller) decides to break him out. To do that he has to deliberately get himself arrested and sent to Fox River prison. USA, shown in Poland.

Prison Without Bars (1938). Based on a French film *Prison sans barreaux* concerning a romance in a reformatory school between an inmate, the doctor and the school superintendent. Britain.

Prisoner [*aka Prisoner: Cell Block H*] (1979–86). Australian soap opera set in a women's prison, Wentworth, over eight series and 692 episodes for Network Ten—see also *Wentworth* (qv). Australia.

Probation Officer (1959–62). Series following the problems faced by a team of probation officers dealing with ex-prisoners. Britain.

Profilage (TF1, 2009–). Police drama of over five seasons and 54 episodes, centring on the investigations of Chloé Saint-Laurent, a psychologist specialising in criminology. Her qualifications help the judicial police identify criminals by decoding their motivations. France.

Psych (USA, 2006–14). Shawn Spencer, trained by his police officer father to be exceptionally observant, uses his skills to pass himself off as a psychic detective and opens up a psychic detective agency with the help of his best friend, pharmaceutical salesman Burton Guster. USA.

Public Defender [*Turno de oficio*] (TVE, season 1: 1986; season 2: 1996). Three lawyers take it in turns to fight for justice. The cases are anything from petty crimes of the socially disadvantaged to medical negligence, rape, domestic violence and miscarriages of justice. Due to its huge success the show returned 10 years later, when the storyline is mainly driven by Cosme, who returns to Madrid as a judge-cum-detective. Spain.

Punta Escarlata [*Punta Escarlata*] (Telecinco, 2011). In the most successful Telecinco series of 2011, Bosco Ruiz and Max Vila are two police officers who investigate the disappearance of two children and move to Punta Escarlata, a small fictitious coastal town, where their investigation becomes increasingly complicated and the list of suspects becomes longer in each episode. Spain.

Quai no 1 (France 2, 1997–2006). French police series focusing on the work of Marie Saint-Georges. An orphan, she was found in an abandoned railway station and now works as a police inspector with her colleague, Captain Max Orteguy. France.

A Question of Conscience [*Un caso di coscienza*] (Rai 2 and Rai 1, 2003–13). The lawyer Tasca, the most successful Italian variant of the much-imitated *Perry Mason*, discovers the terrible truth beneath the surface of cases and gets a confession from the culprits, re-establishing the values of justice and solidarity in an increasingly greedy and cynical society. Italy.

Questions à la justice (Antenne 2, 1985). Talk show centred on legal issues, France.

Rake (2010–). Follows Cleaver Greene, an intelligent but self-destructive Sydney barrister as he defends his (usually guilty) clients. Australia.

Rake (FOX, 2014–). Keegan Dean is a brilliant but self-destructive criminal defence attorney. He specialises in the most difficult and hopeless cases, defending the most eccentric clients from bigamists to cannibals. USA, shown in Poland.

Ramat Aviv G (Channel 2, 1995). A very successful and popular series that is considered the first Israeli soap opera. Israel.

Razzia (2013). Danish documentary series about various Danish government agencies (eg, Tax, Environment Agency, Food) making surprise visits. Denmark.

Recht op Recht (1998–2002). Popular courtroom drama for the Flemish Public Broadcasting channel with high ratings. The title means 'the right to justice'. Belgium.

Rejseholdet [*Unit One*] (2000–04). Prize-winning Danish drama series in 32 episodes about a special police unit travelling all over Denmark to solve complex crimes. The crimes in the series are based on actual cases from Rejseholdet. Denmark.

Republic of Doyle (CBC, 2010–). In this one-hour dramedy, Jake Doyle and his father Malachy run a private investigation agency in St John's, Newfoundland.

Their cases involve them in all sorts of dealings—not all of them on the right side of the law. Canada.

Richard Diamond (CBS, 1957–59; NBC, 1959–60). David Janssen starred as private investigator Richard Diamond (Dick Powell had starred in the radio series). For the first two seasons, set in New York, the show had a somewhat noir flavour, but in season three, the show moved to LA and took on a glitzier appearance. USA.

Richter Alexander Hold [*Judge Alexander Hold*] (Sat.1, 2001–13, 2038 episodes). Follows the same concept as the trendsetting *Richterin Barbara Salesch*. Germany.

Richterin Barbara Salesch (Sat.1, 1999–2012, 2147 episodes). German version of *Judge Judy*. Ex real-life judge Barbara Salesch presides over a criminal court and decides fictitious cases. The style is pseudo-realistic, although the presentation seems always somewhat stage-bound. Besides the juristic personnel the cast mostly consists of lay actors. Germany.

Right or Wrong? The Final Verdict [*Torto o ragione? Il verdetto finale*] (Rai 1, 2008–). One of two Italian reality court shows, it explicitly imitates the American trial procedure, transforming the public into one big jury that gives the final verdict. Italy.

Ripoux Story (2012). This documentary explores the confused relationship between certain police members and organised crime. Ripoux is French slang for '*pourri*' (rotten) which basically describes a corrupt policeman who uses his position inside the judicial system to avoid being suspected of associating with known criminal organisations. France.

The Rockford Files (NBC, 1974–80). An atypical private investigator series, featuring James Garner as ex-con (wrongfully convicted) Jim Rockford, who normally took only cold cases and insurance cases in order to avoid dealing with law enforcement. USA.

Rookie Blue (2010–15). The stakes are high for five young cops fresh out of the Academy and ready for their first day with one of the most elite units in the city. Under the watchful guidance of their officers, Andy McNally and her four fellow rookies quickly learn that no amount of training could prepare them for this new world. Each case they tackle and choice they make will impact their lives, but it's their personal relationships that may play an even greater role in defining the cops they become. One-hour crime drama. Canada.

Rough Justice (1982–2007). BBC series with some 40 separate programmes investigating alleged miscarriages of justice resulting in at least 18 people being released from prison and the setting up of the Criminal Cases Review Commission. Britain.

Rumpole of the Bailey (1975–92). Courtroom drama centred on an ageing junior barrister always committed to defence work and showing his home life. ITV1 originally in prime time. Britain.

Rush (2008–11). Police drama set in Melbourne. It follows the personal and professional lives of the members of a police tactical response team, based on the real life Victoria Police Critical Incident Response Team. Australia.

The Ruth Rendell Mysteries (1987–2000). Police detective work of Rendell's Chief Inspector Wexford from ITV over 55 episodes along with a further 25 episodes based on other stories in which Wexford does not feature. Shown on ITV1 prime-time. Britain.

Sąd rodzinny [*Family Court*] (2008–2011). A Polish documentary TV show taking place in a courtroom. Each episode presents a trial of a different family case. Poland.

Salamander (2012–13). Co-production of VRT (Flanders Public Broadcasting) RTL crime (commercial channel, the Netherlands) and NPO1 (public broadcasting channel, the Netherlands) about a police inspector from the federal police in Brussels, trying to solve a bank heist. Belgium.

Sargeant Thanasis Papathanasis (ANT1, 1990). The life and professional adventures of an honest and decent police officer, who is waiting his promotion that never comes. Greece.

Scales of Justice (1983). A controversial three-part miniseries, portraying entrenched, systematic corruption at all levels of Australian law enforcement. Australia.

Schnell ermittelt [*Fast Forward*] (AU/ORF1, 2009–12, 40 episodes). Crime drama series focusing on the female chief inspector of the homicide division in Vienna who usually solves the committed crimes with intuition and empathy, often going through extensive daydreams that place her in the situations of the murder victims. Austria.

Schneller als die Polizei erlaubt [*Faster than the Police Allows*] (Vox, 2008–10, 100 epidsodes). Reality show about the work of the traffic police; usually focused on offences like speeding and located most often on the vast highway network. Germany.

Die Schulermittler [*The School Detectives*] (RTL, 2009–13, 364 episodes). Reality-style show concentrating on offences and minor crimes (theft, drug use, mobbing) near schools. All episodes are staged in the scripted reality-style manner, meaning lay actors, simple language, sometimes frantic camera movements etc. Germany.

Schweizer im Stasi-Knast [*Swiss Citizens in Stasi-Prison*] (2014). Part of the documentary series *Dok*. Tells the story of a Swiss citizen and his girlfriend who were sentenced to several years in prison in the German Democratic Republic. The documentary does not only address the protagonists' time in prison, but takes a closer look at the repressive system of the GDR as a whole and the resistance against it. Switzerland.

Scott and Bailey (ITV1, 2011–). Police detective work of two principal detectives and their female boss interacting over a range of crimes over four series and 30 episodes on late night ITV1. Britain.

SeaChange (1998–2000). Laura Gibson, a successful city-based corporate lawyer, suffers a series of personal crises. She subsequently moves with her two children to the small coastal town of Pearl Bay, and takes the position of local magistrate. Australia.

Sedes & Belli (2002–04). Flemish police detective series about private investigators Frank Sedes and Lena Belli, working Vic Moens' security firm. They deal with several cases brought on by private clients but resulting in criminals being caught. Belgium, Flemish.

Sędzia Anna Maria Wesołowska [Judge Anna Maria Wesołowska] (2006–11). It is a courtroom-based series and in each episode viewers are presented with a different criminal case. Poland.

Sherlock Holmes (1954–55). British television series based on the characters of Holmes and Watson, with the addition of inspector Lestrade, a baffled policy officer. Britain, shown in Flanders, Belgium.

Silk (2011). It is courtroom drama focusing on the work of a dedicated, working class, ambitious female barrister and her competition with a smooth male rival for promotion from junior barrister to QC at the English Bar. Always features defence work with a different client. Each episode on BBC1 prime time over three series, tracing her successes and frustrations, professional and personal. Britain.

Simone Veil: une loi au nom des femmes (France 2, 2010). Almost 40 years after the legalisation of abortion in France, this documentary centres on Simone Veil, a former minister of gender equality and her struggles for women's rights. France.

Sirens [Sirenot] (Channel 1, 2014). A criminal-legal news magazine covering current criminal issues and discussing their legal implications. Israel.

Siton (Channel 1, 1995). It is one of the first lawyer-focused Israeli dramas, telling the story of a lawyer and his daily life struggles. Israel.

Soeur Thérèse (TF1, 2002–11). Soeur Thérèse is a former police officer who decided to become a member of the clergy, but her ex-husband, a police inspector, often needs her point of view to solve cases. Moreover, the Mother Superior of the convent who is fond of detective novels encourages Soeur Thérèse in her investigations. The series is composed of over 10 seasons of 21 irregular episodes. France.

Softly Softly (1966–76). Spin-off detective series from *Z Cars* (*qv*) following a specialist squad tackling major criminals. Britain.

SOKO 5113 (ZDF, 1978–, 547+ episodes). The German series that began rather unspectacularly on the evening slot of the ZDF. But over the course of three decades became a staple of this channel's crime programmes. *SOKO*, standing for Sonderkommission (special commission), offers police work away from the usual routines. Sometimes going undercover the officers of SOKO solve an assortment of major crimes. The original series was inspired by a book by an ex-police commissioner who complained about the unrealistic portrayal of police work in fictional TV programmes. Spin-offs located in the cities of Leipzig (since 2001) and Wismar (since 2004) as well as in Cologne (since 2001), Stuttgart (since 2009) and even in Austria's Kitzbühel (since 2001) and Vienna (since 2005) followed suit. Germany.

SOS [S.O.S.] (1974). A radio reporter and journalist Rafał Kostroń runs a radio show called S.O.S. in which he tries to investigate and deal with situations and people that need help or advice. While gathering information for his next episode he comes accross a case involving life of his daughter. Poland.

The Source [Hamakor] (Channel 10, 2009) is Channel 10's leading newsmagazine, also following 60 Minutes' reporter-centered investigation style. Israel.

The Special Unit [Ha'meyuchedet] (Channel 2, 2012). This police drama revolves around a special unit that was established for the purpose of solving complex cases. Israel.

Sporløs [Without a Trace] (1999–). Danish documentary series about real people trying to find their long-lost family members. Denmark.

Der Staatsanwalt hat das Wort [The Public Prosecutor has the Word] (DFF1, 1965–91, 140 episodes). Long-running crime series of the German Democratic Republic, told from the viewpoint of the public prosecutor. Each episode told its story in a documentary style, focusing on the social circumstances that lead to the crime. Usually the series dealt with minor offences as the party doctrine stated that major crimes such as murder are (almost) impossible in a socialist society. The programme focused also on rehabilitation and stressed the principle that ex-convicts should be reintegrated into society as soon as possible. Germany.

Starsky and Hutch (ABC, 1975–79). Southern California detective series focusing on the eponymous heroes work in their Ford Gran Torino over four series and 93 episodes for ABC. USA.

Station 2 (1993–). A Danish crime (news) documentary series about actual and present crimes. Seen for the first time on 18 September 1993 with various Danish news readers as hosts. The purpose is to help the police solve their crimes and viewers can call and help the police if they have seen something suspicious. Denmark.

Stingers (1998–2004). A gritty series following undercover police officers and their various cases and false identities. Australia.

STOP Drogówka [*STOP Street Patrol*] (2014–). A documentary TV series show-ing interesting police interventions taking place in different cities around Poland. Programme reveals sometimes brutal events and actions of the patrolling police officers. Poland.

Das Strafgericht [*The Criminal Court*] (RTL, 2002–08, 1058 episodes). Pseudo-realistic courtroom series moulded after the same pattern as *Richterin Barbara Salesch* and *Richter Alexander Hold*. The depicted cases are—as is usual on this kind of show—on the spectacular side. Germany.

Street Legal. Ran from 1987 to 1994 on CBC. *Street Legal* focused on the profes-sional and private lives of the partners in a small Toronto law firm. The primary stars were Sonja Smits as Carrington Barr, Eric Peterson as Leon Robinovitch and C David Johnson as Chuck Tchobanian. Produced at the same time as *LA Law* in the USA, *Street Legal* was distinctively Canadian in its use of Canadian court cus-toms and procedures. Canada.

The Streets of San Francisco (ABC, 1972–77). Police detectives Mike Stone and his young assistant Steve Keller investigating murders in San Francisco over five series and 121 episodes for ABC television. USA.

Strike [*Shvita*] (Yes, 2012). Focuses on the lives and struggles of workers in an oil factory on the outskirts of Jerusalem whose work conditions force them to go on strike. Israel.

Stufe Drei [*Stage Three*] (2013). Short comedy movie about a young man sen-tenced to social service in an institution for mentally handicapped and making friends with the residents. Germany.

Suits (2011–). Smooth, successful corporate lawyer/deal closer who works along-side his hyper-smart protégé (who is not actually the Harvard law graduate he pretends to be). Only his boss and an assistant know this, and they all work for a strong African-American female boss. The series follows the adventures of the pair as they bend or break ethical rules in order to keep the secret while trying cases. USA.

The Superintendent [*El comisario*] (Telecinco, 1999–2009). The long-running *The Superintendent* is set in the small fictitious police station of San Fernando, Madrid. Comisario Castilla and his officers handle a vast array of cases: sexual harassment, street violence, drugs, and violence in old people's homes, human trafficking, Latin American crime gangs and property speculation. Spain.

Supreme Court Hearings. Live televised hearings at the Supreme Court of Canada in Ottawa, Ontario, Canada. Canada.

Suspect [*Hashuda*] (Channel 10, 2015). Is a miniseries which revolves around a female lawyer 'who never lost a case', haunted by her husband's suicide. Israel.

Suspect Zero (2004). Feature movie about an FBI agent who chases a serial killer who chases serial killers himself. USA.

The Sweeney (1975–78). Police series focusing on two members of the Flying Squad, a branch of the London Metropolitan Police dealing with armed robbery and violent crime. The programme's title derives from Sweeney Todd, which is Cockney rhyming slang for 'Flying Squad'. Britain.

Taking Lives (2004). Feature movie about FBI Profiler Illeana Scott, helping the Montreal Police to find a serial killer who take on the identity of his victims. USA/Australia.

Tak czy nie? [*Yes or No?*] (2003). The first Polish interactive TV-series following the investigation on a tragic accident of Sławomir Melanowski. At the end of each episode viewers were asked a yes or no question connected to the case. The answer was to be figured out of the material shown in the episode and evidence available on the show's webpage. Poland.

Tanuchi [*Relax*] (HOT, 2012). A daily sitcom whose protagonists are four women that played leading roles in previous television series. This reflective show is embedded with inter-textual references to other past or ongoing television shows broadcast in Israel and is known for its ironic approach towards the television industry. Israel.

Tatort [*Crime Scene*] (ARD, 1970–, 948+ episodes). The flagship of German crime shows sets the standards in almost every department. It is the longest-running series, has the greatest numbers of investigators in the greatest variety of locales (apparently almost every major city in Germany was at least once the backdrop of a *Tatort* episode), as well as the highest ratings. The start of each 90-minute episode is usually a complicated murder case, resulting often in a cat and mouse situation between police officer and culprit. Spanning more than four decades the array of investigators is ranging from introvert intellectual to controversial action man with an increasing number of female investigators. The plots often reflect the Zeitgeist, ranging from the bleak to the more light hearted. Germany.

Temida [*Themis*] (1985–87). Polish criminal mini-series that take place during interval period. The main topic of each of three episodes is a different case. The plot focuses on a trial connected to the crime. Poland.

Tenth Commandment [*Dekati Entoli*] (Alpha 2004–06, 96 episodes). Self-contained stories based on major cases as they were portrayed in newspapers. Greece.

Tequila and Bonetti (CBS, 1992). Nico Bonetti (Jack Scalia) is a police officer of Italian descent from New York City. He is partnered with Tequila, a specially trained police dog. Together with officer Angela Garcia (Mariska Hargitay), the three of them battle crime in the streets of Los Angeles. USA, shown in Poland.

Territory Cops (2012–). Day to day activities of police officers in Australia's Northern Territory, with a focus on the unique problems of the area. This includes drug and alcohol issues in remote communities, large distances between towns and native wildlife. Australia.

Texas Ranger (CBS, 1993–2001). Cordell Walker (Chuck Norris) is a Texas Ranger. With the help of his partner James Trivette (Clarence Gilyard Jr) and prosecutor Alex Cahill Walker (Sheree J Wilson) he fights crime all around the state of Texas. USA, shown in Poland.

They Stand Accused (DuMont Television Network, 1949–52, 1954). A TV series which dramatised real cases; the producers then chose a jury from the audience asked them to issue a verdict. Also known as *Cross Question*. USA.

Thierry la Fronde (RTF, 1963–64; ORTF, 1964–66). A Robin Hood type story mixing arrests, investigations, prison escapes, etc. France.

This is Wonderland was a legal drama with comedic elements which aired on CBC from 2004 to 2006. It highlighted the multicultural nature of Toronto and demonstrated the shortcomings of the judicial system, regularly depicting it as a blunt instrument ill-equipped to respond to the needs of a diverse and changing society. Canada.

Thorberg (2012). Documentary portraying the fate of inmates in the Swiss high security facility Thorberg. Switzerland.

Thriller Club. Invitation to the Crime Story [*Giallo Club. Invito al poliziesco*] (Rai 1, 1959–61). Police drama mixed with a quiz, with studio guests who had to guess the identity of the culprit. The main character was lieutenant Sheridan, the archetype of the Italian investigator despite his ostensibly American persona. He was a 'sad detective who used his fists a little and his brain a lot' (Veltroni (1992) 109). Italy.

To Catch a Predator (NBC, 2004–07). This documentary-style show originated as a Dateline NBC segment. The network then spun it off into a series. Those working with the programme would, while pretending to be minors, engage possible sex offenders in interactions usually on social media; if the potential offenders pursued the opportunity, then the adults, still pretending to be underage, would arrange a face-to-face meeting. The host of the programme, Chris Hansen, would then confront the potential offenders. At the beginning of the series, the show did not depict involvement of law enforcement; eventually police were shown chasing or arresting potential offenders. USA.

Top of the Lake (2013–). The series follows Inspector Robin Griffin. In the first season (2013), set in a small town in New Zealand, she investigate the disappearance of a suicidal, pregnant 12-year-old and finds herself knee-deep in small-town secrets. For 2016, a second season, set in Hong Kong, is announced. Australia/USA/UK, shown in Switzerland.

To Serve and Protect (1985–). Documentary that depicts the day to day events of police officers in Canadian cities such as Edmonton, Winnipeg, Vancouver as well as several other Royal Canadian Mounted Police (RCMP) detachments in British Columbia. Since its debut in 1992 the series spotlights the efforts of national and local members of law enforcement in major cities in Canada, offering a realistic portrayal of keeping the peace. Episodes contain actual police investigation footage. Canada.

Toto & Harry (Kabel 1, 2002–, 22+ episodes). Documentary-style series about two cops in the city of Bochum. Germany.

A Touch of Frost (ITV1, 1992). Detective series set in a gritty fictional south Midlands town with some comic touches amongst the parade of murder investigations carried out by Detective Inspector Frost and his Detective Sergeant assistant. Britain.

Tout la Verité a show about Crown Prosecutors which debuted in Québec in April 2014. Canada.

The Trace of the Crime [*La huella del crimen*] (TVE, season 1: 1985; season 2: 1991; season 3: 2009). The format is refreshingly different in that we do not witness the solution of the case or the apprehension of the suspect, but we are told the story of why and how the crime was committed in the first place. Every episode is based on one of the most famous criminal cases in Spanish history. Spain.

The Trials of Rosie O'Neill (1990–92). A conflicted young woman lawyer agonises over her professional and personal problems whilst seeking counsel from a variety of sources in this vehicle for Sharon Gless from *Cagney and Lacey*. USA, shown in Britain.

The Untouchables (ABC, 1959–1963). American crime series based on the story of Eliot Ness, crime fighter during the prohibition period in Chicago. USA. (In France the series appeared as 'Les Incorruptibles' from 1964 with reruns thereafter).

Tribunal (TF1, 1988–1990 with reruns through 2000). A fictional trial series, each episode a different case. France.

Die Trovatos Detektive decken auf [*The Trovatos Detectives Reveal*] (RTL, 2009–, 330+ episodes). Scripted reality programme about a real-life detective agency in Mönchengladbach and their investigations of minor crimes and offences. The personnel consists of lay actors and the cases are fictitious. Germany.

True Justice (2011–). Undercover police series with Steven Seagal heading a special task force centred on an economically depressed part of Seattle over two series and 26 episodes to date. USA.

Trust (BBC1, 2004). Lawyer-focused series about a London law firm and the struggles of a bunch of corporate lawyers with a varied ethnic, age and gender mix. Britain.

Trzeci Oficer [*The Third Officer*] (2008). Officers from the Polish Central Bureau of Investigation come across information about a nuclear weapon and try to prevent it from falling into the hands of a group of terrorists. Poland.

Twin Peaks (1990–1991). Iconic series about the death of Laura Palmer, who's body is found on a beach near Twin Peaks. Key investigator is FBI Special Agent Dale Cooper who is drawn into a web of intrigue. USA, shown in Flanders, Belgium.

De Udvalgte (2001–). Danish documentary about how the Immigration Service chooses which refugees can be part of Danish society. Denmark.

UK Border Force (2008–09). The series followed officers at London Heathrow Airport and the ports of Dover and Calais. It followed enforcement teams operating within the UK to detect illegal workers and highlighted the work of entry clearance officers at British Missions overseas. Britain.

Underbelly (2008–13). A popular true-crime drama, each season focusing on a different underworld figure. Australia.

Une femme à la gendarmerie royale du Canada (Arte, 2014). This documentary is co-produced by France and Germany and centres on the recruitment conditions of the Royal Canadian Mounted Police. France/Germany.

Une femme d'honneur (TF1, 1996–2008). Police drama set in the 'gendarmerie' (national army police force) relates the trials and tribulations of a woman lieutenant balancing pending investigations and her family life. France.

Understanding the Law, a series of half hour animated National Film Board films about landmark legal decisions, such as *The Worm*, about the classic tort case *Donohue v Stevenson*. Canada.

Unforgettable (CBS, 2011–14; A&E, 2015–). Carrie Welles (Poppy Montgomery) is a police detective in New York City. She has a unique ability to remember every detail around her, which helps her solve criminal cases. USA, shown in Poland.

Unknown War [*Agnostos Polemos*] (YENED, 1970–74, 226 episodes). A spy drama taking place during the Second World War. The main character is colonel Vartanis of the Greek counter-intelligence against the Germans. It is up to the present the Greek series with the highest ever audience, 76%. Greece.

An Unleashed Dog [*Un cane sciolto*] (Rai 1, 1990–92). De Santis is a 'credible magistrate', free and independent (even with respect to the judiciary's internal hierarchy), with an instinctive and non-ideological sense of justice. He struggles with the difficulties of implementing justice, but in the end he succeeds in defending the rights of individuals and the community. Italy.

The Untouchables. Crime fighting series set in Chicago in the 1930s. Special agent Elliott Ness and his team work—at great personal risk—to framecurb the power of the alcohol Mafia which featured Al Capone. USA, shown in Greece and Belgium.

US Bounty Hunters (2003–). A reality television show about bounty hunters, in the style of *COPS*. USA.

Våbensmuglingen [*Weapon Smuggling*]. Danish 2011 documentary about the Dane Niels Holck and how he took four tons of weapons into India. Denmark.

Vaugand (France 2, 2013–, still in production, so far three episodes). Courtroom drama based on the work of a lawyer, his young assistant and a police detective. France.

Vallanzasca—Gli angeli del male (Evil Angel, 2010). Feature movie about the life of Italian gangster Renato Vallanzasca. Italy/France/Romania.

Vera (2009–). Non-glamorous, middle-aged, down-to-earth Detective Vera Stanhope solves crime in rural and urban North East England. Britain.

Verdachtsfälle (*Suspicious Cases*) (2009–). In now nine seasons, this series produced by RTL dramatizes different types of suspicions about possible crime. There are offsprings in other countries. Germany.

Verdict [*Veredicto*] (Telecinco, 1993–94). First court show fronted by Ana Rosa Quintana, a well-known presenter, and the former Supreme Court judge Diego Rosas Hidalgo. Spain.

Vérité Oblige (TF1, 1997–2002). This legal series was originally broadcast on TF1 and currently reruns are on NRJ12. The series follows the work of Pierre Chevalier, magistrate and law professor, whose respect for justice often brings him into conflict with his peers. France.

Verkehrsgericht [*Traffic Court*] (1983–2001). Traffic offences and their consequences discussed. Germany.

Verklag mich doch! [*Sue me!*] (Vox, 2011–13, 100+ episodes). Documentary-style drama series featuring a team of lawyers who work and comment on a variety of criminal cases. At the end of each episode the case is closed and the audience is informed about the further consequences for the participants. All plots are fictitious, the actors are amateurs. Germany.

Vermist (2007–12). Flemish TV show produced by SBS-Belgium, following the release of a pilot movie and dramatising fictional stories about the missing persons unit of the federal police. Ran for seven seasons. Belgium.

The Vice (1999–2003). Drama series about the work of a police vice unit in London over five series and 28 episodes. Britain.

Vice Squad [*Tmima Ethon*] (ANT1, 1992–95, 116 episodes). Police drama focusing on the vice squad and their fight against prostitution, gambling and drugs. Greece.

Viol, elles se manifestent (France 2, 2012). Every year in France, more than 75,000 women are sexually assaulted. This documentary focuses on the difficulty of being a woman in contemporary society. Echoing the 'Manifeste des 343' published in 1971 (a petition signed by 343 women among them, Simone de Beauvoir and Catherine Deneuve), the film-maker offers victims' testimonies. France.

Virgins [Betulut] (Hot, November 2014). Tells the story of a police woman in Eilat, the most southern city in Israel, who is involved in the investigation of the mysterious death of her sister. Israel.

Vol special [Special Flight] (2011). Documentary, co-produced by Radio Télévision Suisse (the francophone section of the SRG). Award-winning movie about asylum seekers whose requests have been denied and are now in pre-deportation detention. Switzerland.

Von Gangstern, Huren und weissen Westen [Of Gangsters, Whores and Clean Slates] (2006). Part of the documentary series *Reporter*. The movie portrays red-light district attorney Valentin Landmann. Switzerland.

W11—Wydział Śledczy [W11—Investigation Department] (2004–). First Polish docu-crime TV series, based on German *K11—Kommissare im Einsatz*. Show follows the everyday work of three real-life police officers' teams. Most of the characters are played by non-professional actors. In each episode viewers are able to witness crime scene examinations, stakeouts, arrests and line-ups. Poland.

Wachtmeister Studer [Constable Studer] (1939–46, 1976–80, 2001–07). Three series of TV movies adapting the *Wachtmeister Studer* novels by Swiss author Friedrich Glauser. Switzerland.

Wallander (2005–13). TV show about Henning Mankell's gloomy police detective Kurt Wallander following his work solving murders over three series and 32 episodes. Sweden.

Wallander (BBC1, 2008–14). British adaptation of the Mankell character with Kenneth Branagh as Wallander over four series and 12 episodes to date and shown on BBC1. Britain.

The Wanninkhof Case [El caso Wanninkhof] (TVE, 2008). A two-part miniseries which deals with one of the most serious miscarriages of justice in recent Spanish history. Spain.

Wataha [The Border] (2014). Captain Wiktor Rebrow (Leszek Lichota) is trying to solve the mystery of a bombing that killed his friends from the border guard in Bieszczady. Poland.

Water Rats (1996–2001). A police procedural following the Sydney Water Police, investigating crimes at picturesque Sydney Harbour locations. Australia.

Wedding Rings [Anillos de oro] (TVE, 1984). This highly acclaimed and award-winning TV show is set in the early period of Spanish democracy after Franco. Lola Martínez Luque and Ramón San Juan specialise in divorce cases. Spain.

Wentworth (2013–) (aka *Wentworth Prison*). Australian series set in a female prison. The 25 episodes thus far focus on the life on remand in prison of a woman charged with the murder of her husband. There are also German and Dutch versions. Australia.

White Collar [*Ladrón de guante blanco*] (La Sexta, 2014). Depicts the unlikely partnership between an FBI agent and a con artist who offers his know-how to catch white-collar criminals. Spain.

White Collar Blue (2002–03). A drama focused on the work and personal lives of police officers in the city of Sydney. Australia.

White Glove [*Guante blanco*] (TVE, 2008). Mario Pastor is a con artist, who is usually at least one step ahead of Inspector Bernardo Valle. Both men have a whole team to help commit and solve the crimes, respectively. Crimes committed include the theft of a Van Gogh painting, a Stradivarius and a Fabergé egg. Spain.

Winter (2015). A mystery/drama/thriller series featuring Detective Sergeant Eve Winters. A spin-off of telemovie *The Killing Field* (2014), which introduced Winters. Australia.

The Whole Truth (USA, 2010). Legal drama following legal cases from the points of view of both the prosecution and defence. USA, shown in Denmark.

Within These Walls (1974–76, 1978). Set in a female prison. Britain.

Without a Trace (2002–09). American police procedure TV series following the Missing Persons Unit (MPU) of the FBI in New York City. USA, shown in Denmark.

Witse (2004–12). Popular Flemish cop show about a chief inspector called Witse, produced for the Flemish Public Broadcasting channel. Also broadcast by the Dutch public channels AVRO and TROS. Belgium.

The Women's Lawyer [*L'avvocato delle donne*] (Rai 2, 1997). Irene is a mother who runs a law firm in Rome. She is outraged by abuses against women by violent husbands and the cynicism of male lawyers who accuse helpless women in order to defend their guilty clients. The series courageously deals with serious social issues, and the feminist perspective is clear. Italy.

Wonderful Divorce [*Gerushim Niflaim*] (Yes, 2010). Is one of the few lawyer-focused Israeli dramas, telling the story of a law firm practising family law. Israel.

World's Dumbest Criminals (TruTV, 2008–14). Originally called *The Smoking Gun Presents World's Dumbest Criminals*, and then *TruTV Presents World's Dumbest Criminals*, this reality-style series presents clips of funny, idiotic and witless lawbreakers. USA.

World's Wildest Police Videos (1998–2002, 2012). Police videos following car chases, subsequent arrests, robberies, riots and other crimes appear on the show. In 2012, 13 new episodes were recorded. USA.

Wycliffe (ITV1, 1994–98). Detective series set in rural English west country county of Cornwall following the murder investigations of Chief Superintendent Wycliffe and his two DIs over five series and two specials and 38 episodes. Britain.

Yarkon District [*Merchav Yarkon*] (Channel 2, 1997). This is one of the first police-focused dramas produced in Israel telling the story of a leading youth division female detective in one of the police districts in the city of Tel Aviv. The show was praised by the critics, but lasted only five episodes. Israel.

Young Lions (2002). A police drama focused on the work and personal lives of rookie detectives in a Sydney police station. Australia.

Zagadki kryminalne [*Criminal mysteries*] (2014–). A documentary TV series show-ing interesting crime, assaults and robbery cases and difficult investigations and police operations that lead to catching dangerous criminals. Viewers get to see the ruthless behaviour of the criminals, dramatic experiences of their various victims and different methods of police work. Poland.

Zbrodnia [*The Crime*] (2014). The peaceful existence of the people living on the Hel peninsula is suddenly interrupted by a mystery from the past. Following events turn out to be in relation to the unsolved murders that happened years ago. Poland.

Z Cars (1962–65). Innovative series following a number of mobile police duos in a working-class area. Britain.

Zdaniem obrony [*According to Defence*] (1984–86). A mini-series consisting of five episodes. Each episode follows a different criminal case and centers on an attor-ney—detective Sokor (Emil Karewicz) who, in order to prove his clients inno-cence, has to lead his own investigation and find the real criminals. Poland.

Zinzana (Channel 2, 2000). Probably one of the most influential Israeli TV shows, and one of the few focusing on prisoners' lives, both in men's and women's prisons. Israel.

Zone Stad (VTM, 2003–13). Police show about law enforcement officers of the local police in Antwerp, city central division (Zone Stad), eight seasons of 13 episodes each, produced for VTM, Flemish commercial channel. Belgium.

Życie na gorąco [*Life Heated*] (1979). Polish reporter Maj (Leszek Teleszyński) fol-lows around the world trails of a secretive, nazi organisation called W. The aim of the organisation lead by doktor Gebhardt is to trigger international conflicts and aquire weapon of mass destruction. Thanks to Maj all their operations fail. Poland.

Zorro (ABC, 1957–1961). The adventures of a young noble in masked disguise, fighting the abuse of power by local government in the 19th century while Califor-nia was under Spanish rule. USA.

INDEX

Ingram Content Group UK Ltd.
Milton Keynes UK
UKHW020610080323
418160UK00004B/113